Rhetoric of Inquiry

General Editor:

Kirsten F. Benson

Contributing Editors:

Sean Barnette

Deidre Garriott

Meredith McCarroll

Contributors:

Beth-Ann Duncan

Hannah Esworthy

Casie Fedukovich

Teresa Hooper

Jessie Janeshek

Misty Kreuger

Michael Levan

Morgan Livingston

Marcos Loe

Rachel Radom

Mary Jo Reiff

Kelly Rivers

Teresa Saxton

Christopher Sharpe

Caitlin Siminerio

Brittany Stanford

James Winston

Carolyn Wisniewski

Ryan Woldruff

Karen Wolf

Rhetoric of Inquiry

THIRD EDITION

English 102
The University of Tennessee, Knoxville

Edited by Kirsten F. Benson

Content taken from:

The Bedford Researcher, Third Edition
By Mike Palmquist

Joining the Conversation
By Mike Palmquist

The St. Martin's Handbook, Fifth Edition
By Andrea A. Lunsford

A Pocket Guide to Writing in History, Sixth Edition
By Mary Lynn Rampolla

FieldWorking: Reading and Writing Research, Third Edition
By Bonnie Stone Sunstein and Elizabeth Chiseri-Strater

Bedford/St. Martin's

Boston ◆ New York

Content taken from:

The Bedford Researcher, Third Edition
By Mike Palmquist
Copyright © 2011 by Bedford/St. Martin's

Joining the Conversation
By Mike Palmquist
Copyright © 2010 by Bedford/St. Martin's

The St. Martin's Handbook, Fifth Edition
By Andrea A. Lunsford
Copyright © 2003 by Bedford/St. Martin's

A Pocket Guide to Writing in History, Sixth Edition
By Mary Lynn Rampolla
Copyright © 2010 by Bedford/St. Martin's

FieldWorking: Reading and Writing Research, Third Edition
By Bonnie Stone Sunstein and Elizabeth Chiseri-Strater
Copyright © 2007 by Bedford/St. Martin's

Copyright © 2012, 2009, 2007 by Bedford/St. Martin's

Manufactured in the United States of America.

6 5 4 3 2 1
f e d c b a

For information, write: Bedford/St. Martin's, 75 Arlington Street, Boston, MA 02116
(617-399-4000)

ISBN: 978-1-4576-0843-8

Cover art: Trisha Gene Brady, University of Tennessee Libraries

Acknowledgments
Acknowledgments and copyrights can be found at the back of the book on page 433, which constitutes an extension of the copyright page.

Brief Contents

Contents

3   DEVELOPING A RESEARCH QUESTION AND LOCATING SOURCES   47

PART TWO: HISTORICAL RESEARCH   83

4 AN INTRODUCTION TO HISTORICAL RESEARCH AND USING PRIMARY SOURCES   85

7 CONDUCTING INTERVIEWS, OBSERVATIONS, AND SURVEYS   197

PART FOUR: RESEARCH USING SECONDARY SOURCES   227

8 AN INTRODUCTION TO RESEARCH USING SECONDARY SOURCES   229

9 CONDUCTING SECONDARY SOURCE RESEARCH 249

APPENDIXES 289

 **A** DRAFTING YOUR RESEARCH PAPER 291

D SAMPLE STUDENT WORK 373

Rhetoric of Inquiry

PART ONE

Framing Inquiry

1 Inquiry, Research, and Writing in English 102

Introduction to English 102

Welcome to English 102! As a follow up to your English 101 course, 102 is designed both to build on the skills of critical reading, analysis, and argumentation that you practiced in English 101 and to give you the chance to research and produce your own rhetorically effective projects. Overall, English 102 focuses on how writers— through their reading, research, and writing—enter into the "conversations" that go on in particular disciplinary communities or groups, learning the appropriate ways (also called "conventions") of discovering knowledge and participating in that dialogue. As you explore various ways to inquire into a subject, you will learn about differences in the kinds of questions that can or cannot be answered with a particular research method, what constitutes evidence ("data"), and how that evidence is used. You will have the chance to investigate and write about your course topic from various disciplinary perspectives.

In English 101, you learned about *rhetoric*—about what makes a text persuasive, how a Web site works to engage its readers, and how combinations of images and words appeal to audiences. You learned strategies for constructing valid arguments, supported by convincing evidence, that appeal to the audience's reason (logos); strategies for appealing to the audience's emotions in order to make a persuasive point (pathos); and strategies for appealing to shared values (ethos). In other words, you learned how all acts of communication take place in a *rhetorical situation*—a situation in which writers, readers, and texts dynamically interact as writers shape their messages to carry out their purposes and influence their readers.

As you will learn in English 102, the rhetorical situation also guides research. Your purpose as a writer (guided by a research question) helps you make choices about your research sources and methods. For instance, if your goal is to find out more about the rising costs of college tuition and the federal response in terms of financial aid, loans, and grants, you might consult national sources, like *U.S. News & World Report*, *The Chronicle of Higher Education*, or *Congressional Quarterly*. But if your purpose is to focus your research locally—on the rising costs of tuition at UT— you might instead consult the UT Office of Financial Aid, explore the Tennessee Legislature Web site, or research local sources, such as the *Knoxville News Sentinel*, and their coverage of the state lottery scholarships. In addition to a well-defined purpose guiding your selection of sources, knowing the audience you are writing for will help you evaluate your sources. For instance, Wikipedia might be a fine source to consult when discussing a topic with friends or when doing general background research; however, for the purposes of addressing an academic audience in an academic argument, the use of Wikipedia as a research source is not credible. Building, then, on what you have learned in English 101 about analyzing and writing rhetorically forceful arguments, English 102 will teach you to produce new knowledge on a subject through various methods of inquiry and to share that research knowledge with both general and specialized audiences.

In addition to analyzing the rhetorical situations that texts respond to, you also learned in English 101 how the social and cultural contexts in which print, digital, and visual texts appear shape the way messages are presented, and you used this knowledge to, in turn, shape your own arguments. In English 102, you will learn how research and research methods are situated in larger disciplinary contexts and communities that may affect how and what information is gathered and presented. For example, if you are conducting a research project on an environmental issue, you will quickly learn that there are multiple perspectives on this issue, such as scientific perspectives on climate change, invasive species, or renewable energy; economic perspectives on the production of green products or the environmental impact of world trade; sociological perspectives on public environmental movements or social attitudes toward conservation; medical perspectives on the effects of pollution on public health; or political science perspectives on legislation such as emissions caps for big business, policies on offshore drilling, or proposals for new fuel efficiency standards. While scientific reports will rely on facts and statistics, sociological studies might rely on interviews with the public or observations of their efforts, and political perspectives might rely on government documents or congressional testimonies.

In addition to these multidisciplinary approaches, you will learn different types of research methods—both inside and outside the library—and will draw on a range of sources and texts as you investigate your 102 topic of inquiry. As part of your exploration of complex issues and multiple viewpoints, you will encounter a variety of "texts," such as published academic articles, Web sites, blogs, and films. Additionally, because varying types of texts are commonly used by different disciplines, your instructor may ask you to experiment with a range of genres such as letters, proposals, speeches, Web sites, multimedia texts, posters, and research article reports to present your research.

Overall, rather than taking a generic approach to inquiry and research, English 102 will teach you to conduct research that utilizes multiple research methods in order to prepare you for the varied research and writing assignments you will encounter in courses outside of English and in your major field of study. While individual English 102 sections will focus on different inquiry topics, all course sections share the same objectives or outcomes (see Box 1.1) and the same three core units focused on particular research approaches. While some instructors may present these research units in a different sequence, they are presented in this book in the following order: historical, qualitative, and secondary source research.

The historical research unit (see Part Two of this book) will ask you to explore the past in order to answer questions about the accuracy of past accounts or to inform and enlarge your understanding of the historical context of a given issue or event. You may be asked to examine artifacts (primary sources), visit a museum or historical society, consult library archives, dig through old boxes from your attic, or interview someone who can provide an historical perspective on the question being asked.

The qualitative research unit (see Part Three of this book) will teach you to explore people's thoughts and actions in order to find answers to certain kinds of research questions. This type of research (sometimes called "hands-on" or "field" research—which refers to participatory research that takes place in a particular setting, referred to as "the field") will teach you to gather information about people through interviews, surveys, or observations of and note-taking on an event or gathering. The idea is for you to understand people's perceptions and actions by gathering data on your own and then presenting what you discover in your writing; most students find this type of research to be truly engaging.

The unit on secondary source research (see Part Four of this book) focuses upon how to gather print and digital material from library, electronic database, and Internet sources. This unit will prepare you to undertake academic research projects in any of your future courses: you will learn how to conduct a thorough, targeted search for sources; how to evaluate their relevance and credibility; and how to use them in a rhetorically effective way to accomplish your purpose, whether that is to inform, change someone's mind, and/or prompt someone to take action.

Overall, English 102 focuses on active research. It encourages your engagement with a topic and your development of research questions that genuinely interest you. Rather than teaching the decontextualized approach to research that you might remember from high school (with piles of note cards and a paper so crowded with

Box 1.1: English 102 Outcomes

By the end of English 102, students should be able to:

- read critically to identify, define, and evaluate problems/complex issues, taking into account multiple points of view and varying disciplinary and cultural contexts;

- recognize the research methods and textual genres used by different disciplinary and expert communities;

- enter and participate in different ongoing expert conversations using a range of written and visual texts;

- frame research questions that will guide formal inquiry; select appropriate research methods that will lead to answers to those questions; and evaluate the usefulness and quality of sources;

- use multiple investigative methodologies and sources of data (including interviews, surveys, and observations, as well as historical and library research) to investigate research problems and questions;

- construct effective arguments that participate in scholarly and intellectual conversations; answer research questions, present evidence-based support for claims, and integrate information effectively;

- draft and revise arguments to take into account possible objections/critiques and to shape content, tone, organization, and style to correspond appropriately with the rhetorical situation and context;

- present research effectively, selecting textual genres and rhetorical appeals appropriate to audience and purpose and drawing on various modes of communication (written, digital/visual, oral).

other voices that it pushes out your own), this course gives you the tools to utilize multiple methods of research in order to find out about and define positions on issues of your own choosing. As you move from English 102 to your third required writing course at UTK (a "Communicating through Writing," or "WC," course that may be in your major or in a discipline outside of English), we hope that you will take with you a greater awareness of how different disciplines and communities construct knowledge, gather data, and marshal evidence to support their claims. Our goal is for you to transfer the research and writing skills you learn in 102 to your later courses and especially to courses in your major.

Exercise 1.1

Write a one-page description of your previous experiences with research-based writing, in your high school courses, your English 101 course, or other college courses. What do you like most about researching a topic? What do you like least? How familiar are you with using the Hodges Libraries? What resources (either in the library or outside the library) have you consulted to do research on a topic related to one of your courses? After you explain your previous research experiences, describe the skills you would like to work on in your English 102 course.

Exercise 1.2

The expectations of your English 102 course are spelled out in a formal institutional genre, the syllabus, which functions as a contract of sorts between you and your instructor. After examining your 102 syllabus, explain what it tells you about the goals and objectives of the course, the structure of the course, the research and writing you will be doing, and the way your research and writing will be evaluated. What questions do you have, or what terms or information are you uncertain about? Bring any questions you have back to the larger class for discussion.

Exercise 1.3

Read the course goals and objectives and/or the description of the course, which should be at the beginning of the course syllabus. In your own words, explain what the course is about. Your course focuses on a specific topic. Based on your reading of the syllabus, what do you see as the relationship between the course topic and the objectives of research and writing? Be prepared to share your interpretation with your classmates, in either small groups or large class discussion, and identify areas of similarity and difference in your interpretations.

Exercise 1.4

See Box 1.1, "English 102 Outcomes." An "outcome" is a measure that all students should be able to meet upon successfully completing English 102. Which, if any, of the outcomes seem related to skills you learned in English 101? Which do you think will be applicable to courses outside of English 102? Explain your responses.

Exercise 1.5

Break up into small groups. Your instructor will assign each group one of the outcomes from Box 1.1. In your group, work to define what you think the outcome means and to provide an example. Your instructor will visit each group to offer assistance, but begin with your own definition and interpretation, backed up by evidence from the syllabus, course materials, textbooks, or any notes from class discussion or your instructor's lectures. Be prepared to report on your outcome and its meaning—either in a short written text or a brief presentation to the class.

Bringing Your Knowledge to the Course Topic

While registering for English 102, you probably realized that individual sections of the course focus on different topics ("Inquiry into Self," "Inquiry into Music and Culture," "Inquiry into Fear," and many others). It's also likely that you registered for your specific section based on your interest in the topic. Regardless of whether you consider yourself an expert, a fan, or a novice, you doubtless know both more *and* less about your section's topic than you realize. English 102 should be a class in which you build on your existing interest and knowledge and also ask new questions in order to learn more about your topic.

You've already read the syllabus provided by your instructor, which includes a brief course description and, along with other background material your instructor provided, gave you an idea of how your instructor imagines the topic you'll explore during the semester. The following list of basic questions is designed to get you thinking about what *you* already know about the course topic:

- When you think of the course title, "Inquiry into _____," what words, phrases, names, or ideas come to mind?

- Why are you interested in this course topic?

- What has been your experience with or knowledge of the course topic?

- In what ways, if any, did the course topic come up in previous classes?

- In what ways, if any, has the course topic come up where you work?

- If you know a lot about the course topic, what are some basic things you'd tell someone who's new to it?

- If you're new to the course topic, what are at least two things you'd like to know about it?

- Think about the last few weeks. What do you recall reading, hearing, or seeing related to the course topic?

- Who might specialize in this topic, or whom would you turn to for answers to your questions?

- In addition to the specialists you mentioned above, what other type of person or groups of people would you expect to be interested in this topic?

- What movie, book, magazine, or Web site offers a good introduction to the course topic?

- If you had to search for more information on the course topic using Google or another Internet search engine, what keywords or phrases would you use?

Answering these questions won't make you an expert in the topic, but the process will lead you and the rest of the class to additional questions. Some basic questions may be answered quickly as you complete background reading assigned by your instructor. But in order to answer more complex questions, you'll need to turn to additional, individualized reading and the historical, qualitative, and secondary source research methods you'll explore throughout the semester.

Exercise 1.6

Compose a list of three questions you have about the course topic (these might come from reading the course description or from your answers to the questions in the previous section of this chapter). Ask the same questions of three other people in your class. What overlap exists in their responses? In what ways are their responses different?

Exercise 1.7

Write a paragraph that explains what you currently know about your 102 course topic and what you would like to learn about the topic during the semester. Can you already think of some avenues of research that you would like to explore? Be prepared to share your response with the rest of the class.

Exercise 1.8

Write a paragraph that analyzes how your background, previous experiences, and prior knowledge may inform your research on your 102 topic. If you chose your 102 section based on its topic, why did you choose this topic? What personal facts (such as your age, gender, race, class, nationality, family background, belief system) may affect your perceptions of the topic, and how? What subjective positions (life history and personal experiences) may inform your research?

Understanding Disciplinary Writing and Research

You may have chosen to take the section you enrolled in because of a personal interest of some kind in the topic. Of course, you are not alone in finding something compelling about it — others have thought about, researched, and written about it before now. Below you will come across a well-known metaphor for how people find out about and share knowledge that was created by the rhetorician Kenneth Burke (see "Understanding Disciplinary Vocabularies," p. 13). Like a social gathering in a room (or "parlor") where people are moving from conversation to conversation, listening in and sometimes participating in the discussion, research and writing often take place across a spectrum of groups or academic disciplines, each with its own way of weighing in on a subject and furthering the conversation. In English 102, you will participate in your own classroom "parlor," engaging in various discussions about your inquiry topic, finding out new information, and providing your own input into the conversation by way of the papers you write; you will begin to enter new "disciplinary discourse communities."

When you register for courses each semester, you probably notice that you have several "general education" requirements, the purpose of which is to introduce you to knowledge and conventions of the humanities, the social sciences, and the natural sciences. While English 102 cannot teach you how to be successful in all of those areas, it aims to help you to see that different disciplines understand, investigate, and produce knowledge in different ways and to know that you will be expected to read and write in many different ways across the range of courses you will encounter as an undergraduate student. To better prepare you to do that, your 102 assignments will ask you to investigate and write about your topic in ways that are characteristic of humanities courses such as history and English and of social science courses such as sociology and anthropology. The following section will help you begin to identify the distinct identities of various disciplines by showing you how to think about and examine the differing vocabularies, styles, uses of evidence, and ways of presenting evidence in other fields.

Understanding Disciplinary Discourse

RECOGNIZING THE CRITICAL ROLE THAT WRITING PLAYS IN ALL DISCIPLINES

Students in the humanities tend to expect that writing will play a central role in their education; students in other areas sometimes imagine that writing will be of secondary importance to them. Yet faculty working in the sciences, social sciences, business, and other areas have a different understanding. Here, for example, is what some faculty members in chemistry have to say:

> Is writing important in chemistry? Don't chemists spend their time turning knobs, mixing reagents, and collecting data? They still get to do those things, but professional scientists also make presentations, prepare reports, publish results, and submit proposals. Each of these

"Understanding Disciplinary Discourse" is taken from Andrea A. Lunsford, *The St. Martin's Handbook*, Fifth Edition, pp. 860–69 (Chapter 63, "Understanding Disciplinary Discourse").

activities involves writing. If you remain skeptical about the need for writing skills, then ask your favorite professor, or any other scientist, to track the fraction of one workday spent using their word-processing program. You (and they) may be surprised at the answer.

—Oregon State University, *Writing Guide for Chemistry*

As this statement suggests, writing is central to learning regardless of the discipline you are in.

ANALYZING ACADEMIC ASSIGNMENTS AND EXPECTATIONS

Since academic assignments vary widely from course to course and even from professor to professor, the tips this section offers can only be general. The best advice, however, is really very simple: make sure you are in control of the assignment rather than letting the assignment be in control of you. To take control, you need to understand the assignment fully and to understand what professors in the particular discipline expect in response.

When you receive an assignment in *any* discipline, your first job is to make sure you understand what that assignment is asking you to do. Some assignments may be as vague as "Write a five-page essay on one aspect of the Civil War" or "Write an analysis of the group dynamics at play in your recent collaborative project for this course." Others, like this psychology assignment, will be fairly specific: "Collect, summarize, and interpret data drawn from a sample of letters to the editor published in two newspapers, one in a small rural community, and one in an urban community, over a period of three months. Organize your research report according to APA requirements." Whatever the assignment, you must take charge of analyzing it. Answering the following questions can help you do so.

Box 1.2: Analyzing an Assignment in Any Discipline

1. **What is the purpose of the assignment?** Does it serve an informal purpose, as a basis for class discussion or as a way to brainstorm about a topic? Or is the purpose more formal, a way to demonstrate your mastery of certain material and your competence as a writer?

2. **What is the assignment asking you to do?** Are you to summarize, explain, evaluate, interpret, illustrate, define? If the assignment asks you to do more than one of these things, does it specify the order in which you are to do them?

3. **Do you need to ask for clarification of any terms?** Students responding to the preceding psychology assignment might well ask the instructor, for instance, to discuss the meaning of *collect* or *interpret* and perhaps to give examples. Or they might want further clarification of the term *urban community* or the size of a suitable *sample*.

Box 1.2: *continued*

4. **What do you need to know or find out to do the assignment?** Students doing the psychology assignment need to develop a procedure — a way to analyze or categorize the letters to the editor. Furthermore, they need to know how to do simple statistical analyses of the data.

5. **Do you understand the expectations regarding background reading and preparation, use of sources (both written and visual), method of organization and development, format, and length?** The psychology assignment mentions no reading, but in this field an adequate statement of a problem usually requires setting that problem in the context of other research. A student might well ask how extensive this part of the report is to be.

6. **Can you find an example of an effective response to a similar assignment?** If so, you can analyze it and perhaps use it as a model for developing your own approach to the current assignment.

7. **Does your understanding of the assignment fit with that of other students?** Talking over an assignment with classmates is one good way to test your understanding.

Exercise 1.9

Below is an assignment from a communications course. Read it carefully, and then use the seven questions above to analyze it.

Assignment: Distribute a questionnaire to twenty people (ten male, ten female) asking these four questions: (1) What do you expect to say and do when you meet a stranger? (2) What don't you expect to say and do when you meet a stranger? (3) What do you expect to say and do when you meet a very close friend? (4) What don't you expect to say and do when you meet a very close friend? When you have collected your twenty questionnaires, read them over and answer the following questions.

- What, if any, descriptions were common to all respondents' answers?

- How do male and female responses compare?

- What similarities and differences were found between the responses to the stranger and to the very close friend?

- What factors (environment, time, status, gender, and so on) do you think have an impact on these responses?

- Discuss your findings, using concepts and theories explained in your text.

UNDERSTANDING DISCIPLINARY VOCABULARIES

The rhetorician Kenneth Burke describes how people become active participants in the "conversation of humankind" in the following way. Imagine, he says, that you enter a crowded room in which everyone is talking and gesturing animatedly. You know no one there and cannot catch much of what is being said. Slowly you move from group to group listening, and finally you take a chance and interject a brief statement into the conversation. Others listen to you and respond. Thus, slowly but surely, you come to *participate* in, rather than to observe, the conversation. Entering into an academic discipline or a profession is much like entering into such a conversation. At first you feel like an outsider, and you do not catch much of what you hear or read. Trying to enter the new "conversation" takes time and careful attention. Eventually, however, the vocabulary becomes familiar, and participating in the conversation seems easy and natural.

Of course, this chapter cannot introduce you to the vocabulary of every field. The point is that *you* must make the effort to enter into the conversation, and that again means taking charge of the situation. To get started, one of the first things you need to do is to study the vocabulary of the field you are most interested in.

Try to determine how much of what you are hearing and reading depends on specialized or technical vocabulary by highlighting key terms in your reading or your notes to help you distinguish the specialized vocabulary. If you find little specialized vocabulary, try to master the new terms quickly by reading your textbook carefully, by asking questions of the instructor and other students, and by looking up key words or phrases.

If you find a great deal of specialized vocabulary, however, you may want to familiarize yourself with it somewhat methodically. Any of the following procedures may prove helpful:

- Keep a log of unfamiliar or confusing words *in context*. To locate definitions, check the terms in your textbook's glossary or index or consult a specialized dictionary.

- Review your class notes each day after class. Underline important terms, review their definitions, and identify anything that is unclear. Use your textbook or ask questions to clarify anything confusing before the class moves on to a new topic.

- Check to see if your textbook has a glossary of terms or sets off definitions in italics or boldface type. Study pertinent sections to master the terms.

- Try to start using or working with key concepts. Even if they are not yet entirely clear to you, working with them will help you come to understand them. For example, in a statistics class, try to work out (in words) how to do an analysis of *covariance*, step by step, even if you are not sure of the precise definition of the term. Or try to plot the narrative progression in a story even if you are still not entirely sure of the definition of *narrative progression*.

- Find the standard dictionaries or handbooks of terms for your field. Students beginning the study of literature, for instance, can turn to such guides as *A Handbook to Literature*, Ninth Edition, or *A Handbook of Critical Approaches to Literature*. Those entering the discipline of sociology may refer to the *Dictionary of the Social Sciences*, while students beginning statistical analysis may turn to *Statistics without Tears*. Ask your instructor or a librarian for help finding the standard references in your field.

- If you belong to online Listservs or discussion groups — or even if you are browsing sites on the Internet and World Wide Web related to a particular field — take special note of the ways technical language or disciplinary vocabulary is used there. Sometimes, you can find definitions of terms on a Web site's FAQ page, if one exists.

Whatever your techniques for learning a specialized vocabulary, begin to use the new terms whenever you can — in class, in discussions with instructors and other students, and in your assignments. This ability to *use* what you learn in speaking and writing is crucial to your full understanding of and participation in the discipline.

IDENTIFYING THE STYLE OF A DISCIPLINE

Becoming familiar with technical vocabulary is one important way to initiate yourself into a discipline or field of study. Another method is to identify stylistic features of the writing in that field. You will begin to assimilate these features automatically if you immerse yourself in reading and thinking about the field. To get started, study some representative pieces of writing in the field with the following questions in mind:

- How would you describe the overall *tone* of the writing? Is it very formal, somewhat formal, informal?

- To what extent do writers in the field strive for a somewhat distanced, objective stance?

- In general, how long are the sentences? How long are the paragraphs?

- Are verbs generally active or passive — and why?

- Do the writers use first person (*I*) or prefer terms such as *one* or *the investigator*? What is the effect of this choice?

- Does the writing use visual elements such as graphs, tables, charts, computer-based graphics, visuals, or maps? How are these integrated into the text?

- What role, if any, do headings and other formatting elements play in the writing?

- What bibliographic style (such as MLA, APA, CSE, or *Chicago*) is used?

Of course, writings within a single discipline may have different purposes and different styles. Although a research report is likely to follow a conventional form, a speech greeting specialists at a convention may well be less formal and more personal no matter what the field. Furthermore, answering questions such as the preceding ones will not guarantee that you can produce a piece of writing similar to the ones you are analyzing. Nevertheless, looking carefully at writing in the field brings you one step closer to writing effectively in that discipline.

UNDERSTANDING THE USE OF EVIDENCE

"Good reasons" form the core of any writing that argues a point; they provide the launching pad for the specific *evidence* for the argument. However, what is acceptable and persuasive evidence in one discipline may be more or less so in another. Observable, quantifiable data may constitute the very best evidence in, say, experimental psychology, but the same kind of data may be less appropriate—or even impossible to come by—in a historical study. As you grow familiar with any area of study, you will develop a sense of just what it takes to prove a point in that field. You can speed up this process, however, by doing some investigating and questioning of your own. As you read your textbook and other assigned materials, make a point of noticing the use of evidence. The following questions are designed to help you do so:

- How do writers in the field use precedent and authority? What or who counts as an authority in this field? How are the credentials of an authority established?

- What use is made of quantitative data (items that can be counted and measured)? What kinds of data are used? How are such data gathered and presented?

- What use is made of qualitative data (items that can be systematically observed)?

- How are statistics used and presented? Are tables, charts, or graphs common? How much weight do they carry?

- How is logical reasoning used? How are definition, cause and effect, analogy, and example used in this discipline?

- How does the field use primary and secondary sources? What are the primary materials—the firsthand sources of information—in this field? What are the secondary materials—the sources of information derived from others? How is each type of source likely to be presented?

- What other kinds of textual evidence are cited? Web sites? electronic journals or databases? video or audio? visual images? personal experiences or personal correspondence?

- How are quotations used and integrated into the text?

In addition to carrying out your own investigation, ask your instructor how you can best go about making a case in this field.

Exercise 1.10

Do some reading in books and journals [recommended by your instructor] associated with your prospective major or a discipline of particular interest to you, using the preceding questions to study the use of evidence in that discipline. If you are keeping a writing log, make an entry in it summarizing what you have learned.

USING CONVENTIONAL DISCIPLINARY PATTERNS AND FORMATS

You can gather all the evidence in the world and still fail to produce effective writing in your discipline if you do not know the field's generally accepted formats for organizing and presenting evidence. Again, these formats vary widely from discipline to discipline and sometimes from instructor to instructor, but patterns do emerge. The typical laboratory report, for instance, follows a fairly standard organizational framework whether it is in botany, chemistry, or parasitology. A case study in sociology or education or anthropology likewise follows a typical organizational plan.

Your job in any discipline is to discover its conventional formats and organizing principles so that you can practice using them. This task is easy enough to begin. Ask your instructor to recommend some excellent examples of the kind of writing you will do in the course. Then analyze these examples in terms of format and organization. You might also look at major scholarly journals in the field to see what types of formats seem most common and how each is organized. Study these examples, and keep in mind these questions about organization and format:

- What types of essays, reports, or documents are common in this field? What is the purpose of each type? Are these types produced mainly in print or mainly online?

- What can a reader expect to find in each type? What does each type assume about its readers?

- How is a particular type of text organized? What are its main parts? Are they labeled with conventional headings? What logic underlies this sequence of parts?

- How does a particular type of essay, report, or document show the connections among ideas? What assumptions of the discipline does it take for granted? What points does it emphasize?

Remember that there is a close connection between the writing patterns and formats a particular area of study uses and the work that scholars in that field undertake. Here are statements from two writing guides that were developed for students by faculty members in philosophy and microbiology. What do these statements suggest about disciplinary patterns and formats?

Philosophy

Like baking a pie, planning a vacation, or raising a child, good writing in philosophy requires creativity, thought, and a set of basic skills. This section . . . identifies and exemplifies eight skills that you will frequently make use of in your philosophy writing assignments. These include (1) identifying a philosophical problem; (2) organizing ideas; (3) defining concepts; (4) analyzing arguments; (5) comparing and contrasting; (6) giving examples; (7) applying theory to practice; and (8) testing hypotheses.

— Oregon State University, *Writing Philosophy Papers: A Student Guide*

Microbiology

The main purpose of most scientific writing is to inform and educate other people about research that has been performed. A scientific report should explain clearly how the research was performed and what results were observed. "Good science" must be repeatable — other scientists should be able to repeat the experiment in order to see if they come up with the same results or not. And, lastly, an argument or opinion might be proposed based on the results obtained.

— Oregon State University, *Writing for Microbiology Majors*

Exercise 1.11: For Collaboration

Pair up with a classmate or friend who intends to major in the same field you are considering. Then do some investigating on your college Web site to identify a faculty member in that field and learn about that professor's scholarly work. Next, call or e-mail the professor, asking for an appointment to conduct an interview. (Have a couple of backup professors on your list in case the first one is not available.) To prepare, read Chapter 7, pages 197–200, on conducting an interview. Then draw up some questions about what doing research in this field is like. You might use the information in this chapter. Conduct the interview, and, afterward, write a brief report for your class about what you have learned.

Exercise 1.12: Thinking Critically

Reading with an Eye for Disciplinary Discourse

The following abstract introduces an article titled "Development of the Appearance-Reality Distinction." This article appeared in *Cognitive Psychology*, a specialized academic journal for researchers in the subfield of psychology that focuses on human cognition. Read this abstract carefully to see what you can infer about the discourse of cognitive psychology—about its characteristic vocabulary, style, use of evidence, and so on.

Young children can express conceptual difficulties with the appearance-reality distinction in two different ways: (1) by incorrectly reporting appearance when asked to report reality ("phenomenism"); (2) by incorrectly reporting reality when asked to report appearance ("intellectual realism"). Although both phenomenism errors and intellectual realism errors have been observed in previous studies of young children's cognition, the two have not been seen as conceptually related and only the former errors have been taken as a symptom of difficulties with the appearance-reality distinction. Three experiments investigated 3- to 5-year-old children's ability to distinguish between and correctly identify real versus apparent object properties (color, size, and shape), object identities, object presence-absence, and action identities. Even the 3-year-olds appeared to have some ability to make correct appearance-reality discriminations and this ability increased with age. Errors were frequent, however, and almost all children who erred made both kinds. Phenomenism errors predominated on tasks where the appearance versus reality of the three object properties were [*sic*] in question; intellectual realism errors predominated on the other three types of tasks. Possible reasons for this curious error pattern were advanced. It was also suggested that young children's problems with the appearance-reality distinction may be partly due to a specific metacognitive limitation, namely, a difficulty in analyzing the nature and source of their own mental representations.

—John H. Flavell, Eleanor R. Flavell, and Frances L. Green, *Cognitive Psychology*

THINKING ABOUT YOUR OWN WRITING IN A DISCIPLINE

Choose a piece of writing you have produced for a particular discipline—a hypertext history essay, a laboratory report, a review of the literature in some particular field, or any other written assignment. Examine your writing closely for its use of that discipline's vocabulary, style, methods of proof, and conventional formats. How comfortable are you writing a piece of this kind? In what ways are you using the conventions of the discipline easily and well? What conventions give you difficulty, and why? You might talk to an instructor in this field about the conventions and requirements for writing in the discipline. Make notes about what you learn about being a better writer in the field.

As you may have noticed already, throughout the body of this chapter there are "Exercises" that encourage you to think further about the concepts discussed. Also, at the end of this and every chapter you will find "Questions and Activities" that ask you to reflect upon or apply the information or skills you read about. Your instructor may assign some of the activities in class or for homework. Since they are intended to help you practice the reading, research, and writing skills you are developing in this course, we encourage you to try them out on your own, too, whenever possible. At the end of the book, in Appendices A, B, C, and D, you will find additional resources to help you through the process of conducting and writing your research papers, as well as sample papers written by former English 102 students. We hope that your performance in the course will be so successful that your work, too, could appear in a future edition of this book!

✱ Questions and Activities for Chapter 1

1. In a one- to two-page response, reflect on your background as a writer and researcher. You might:

a. Describe your previous academic writing and research experiences, specifying the types or genres of writing you have done (for example, literary analyses, reports, case studies, poems, research papers, short stories, articles, etc.). What were the subjects of some of these papers/projects? Were any particularly memorable? Why?

b. Describe any nonacademic writing experiences you have had. For example, do you have or have you had jobs that require writing? What sorts of writing/communication do you envision doing in the profession or career you plan to enter? What other writing outside of school assignments have you done?

c. Explain what you perceive as both your strengths and weaknesses as a writer/researcher. What do you do well, and what do you need to work on and improve during the semester?

d. Keeping in mind your 102 course topic, describe the subjects you are interested in and might be interested in writing about during the semester.

e. Explain what you hope to accomplish in this course and what you hope to gain as a researcher and writer.

2. Briefly research an aspect of your course topic that interests you, and present a short, factual account to the class, introducing your classmates to what you find. Include a source from a humanities, social science, or natural and applied sciences discipline. In addition to reporting on your topic, explain to the class how you went about finding information and what resources were most or least helpful (and why).

3. Make a list of the courses that you have taken (or are taking) that satisfy some of your general education requirements. Then, discuss what differences you have come across regarding the types of knowledge that seems to be valued in those different disciplines.

4. Go to the UT Libraries' Web page; under "Databases," select "General Topics," and then click on *CQ Researcher*. Associated with *Congressional Quarterly*, this database "provides researchers with an introductory overview; background and chronology on the topic; an assessment of the current situation; tables and maps; pro/con statements from representatives of opposing positions; and bibliographies of key sources." Choosing a topic you are discussing in class (or a related theme or topic), do a "Quick Search" of the topic. After selecting a report, reflect on the various sources of information in the report, paying careful attention to both textual and graphic resources (charts, tables, visuals). Describe the multiple perspectives represented and the multiple sources incorporated, paying careful attention to how these sources are synthesized and integrated. Write a one-page analysis of the report you found and its use of data.

5. Apply the questions in the section on "Understanding the Use of Evidence," to at least two scholarly articles or sources your instructor has assigned for your 102 course topic (or that you find on your own from Library databases). Based on your analysis of evidence, would you say that the evidence for the argument stems mainly from humanities, social sciences, or applied sciences? How do you know? Explain.

2 Entering a Research Conversation

Your instructor will most likely begin inquiry into your English 102 course topic by helping you become familiar with the written conversations that various people are having about it. That means you'll be reading a variety of texts about your topic from the very beginning of the course. This chapter offers useful strategies for active, critical reading and for evaluating the relevance and quality of texts that will prepare you to enter a research conversation and begin identifying your own interests and questions about your topic. You will learn how to skim a text or Web site to get an overview of its contents, how to read for the "main point," and how to make good notes or annotations in the margins. Also, since instructors in all undergraduate courses will ask you to critically evaluate what you read, the section "How Can I Evaluate Sources?" provides helpful advice for doing that. Finally, templates for writing different kinds of summaries and responses are included in the section "How Can I Read Like a Writer?"

Your goal in the early stages of any of the research projects you do in English 102 will be to become familiar with what others have said about your topic, so you will be able to apply the strategies described in this chapter to the reading you do throughout the semester (and to later undergraduate coursework).

How Can I Read Critically?

Reading critically means reading with an attitude. It also means reading with your writing situation in mind. Through critical reading, you can quickly recognize the questions—points of disagreement, uncertainty, concern, or curiosity—that are under discussion in a written conversation as well as think about how you'll respond to one of these questions.

Check out Appendix C, Work-in-Progress Research and Writing Activities, to find additional practical suggestions to help you read, research, and write successfully.

Chapter 2, "Entering a Research Conversation" is taken from Mike Palmquist, *Joining the Conversation*, pp. 50–73 (Chapter 3, "Reading to Write").

Read with an Attitude

As you learn about and prepare to contribute to a written conversation, both your point of view and your attitude are likely to change. Initially, your attitude might be one of curiosity. You'll note new information in your sources and mark key passages that provide insights. You'll adopt a more questioning attitude as you determine whether sources fit into the conversation or are reliable. Later, after you begin to draw conclusions about the conversation, you might take on a more skeptical attitude, becoming more aggressive in challenging the arguments made in sources than you were at first.

Growing familiarity with and understanding of an issue ⟶

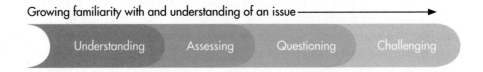

Regardless of where you are in your writing process, you should always adopt a critical attitude. Accept nothing at face value; ask questions; look for similarities and differences among the sources you read; examine the implications of what you read for your writing project; be on the alert for unusual information; and note relevant sources and information. Most important, be open to ideas and arguments, even if you don't agree with them. Give them a chance to affect how you think about the conversation you've decided to join.

Be Aware of Writing Situations

Reading critically involves approaching each source with an awareness not only of your own writing situation but also of the writing situation that shaped the source. Keep in mind that each document you read was written to accomplish a particular purpose and was intended for a particular group of readers. Realize that the physical, social, and cultural settings in which the document was produced affected how the writer presented information, ideas, and arguments. And remember that the writing situation that helped produce the source might differ significantly from your own writing situation.

As you read, remember what you are trying to accomplish. Your purpose will affect your assessment of the information, ideas, and arguments you encounter. Moreover, your readers' purposes, needs, interests, and backgrounds will affect your assessment of what you read.

Finally, and perhaps most important, remember that you are working on your writing project to make a contribution, to shape your readers' thinking about your subject. Avoid being overly deferential to the authors who have written before you. You should respect their work, but don't assume that their conclusions about the subject are the last word. Be prepared to challenge their ideas and arguments. If you don't do this, there's little point in writing, for you'll simply repeat the ideas of others instead of advancing your own.

What Strategies Can I Use to Read Actively?

Once you've thought about your writing situation and the writing situations that shaped your sources, you're ready to start reading actively. Reading actively means interacting with sources and considering them in light of the conversation you've decided to join. When you read actively, you might do one or more of the following:

- skim the source to get a general sense of what it's about
- write questions in the margins
- jot down your reactions
- identify key information, ideas, and arguments
- note how you might use information, ideas, and arguments in your document
- visually link one part of the source to another
- identify important passages for later rereading

To read actively, focus on three strategies: skimming, marking and annotating, and examining sources closely.

Identify the type of document to remind yourself of typical purposes, forms of evidence, and conventions of a genre. This page is part of an article from the professional journal *Adweek*.

Check the title (and table of contents, if one is provided) for cues about content.

Skim opening paragraphs to learn about the purpose and scope of the document.

Check headings and subheadings to learn about content and organization.

Skim captions of photos and figures, which often highlight important arguments, ideas, and information.

Look for pull quotes (quotations or passages called out into the margins or set in larger type) for a sense of the writer's main idea.

Read the first and last sentences of paragraphs to find key information

↥ How to Skim a Print Document

Skim for an Overview

Before investing too much time in a source, skim it. Skimming—reading just enough to get the general idea of what a source is about—can tell you a great deal in a short amount of time and is an important first step in reading a source critically. To skim sources, glance at surface elements without delving too deeply into the content.

Megan Martinez, a student working on an informative essay about social-networking sites such as Facebook and MySpace, used skimming to gain a quick overview of the information, ideas, and arguments that had been published on the subject. Using one of the databases available through her school's library, she found and skimmed an article in *Adweek* that explored the Marine Corps's use of MySpace for recruiting. She also skimmed a discussion of social networking and privacy on the University of Texas at Austin's Information Technology Services Web site.

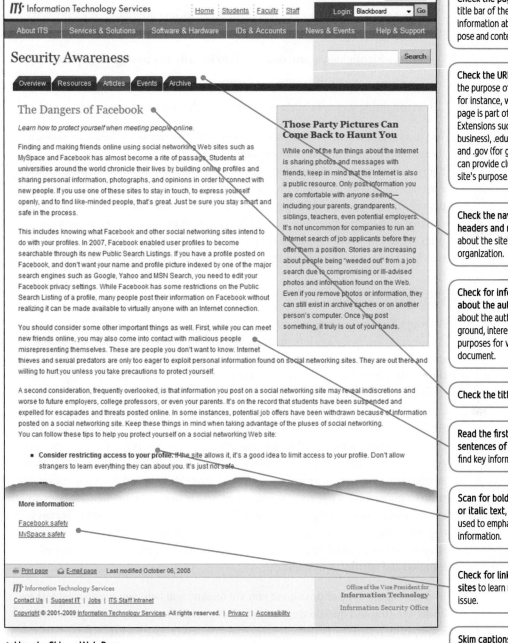

The University of Texas at Austin

ITS Information Technology Services

Home Students Faculty Staff

Service Alerts

Login: Blackboard ▼ Go

About ITS | Services & Solutions | Software & Hardware | IDs & Accounts | News & Events | Help & Support

Security Awareness

Search

Overview | Resources | Articles | Events | Archive

The Dangers of Facebook

Learn how to protect yourself when meeting people online.

Finding and making friends online using social networking Web sites such as MySpace and Facebook has almost become a rite of passage. Students at universities around the world chronicle their lives by building online profiles and sharing personal information, photographs, and opinions in order to connect with new people. If you use one of these sites to stay in touch, to express yourself openly, and to find like-minded people, that's great. Just be sure you stay smart and safe in the process.

This includes knowing what Facebook and other social networking sites intend to do with your profiles. In 2007, Facebook enabled user profiles to become searchable through its new Public Search Listings. If you have a profile posted on Facebook, and don't want your name and profile picture indexed by one of the major search engines such as Google, Yahoo and MSN Search, you need to edit your Facebook privacy settings. While Facebook has some restrictions on the Public Search Listing of a profile, many people post their information on Facebook without realizing it can be made available to virtually anyone with an Internet connection.

You should consider some other important things as well. First, while you can meet new friends online, you may also come into contact with malicious people misrepresenting themselves. These are people you don't want to know. Internet thieves and sexual predators are only too eager to exploit personal information found on social networking sites. They are out there and willing to hurt you unless you take precautions to protect yourself.

A second consideration, frequently overlooked, is that information you post on a social networking site may reveal indiscretions and worse to future employers, college professors, or even your parents. It's on the record that students have been suspended and expelled for escapades and threats posted online. In some instances, potential job offers have been withdrawn because of information posted on a social networking site. Keep these things in mind when taking advantage of the pluses of social networking. You can follow these tips to help you protect yourself on a social networking Web site:

- **Consider restricting access to your profile.** If the site allows it, it's a good idea to limit access to your profile. Don't allow strangers to learn everything they can about you. It's just not safe.

Those Party Pictures Can Come Back to Haunt You

While one of the fun things about the Internet is sharing photos and messages with friends, keep in mind that the Internet is also a public resource. Only post information you are comfortable with *anyone* seeing—including your parents, grandparents, siblings, teachers, even potential employers. It's not uncommon for companies to run an Internet search of job applicants before they offer them a position. Stories are increasing about people being "weeded out" from a job search due to compromising or ill-advised photos and information found on the Web. Even if you remove photos or information, they can still exist in archive caches or on another person's computer. Once you post something, it truly is out of your hands.

More information:

Facebook safety
MySpace safety

Print page | E-mail page | Last modified October 06, 2008

ITS Information Technology Services

Contact Us | Suggest IT | Jobs | ITS Staff Intranet

Copyright © 2001-2009 Information Technology Services. All rights reserved. | Privacy | Accessibility

Office of the Vice President for
Information Technology
Information Security Office

Check the page title in the title bar of the browser for information about the purpose and content of the page.

Check the URL to learn about the purpose of a Web page — for instance, whether the page is part of a larger site. Extensions such as .com (for business), .edu (for education), and .gov (for government) can provide clues about the site's purpose.

Check the navigation headers and menus to learn about the site's content and organization.

Check for information about the author to learn about the author's background, interests, and purposes for writing the document.

Check the title.

Read the first and last sentences of paragraphs to find key information.

Scan for boldface, colored, or italic text, which might be used to emphasize important information.

Check for links to other sites to learn more about the issue.

Skim captions of photos and figures, which often highlight important arguments, ideas, and information.

↰ **How to Skim a Web Page**

Mark and Annotate

Marking a source to identify key information, ideas, and arguments is a simple yet powerful active-reading strategy. Common marking techniques include

- using a highlighter, a pen, or a pencil to identify key passages in a print source
- attaching notes or flags to printed pages
- highlighting passages in electronic texts with your word-processing program

You can further engage with your sources by writing brief annotations, or notes, in the margins of print sources and by using commenting tools for electronic sources. Many writers, such as Megan Martinez, whose notes are illustrated on page 27, use annotations in combination with marking. For instance, if you have highlighted a passage (marking) with which you disagree, you can write a brief note about why you disagree with the passage (annotating). You might make note of another source you've read that could support your argument, or you might write yourself a reminder to look for information that will help you argue against the passage.

Pay Attention

Although writing projects can differ greatly, you'll want to examine at least some documents closely for key information, ideas, and arguments. Noting various aspects of a written work during your active reading will help you better understand the source, its role in the conversation you've decided to join, and how you might use it in your own writing.

RECOGNIZE THE TYPE OF DOCUMENT

One of the most important things to pay attention to is the type of document—or genre—you are reading. For example, if a source is an opinion column rather than an objective summary of an argument, you're more likely to watch for a questionable use of logic or analysis. If you are reading an article in a company newsletter or an annual report, you'll recognize that one of the writer's most important concerns is to present the company in a positive light. If an article comes from a peer-reviewed scholarly journal, you'll know that it's been judged by experts in the field as well founded and worthy of publication.

Recognizing the type of document you are reading will help you create a context for understanding and questioning the information, ideas, and arguments presented in a source.

In America, we live in a paradoxical world of privacy. On one hand, teenagers reveal their intimate thoughts and behaviors online and, on the other hand, government agencies and marketers are collecting personal data about us. For instance, the government uses driver license databases to find "dead-beat dads" or fathers who are behind on their child support payments. Many government records have been turned into digital archives that can be searched through the Internet. Every time we use a shopping card, a retail store collects data about our consumer spending habits. Credit card companies can create even larger profiles of our shopping behaviors. Locked away on hundreds of servers is every minute detail of our daily lives from our individual buying preferences to personal thoughts. Galkin (1996) states: "Much of the information that people would like to keep secret is already lawfully in the possession of some company or government entity, and what we want is to stop further disclosure without authorization." [14] Many people may not be aware of the fact that their privacy has already been jeopardized and they are not taking steps to protect their personal information from being used by others.

Are we being tricked into thinking privacy is real?

Megan has highlighted key passages and has written notes in the margin.

In an age of digital media, do we really have any privacy?

In an age of digital media, do we really have any privacy? From Oscar Gandy's (1993) perspective, we probably do not. Using the metaphor of a Panopticon—an architectural design that allowed prisoners to be monitored by observers—Gandy argues that surveillance systems can exert the same type of control in contemporary culture. He states: "the panoptic sort is an antidemocratic system of control that cannot be transformed because it can serve no purpose other than that for which it is designed—the rationalization and control of human existence." [15] He calls for an agency that will be charged with ensuring the survival of privacy.

Look this up.

Might be a good idea.

In post 9/11 America, government agencies appear to be doing the opposite. In 2005, the Department of Defense proposed to create a marketing and recruitment database to track students for military recruitment. According to the Electronic Frontier Foundation (2005), "Among the information kept on students were ethnicity, phone numbers, e-mail addresses, intended fields of study and extracurricular activities. The record system even included parents' attitudes about military recruitment." [16] But, the system was set up before notifying the public, a violation of the Privacy Act. Thus, establishing government agencies may not be a solution to the privacy dilemma. In a post 9/11 world, the U.S. government utilizes computer technology to exert some degree of control over its citizens, rather than protect their privacy.

Check out the EFF.

Megan has identified a key point with highlighting and an annotation.

Can we trust the government?

ᒪ **Marking and Annotating a Source**

IDENTIFY THE MAIN POINT

Most sources make a main point that you should pay attention to. An editorial in a local newspaper, for example, might urge voters to approve financing for a new school. An article might report a new advance in automobile emissions testing, or a Web page might emphasize the benefits of a new technique for treating a sports injury. Often the main point will be expressed in the form of a thesis statement. As you read critically, make sure you understand what the writer wants readers to accept, believe, or do as a result of reading the document.

FIND REASONS AND EVIDENCE THAT SUPPORT THE MAIN POINT

Once you've identified the main point, look for the reasons given to accept it. If an author is arguing, for instance, that English should be the only language used for official government business in the United States, that author might support his or her argument with the following reasons:

> The use of multiple languages erodes patriotism.
>
> The use of multiple languages keeps people apart — if they can't talk to one another, they won't learn to respect one another.
>
> The use of multiple languages in government business costs taxpayers money because so many alternative forms need to be printed.

Reasons can take a wide range of forms and are often presented in forms that appeal to emotions, logic, principles, values, or beliefs. As persuasive as these reasons might seem, they are only as good as the evidence offered to support them. In some cases, evidence is offered in the form of statements from experts on a subject or people in positions of authority. In other cases, evidence might include personal experience. In still other cases, evidence might include firsthand observations, excerpts from an interview, or statistical data.

In many cases, writers will present general conclusions based on evidence rather than a detailed discussion of the evidence. For example, a writer is much more likely to point out that more than half of the respondents to a survey agreed with a particular solution to a problem, rather than explain that 11 percent strongly disagreed, 22 percent disagreed, 7 percent had no opinion, 42 percent agreed, and 18 percent strongly agreed. When you use empirical evidence in a source, consider where the evidence comes from and how it is being used. If the information appears to be presented fairly, ask whether you might be able to use it to support your own ideas, and try to verify its accuracy by consulting additional sources.

A New Face for Schools

by Laura Lefkowits

Choice is ubiquitous in our lives. From on-demand TV programs to music downloads to "fast" gourmet restaurant chains that let customers build their ideal burrito, we like "having it our way."

This trend toward using technology to support individualization and customization has been immersing itself in our culture for the past decade, along with fears that such technologies would isolate us from one another, severely restricting face-to-face communications. Now, however, our fears are subsiding as another trend emerges—the rise of dozens of new voluntary communities, or social networks, that are bringing us together in unique, technology-driven ways.

Ask students about social networks, and they'll tell you that, whatever their geographic locale, they are a mere breath away from each other on Facebook. They regularly negotiate sales of everything from video games to car parts on eBay, prefer to share vacation memories and weekend photos on Flickr, and of course, create their alter-egos on MySpace.

The participation and active contribution of users is what makes these networks powerful, purposeful communities. My organization, the Denver-based Mid-continent Research for Education and Learning (McREL), believes these communities can have a powerful effect on student achievement in our 21st-century schools.

How "purposeful communities" work

In their work on school leadership, McREL researchers identify "purposeful community" as a critical component of successful education systems. In K–12 education, this community includes students, parents, teachers, school staff members, central office administrators and support personnel, the school board, other social agencies, and businesses.

A purposeful community has the collective ability to develop and use all available assets to accomplish purposes and produce outcomes that matter to all community members. Members come together to accomplish outcomes that individuals could not accomplish on their own, such as increasing graduation rates or reducing absenteeism.

Purposeful communities use both tangible assets (such as media centers and textbooks) and intangible assets (such as parent involvement and community support) to achieve their purposes. They also have agreed-upon processes for working together, which include both articulated and tacit operating principles governing their interactions.

These processes ensure the viability of the community and increase the likelihood of meeting shared goals. Finally, purposeful communities exhibit a sense of collective efficacy; they really do believe that together they can make a difference.

Compare the characteristics of a purposeful community to many social networking tools, and you find many similarities.

The power of social networks

Social networking sites are established for a specific purpose and depend on users adhering to agreed-upon processes to achieve common goals and to self-regulate on behalf of the community's interests. On Facebook (www.facebook.com), for example, you may only view another's profile if you have been "friended" by that person. This promotes a level of privacy with which all users are comfortable.

Most sites also have mechanisms that allow community members to flag posted items that they believe are inappropriate or outside the terms of use. For example, on the free classified advertising site Craig's List (www.craigslist.org), users looking for a new home can select a list of houses for sale by owner or a separate list for sale by agent. If an unscrupulous agent lists a house in the "for sale by owner" section, an observant user can flag the item, warning fellow users about the infraction. When an item receives a certain number of flags, it is pulled from the site.

Most "terms of use" statements do not specify each and every possible infraction warranting a flag. Rather, it is up to users themselves to set the standards, and over time, each virtual community develops its own set of tacit agreements and operating principles to guide its online behavior.

Perhaps the most powerful similarity between social networking and purposeful communities is the notion of collective efficacy. Writers such as Howard Rheingold and James Surowiecki have discussed the power inherent in online communities. Rheingold coined the term "smart mobs," and Surowiecki identified this phenomenon as the "wisdom of crowds." One only has to look at the impact of the Internet on the fundraising abilities of our presidential candidates to understand the strength inherent in a community of likeminded people joining together in a virtual world to support a shared goal.

And how can anyone deny the sense of collective efficacy at play this past March, when hundreds of California high school students, responding to text messages, walked out of school to protest budget cuts made by the school board that very morning? Students, particularly angered over the 50 percent cut to the sports programs, gathered at the high school and walked to the district offices carrying hastily prepared protest signs.

Ultimately, the students were invited to meet with school officials to discuss the possibility of initiating a ballot issue to raise funds for the sports program.

Social networking, school improvement

Could Facebook be a model for a 21st-century purposeful student community designed for school improvement? Possibly, but evidence suggests that education is not prepared to accept the dimension of purposeful communities offered by social networks.

In its 2007 report *Creating & Connecting*, the National School Boards Association revealed that 96 percent of students with online access spend nearly as much time using social networking technologies as watching television—nine hours and 10 hours respectively each week. Moreover, more than half of the respondents indicated that they use social networking tools to talk about education and collaborate on school projects, yet associated interviews with district leaders revealed that most K–12 school systems have strict rules against nearly all forms of online social networking while at school.

What's wrong with this picture?

Perhaps we should take a lesson from our students. They are, in fact, organically forming purposeful communities throughout cyberspace every day. Rather than restricting the most highly engaging form of communication and community-making available to students, what if schools embraced this technology and made use of its natural educational advantages?

True purposeful communities are composed of students, parents, teachers, and many others. Together, stakeholders' contributions to school improvement strategies could grow exponentially and virally in the same way one adds friends on Facebook. Imagine what the next generation of schools might look like when they are led by today's students, whose lives are filled with choice and whose communities are inherently purposeful.

Laura Lefkowits (llefkowits@mcrel.org) is vice president for policy and planning services at McREL. She served as an at-large member of the Denver Public Schools Board of Education from 1995 to 1999.

This article is adapted from one that originally appeared in the Winter 2008 issue of McREL's Changing Schools *(www.mcrel.org/topics/products/339).*

Reprinted with permission from American School Board Journal, *July 2008.*

Working Together: Identify Information in a Source

Working with a group of classmates, identify the main point, reasons, and evidence in Laura Lefkowits's article "A New Face for Schools."

1. **List the main point at the top of your page.** Determine what the author is asking you to know, believe, or do.

2. **Briefly list each reason to accept the main point** in the order in which it appears in the source. You might want to brainstorm lists individually based on your reading of the article and then share your ideas to create the group's list.

3. **Identify the most important evidence offered as proof for each reason.** Once you've agreed on the reasons, work together to identify the evidence used to support each reason.

@ Download or print this Working Together activity at **bedfordstmartins.com/conversation.**

CONSIDER ILLUSTRATIONS

A growing number of documents are using illustrations — photographs and other images, charts, graphs, tables, animations, audio clips, and video clips — in addition to text. Illustrations are typically used to demonstrate or emphasize a point, help readers better understand a point, clarify or simplify the presentation of a complex concept, or increase the visual appeal of a document. Illustrations can also serve as a form of argument by presenting a surprising or even shocking set of statistics or setting an emotional tone. As you read, be aware of the types of illustrations and the effects they produce. The types of illustrations you are likely to encounter include the following:

- **Photographs and images.** Photographs and other images, such as drawings, paintings, and sketches, are frequently used to set a mood, emphasize a point, or demonstrate a point more fully than is possible with text alone.

- **Charts and graphs.** Charts and graphs provide a visual representation of information. They are typically used to present numerical information more succinctly than is possible with text alone or to present complex information in a compact and more accessible form.

- **Tables.** Tables provide categorical lists of information. Like charts and graphs, they are typically used to make a point more succinctly than is possible with text alone or to present complex information in a compact form. Tables are frequently used to illustrate contrasts among groups, relationships among variables (such as income, educational attainment, and voting preferences), or change over time (such as growth in population during the past century).

- **Digital illustrations.** Digital publications, such as PowerPoint presentations and Web pages, can include a wider range of illustrations than print documents can. Illustrations such as audio, video, and animations differ from photographs, images, charts, graphs, and tables in that they don't just appear on the page — they do things.

RECORD NEW INFORMATION AND CHALLENGING IDEAS

As you read, mark and annotate passages that contain information that is new to you. In your writer's notebook, record new information in the form of a list or as a series of brief descriptions of what you've learned and where you learned it.

You might be tempted to ignore material that's hard to understand, but if you do, you could miss critical information. When you encounter something difficult, mark it and make a brief annotation reminding yourself to check it out later. Sometimes you'll learn enough from your continued reading that the passage won't seem as challenging when you come back to it. Sometimes, however, you won't be able to figure out a passage on your own. In that case, turn to someone else for help — your instructor, a librarian, members of an online forum or a newsgroup — or try searching a database, library catalog, or the Web using key words or phrases you didn't understand.

How Can I Evaluate Sources?

At the beginning of a writing project, you'll usually make quick judgments about the sources you come across. Skimming an article, a book, or a Web site (see p. 24) might be enough to tell you that spending more time with the document would be wasted effort. As you prepare to write, however, you should evaluate potential sources in light of your writing situation and your needs as a writer. Evaluating a source means examining its relevance, evidence, author, publisher, timeliness, comprehensiveness, and genre.

Determine Relevance

Relevance is the extent to which a source provides information you can use in your writing project. Remember your purpose when you evaluate potential sources. Even if a source provides a great deal of information, it might not meet your needs. For example, an analysis of the printing features in word-processing programs might contain a great deal of accurate and up-to-date information—but it won't be of much use if you're writing about color laser printers for college students.

Your readers will expect information that meets their needs as well. If they want to read about personal printers for college students, for instance, pass up sources that focus on high-capacity office printers.

Consider the Use of Evidence

Evidence is information offered to support a point. Statistics, facts, expert opinions, and firsthand accounts are among the many types of evidence you'll find. As a writer, you can evaluate not only the kinds of evidence in a source but also the quality, amount, and appropriateness of that evidence. Ask yourself the following questions:

- **Is enough evidence offered?** A lack of evidence might indicate fundamental flaws in the author's argument.

- **Is the right kind of evidence offered?** More evidence isn't always better evidence. Ask whether the evidence is appropriate for the reasons being offered and whether more than one type of evidence is being used. Many sources rely far too heavily on a single type of evidence, such as personal experience or quotations from experts.

- **Is the evidence used fairly?** Look for reasonable alternative interpretations, questionable or inappropriate use of evidence, and evidence that seems to contradict points made elsewhere in a source. If statistics are included, are they interpreted fairly or presented clearly? If a quotation is offered to support a point, is the quotation used appropriately?

- **Are sources identified?** Knowing the origins of evidence can make a significant difference in your evaluation of a source. For example, if a writer quotes a political poll but doesn't say which organization conducted the poll, you might reasonably question the reliability of the source.

Identify the Author

The significance of authorship is affected by context. For example, take two editorials that make similar arguments and offer similar evidence. Both are published in your local newspaper. One is written by a fourteen-year-old middle school student, the other by a U.S. senator. You would certainly favor the senator's editorial if the subject was U.S. foreign policy. If the subject was student perceptions about drug abuse prevention in schools, however, you might value the middle school student's opinion more highly.

Ask the following questions about the author of a source:

- **Is the author knowledgeable?** An author might be an acknowledged expert in a field, a reporter who has written extensively about an issue, or someone with firsthand experience. Then again, an author might have little or no experience with a subject beyond a desire to say something about it. How can you tell the difference? Look for a description of the author in the source. If none is provided, look for biographical information on the Web or in a reference such as *Who's Who*.

- **What are the author's biases?** We all have biases—a set of interests that shapes our perceptions. Try to learn about the author's affiliations so that you determine the extent to which his or her biases affect the presentation of arguments, ideas, and information in a source. For instance, you might infer a bias if you know that an author writes frequently about gun control and works as a regional director for the National Handgun Manufacturers Association.

Learn about the Publisher

Publishers are the groups that produce and provide access to sources, including books, newspapers, journals, Web sites, sound and video files, and databases. Like authors, publishers have biases. Unlike authors, they often advertise them. Many publishers have a mission statement on their Web sites, while others provide information that can help you figure out their priorities. You might already be familiar with a publisher, particularly in the case of major newspapers or magazines, such as the *New York Times* (regarded as liberal) or *U.S. News and World Report* (regarded as conservative). If the publisher is a scholarly or professional journal, you can often figure out its biases by looking over the contents of several issues or by reading a few of its editorials.

Establish Timeliness

The importance of a source's date of publication varies according to your writing situation. For example, if you're writing a feature article on the use of superconducting materials in new mass-transportation projects, you probably won't want to spend a lot of time with articles published in 1968. However, if you're writing about the 1968 presidential contest between Hubert Humphrey and Richard Nixon, then sources published during that time period will take on greater importance.

Print sources usually list a publication date. However, it can be difficult to tell when Web sources were created. When in doubt, back up undated information found on the Web with a dated source.

Assess Comprehensiveness

Comprehensiveness is the extent to which a source provides a complete and balanced view of a subject. Like timeliness, the importance of comprehensiveness varies according to the demands of your writing situation. If you are working on a narrowly focused project, such as the role played by shifts in Pacific Ocean currents on snowfall patterns in Colorado last winter, comprehensiveness in a source might not be important — or even possible. However, if you are considering a broader issue, such as the potential effects of global climate change on agricultural production in North America, or if you are still learning as much as you can about your subject, give preference to sources that provide full treatment.

Recognize Genre

Knowing the genre of a source can help you understand a great deal about its intended readers, the kind of evidence it is likely to use, and the kind of argument it is likely to make. An article in a professional journal, for example, will almost certainly rely on published sources or original research, and it will carefully document its sources so that readers can easily locate related documents. In contrast, a blog entry is more likely to rely on personal observation and reflection.

By understanding the conventions of a particular genre, you can understand whether the information, ideas, and arguments found in it might be of use to you as you work on your writing project. To evaluate a genre, carry out the following activities:

- **Analyze the writing style.** Determine how formally (or informally) the document is written. Check for the use of specialized terms that might be unfamiliar to general readers. Try to understand how the writer views himself or herself in relation to readers.

- **Consider how evidence is used.** Identify numerical information; quotations and paraphrases; summaries of other documents; charts, graphs, and tables; and images and other illustrations. Ask yourself why the writer chose the types of evidence you've found in the document.

- **Look at the organization.** Try to break the document into major sections. Ask whether you've seen this type of organization used in other documents, and think about the purposes of those documents. Documents within a genre often follow a similar structure.

- **Identify citation styles.** Determine whether the sources of information, ideas, and arguments are identified in the document.

- **Consider design.** A document's appearance can tell you a lot about its purpose, intended readers, and likely means of distribution. Is the document's medium print or digital? Does it use color, columns of text, and images or other illustrations? What types of readers might appreciate the use of these design elements? And what effect might these elements have on potential readers?

Examine Electronic Sources Closely

You can apply the general evaluative criteria discussed above to most types of sources. However, electronic sources can pose special challenges. Because anyone can create a Web site, start a blog, or post a message to a newsgroup, e-mail list, or Web discussion forum, approach these sources with more caution than you would reserve for print sources such as books and journal articles, which are typically published only after a lengthy editorial review process.

WEB SITES AND BLOGS

To assess the credibility of a Web site or a blog, consider its domain (.edu, .com, and so on), and look for information about the site (often available on the "About This Site" or "Site Information" page).

NEWSGROUPS, E-MAIL LISTS, AND DISCUSSION FORUMS

To assess the relevance and credibility of a message on a newsgroup, an e-mail list, or a Web discussion forum, check for a "signature" at the end of the message, and try to locate a Frequently Asked Questions (FAQ) list. A signature can provide information about the sender, such as a professional title, and the URL for a personal home page where you can learn more about the author. FAQs can tell you about the purpose of a newsgroup, an e-mail list, or a discussion forum; whether messages are moderated (reviewed before being posted); and whether membership is open or restricted to a particular group.

WIKIS

Wikis are Web sites that can be added to or edited by visitors to the site. Reference sites such as Wikipedia (en.wikipedia.org) have grown in importance on the Web, and many are highly ranked by search sites such as Ask, Yahoo!, and Google. Unfortunately, it can be difficult to evaluate the credibility of wiki pages because changes occur quickly and repeatedly, with no guarantee of accuracy or credibility. You might want to use wikis when you are beginning to learn about a topic, but avoid citing them as the "last word" on a topic. In fact, those "last words" might change before you submit your final draft.

Check the domain to learn about the site's purpose and publisher:

.biz, .com, .coop: business   .mil: military
.edu: higher education   .gov: government
.org: nonprofit organization   .net: network organization

Check the title bar and page headers or titles to learn about the site's relevance and publisher.

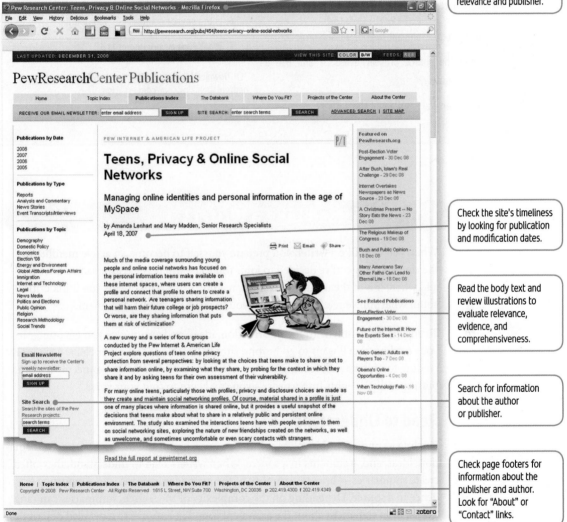

Check the site's timeliness by looking for publication and modification dates.

Read the body text and review illustrations to evaluate relevance, evidence, and comprehensiveness.

Search for information about the author or publisher.

Check page footers for information about the publisher and author. Look for "About" or "Contact" links.

⌐ **How to Evaluate a Web Site**

Practice: Evaluate a Source

Select a source you have found as you've learned about a topic. In your writer's notebook, respond to the following questions:

1. Is the source relevant to your writing project?

2. Does the source present evidence and use it appropriately?

3. What can you learn about the author?

4. What can you learn about the publisher?

5. Is the source timely?

6. Is the source comprehensive enough?

7. What type of document is it?

@ Download or print this Practice activity at bedfordstmartins.com/conversation.

How Can I Read Like a Writer?

When you read like a writer, you prepare yourself to become an active member of the conversation you've decided to join. You learn where the conversation has been — and where it is at the moment. In short, reading like a writer helps you think critically about what you've read and prepares you to write your own document.

To engage more fully with the information, ideas, and arguments you encounter in your reading, you'll want to go beyond simply knowing what others have written. By reading to understand, reading to respond, and reading to make connections — and putting your thoughts into words — you can begin to find your voice.

Read to Understand

Reading to understand involves gaining an overview of the most important information, ideas, and arguments in a source. When writers read to understand, they often create summaries — brief descriptions of the main idea, reasons, and supporting evidence in a source. Depending on the complexity of the source, summaries can range from a brief statement about the argument found in a source to a detailed description of the key points and evidence it provides.

Many writers believe that a summary should be objective. It would be more accurate to say that a summary should be accurate and fair. That is, you should not misrepresent the information, ideas, or arguments in a source. Achieving accuracy and fairness, however, does not necessarily mean that your summary will be an objective presentation of the source. Instead, your summary will reflect your purpose, needs, and interests and—if you're writing for an audience—those of your readers. You'll focus on information, ideas, and arguments that are relevant to your writing situation. As a result, your summary is likely to differ from one written by another writer. Both summaries might be accurate and fair, but each one will reflect its writer's writing situation.

As you read to understand, highlight key points in the source, and note passages that include useful quotations or information you might use to add detail to your summary. If you are writing a summary for a class, it will typically take one of three forms: a main-point summary, a key-point summary, or an outline summary.

Megan Martinez found the article on page 40 during her search for information about social networking. Published by the Times Online, a Web site owned by leading British newspaper companies, the article suggested another way of looking at the benefits and drawbacks of social-networking sites.

MAIN-POINT SUMMARIES

A main-point summary reports the most important information, idea, or argument presented in a source. You can use main-point summaries to keep track of the overall claim made in a source, to introduce your readers to a source, and to place the main point of that source into the context of an argument or a discussion of a subject. Megan might have written the following main-point summary of Bernhard Warner's article:

> In his article "Is Social Networking a Waste of Time?" Bernhard Warner argues that the use of social-networking sites and other Web 2.0 media by students will ultimately benefit society — and the students themselves.

Main-point summaries are brief. They identify the source and its main point.

KEY-POINT SUMMARIES

Like a main-point summary, a key-point summary reports the most important information, idea, or argument presented in a source. However, it also includes the reasons (key points) and evidence the author uses to support his or her main point. Key-point summaries are useful when you want to keep track of a complex argument or understand an elaborate process.

> In his article "Is Social Networking a Waste of Time?" Bernhard Warner argues that the use of social-networking sites and other Web 2.0 tools by students will ultimately benefit society — and the students themselves. He notes that concerns expressed by members of the business community about lost productivity should not be extended to students' use of social-networking sites and tools. In fact, he points out that while adults tend to view the use of these sites and tools

The author, source, and main point are identified.

The concerns of people on the other side of the issue are briefly presented.

Is Social Networking a Waste of Time?

by Bernhard Warner

There has been much fuss of late over the loss of productivity brought on by employees multi-tasking between actual work and social networking. One estimate puts the cost to British industry at £6.5 billion per annum in lost productivity and questionable bandwidth usage. Another survey estimates that Britain's social media fanatics are spending as much as 12 hours per week on these sites, no doubt eating into valuable work time.

But what is the impact of this collective Facebook/MySpace/Bebo addiction on high school and university students, our bright future? A new survey this week by IT specialists Global Secure Systems (the ones who took a look at the impact on businesses and arrived at the £6.5 billion figure) says students are also guilty of sneaking in a fair bit of social networking during the school day.

In their survey of 500 English schoolchildren between the ages of 13 and 17, 51 percent confess to checking their social network profiles during lessons. Over a quarter admit their in-school daily social network fix exceeds over 30 minutes each day.

If this sounds surprising, you haven't been to school lately. Laptop-toting school kids are the norm these days, as are Wifi-enabled campuses. And when the laptop is in the locker, there are net-enabled smart phones at the ready. Add to the equation the rocket-fast texting ability of your typical 16-year-old and you get an explosion of social networking opportunities at the most unlikely points in the school day.

No educator would knowingly allow such a distraction in their classroom, and yet it appears to be happening right under their noses. It's hard enough getting the PlayStation generation to focus for even a half-hour on a lecture of, say, King John and the Magna Carta. Try competing with the latest lunchroom gossip being broadcasted to mobiles, Facebook, and Twitter. The significance of establishing modern-day democracy pales in comparison.

Before you shake your head and mutter something starting with the phrase "In my day . . . ," admit it—how many of you have shirked off work on an important business project to tend to a personal e-mail, text, or, these days, a Facebook query? How many of you have done it today? How many of you are doing it now?

We adults might regard tidying up our profile, sending messages to friends or contacts, joining the odd (or oddball) group, or participating in a movie knowledge quiz to be a harmless distraction, the kind of thing that keeps us sane during the workday. (While writing this column, I have been twice drawn to my Facebook profile to attend to small matters, but that's it. No more for me today. Okay, maybe after lunch.) But teens are deadly serious about social networks. For them, failing to attend to these duties could end friendships, sink reputations, and mean missed opportunities to climb the fickle and precarious social ladder of young adulthood. I say we ought to go easy on them if they are neglecting some of their responsibilities while they fuss around with their online persona.

As a university lecturer at John Cabot University in Rome I encourage my students, all in their early twenties, to embrace social media and every other Web 2.0 application out there. Yes, posting photos of you and your semi-clad friends boozing it up late at night could sink your chances with a prospective employer, who will no doubt be snooping around for this very type of incriminating evidence. But the good far outweighs the bad. I encourage the students to be creative, to promote our online student newspaper, which just over a year from launch is pulling in steadily rising traffic. No doubt all the blog, Facebook, and MySpace mentions are helping. I've had students who use social networking sites to build and promote projects on fighting poverty and eradicating hunger, organizing music gigs, art and photo exhibitions, plus coordinating meetups for political rallies.

I admire the growing number of young students who dedicate hours to designing complicated widgets and applications too. Yes, they're probably neglecting their history paper to complete it, but the end product is a far more valuable lesson learned in creativity, courage, and computer coding. When I look at all the creativity, the collaboration, and the activism being generated in these networks, I am hopeful for the future. Perhaps it is we educators who need to learn how to harness this power into our everyday classroom lessons.

Bernhard Warner, a freelance journalist and media consultant, writes about technology, the Internet, and media industries. He can be reached at techscribe@gmail.com.

as "a harmless distraction," many students fear that not using them "could end friendships, sink reputations, and mean missed opportunities to climb the fickle and precarious social ladder of young adulthood" (para. 7). Overall, Warner argues, the advantages of using social-networking sites and other Web 2.0 tools — in terms of "the creativity, the collaboration, and the activism being generated in these networks" — far outweigh the disadvantages (para. 9).

OUTLINE SUMMARIES

Sometimes called a plot summary, an outline summary reports the information, ideas, and arguments in a source in the same order used in the source. In a sense, an outline summary presents the overall "plot" of the source by reporting what was written in the order in which it was written. Outline summaries are useful when you need to keep track of the sequence of information, ideas, and arguments in a source.

In his article "Is Social Networking a Waste of Time?" Bernhard Warner argues that despite concerns expressed by members of the business community about lost productivity, we should not discourage students from using social-networking sites and tools. Warner reports that a recent survey of 500 English students between the ages of 13 and 17 indicates that more than half check social-networking sites during lessons and that more than a quarter spend more than 30 minutes each day on social-networking sites. Yet he points out that these behaviors are similar to those of adults, who tend to view the use of social-networking sites and other Web 2.0 tools as "a harmless distraction." Moreover, he notes that failing to use these tools can have significant consequences for students, many of whom fear that not using them "could end friendships, sink reputations, and mean missed opportunities to climb the fickle and precarious social ladder of young adulthood" (para. 7).

> The author, source, and main point are identified.

> The summary identifies each of the major points made in the article in the order in which they were made.

> The author's name is mentioned whenever information from the source is used.

> Terms such as "moreover" and "overall" provide a sense of movement through the source.

Warner, himself a teacher, argues that rather than trying to reduce students' use of social-networking sites and tools, we should instead channel them in productive ways. He reflects on his own successful use of social-networking tools and sites to support learning projects focused on "fighting poverty and eradicating hunger, organizing music gigs, art and photo exhibitions, plus coordinating meet-ups for political rallies" (para. 8). Overall, Warner argues, the advantages of using social-networking sites and other Web 2.0 tools — in terms of "the creativity, the collaboration, and the activism being generated in these networks" — far outweigh the disadvantages (para. 9).

Practice: Summarize a Source

Using the following guidelines, write an outline summary of Laura Lefkowits's article "A New Face for Schools" (p. 29):

1. Record the author and title of the source.

2. Identify the main point and key points made by the writer. Present the main point and key points in the order in which they appear in the source. For each point, briefly describe the evidence provided to back it up.

3. Clearly credit the author for any information, ideas, and arguments you include in your summary: use quotation marks for direct quotations, and identify the page from which you've drawn a paraphrase or quotation. (See Appendix B for guidelines on documenting sources.)

@ Download or print this Practice activity at bedfordstmartins.com/conversation.

Read to Respond

Reading to respond allows you to begin forming your own contribution to a conversation. Your response will help you focus your reactions to the information, ideas, and arguments you've encountered in a source. To prepare to write a response to a source, note passages with which you agree or disagree, reflect on interesting information and ideas, and record your thoughts about the effectiveness of the argument advanced in the source.

AGREE/DISAGREE RESPONSES

If you want to explore an idea or argument in a source, try freewriting about why you agree or disagree with it. In your response, clearly define the idea or argument to which you are responding. Then explain whether you agree or disagree with the idea or argument — or whether you find yourself in partial agreement with it — and why.

REFLECTIVE RESPONSES

A reflective response allows you to consider the meaning or implications of what you read. You might focus on a key passage or idea from a source, explaining or elaborating on it. Or you might reflect on your own experiences, attitudes, or observations in relation to a piece of information, an idea, or an argument. You can also use a reflective response to consider how an idea or argument might be interpreted by other readers, how it might be applied in a new context, or how it might be misunderstood.

ANALYTIC RESPONSES

An analytic response focuses on the important elements of a source, such as its purpose, ideas, argument, organization, focus, evidence, and style. For example, you might ask whether the main point is stated clearly, or whether appropriate types of evidence are used to support an argument. You might also analyze the logic of an argument or map its organization. Or you might offer suggestions about how an author could have made the source more effective.

Even when writers choose a particular type of response, they often draw on the other types to flesh out their ideas. For example, you might consider why you disagree with an argument by analyzing how effectively the source presents the argument. Or you might shift from agreeing with an idea to reflecting on its implications.

Practice: Respond to a Source

Putting your response into words can help you sort out your reactions to the ideas, information, and arguments in a source. Use the following guidelines to write an informal response to Bernhard Warner's essay (p. 40) or Laura Lefkowits's article (p. 29):

1. Identify a focus for your response. You might select important information, an intriguing idea, or the author's overall argument.

2. Decide what type of response you are going to write: agree/disagree, reflective, analytical, or some combination of the three types.

3. Write an introduction that identifies the information, idea, argument, or source to which you are responding, lays out your overall response (your main point), and identifies the source's author and title.

4. Provide reasons to support your main point and evidence to support your reasons.

5. Clearly credit the sources of any information, ideas, or arguments you use to support your response: use quotation marks for direct quotations, and identify the page or paragraph from which you've drawn a paraphrase or quotation. (See Appendix B for guidelines on documenting sources.)

@ Download or print this Practice activity at bedfordstmartins.com/conversation.

Read to Make Connections

You can learn a lot by looking for similarities and differences among the sources you read. For example, you might identify a group of authors with a similar approach to a subject, such as favoring increased government support for wind energy. You could then contrast this group with other groups of authors, such as those who believe that market forces should be the primary factor encouraging wind power, or those who believe we should focus on other forms of energy. Similarly, you can take note of information in one source that supports or contradicts information in another. These notes can help you build your own argument or identify information that will allow you (and your readers) to better understand a conversation.

As you read more and more about a subject, you'll start to notice common themes and shared ideas. Recognizing these connections among groups of authors can help you understand the scope of the conversation. For example, knowing that people involved in your conversation agree on the overall definition of a problem might lead you to focus your efforts on either challenging that definition with an alternative

---

Working Together: Make Connections among Sources

Work together with a group of classmates to identify general approaches to the subject of social networking. To prepare for the group activity, each member should read, mark, and annotate the articles, Web pages, and reports on social networking in this chapter. During class, you should carry out the following activities:

1. Members of the group should take turns reporting what they've learned about one of the sources.

2. As each report is made, the other members of the group should take notes on the key ideas highlighted by the reporter.

3. When the reports have been completed, the group should create an overall list of the key ideas discussed in the individual reports.

4. Identify sources that seem to share similar approaches to the issue. Give each group of sources a name, and provide a brief description of the ideas its authors have in common.

5. Describe each group in detail. Explain what makes the authors part of the same group (their similarities) and how each group differs from the others you've defined.

Once you've completed the activity, consider how you would respond to each group of authors. Ask whether you agree or disagree with their approach, and describe the extent to which you agree or disagree. Consider whether you would want to join a group, whether you would want to refine a particular approach to better fit your understanding of the subject, or whether you would rather develop a new approach.

@ Download or print this Working Together activity at bedfordstmartins.com/conversation.

one or suggesting a possible solution. If you find yourself agreeing with one group of authors, you might start to think of yourself as a member of that group—as someone who shares their approach to the subject. If you don't agree with any of the groups you've identified, perhaps you are ready to develop a new approach to the subject.

To make connections among authors, jot down notes in the margins of your sources or in your writer's notebook. Each time you read a new source, keep in mind what you've already read, and make note of similarities and differences among your sources. When you notice similar themes in some of your sources, review the sources you've already read to see whether they've addressed those themes.

Beyond a collection of notes and annotations, reading to make connections might also result in longer pieces of freewriting. In some cases, you might spend time creating a brief essay that defines each group, identifies which authors belong to each group, and reflects on the strengths, weaknesses, and appropriateness of the approach taken by each group.

In Summary: Entering a Research Conversation

✦ Read with a purpose (p. 21).

✦ Become an active reader (p. 23).

✦ Evaluate potential sources in light of your writing situation (p. 32).

✦ Summarize useful ideas, information, and arguments (p. 38).

✦ Respond to what you read (p. 42).

✦ Explore connections among sources (p. 44).

✱ Questions and Activities for Chapter 2

1. Write a journal entry in which you begin to identify aspects of the course topic that interest you the most. In your journal entry, include responses to the following questions:

   a. What are the three most important issues you have identified so far?

   b. Of these issues, which one do you have the most previous knowledge about?

    c. Identify some issues concerning your course topic about which people disagree.

    d. What questions or concerns do you have about this inquiry topic?

    e. Thus far, what issue are you most interested in exploring further? Why?

2. Look at the illustration "How to Skim a Print Document" (p. 24), and apply the instructions in each of the callout boxes to skim a text you are reading. For example, what does the title reveal about the subject and main point of the text? If you read only the first and last sentences of each paragraph, what do you find out about the content of the text? Write down your responses.

3. Using the callout boxes in the illustration "How to Skim a Web Page" (p. 25) as a guide, skim a Web site that seems to offer relevant information on your emerging topic. Write down your responses.

4. Evaluate a text you are reading by responding to each of the following questions, from the section "How Can I Evaluate Sources?": What is its relevance, how is evidence used, who is the author, who is the publisher, when was it published, and what type of document is it? (See the "Practice: Evaluate a Source" activity on p. 38 for another version of this question.)

5. Analyze the evidence and reasons offered by the writer of a text you're reading. Make a list of those reasons on a page for discussion in class. (Alternatively, complete the activity on p. 31, "Working Together: Identify Information in a Source.")

6. Writing a summary of a text is an excellent way to develop your reading comprehension and to practice using succinct, precise language. Write a one-paragraph (150 words) summary of the content of one of your readings, using either the main-point/key-point or outline summary technique. Refer to the section "How Can I Read Like a Writer?" (p. 38) for more details regarding these different summary strategies.

7. Complete the activity "Practice: Respond to a Source" (p. 43) using either of the short texts included in this chapter, another text assigned by your instructor, or one that you came across in your own reading.

3 Developing a Research Question and Locating Sources

Exploring a topic through reading, developing a research question, and conducting a targeted search for additional source material: these are activities you will engage in during each of the projects you do in English 102. In later pages of this book, you'll find many references to the skills detailed in this chapter — framing research questions, deciding upon the kinds of sources you'll need, and keeping track of and understanding what you discover — and that's a good indicator of how crucial these skills are to becoming a good researcher. While the particular types of questions you ask and sources you look for will differ from project to project, the information from this chapter will be useful to each of your 102 assignments.

The more "formal" stage of research starts at the point when you realize you don't know or understand something, when the desire to *find out* starts to percolate in your mind. The section "How Should I Focus My Search for Sources?" will help you identify and formulate a strong research question, which may be about something that you don't understand; something that doesn't seem to correspond with your experience or with what you already know; something about the perspectives, information, or opinions of important groups of people that appear to have been left out of the conversation; something that has to do with historical background and context; and/or something about which you simply are curious and want to know more. Experimenting with different ways to frame a research question will enable you to better understand what you're trying to find out — and has the added (and time-saving!) benefit of helping you formulate a more targeted search for additional sources.

Once you have a better-defined idea of what you want to investigate, you face the challenge of deciding what kinds of source material will best help you answer your question and which — among the many you will come across — are relevant, useful, and credible. The section "How Can I Develop a Search Plan?" will help you negotiate that challenge.

Check out Appendix C, Work-in-Progress Research and Writing Activities, to find additional practical suggestions to help you read, research, and write successfully.

Chapter 3, "Developing a Research Question and Locating Sources," is taken from Mike Palmquist, *Joining the Conversation*, pp. 460–78 (Chapter 11, "Preparing to Use Sources in an Academic Essay"), and Mike Palmquist, *The Bedford Researcher*, Third Edition, pp. 44–46 (Chapter 3, "Developing Your Research Question and Proposal").

If you've done a research paper before, you know that it can be hard to remember which sources include the information you need — and sometimes that can make research feel frustrating, even overwhelming. The section "How Can I Keep Track of My Sources?" offers useful strategies for understanding and recalling the important information in your research materials. It also includes information on one of the most common English 102 assignments, the annotated bibliography.

Finally, the last section of the chapter, "What Is a Research Proposal and How Can I Create One?," provides guidelines for putting together a research proposal, a very common assignment in English 102 and in other courses across the university. Also included is a Sample Student Research Proposal written by a previous English 102 student.

How Should I Focus My Search for Sources?

As you prepare to search for sources, it's best to have an idea of what you're looking for. Focus your efforts to collect, read, evaluate, and take notes on sources by developing a research question—a brief question that asks about a specific aspect of your subject, reflects your writing situation, and is narrow enough to allow you to collect information in time to meet your deadlines.

Your research question will reflect the role you've adopted as a writer. To develop your research question, you'll generate ideas for potential research questions and assess each one in light of your interests, role, and writing situation.

Generate Potential Research Questions

Start to develop your research question by generating a list of questions about the conversation you've decided to join. Most research questions begin with the word *what*, *why*, *when*, *where*, *who*, or *how*. Some research questions use the word *would* or *could* to ask whether something is possible. Still others use the word *should* to analyze the appropriateness of a particular action, policy, procedure, or decision. Questions can focus on the following:

- **Information:** what is known—and not known—about a subject
- **History:** what has occurred in the past that is relevant to a subject
- **Assumptions:** what conclusions—merited or not—writers and readers have already made about a subject

- **Goals:** what the writers and readers involved in this conversation want to see happen (or not happen)

- **Outcomes:** what has happened so far, or what is likely to happen

- **Policies:** what the best procedures are for carrying out actions or for making decisions

Questions can also lead you to engage in the following kinds of thinking processes:

- **Reflecting:** considering the significance of a subject

- **Reporting:** seeking information; conveying what is known about a subject

- **Analyzing:** looking for similarities and differences among subjects or aspects of a subject; asking what leads to a specific result; asking about a series of events

- **Evaluating:** asking about strengths and weaknesses, advantages and disadvantages, or appropriateness

- **Problem solving:** defining problems, considering the outcomes of a problem, assessing potential solutions, and/or offering solutions

- **Advocating:** advancing arguments about a subject

By combining a specific focus, such as assumptions, with a specific type of thinking process, such as problem solving, you can create carefully tailored research questions, such as the ones that student writer Jennie Tillson considered for an essay about the cost of college.

> What assumptions have shaped debates about rising tuitions?
>
> What assumptions have worked against a resolution of this problem?
>
> Why have college administrators been unable (or unwilling) to control tuition hikes?
>
> Why do so many families take out loans to pay for a college education?
>
> What can the government do to help reduce tuition costs?
>
> What can students do to manage tuition costs?

As you begin to generate potential research questions, ask yourself whether you are interested in focusing on such concerns as the current state of knowledge about your subject, its history, the assumptions informing the conversation about the subject, the goals of writers involved in the conversation, its likely outcomes, or policies associated with the subject. Then reflect on the range of options you have for thinking about these concerns. Are you interested, for example, in learning what others have done or are doing? Do you want to conduct analyses such as comparing alternatives, looking for cause-and-effect relationships, or tracing a sequence of events? Are you intrigued by the prospect of defining or solving problems?

Specific question words might also help you get started. If you are interested in conducting an analysis, for example, ask questions using the words *what, why, when, where, who,* and *how.* If you want to explore goals and outcomes, use the word *would* or *could.* If the conversation focuses on determining an appropriate course of action, generate questions using the word *should.* Consider the differences among these questions:

> **What** are the benefits of a college education?
>
> **Would** it be feasible to require colleges and universities to commit 5 percent of their endowments to financial aid?
>
> **Should** the U.S. Congress pass legislation to control tuition costs?

Each question would lead to differences in how to search for and select sources of information, what role to adopt as a writer, and how to organize and design the document.

Select and Refine Your Question

After reviewing your potential research questions, select a question that interests you, is consistent with the role you have adopted, and is appropriate for your writing situation. Then refine your question by referring to shared assumptions and existing conditions, narrowing its scope, and conducting preliminary searches.

REFLECT ON YOUR WRITING SITUATION

As you consider potential research questions, pay attention to your purpose and role. Your efforts to collect information should help you accomplish your purpose and address your readers' needs, interests, values, and beliefs. Keep in mind, however, that as you learn more about your subject, you might refine your purpose. In turn, that might lead to changes in your research question. If you think of your research question as a flexible guide—as a question subject to revision—you can increase the effectiveness of your document.

Sources help writers refine their purposes and create research questions that address their readers' needs, interests, values, and beliefs.

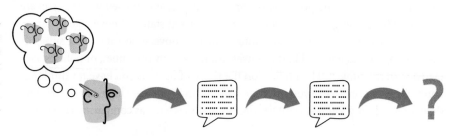

REFER TO SHARED ASSUMPTIONS AND EXISTING CONDITIONS

You can refine your research question by calling attention to assumptions that have been made by the community of writers and readers who are addressing your subject, or by referring to existing conditions relevant to your subject. Note the difference among these three versions of student writer Ali Bizzul's research question about the health risks associated with weight gain among football players.

Original Question:
Why would football players risk their health — and even their lives — by putting on extra weight?

Alternative 1:
Given the widespread belief among coaches that extra bulk might reduce performance on the field, why would football players risk their health — and even their lives — by putting on extra weight?

Alternative 2:
In the face of recent high-profile deaths among college and professional football players, why would football players risk their health — and even their lives — by putting on extra weight?

As you refine your research question, experiment with using qualifying words and phrases such as the following:

Mix . . .	and Match
Although	we know that . . .
Because	it is uncertain . . .
Even though	it is clear that . . .
Given that	studies indicate . . .
If	recent events . . .
Now that	it has been shown . . .
Since	the lack of . . .
While	we cannot . . .

NARROW YOUR SCOPE

Early research questions typically lack focus. You can narrow the scope of your question by looking for vague words and phrases and replacing them with more specific words or phrases. The process of moving from a broad research question to one that might be addressed effectively in an academic essay might produce the following sequence:

Original Question:
What is behind the increased popularity of women's sports?

Refined:
What has led to the increased popularity of women's sports in colleges and universities?

Further Refined:
How has Title IX increased opportunities for women athletes in American colleges and universities?

In this example, the writer has narrowed the scope of the research question in two ways. First, the writer has shifted its focus from women's sports in general to women's sports in American colleges and universities. Second, the writer has moved from a general focus on the increased popularity of women's sports to a more specific focus on the opportunities brought about by Title IX, the federal legislation that mandated equal opportunities for women athletes.

CONDUCT PRELIMINARY SEARCHES

One of the best ways to test your research question is to conduct some preliminary searches in an online library catalog or database or on the Web. If you locate a vast amount of information in your searches, you might need to revise your question so that it focuses on a more manageable aspect of the subject. In contrast, if you find almost nothing, you might need to expand the scope of your question.

How Can I Develop a Search Plan?

Once you've created your research question, you'll need to make decisions about

- the types of sources you want to collect (such as books, articles, and opinion columns)
- the types of search tools (such as library catalogs, databases, and Web search sites) and research methods (such as browsing library shelves, consulting librarians, or conducting surveys) you will use
- the schedule you will follow as you conduct your search

Your decisions will become the heart of your search plan—a brief, informal plan that records your ideas about how to locate and collect information on a specific conversation about your subject. As you develop your plan, keep your research question in mind. Doing so will help you determine what types of sources, resources, and search strategies will be most productive.

Identify Relevant Types of Sources

Writers use information found in a variety of sources—electronic, print, and field—to support the points they make in their documents. To identify relevant sources for your writing project, consider the nature of the conversation you are joining, the scope and timeliness of your subject, the information you'll need to develop your ideas, and the evidence you'll need to support your points.

CONSIDER YOUR CONVERSATION

Ask yourself about the conversation you've decided to join. Does it focus on a highly specialized issue within a scholarly discipline, such as a discussion of gene splicing in biology? If so, the best sources usually are scholarly books and journal articles. Does it address a subject that has broad appeal, such as transportation problems in your state or region? If so, you can draw on a much wider range of sources, including newspaper and magazine articles, editorials and opinion columns, blogs, and Web sites.

CONSIDER THE SCOPE AND TIMELINESS OF YOUR SUBJECT

Is your subject broad, or is it highly focused? Is it of enduring interest? Some subjects, such as funding for higher education or reducing alcohol consumption by college students, tend to be discussed over an extended period of time in a wide range of sources. If your subject focuses on a recent event, however, it might be best to turn to magazine and newspaper articles, the Web, blogs, observation, surveys, or interviews.

CONSIDER WHAT YOU NEED TO LEARN

If your subject is unfamiliar to you, look for sources that offer general overviews or discuss important aspects of the subject. For example, the introductory chapters of scholarly books often provide general overviews of a subject, even when the rest of the book focuses on a narrow aspect of the subject. You can also look for overviews of a subject in magazine articles, in professional journal articles, and on the Web.

CONSIDER THE EVIDENCE YOU'LL NEED

As you consider what you want to say about your subject, think about the kind of evidence other writers have used to make their points. If most writers have used numerical data found in scholarly research reports, for example, be sure to search for those kinds of reports. Similarly, if you notice that writers tend to refer to expert opinion, search for documents written by recognized experts in the field.

Identify Appropriate Search Tools and Research Methods

Once you've identified the types of sources that seem most relevant, determine which search tools and research methods you might use to locate those sources. In general, you can use three sets of resources to locate information.

- **Electronic search tools,** such as online library catalogs, databases, and Web search sites, allow you to search and browse for sources using a computer. Electronic search tools provide access to publication information about—and in some cases to the complete text of—print and digital sources.

- **Print resources,** such as bibliographies, indexes, encyclopedias, dictionaries, handbooks, almanacs, and atlases, can be found in library reference and periodical rooms. Unlike electronic search tools, which typically cover recent publications, many print resources provide information about publications over several decades—and in some cases over more than a century.

- **Field research methods** allow you to collect information firsthand. These methods include conducting observations, interviews, and surveys; corresponding with experts; attending public events and performances; and viewing or listening to television and radio programs.

Student writer Hannah Steiner, who wrote an informative essay about the use of hydrogen fuels, knew that her topic would require recent sources. As she put together her search plan, she decided to search databases for recent scholarly articles and to look for Web sites that reported recent research. To obtain the most up-to-date information, she also scheduled an interview with a professor of engineering at her university who had expertise in the area.

Review Your Plan

Your search plan might be an informal set of notes that will guide you as you gather information, or it might be a set of step-by-step instructions complete with details such as keywords to search, interview questions to ask, and observation forms to fill out. The choice is yours, but no matter how informal your plan, you should write it down. Doing so will help you remember the decisions you've made as you've prepared to collect your sources.

After developing your search plan, schedule time to search for and collect information. Next to each activity — such as searching databases, searching the Web, searching a library catalog, browsing library shelves, and conducting an interview—identify start dates and projected completion dates. Creating a schedule will help you budget and manage your time.

Share your plan with your instructor, your supervisor, your classmates, or a librarian. Each might suggest additional search tools, research methods, shortcuts, and alternative research strategies for your project. Take notes on the feedback you receive, and, if necessary, revise your plan.

How Can I Keep Track of My Sources?

If you've ever forgotten a phone number or misplaced tickets to a concert, you know how frustrating it can be to lose something. It can be just as frustrating to lose your interview notes or forget where you found a quotation or fact. Your writer's notebook is a good place to keep track of the information you collect during a writing project. You can also organize and save your sources, create a working bibliography, and create an annotated bibliography.

Manage Print Materials

Depending on the scope of your writing project, you might accumulate a great deal of print information, such as

- your written notes (in a notebook, on loose pieces of paper, on sticky notes, and so on)
- printouts from Web pages and databases
- articles sent through a library's fax-on-demand or interlibrary loan service
- printed word-processing documents, such as your outline and rough drafts
- books, magazines, newspapers, brochures, pamphlets, and government documents
- photocopies of articles, book chapters, and other documents
- letters, printed e-mail messages, and survey results

Rather than letting all this material build up in messy piles on your desk or stuffing it into folders in your backpack, create a filing system to keep track of your print documents. Filing systems can range from well-organized piles of paper labeled with sticky notes to three-ring binders to file cabinets filled with neatly labeled file folders.

Regardless of the approach you take, keep the following principles in mind:

- **Create an organizational scheme that allows you to locate your print materials.** Decide whether you want to group materials by topic, by date, by argument, by type of material (Web pages, photocopies, original documents, field sources, and so on), or by author.
- **Stick with your organizational scheme.** You'll find it difficult to locate materials if you use different approaches at different points in your writing project.

- **Make sure printed documents provide complete publication information.** If a source doesn't contain publication information, write it on the document. Publication information includes author, title, publisher, place and date of publication, and—for a Web source—sponsoring organization and URL.

- **Date your notes.** Indicating the date when you recorded information can help you reconstruct what you might have been doing while you took the note. Dates are also essential for documenting Web sources and other online sources.

- **Write a brief note on each of your print materials.** Indicate how it might contribute to your project.

Manage Digital Materials

As you gather digital information, keep it organized. The simplest strategy is to store notes and copies in a single computer folder. Use descriptive file names to save your work. Rather than naming a file "Notes 1.doc," for instance, name it "Interview Notes from John Garcia, April 22.doc." However, the single-folder approach might not work well for larger projects. Scrolling through a long list of files in the folder will make it difficult to find a single document easily. As a result, you might find it more efficient to create multiple folders to hold related files.

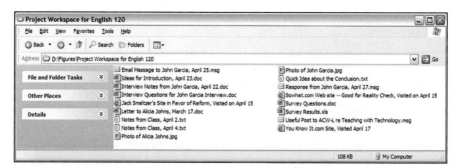

⌞ **Saving Work in a Single Folder**

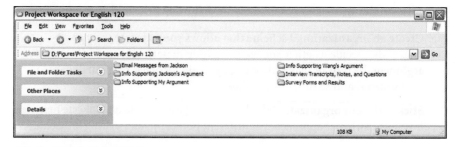

⌞ **Saving Work in Multiple Folders**

To save electronic sources, you can copy and paste; download; or use e-mail, bookmarking tools, or capture tools.

Copying and Pasting. You can use the Copy and Paste commands in your browser and word-processing program to save electronic documents and graphics. Be sure to copy and paste the URL and record the date when you accessed a Web page so that you can return to it if necessary and cite it appropriately.

Downloading. Downloading electronic sources to a hard drive, a flash drive, or a writable CD or DVD allows you to open them in a Web browser or word-processing program at a later point. This might save you time toward the end of your writing project, particularly when you are drafting your document.

The method for downloading copies of sources will vary according to the type of electronic source you're viewing.

- You can save Web pages using the File > Save As . . . or File > Save Page As . . . menu in your browser.

- You can save images and other media materials from the Web by right-clicking (in Windows) or command-clicking (on the Macintosh) on the item you want to save and selecting Save Image As . . . or Save Picture As . . . (or some similar command) from the pop-up menu.

- You can mark and save database records returned by a search.

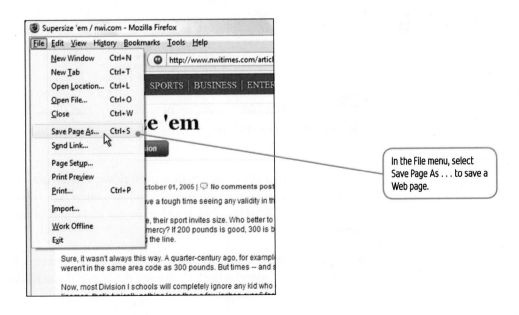

In the File menu, select Save Page As . . . to save a Web page.

Remember that saving a source does not automatically record the URL or the date on which you viewed the source for the first time. Be sure to record that information in your writing log, in your working bibliography (see p. 62), or in a document in the folder where you've saved your files.

Using E-mail. You can e-mail yourself messages containing electronic documents you've found in your research. Some databases, such as those from EBSCO and OCLC/FirstSearch, allow you to e-mail the text of selected records directly from the database.

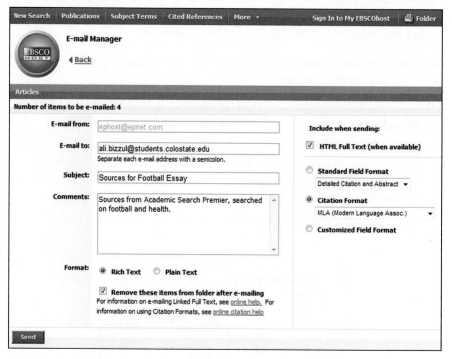

⌐ Sending E-mail from a Database

Saving Bookmarks and Favorites in Your Browser. You can use your Web browser's Bookmarks or Favorites list to keep track of online sources. Keep these lists organized by putting related items into folders and giving the items on your list descriptive names.

Be aware that there are some drawbacks to storing your sources in a Bookmarks or Favorites list. First, pages on the Web can and do change. If you suspect that the page you want to mark might change before you complete your writing project, download or print it so that you won't lose its content. Second, some Web pages are generated by database programs. In such cases, you might not be able to return to the page using a Bookmarks or Favorites list. A URL like the following usually indicates that a Web page is generated by a database program:

http://firstsearch.oclc.org/FUNC/QUERY:%7Fnext=NEXTCMD%7F%22/FUNC/SRCH_RESULTS%22%7F
entityListType=0%7Fentitycntr=1%7FentityItemCount=0%7F%3Asessionid=1265726%7F4%7F/fsres4.txt

Although the beginning portion of this long string of characters looks like a normal URL, the majority of the characters are used by the database program to determine which records to display on a page. In many cases, the URL works only while you are conducting your search. If you add such a URL to your Bookmarks or Favorites list, there's a good chance it won't work later.

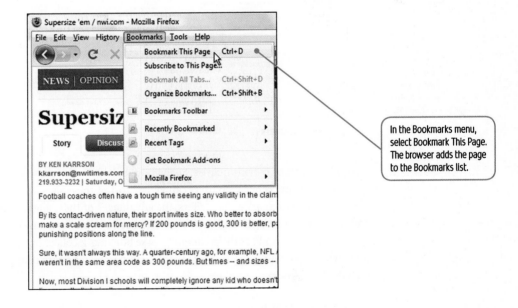

In the Bookmarks menu, select Bookmark This Page. The browser adds the page to the Bookmarks list.

Using Personal Bookmarking Sites. Personal bookmarking sites allow you to save your bookmarks to a Web site at no charge and view them from any computer connected to the Web. Some of these sites, such as Google Bookmarks, allow you to access your bookmarks through a toolbar. The Google toolbar (toolbar.google.com) provides access to your bookmarks as well as tools for organizing them, such as labels.

If you use more than one computer, you can benefit from the following sites:

Ask.com's MyStuff: mystuff.ask.com

Google Bookmarks: www.google.com/bookmarks/

Yahoo! Bookmarks: bookmarks.yahoo.com

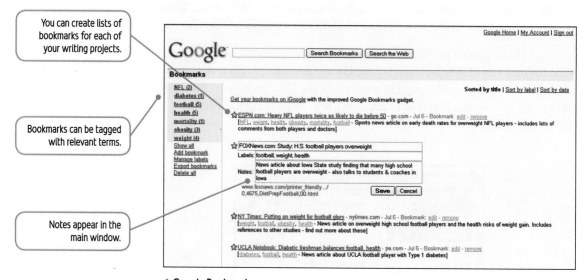

You can create lists of bookmarks for each of your writing projects.

Bookmarks can be tagged with relevant terms.

Notes appear in the main window.

ⵏ Google Bookmarks

Using Social Bookmarking Sites. Social bookmarking sites allow you to create lists of bookmarks that other Web users can view. Most of these sites also allow you to create private bookmarks. For writers, the advantages of these sites include: (1) the ability to save bookmarks and then view them at any time from any computer connected to the Web and (2) the ability to browse bookmark collections created by other users who share your interest in a subject. Leading social bookmarking Web sites include the following:

BlinkList: www.blinklist.com

ClipMarks: www.clipmarks.com

Delicious: delicious.com

StumbleUpon: www.stumbleupon.com

Using Web Capture Tools. A wide range of programs have been created to help writers keep track of the information they find online. Some of these programs work with your browser as toolbars or "add-ons" (a term used for programs that work within the Firefox browser). For example, most leading social bookmarking sites have created free tools that can be added to Internet Explorer and Firefox. By clicking on the ClipMark button, for instance, you can add a Web page—or portions of a page—to your collection of materials on ClipMarks. Some add-ons in Firefox offer powerful sets of tools for managing information. Both Zotero and ScrapBook allow you to save entire pages or parts of pages to your local computer. In addition, Zotero provides support for citing sources. Leading, no-fee Web capture tools include the following:

BlinkList Button: www.blinklist.com

ClipMarks Toolbar: clipmarks.com/install/

Delicious Tools: delicious.com/help/tools

ScrapBook Firefox Add-on: amb.vis.ne.jp/mozilla/scrapbook/

Zotero Firefox Add-on: www.zotero.org

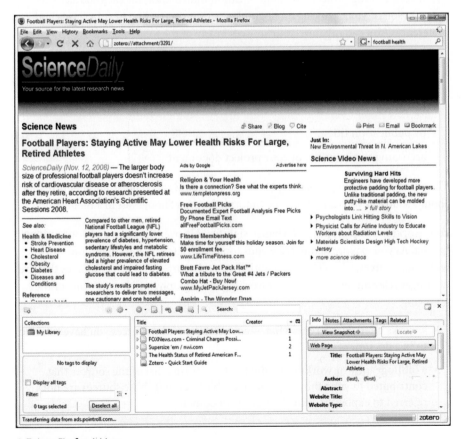

ㄴ Zotero Firefox Add-on

Backing Up Your Files. Whatever strategies you use to save and organize digital materials, replacing lost information takes time and effort. Avoid the risk of lost information by taking the time to make copies of your electronic files, saved Web pages, e-mail messages, and Bookmarks or Favorites lists.

Create a Working or an Annotated Bibliography

A bibliography is a list of sources with complete publication information, usually formatted according to the rules of a documentation system such as the Modern Language Association system or the American Psychological Association system. As you start collecting information, create a working bibliography or an annotated bibliography to keep track of the sources you are using.

WORKING BIBLIOGRAPHIES

A working bibliography is a running list of the sources you've explored and plan to use in your writing project — with publication information for each source. The organization of your working bibliography can vary according to your needs and preferences. You can organize your sources in any of the following ways:

- in the order in which you collected your sources
- in categories
- by author
- by publication title
- according to an outline of your project document

The entries in a working bibliography should include as much publication information about a source as you can gather (see "Information You Should List in a Bibliography").

Your working bibliography will change significantly over the course of your writing project. As you explore and narrow your topic and, later, as you collect and work with your sources, you will add potentially useful sources and delete sources that are no longer relevant. Eventually, your working bibliography will become one of the following:

- **a works cited or references list** — a formal list of the sources you have referred to in a document
- **a bibliography or works consulted list** — a formal list of the sources that contributed to your thinking about a subject, even if those sources are not referred to explicitly in the text of the document

TABLE 3.1
Information You Should List in a Bibliography

Type of Source	Information You Should List
All Sources	• Author(s) • Title • Publication year • Brief note—or annotation—describing or commenting on the source, indicating how you might use it in your document, or showing how it is related to other sources (for annotated bibliographies only)
Book	• Editor(s) of book (if applicable) • Publication city • Publisher • Series and series editor (if applicable) • Translator (if applicable) • Volume (if applicable) • Edition (if applicable)
Chapter in an Edited Book	• Chapter title • Publication city • Publisher • Editor(s) of book • Book title • Page numbers
Journal, Magazine, and Newspaper Article	• Journal title • Volume number or date • Issue number or date • Page numbers
Web Page, Blog Entry or Reply, Discussion Forum or Newsgroup Post, E-mail Message, and Chat Transcript	• URL • Access date (the date you read the source) • Sponsoring organization, if listed
Field Research	• Title (usually a description of the source, such as "Personal Interview with Ellen Page" or "Observation of Reid Vincent's Class at Dunn Elementary School") • Date (usually the date on which the field research was conducted)

@ The *Student Center for Joining the Conversation* Web site (**bedfordstmartins .com/conversation**) provides access to tools that allow you to save bibliographic information about each of your sources. With these tools, you can create a working bibliography formatted in either MLA or APA style.

Keeping your working bibliography up to date is a critical part of your writing process. It helps you keep track of your sources and increases the likelihood that you will cite all the sources you use in your document—an important contribution to your efforts to avoid plagiarism.

The first five sources from student writer Ali Bizzul's working bibliography are shown in the following illustration.

Entries follow APA style.

Bailes, J. E., Cantu, R. C., & Day, A. L. (2002). The neurosurgeon in sport: Awareness of the risks of heatstroke and dietary supplements. *Neurosurgery, 51*, 283–288. doi:10.1097/00006123-200208000-00002

Groeschen, T. (2008, October 17). Growing concern: Supersize me. *Cincinnati Enquirer*. Retrieved from http://news.cincinnati.com

Harp, J. B., & Hecht, L. (2005). Research letter: Obesity in the National Football League. *Journal of the American Medical Association, 293*, 1061–1062. doi:10.1001/jama.293.9.1061-b

Korth, J. (2006, January 29). A huge problem. *St. Petersburg Times*. Retrieved from http://tampabay.com/

Longman, J. (2007, November 30). Putting on weight for football glory. *New York Times*. Retrieved from http://www.nytimes.com

ʟ **Part of Ali Bizzul's Working Bibliography**

ANNOTATED BIBLIOGRAPHIES

An **annotated bibliography** provides a brief note about each of the sources you've listed, in addition to complete citation information. These notes, or annotations, are typically no longer than two or three sentences. The content, focus, and length of your annotations will reflect your purposes for creating an annotated bibliography.

- In some writing projects, you will submit an annotated bibliography to your instructor for review and comment. In this situation, your instructor will most likely expect a clear description of the content of each source and some indication of how you might use the source.

- In other writing projects, the annotated bibliography serves simply as a planning tool—a more detailed version of a working bibliography. As a result, your annotations might highlight key passages or information in a source, suggest how you can use information or ideas from the source, or emphasize relationships between sources.

- In still other projects, the annotated bibliography will be the final result of your efforts. In such cases, you would write your annotations for your readers, keeping their purposes, needs, interests, and backgrounds in mind.

An annotated bibliography is a useful tool even if you aren't required to submit it for a grade. By turning your working bibliography into an annotated bibliography, you can remind yourself of each source's information, ideas, and arguments and how the source might be used in your document.

The following annotated bibliography provides information that an instructor could use to assess a student's progress on a writing project.

Bailes, J. E., Cantu, R. C., & Day, A. L. (2002). The neurosurgeon in sport: Awareness of the risks of heatstroke and dietary supplements. *Neurosurgery, 51,* 283–288. doi:10.1097/00006123-200208000-00002

Bailes, Cantu, and Day discuss the rising numbers of heatstroke injuries and deaths among football players in the United States, and their study links some of these incidents to the use of dietary supplements. This source may help explain some of the extreme measures football players will take to gain or maintain weight, and the possibly fatal consequences of their decisions.

> Annotations provide brief summaries of the purpose and content of the sources.

Groeschen, T. (2008, October 17). Growing concern: Supersize me. *Cincinnati Enquirer.* **Retrieved from http://news.cincinnati.com/**

Groeschen interviews local experts in the Cincinnati area, including former NFL players, coaches, and team physicians, about the problem of weight gain among football players. He also cites alarming statistics from studies about obesity in young players. This article will help explain the perspectives of players and coaches themselves, showing that they regret focusing so much on their weight and that they're trying to help today's players stay healthy.

> Annotations are intended for the writer and the instructor. They indicate how and where the writer will use the source in the document.

Harp, J. B., & Hecht, L. (2005). Research letter: Obesity in the National Football League. *Journal of the American Medical Association, 293,* **1061-1062. doi:10.1001/jama.293.9.1061-b**

Harp and Hecht studied obesity levels among NFL players during the 2003–2004 season. Their discussion includes the higher BMI (body mass index) of linemen and the potential health complications of excess weight for athletes. Their conclusions will help me demonstrate that weight gain is a problem even for professional players and poses serious risks to their health and safety.

⌐ Part of Ali Bizzul's Annotated Bibliography

In Summary: Developing a Research Question and Locating Sources

+ **Develop a research question (p. 48).**

+ **Plan your search for sources (p. 52).**

+ **Get feedback on your plan (p. 54).**

+ **Save and organize print and digital sources (p. 55).**

+ **Keep a working bibliography (p. 62).**

+ **Consider creating an annotated bibliography (p. 64).**

What Is a Research Proposal and How Can I Create One?

A research proposal—sometimes called a prospectus—is a formal presentation of your plan for your research project. A proposal helps you pull together the planning you've done on your project and identify areas where you need additional planning.

Unlike a search plan, which is designed primarily to help *you* decide how to collect information, a research proposal is addressed to someone else, usually an instructor, supervisor, or funding agency. A research proposal typically includes the following parts:

- **A title page** serves as a cover for your research proposal. It should include the working title of your research writing project, your name and contact information, and the date.

- **An introduction** should identify the issue you've decided to address; state your research question and, if you have created one, your preliminary thesis statement; describe your purpose; and identify your readers and describe their needs, interests, values, and beliefs.

- **A review of literature** provides a brief overview of the key information, ideas, and arguments in the sources you've collected so far. You should identify useful sources found during your exploration of your topic and explain why you've found them useful.

- **A plan to collect information** offers a brief description of the types of resources you'll use to locate information relevant to your issue and outlines the steps you'll take to collect it. You should indicate whether you'll consult reference librarians; whether you'll use library catalogs, databases, and Web sites; and whether you'll conduct field research.

- **A project timeline** will give your reader an indication of the range of days, weeks, or months over which you will be completing your research and writing your document.

- **A working bibliography** lists the sources you've collected so far. Sometimes you will be asked to create an annotated working bibliography, which contains a brief description of each source. Your working bibliography should conform to the documentation system (MLA, APA, *Chicago*, CSE) specified by your instructor, supervisor, or funding agency.

Optional elements include the following:

- **An abstract or executive summary** provides a brief summary — usually fifty to two hundred words — of your project. You should identify the issue you've decided to address and your research question. You should also indicate what type of document — such as a research essay, informative Web site, or magazine article — you'll write.

- **An overview of key challenges** encourages you to think about potential problems you will need to address as you work on your project. This section of your research proposal might discuss such difficulties as locating or collecting specific types of sources. It also provides an opportunity for your instructor, supervisor, or potential funder to respond by suggesting strategies for meeting specific challenges.

- **A funding request and rationale** provides a budget that identifies costs for key project activities, such as conducting your search, reviewing the sources you collect, writing and designing the document, and publishing the document.

A formal research proposal allows you to consolidate the work you've done so far and get feedback on your plans to carry out your project.

Practice: Create a Research Proposal

Use the following activity to create a formal research proposal.

1. Provide the working title for your project.

2. Describe your issue.

3. Describe your purpose for working on this project.

4. Describe your readers' needs, interests, values, and beliefs.

5. State your research question.

6. Briefly review key findings about your issue from the sources you found as you explored your topic.

7. Indicate how you'll locate additional information, ideas, and arguments about your issue.

8. Include your project timeline.

9. Include your working bibliography.

10. Discuss the key challenges you face (optional).

11. Identify specific funding requests (optional).

@ You can download or print this activity at **bedfordresearcher.com**. Click on Activities > Create a Research Proposal.

Sample Student Research Proposal

English 102 instructor Teresa Saxton, whose course was titled "Inquiry into Your Generation," gave the following assignment:

Objective

To define your research question and outline a research plan for answering it.

Procedure

1. Choose your topic of inquiry. The only topic stipulation is that it must focus on and research about some aspect of Millennial life. It is best to choose a topic that you are interested in since you will be thinking about and studying it for the rest of the semester.

2. Formulate a hypothesis about that topic. In other words, what do you think this topic will uncover about the Millennial Generation?

3. Determine what else you will need to learn about the topic or the Millennial Generation in order to prove your hypothesis.

4. Determine *how* you will find that necessary information. Do you need interviews, surveys, field research, and/or secondary source library research to find this information?

5. Put this information into a proposal format with five headings, as shown below.

Sections of Proposal

1. **Background information:** Provide a definition of the topic you have chosen and some background information. This information can include your reasons for choosing the topic.

2. **Hypothesis:** What is your working thesis (or thesis that is not yet proven)? Keep this to one or two sentences.

3. **Research goals:** What specific questions do you hope to answer in your paper?

4. **Required data:** What information will you have to find in order to reach your research goals and answer the questions listed there? What will you need expert opinions to prove? What will you need Millennial opinions to prove? What will you need statistics to show?

5. **Research methods:** How do you plan to obtain this necessary information? This section should include whether you plan to use interviews, surveys, or observations (and the details about each of these) along with what keywords you plan to use for library research.

Remember that you will be spending a large amount of time reading, thinking, and writing about your chosen topic. Be sure to choose something that you are interested in learning more about. I am happy to suggest topics, but you should not feel limited to my suggestions or class discussion. Perhaps the most important thing to remember while choosing your topic is to make it narrow enough to write about. This topic will become a 10-page paper, which may sound like a lot of space to fill but is not.

Siminerio 1

Caitlin Siminerio

Research Proposal

13 Mar. 2010

Millennials and Interactive Video Games

My research paper will focus on Millennials and their desire to play interactive video games. Over the recent years of personal experience I have gained interest in this topic because interactive video games have become extremely popular with today's youth. My brother, I, and our friends play these new video games for countless hours and sometimes all night long. *Dance Dance Revolution*,

Siminerio 2

Guitar Hero, and *Rock Band* are the games that will be carefully examined throughout my research. These games are called interactive because multiple people can play, and they provide a way of fun social interaction. I want to uncover why Millennials are so fascinated by these musical interactive games and what their true feelings are towards these games.

Before performing any further research, I created my hypothesis. I believe the Millennial generation enjoys interactive games because they can be played with multiple players, are enjoyable at social events, and the music is fun to listen to. I also feel that that these games are a way for today's youth to express themselves through music and technology. Even if the players have no musical experience, they can still enjoy the games. If my research proves my hypothesis correct, I will progress with the thesis: Millennials are a generation who use video games to create a social environment with their peers.

I hope to learn and address several points in my paper. Ever since these musical games have become popular with teenagers, I have always wondered who came up with the idea of *DDR*, *Guitar Hero*, and *Rock Band*? Are these games created by teens for teens, or did an adult create them? I would like to learn about the interactive games themselves. I need to know when they were released and how much success they have had in the markets since then. To better understand the games I must see how these games are specifically operated and how they are actually played by Millennials. I will also need to investigate and look into the songs that are being played in these interactive video games. My research would require addressing these songs and seeing why Millennials enjoy playing them so much. I find it odd that the songs played in these musical games are from different generations and yet Millennials still love playing these games. I would like to know how the creators of these games advertise to Millennials. Does this advertising influence the decisions of Millennials to try the games? I need to find out what age groups play these games the as well. Many people I know between the ages of 14 to 23 worship

Siminerio 3

musical games. Why do they play the games? Do they have same or different reasons? My last question would be, will there be any sequels to these games? I hope to successfully determine the answers to my research questions.

In order to prove my hypothesis, there are certain things that must be further researched. In order to find information about the designers and developers of the games, I must look at the products' official Web sites. From an official Web site I can surely find information about the game, like when and where it was released. *Consumer Reports* will help show how people actually feel about the games. I will also have to look at reviews of the games and to see how people actually describe them. On the internet, I want to go to Facebook and search *Guitar Hero, Rock Band*, and *DDR* to see if people are hosting parties with these games. To fully understand how Millennials play these games, I will have to observe them in this act. I also think some statistics on what age groups play these games would help prove my hypothesis. I also want to look at statistics that involve consumer rates and success of the products.

I plan on obtaining this information through a variety of methods. In order to find the reviews of these interactive games I plan on looking into some Web sites, such as the products' main sites (*Guitar Hero, Rock Band*, and *DDR*), game system sites, and the sites of the creators of the products. I also plan on looking through PlayStation and Xbox magazines to examine the advertisements and articles about the games. To gather some statistics about game use and users, surveys will help my research. The questions in my surveys will be short and simple, such as: Have you ever played with interactive games? If so, which ones? Why do you like interactive video games? Do you play self-involved games such as *World of Warcraft, Call of Duty*, or others? I would also like to observe Millennials actually playing the interactive games. While the game is playing I want to study Millennial expressions, actions, and verbal responses to these particular games. I not only want to inspect the Millennials playing a game but also the Millennials watching a game. Once I am done

Siminerio 4

examining the Millennials, I would like to further examine the games themselves. I want to see the displays, colors, and characters of the games. While
observing the game I want to take time to listen and study the songs. I will
have to look up when these songs were created and the groups that created
them. The controllers are another major part of the game that will have to
be inspected. The controllers are actually instruments or mats that are color-
coded. I want to see if there is a difference when Millennials play with the
musical-looking controller or a basic controller. I plan on interviewing Millennials about the games as another method to gather more information. I would
like to interview two to four Millennials from the ages of 16 to 23 to see why
each particular age group enjoys the game so much. Finally, I will perform
library research to obtain more information. My search will be broad, and I will
be specifically looking at interactive gaming, teaching with technology, marketing information from databases, and video game isolation and violence.
With all the technology Millennials have in this world, I find it fascinating that
interactive games are becoming more popular.

Sample Student Annotated Bibliography

English 102 instructor Teresa Saxton, whose course was titled "Inquiry into Your
Generation," gave the following assignment and guidelines for the student sample
annotated bibliography that follows:

The Basics

This assignment is designed to help you gather your research for the final paper into a usable form.
You will assemble ten sources that you believe will be useful for your final paper into a bibliography
and then annotate, or summarize, the sources. See the "Guidelines for Annotated Bibliography" for
further information on the format of the bibliography.

The Sources

The sources used in this bibliography can and should include the sources you plan to use in your final paper. Among these sources, nonlibrary sources (such as interviews and Web sites discussed in your research proposals) can be included in these annotations. However, five sources must be library sources, and one of these five must be a book. The other five may be either library or nonlibrary sources.

Primary vs. Secondary Sources

Primary sources are original documents or data that you analyze yourself. When you analyze them, note that you will be approaching them in a way that is unlike the way they were originally intended to be read. For example, if you are writing a paper on Millennials' use of Wikipedia, you would use the Web site itself as a source. However, you would not be using the source to learn information about certain entries; instead, you would be looking at the format of the page, the methods for posting information, how users contest information, what topics are included in the entries, what topics are linked, how the links aid learning (or not), and so on. In other words, you are not using Wikipedia as the reference it is meant to be, but as a researchable item itself.

Secondary sources are published works whose authors have done their own analysis of a primary source. So, if you are studying Wikipedia, a newspaper article about how the site is being used at the workplace, a technology journal's article about how the site originated, or a communications journal's editorial about the accuracy of the information posted will all be potentially useful secondary material. Obviously, if you plan to use someone else's analysis of your subject, you want that writer to be an informed, intelligent person and not a 12-year-old who thinks the site is "way cool" because it has an entry on her favorite video game.

Online Sources

Using Web sites for secondary sources can be tricky. Searching with Google rarely works out the way you'd like it to and often takes five times as long to find valid information as it would if a library database was used. There are wonderful sites on many subjects that you can find with Google, but they are mixed in with personal journals and blogs that are less usable (unless the blogger is famous). Yes, Google Scholar can help, but it still leaves much to be desired. I would suggest starting with library research first and then looking at the sources cited in those library sources. Chances are if there is a wonderful Web site on your topic out there, someone else has found it for you and used it in his or her article. Also, looking for .edu sites rather than .com sites can be helpful. In other words, be careful with the Internet; it has broadened our horizons . . . but sometimes too much. If you decide to use a Web site as a secondary source, there should be compelling reasons to do so that you can articulate in a conference about your paper.

Guidelines for Annotated Bibliography

Bibliography

- Alphabetize entries according to the last name of the author. If there is no author, use the first letter of the title to alphabetize.

- Double-space lines within entries; use regular double-space between entries (in other words, everything is double-spaced, with no extra spacing between entries).

- Do not number the entries.

- The first line of each entry should be flush with the left margin; subsequent lines should be indented five spaces to emphasize the last name of the author (a format opposite to that of paragraphs).

- Use MLA style for your entries. This style is outlined in your *Harbrace* and available online through the OWL at Purdue. This style should also be used to format your page.

Annotation

- Your purpose in this assignment is to summarize and evaluate each source and decide how it will be useful in writing your final paper. Not all of your sources need to be used in your final paper, but all that you choose to annotate should be useful in thinking about the topic and helping you form your ideas about your argument. These annotations should then be useful for you to return to as you write your paper.

- Use the author's last name and present tense verbs in your annotation.

- There are many different ways to write an annotation. Here, I'd like you to use a three-point method, as follows:

   Sentence 1: Provide a broad generalization. This sentence should provide the reader with a general summary of what the material is about, but with some detail (saying *Nickle and Dimed* is about the working class is not enough). When summarizing articles and critical books, make sure you include the overall thesis and perhaps main points in this general summary. Example: "Frye compares Old and New Comedy and concludes that 'Shakespeare's comedies conform for the most part to a romantic development of New Comedy.'"

   Sentence 2: Provide a more detailed summary. Give some detail to flesh out the general. Example: "Frye argues that the New Comedy creates a narrative in which an alienated love moves toward rebirth through a quest and/or marriage, and a new society is formed during the last scenes of the play."

   Sentence 3: Evaluate the use of the text. Describe how the information in the text will be useful to the intended readers. Stay focused on other readers here. Example: "Those interested in how working-class wages affect real-life individuals will find Ehrenreich's descriptions particularly helpful and interesting, even moving."

Winston 1

James Winston

4 Apr. 2010

Annotated Bibliography

Babbage, Keen. *Extreme Economics: The Need for Personal Finance in the School Curriculum*. Lanham, MD: Rowman & Littlefield Education, 2007. Print. Babbage writes about the importance of teaching personal finance to students in all levels of schooling. The author includes ways to teach students about managing funds. Parents and teachers alike would find her lessons useful in teaching their children or students.

Baker, Murray. *The Debt-Free Graduate: How to Survive College without Going Broke*. New York: The Career Press, 2000. Print. Baker describes methods and shares advice for students with limited amounts of money. Specifically, Baker proposes ways for a college student to graduate debt-free or with only a limited amount of debt. Students looking for more cost-efficient ways to survive college will greatly benefit from Baker's suggestions, and his finance tips will even be useful well after college.

Duncan, Jr., John J. "Legislative Update." *Washington Report*. The American Educational Trust, Feb. 2008. Web. 15 Mar. 2010. Congressman Duncan, representative for the second congressional district of Tennessee, which includes Knoxville, writes in his quarterly newsletter about events and issues currently affecting the United States legislature and his own constituents. Specifically, Duncan notes the current state of the economy and the importance of fiscal responsibility for government and individuals. Those interested in Duncan's activities on and off Capitol Hill will find his newsletter rather interesting. Duncan's opinions are especially important to those who want an inside opinion of those in Washington, D.C.

Winston 2

United States. Dept. of Labor. *Final Report of the 2002 National Summit on Retirement Savings*. 1 Mar. 2002. Web. 2 Apr. 2010. The 2002 summit brought together leaders from Congress, the president's cabinet, and private businesses, and this report is the result of their work. The report focuses on the importance of saving, and it addresses ways to market saving to individuals of each generation, from the Silent to the Millennial. Those interested in the opinions of national leaders on the issue of saving money would find this report very useful. Those trying to propose the idea of saving money to people would find the analysis and specific ideas for each generation rather helpful.

Gwartney, James D., Richard L. Stroup, and Dwight R. Lee. *Common Sense Economics: What Everyone Should Know about Wealth and Prosperity*. New York: St. Martin's Press, 2005. Print. Gwartney and his co-authors write to inform the average person about basic economics and how it affects him or her. They explain the key elements of the economy and ways to improve one's personal finances, such as saving more money and relying less on credit cards. Those who want to learn about economics would benefit greatly from the concise and useful explanations the authors provide.

Miller-Adams, Michelle. *Owning Up: Poverty, Assets, and the American Dream*. Washington, D.C.: Brookings Institution Press, 2002. Print. Miller-Adams writes about the ability of the poor and impoverished in America to save money. Specifically, if the immediate rewards are great enough, poor people can save money. Those with limited incomes, such as college students, would find Miller-Adams's ideas and tips very interesting and helpful.

United States. Bureau of Economic Analysis. *Personal Income and Outlays*. 28 Mar. 2008. Web. 29 Mar. 2010. The Bureau of Economic Analysis (BEA) publishes a monthly report on changes in income, spending, and saving in

America. The report highlights statistics and differences between the current and previous months. Those interested in economics will find this report useful for its statistics on such things as fluctuations in income and spending. Businesses looking for signs of economic growth or contraction can readily use the information provided by the BEA.

Scott, Adrian J., Alan Lewis, and Stephen Lea. *Student Debt: The Causes and Consequences of Undergraduate Borrowing in the UK*. Bristol, UK: The Policy Press, 2001. Print. Scott, Lewis, and Lea write about their study on debt, student loans, and the impact for college students in the United Kingdom. They identify the lack of financial planning and knowledge on the part of students, and the long-term effects of over-borrowing on students' financial future. Administrators, parents, and students interested in financial advice about college loans would find their study useful.

Smith, Ashleigh. Personal interview. 1 Apr. 2008. Smith, a recent graduate of Carson-Newman College, describes her efforts to save money when she was in college and now that she is working her first full-time job. She expresses her personal savings philosophy and her thoughts on the importance of saving money. As an older Millennial, her financial knowledge and savings habits serve as an example of young people today. Those interested in what young people think about saving money will find her thoughts rather significant.

Thomas, Keltie. *Kids' Guide to Money Cent$*. Hong Kong: Kids Can Press, 2004. Print. Thomas writes about money, budgeting, and saving for children. She uses her adolescent characters to teach financial lessons to the readers. Children would enjoy the lessons to be learned from her financial planning tips. Parents and teachers can find information and ways to teach their students or children about money.

✳ Questions and Activities for Chapter 3

1. What is the purpose of a having a "research question"? Why is it necessary to frame a research question before designing a research project?

2. To get some experience framing research questions, read the excerpt below and the sample research questions that might arise from it. Then read the additional passages A and B that follow, and come up with three possible research questions for each that would be appropriate for historical, qualitative, and secondary source research.

> During the expedition [to Mt. Everest], more than $10,000 worth of the tents, ropes, and bottled oxygen that my life depended on went missing, some of it turning up later, hidden amid other team members' equipment [. . .]. Expedition members who tried to stand up against their team-mates' thuggish behavior were physically threatened, cut off from the team's power supply, refused food, pelted with rocks, and in one instance, beaten.
>
> — Michael Kodas. *High Crimes: The Fate of Everest in a Time of Greed.*
> New York: Hyperion, 2008, 7–8.

Possible historical research question: Climbing Mt. Everest once seemed to be the "experience of a lifetime" and a sport for mountain-climbing "purists." When did it become an occasion for thievery and thuggishness, and what conditions caused the change? *(Research plan: Read several past and current accounts of climbing Mt. Everest, and look especially for information about the contextual conditions that may have changed since the time Sir Edmund Hillary and Tenzing Norgay first reached the summit.)*

Possible qualitative research question: According to those who have climbed Mt. Everest, what are the hardships and dangers of their climbing experience? *(Research plan: Conduct interviews and/or surveys to ask Mt. Everest climbers about their experiences. First, use library databases or reputable Web sites to find names of people who have climbed Mt. Everest and to find published, firsthand historical accounts written by actual climbers.)*

Possible secondary source research questions: What monetary and physical preparations does a climber need to make to try to reach the summit of Mt. Everest? *(Research plan: Search library databases, books, and reputable Web sites for information an actual climber would use to find out how best to prepare and what he or she needs to know in order to make such an expedition.)*

Passage A: Read the excerpt that follows, and then write three possible research questions.

> Growing up with three sisters, *Little Women* was more than just a book; it was a parallel world. Meg, Jo, Beth, and Amy became templates against which to compare myself. As the youngest I couldn't possibly be Meg, the calm collected oldest. But I was certainly no Amy — vain, spoiled and self-centered. Good, kind-hearted, Beth appealed to me. But in the end, she dies. . . . So, of course, like every other girl who ever read Louisa May Alcott's novel, I wanted to be Jo: creative, strong-minded, and independent. She was an ideal, not only the kind of woman I aspired to be, but also the kind of woman Alcott wanted to be.
>
> — Lynn Neary. "Jo March, Everyone's Favorite Little Woman." *Morning Edition.*
> Natl. Public Radio. 9 June 2008. Transcript. 14 June 2008

Now write down your possible historical research question, your possible qualitative research question, and your possible secondary source research question.

Passage B: Read the excerpt that follows, and then write three possible research questions.

> A piece of music will draw one in, teach one about its structure and secrets, whether one is listening consciously or not. This is so even if one has never heard a piece of music before. Listening to music is not a passive process but intensely active, involving a stream of inferences, hypotheses, expectations, and anticipations. We can grasp a new piece — how it is constructed, where it is going, what will come next — with such accuracy that even after a few bars we may be able to hum or sing along with it. Such anticipation, such singing along, is possible because one has knowledge, largely implicit, of musical "rules" (how a cadence must resolve, for instance) and a familiarity with particular musical conventions (the form of a sonata, or the repetition of a theme). When we "remember" a melody, it plays in our mind; it becomes newly alive.
>
> — Oliver Sacks. "The Abyss: Music and Amnesia." *The New Yorker*,
> 24 September 2007. 14 June 2008

Now write down your possible historical research question, your possible qualitative research question, and your possible secondary source research question.

3. Look back at "Generate Potential Research Questions" (p. 48), and use the list to help you identify some of the things you want to find out about *your* topic or are required to find out by the terms of one of your instructor's assignments. (Think about the *gaps* in your knowledge — what don't you know yet but think you need to know about your topic?) Narrow down the possible areas your inquiry will focus

upon—you might decide you most want to find out matters of information, history, assumptions, goals, outcomes, or policies. (Your instructor's assignment may have asked you to focus on one of these areas, so look at that first to find out.) Construct a preliminary research question that's consistent with your purpose and assignment. Use the research questions in the chapter as models, and adapt them as needed for your topic and area and purpose of inquiry.

4. Review the information presented under "Refer to Shared Assumptions and Existing Conditions" (p. 51). Refine your preliminary research questions according to the suggestions made there. Model your refined research question after the "Alternative 1" or "Alternative 2" examples. Then, refine your question even further by revising it according to the suggestions made under "Narrow Your Scope" (p. 51).

5. According to your instructor's assignment, what type of inquiry approach will you be using for your next paper: historical, qualitative, or secondary source research? Review your research question to make sure it is appropriate for the type of research you will be doing. That is, revise your question as needed to make sure that it is phrased in a way that obviously requires historical, qualitative, or secondary source research. (*Hint*: Even if you do not think your question needs revising, look at it again—most questions need to be revised a few times before they're really effective!)

6. Make a plan for the kinds of sources you need to look for in order to answer your research question. What are you aiming to learn, what kind of evidence do you need, and where will you look for information?

7. When you search for information, how do you keep track of what you find? Describe your process for managing print and electronic materials, and compare your methods to strategies described in the chapter.

8. One of the most common assignments given by instructors across campus is the "annotated bibliography," and information about this is provided in the chapter. What is an annotated bibliography, and what are the purposes and benefits of creating one?

9. Using the examples of annotated bibliography entries in the chapter, those provided in the Web site references in the "How to Write an Annotated Bibliography" activity in Appendix C (p. 338), and those provided on pp. 158–59, create annotated bibliography entries for the sources you've consulted for your project.

10. Create a research proposal. You can either download or print the "Create a Research Proposal" activity at **bedfordresearcher.com**. Click on Activities > Create a Research Proposal, OR simply write it out yourself. See the Sample Student Research Proposal on p. 69 for an example.

11. Write out your research question(s) based on the reading you've done so far, and write a paragraph or two in which you brainstorm or freewrite in response to your question. Then draft a preliminary thesis that responds to your research question. Trade your materials with a classmate, and respond to the following questions: Does the preliminary thesis effectively respond to the research question? Is the preliminary thesis too broad or too narrow? Does it sound like a thesis that would engage you as a reader? Why, or why not? Make suggestions for revision.

PART TWO

Historical Research

 One of the goals of your 102 course will be to situate your inquiry topic within the context of past conversations, communities, and cultures—to gain an accurate historical perspective on the topic. "Simple enough," you might say, "but *why* do this, and how?" So much of what we know and do in the present is informed and affected by past practices and events, and historical research helps us to gain an understanding of that, as well as discover previously unknown, obscured, or "lost" information. (Who doesn't love a great scavenger hunt or feel satisfaction at solving a puzzle? In many ways, those are good analogies to what historical research is and what historical researchers do.) Enlarging our perspective to include knowledge of the past helps us better know how to think about and act in the present. And, since much of what we now read in various texts and media is "filtered" or "prepared" for us, often we don't actually encounter the original, or primary, material and thus can't form completely accurate understandings of what happened. Using historical inquiry methods, you'll be able to understand what primary and archival materials are and how they differ from secondary sources, and you'll use them to study the history of an event, person, or issue or to compare past conversations or actions regarding an issue to those of the present. You'll use primary materials from historical archives, online archives, historical accounts of past events, public records/documents, letters, biographies, and the like to answer your research questions about who, what, where, when, why, or how something happened in the past— which will enlarge your understanding of your topic in the present.

Part Two begins with Chapter 4, "An Introduction to Historical Research and Using Primary Sources." In the first section, "Why Study History?," you'll read about the reasons why people study history, how our view of history changes over time, and you will develop a sense of how historical research expands our understanding of every topic and event. The next two sections, "Primary Sources: Handle with Care, but DO Handle" and "Working with Historical Sources," will introduce you to various kinds of primary materials and how to make use of them for research purposes. In the final section of the chapter, you will find practical information about how to locate primary source material in the UT Libraries.

In Chapter 5, "Conducting Archival Research," you will learn about particular types of primary materials, those stored in various physical and online archives in libraries, museums, and maybe even in your own attic. Also included in the chapter is an example of a student-written transcription of a letter from an archive in the UT Libraries.

As you read these chapters and become familiar with historical methods, remember this: history isn't just for historians. Historical research methods like the ones you'll read about and use in this part of English 102 will be helpful for answering questions in any academic discipline or career.

4 An Introduction to Historical Research and Using Primary Sources

Why Study History?

As any Harry Potter fan knows, the most boring class at Hogwarts School of Witchcraft and Wizardry is History of Magic, taught by the dead (and "deadly dull") Professor Binns. The professor's droning lectures regularly send students into a stupefied trance, from which they emerge just long enough to scribble a few names or dates into their notes. Asked on one occasion about an unsolved mystery involving the school's past, Binns replies, "My subject is History of Magic. . . . I deal with facts, Miss Granger, not myths and legends."[1] Students who take their first college history class with a sense of foreboding often think that real historians, like Professor Binns, are interested only in compiling lists of names, dates, places, and "important" events that happened sometime in the past. But history is much more than this. The historian's goal is not to collect "facts" about the past, but rather to acquire insight into the ideas and realities that shaped the lives of men and women of earlier societies. Some beliefs and institutions of the past may seem alien to us; others are all too familiar. But in either case, when we study the people of the past, what we are really learning about is the rich diversity of human experience. The study of history is the study of the beliefs and desires, practices and institutions, of human beings.

Why should we bother studying the past in our increasingly future-oriented society? There are as many answers to that question as there are historians. First, a thoughtful examination of the past can tell us a great deal about how we came to be who we are. When we study history, we are looking at the roots of modern institutions, ideas, values, and problems. Second, the effort we put into grappling with the worldviews of earlier societies teaches us to see the world through different eyes. The ability to recognize the meaning of events from a perspective other than our own is of inestimable value in our increasingly complex and

> **Check out Appendix C, Work-in-Progress Research and Writing Activities,** to find additional practical suggestions to help you read, research, and write successfully.

[1] J. K. Rowling, *Harry Potter and the Chamber of Secrets* (New York: Scholastic Press, 1999), 148–49.

"Why Study History?" is taken from Mary Lynn Rampolla, *A Pocket Guide to Writing in History*, Sixth Edition, pp. 1–4 (Chapter 1, "Introduction: Why Study History?").

multicultural society. Moreover, an awareness of various perspectives encourages students of history to engage in a critical analysis of their own culture and society and to recognize and critique their own assumptions. Finally, while historians, unlike Hogwarts' Professor Trelawney, don't have crystal balls with which to predict the future, an understanding of how past events have shaped the complex problems of our own times can help us make informed decisions about our future.

History is a complex discipline, and historians are a diverse group. They take different approaches to their material; they interpret events in different ways; they even disagree on such basic issues as whether and to what extent historians can be objective. These debates and disagreements amongst professional historians demonstrate the passion with which they approach their subject and ensure that the study of history will always remain fresh and exciting. Regardless of their approaches, however, all historians see writing as an important tool of inquiry and communication.

Historical Questions

Historians come to their work with a deep curiosity about the past; to satisfy that curiosity, they ask some of the same questions detectives ask: *Who? What? When? Where?* and *Why?* Some of those questions are designed to elicit "the facts" and are relatively easy to answer: *Who* was the emperor of Japan during World War II? *What* tools did eighteenth-century weavers use? *When* did the Vietnamese drive the Khmer Rouge out of Phnom Penh? *Where* was the first successful French settlement in Canada? Other questions, however, are less easy to answer: *Who* was Jack the Ripper? *What* were the religious beliefs of the peasants of twelfth-century Languedoc? *When* did President Nixon learn about the Watergate break-in? *Where* did the inhabitants of the original settlement at Roanoke go? *Why* did the civilization of the ancient Maya collapse? Complex questions such as these have formed the basis of absorbing historical studies.

Historians also need to analyze relationships between historical facts. Many of the questions historians ask, for example, reflect their interest in understanding the *context* in which events occurred. For instance, a historian interested in nineteenth-century science would not simply describe great "advances," such as Charles Darwin's publication of his theory of evolution by means of natural selection. As we know from the heated debates of our own time, science takes place within a social and cultural context, and scientific ideas can have a deep impact on politics, religion, education, and a host of other social institutions. Therefore, the historian would also consider questions about historical context: What role did political issues play in the acceptance or rejection of Darwin's theory? What other theories were current at the time, and how did they influence Darwin's thinking? Why did some theologians find his ideas threatening to religion, while others did not? What impact did larger social, political, and intellectual movements and institutions have on the study of biology in this period? In other words, historians do not examine events in isolation; rather, they try to understand the people and events of the past in terms of the unique historical context that helped shape them.

As they explore the relationships between and among events in the past, historians also examine the *causes* of events. The historical events that you will be studying and writing about can almost never be traced to a single cause, and historians are careful to avoid simplistic cause-and-effect relationships as explanations for events. For example, although the assassination of Archduke Franz Ferdinand is often cited as the event that precipitated World War I, no historian would argue that it *caused* the war. Rather, historians try to uncover the complex multiplicity of causes that grow out of the historical context in which events occurred.

Historians also ask questions about the relationship between *continuity* (events, conditions, ideas, and so on that remain the same over time) and *change*. Many of the questions historians ask reflect this interest. For example, a historian who asks, "What impact did the Black Death have on the economic and legal status of European peasants?" is interested in examining the changes brought about by the bubonic plague against the backdrop of the ongoing institution of serfdom.

Finally, while the past doesn't change, historians' interests—and the questions they ask—do. Historians, like the people they study, are part of a larger context. They are guided in their choice of subject and in their questions by their own interests and by the interests and concerns of their societies. As they ask new questions, historians look at sources in new ways. For example, in the 1950s, many standard U.S. history textbooks described Christopher Columbus as a heroic explorer; modern historians, writing from a more global perspective, have focused attention on the impact Columbus's explorations had on the indigenous peoples of the Americas. Historians may even discover "new" sources—sources that had always existed but had been ignored or dismissed as irrelevant. For example, the civil rights movement helped draw historians' attention to the central role of minorities in U.S. history.

History is a vital and dynamic discipline. We will never know all there is to know about the past because we are constantly posing new questions, and our questions, in turn, help us see the past in new ways. The best way to enter the world of the historian is to ask as many questions as you can about the particular historical issues you are studying. As you seek the answers, be aware of the new and more complex questions that your answers raise, and let those new questions guide your exploration further.

Primary Sources: Handle with Care — but DO Handle

DAVID J. EICHER

Used wisely, they can be rich material for bringing the past to life in both nonfiction and fiction.

It was an ordinary, hot summer afternoon in 2001, and I sat in an ordinary library chair. But suddenly an electric surge of energy raced through me. I was in the manuscript reading room of the U.S. National Archives and Records Administration in Washington, sifting through original Civil War papers for a book project. The archives are a researcher's paradise; surrounded by boxes of Union generals' papers on a cart, gently opening one file at a time to explore clues from the past, I was in an environment that makes a writer's head swim. As I carefully lifted a letter from Joseph B. Carr's file, I saw an ornately written request to commission the New Yorker a brigadier general, and, on the other side, a nice, neatly written endorsement — by President Abraham Lincoln.

Running across Lincoln endorsements is hardly unique or even rare in the National Archives' Civil War papers, but this one stuck out like a sore thumb — or finger. There, on the page, in Lincoln's characteristic dark-brown ink, was a little smudge with a partial fingerprint. This was probably a print of Lincoln's, and the immediacy of history staring right at me was as powerful at that moment as it can ever be. It was almost as stunning as if Lincoln had walked right up and sat down beside me at the desk.

My Civil War research at the National Archives underscored the importance of finding and using good sources to craft meaningful writing. Historical writers in particular — be they creating fact or fiction — draw on a wealth of materials as a basis for what they say. Particularly valuable for such writers, as underscored by Lincoln's fingerprint, are the materials classified as primary sources. Primary sources are the original records created in real time — i.e., created at, or about, the time of the actual events they represent. They are critically important to writing nonfiction, and equally as important to fiction writers who wish to know the baseline facts behind historical events in order to set up a story's climate.

David J. Eicher, "Primary Sources: Handle with Care — but DO Handle." From *The Writer*, April 2007, pp. 34–37.

Primary sources usually fall into these categories:

- letters
- official documents, ranging from appointments and legal briefs to committee reports
- journals and diaries
- newspaper and magazine articles
- images, including photographs, drawings, paintings, sketches and maps.

Strengths and Weaknesses

Primary sources must be used carefully, but by definition they generally are more valuable than interpretive sources produced later. The closer records are to an event and the closer they are to eyewitness participants, then the closer they are, generally speaking, to pristine credibility. This has played itself out time and time again with major historical events, as with the assassination of President John F. Kennedy in Dallas in 1963. Reading the original records, testimony and eyewitness accounts from the scene at Dealey Plaza leads to a very different conclusion about what happened and who was involved than much of the revisionist nonsense that followed would claim.

And yet primary sources themselves vary widely in quality and reliability. History as it is written is subject to human foibles. Problems with the reliability of primary sources stem from carelessness, human nature and outright dishonesty. For example, newspaper reports during the Civil War were notoriously inaccurate. Not only did newspaper journalism have a heritage of political alignments, clouding interpretations of events from paper to paper, but journalistic integrity at the time was so poor that many completely false stories were printed. The outcomes of battles were immediately reported to favor one side or the other independent of the facts; commanders were reported killed or mortally wounded who were still unscathed; and phantom troop movements or even false messages allegedly issued to troops were sometimes printed.

Dishonest motives sometimes color primary sources, too. During the Civil War, after-action reports by officers in command of unsuccessful battles nearly always used euphemistic language or twisted reality slightly to justify their actions and excuse the outcome of a battle or campaign. In the wake of a less than stellar action, "covering one's ass"—as it's now called—played to some extent into nearly every official report.

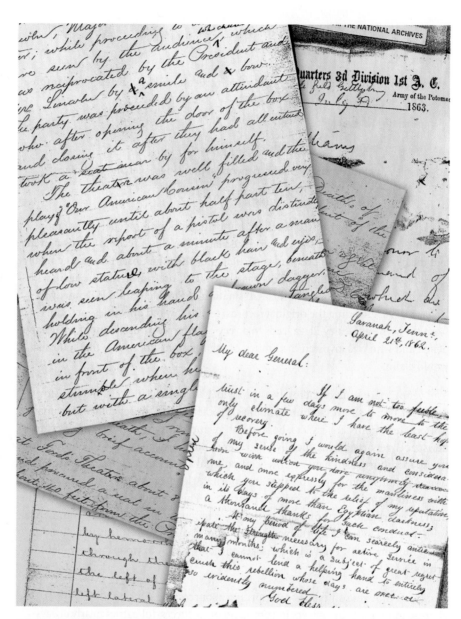

⌐ At top: Part of the account of President Lincoln's assassination by Charles A. Leale, the first physician to reach Lincoln. Bottom: Writing to Civil War commander Henry W. Halleck, Union Gen. Charles F. Smith, ailing from dysentery and a foot infection caused by a fall at Shiloh, hopes for a recovery that never comes.

But far more prevalent was the simple human trait of not recollecting details about important events consistently well, even immediately after an event. There are many examples of this, but one of the most celebrated is the eyewitness testimony of those who were inside Ford's Theatre on the night of April 14, 1865, when Lincoln was assassinated. Although hundreds of people witnessed the event, witnesses told many different stories about what they saw happen—versions that conflicted with each other and could not have occurred the way they were described. In fact, there are so many discrepancies about this sad event that one historian, Timothy Good, wrote a book about the testimony titled *We Saw Lincoln Shot: 100 Eyewitness Accounts*. Good's book is a fascinating examination of the notoriously unreliable human mind.

So, the bottom line for writers using primary sources is to exercise extreme caution. Writers need to sift through sources and determine the truth about what happened, or set a historical scene, by judging the credibility of the various sources. It means you need to be part analytical scientist, part attorney and part psychologist—and the people you're judging are often long gone. But it does make for an interesting challenge.

Some Surprising Treasures One Historian Found in Primary Sources

Searching through files of papers at the U.S. National Archives and Records Administration, the U.S. Library of Congress or any one of dozens of academic and library collections is like the ultimate journey through the candy store. As a writer, you never quite know what gem you'll come across that might either illuminate your current project or add to a future work. It's a collecting adventure, one that hides surprises that sometimes seem to turn up a few times a day and around every corner.

Here are some highlights from one afternoon's exploration in the National Archives, looking through various documents in the Civil War papers of Union officers.

- On crinkled and stained letterhead of the headquarters of the 3rd Division, 1st Army Corps, Maj. Gen. Abner Doubleday—who later popularized (but did not invent) baseball—writes to Brig. Gen. Seth Williams, adjutant general of the Army of the Potomac. On the battlefield during the third day of the battle of Gettysburg, Doubleday asks Williams for command of one of the army's corps. "I think myself entitled by rank," snorts Doubleday, who had briefly taken over command of the 1st Army Corps on the first day at Gettysburg after its commander, Maj. Gen. John F. Reynolds, was shot dead. Now, after the command has been given to another man, Doubleday is in such a snit that he needs to take time out during one of the greatest battles in world history to plead his case for greater command. (In the end, Doubleday did not receive a corps command.)

- In another stained battlefield letter, one of Ulysses S. Grant's early supporters, Maj. Gen. Charles F. Smith, writes Maj. Gen. Henry W. Halleck, in command of the Western theater, from the Shiloh battlefield. Two weeks after that intense bloodbath, Smith is ailing from the effects of chronic dysentery and a foot injury and subsequent infection he received during the opening of the campaign, when he slipped while jumping from one boat to another. Grant admires the older, more seasoned Smith, who looks on Grant as a younger brother. Asking to move to a warmer, more stable climate, Smith writes (see illustration, page 90), "At my period in life I can scarcely anticipate the strength necessary for active service in many months, which is a subject of great regret that I cannot lend a helping hand to entirely crush this rebellion whose days are over or so evidently numbered." Four days later, Smith dies from the infection.

- Shortly before the battle of Shiloh, Grant is embroiled in a controversy involving Gen. Halleck. Previously Grant's superior and jealous of his junior's success at the battle of forts Henry and Donelson, Halleck attempts to smear Grant by spreading stories about the latter's alleged drinking and his absence from his command without leave (presumably on a drinking binge). Although the stories are untrue, they nearly derail Grant's career.

  Having heard these rumors circulating, the adjutant general in Washington, Lorenzo Thomas, writes to Halleck and unwittingly plays into the scheme. "It has been reported that soon after the battle of Fort Donelson," Thomas penned, "Brigadier General Grant left his command without leave. By direction of the President, the Secretary of War desires you to ascertain and report whether General Grant left his command at any time without proper authority, and if so, for how long?"

  In the end, the Halleck-Grant controversy only underscored Grant's value and backfired on Halleck. Grant's stock rose, and when temperance advocates complained about this general who sometimes drank hard spirits, Lincoln finally said, "If you can find out what he likes, I will send a case to all my generals." It was a fitting tribute to his confidence in Grant, who eventually would win the war.

  —D.J.E.

Here are a few questions to ask yourself in evaluating the quality of a primary source:

- Did the writer or speaker have an ax to grind?
- How does this account compare to other accounts?
- What are the writer's reputation and qualifications?

- How well situated was the writer for describing an event?

- How long after an event has an account been written?

- Is the event based on eyewitness observation, or on a second- or third-hand account?

History in Your Hands

There is a big payoff for playing intellectual detective, because there is just nothing like the excitement of handling the documents themselves—to hold the physical pieces that played a part in major world events. In the case of the Lincoln assassination, for example, one of the pieces in a Lincoln file that I held was a handwritten paper by Charles A. Leale, a 23-year-old assistant surgeon in the U.S. Army who happened to be in Ford's Theatre that night. Leale was the first doctor to reach Lincoln after the shooting, and his 11-page manuscript account is amazing to read. (See illustration, page 90.)

"The play of 'Our American Cousin' progressed very pleasantly, Leale wrote, "until about half past ten, when the report of a pistol was distinctly heard and about a minute after a man of low stature, with black hair and eyes, was seen leaping to the stage beneath, holding in his hand a drawn dagger. . . . I then heard cries that the 'President had been murdered,' which were followed by those of 'Kill the murderer.'"

Leale's account of reaching the box is paramount: "When I reached the President," he recalled, "he was in a state of general paralysis; his eyes were closed and he was in a profoundly comatose condition, while his breathing was intermittent and exceedingly stertorous. I placed my finger on his right radial pulse but could perceive no movement of the artery. . . . I commenced to examine his head and soon passed my fingers over a large firm clot of blood. . . ."

Surrounded by a scene of chaos, Leale typified the most reliable of primary-source writers—calm, cool and analytical.

Locating Primary Sources

So, assuming you can identify a useful primary source, where do you find them? You can use the Internet in several ways to begin your search, particularly if you're aware of the individual people or types of source materials you're looking for. You can start by consulting major collections of primary sources on the Web. These include:

- American Memory, the Library of Congress digitized records site, http://memory.loc.gov

- EuroDocs, Western European Primary Historical Documents, http://eudocs. lib.byu.edu

- Making of America, which features 19th-century books and magazines, http:// moa.umdl.umich.edu

- Gallica, digital library of the National Library of France, http://gallica.bnf.fr

- Avalon Project, documents in law, history and diplomacy, http://avalon.law. yale.edu/default.asp

You can also use one of the many Internet search engines to find specific people or documents. Be specific when you search, and don't expect to always find things easily. Sometimes a fair amount of rooting around is necessary to come up with documents buried in collection lists. Try the best search engines first: Google, Altavista and Alltheweb. If that doesn't work, you might try using a history-subject directory, such as:

- History Matters, the U.S. Survey on the Web, http://historymatters.gmu.edu

- World Wide Web Virtual Library: History, http://vlib.iue.it

- History Guide, www.historyguide.de

After you've found primary-source documents, it's not always easy to make use of them. Normally, you need to make a trip to the library or institution where the document is housed to study and photocopy it. Check the Web site and the institution behind it, and gather contact addresses so you can write or e-mail the parties responsible to query them on usage. Generally, you can quote several sentences freely without permission, as defined under "fair use" in federal law. If you think you might ultimately use the whole of a particular document in a book or article, consider questions like these pertaining to rights and permissions: Does it belong to the collection represented by the Web site? Is it a scanned image of a document? Is it a transcribed document? Also, see if there are links to external documents that might prove useful.

Some documents—still a small amount, unfortunately—have been digitized and are available for downloading and commercial use straight from the Web sites, saving you cross-country or trans-world trips. But be careful about checking the rights, fees and permission statements that come along with the imagery and the sites: Because a document (or a copy of a document) exists in someone's collection doesn't necessarily mean they can give you the rights to use it. Meticulously documenting on the back of photocopies where and when you made the copies will help you organize the collection later, when you need to know the specifics of what you have.

Lastly, remember that vast numbers of primary sources exist out there, and many have never been carefully examined. In the Civil War domain, for example, just one record group in the National Archives—telegrams received by general in chief Henry Halleck—contains more than 1 *million* items. You could move into the archives' reading room and spend your whole life researching there without reading them all! Now how could a writer have a more alluring dilemma than that?

Working with Historical Sources

As you begin to think about historical questions, you will find that your search for answers will require you to explore a wide variety of sources. You will look at materials written in the period you are studying, and you will read books and articles written by modern historians. You may examine maps, photographs, paintings, and pottery. Ultimately, you may discover that you need to broaden your knowledge in a wide variety of areas, for history often takes its practitioners into all manner of related fields: literary criticism, art history, and archaeology; political science, economics, and sociology. In any case, you will need to learn how to work with the sources on which the study of history is based.

Identifying Historical Sources

To answer their questions, historians evaluate, organize, and interpret a wide variety of sources. These sources fall into two broad categories: primary sources and secondary sources. To study history and write history papers, you will need to know how to work with both kinds of sources.

PRIMARY SOURCES

Primary sources are materials produced by people or groups directly involved in the event or topic under consideration, either as participants or as witnesses. They provide the evidence on which historians rely in order to describe and interpret the past. Some primary sources are written documents, such as letters; diaries; newspaper and magazine articles; speeches; autobiographies; treatises; census data; and marriage, birth, and death registers. In addition, historians often examine primary sources that are not written, like works of art, films, recordings, items of clothing, household objects, tools, and archaeological remains. For recent history, oral sources, such as interviews with Vietnam veterans or Holocaust survivors and

"Working with Historical Sources" is taken from Mary Lynn Rampolla, *A Pocket Guide to Writing in History*, Sixth Edition, pp. 6–19 (Chapter 2, "Working with Sources").

other such eyewitness accounts, can also be primary sources. By examining primary sources, historians gain insights into the thoughts, behaviors, and experiences of the people of the past.

Sometimes, you may be able to work directly with primary source materials, such as letters or manuscripts in an archive. More often, you will use print or electronic versions of sources, such as edited and/or translated collections of letters or documents, images of maps or paintings, or facsimiles. (For more on evaluating edited and translated sources, see p. 99.) In either case, primary sources provide windows into the past that allow you to develop your own interpretation, rather than rely on the interpretation of another historian.

SECONDARY SOURCES

Historians also use *secondary sources*: books and articles in scholarly journals that comment on and interpret primary sources. Secondary sources are extremely useful. Reading secondary sources is often the simplest and quickest way to become acquainted with what is already known about the subject you are studying. In addition, examining scholarly books and articles will inform you about the ways in which other historians have understood and interpreted events. Reading a variety of secondary sources is also the best way to become aware of the issues and interpretations that are the subject of controversy and debate among professional historians, debates in which you, as a student of history, are invited to participate. In addition, the bibliographies of secondary sources can direct you to primary sources and additional secondary sources that you might find useful.

As valuable as secondary sources are, you should never base a history paper on them alone, unless, of course, you are writing a historiography paper. Whenever possible, you should work from primary sources, studying the events of the past in the words of people who experienced, witnessed, or participated in them.

PRIMARY OR SECONDARY? THE CHANGING STATUS OF A SOURCE

While the definitions provided above seem fairly straightforward, it is not always easy to determine whether a particular text is a primary source or a secondary source. This is because the status of a source as primary or secondary does not depend on how old the source is, but rather on the historical question you are asking. For example, if you are writing about the reign of Julius Caesar (100–44 BCE), Suetonius's *Lives of the Twelve Caesars*, written in the early second century CE, would be a *secondary* source because Suetonius was not a witness to the events he describes. If, however, you are writing about the debates among second-century Romans about the use and abuse of imperial power, Suetonius's work would be a *primary* source. Thus, the status of a source as primary or secondary depends on the focus of your research.

Note: How you access a source does not affect its status as a primary or secondary source. You can find both primary sources (such as collections of letters, newspapers, and photographs) and secondary sources (such as journal articles and books) in your library; you can also find both online. For example, *The Complete Work of Charles Darwin Online*, published by Cambridge University (http://darwin-online .org.uk), includes facsimiles of Darwin's notebooks, letters, and other original documents that would be considered primary sources. Similarly, many scholarly articles, which originally appeared in print journals, can also be accessed through electronic databases or archives such as *JSTOR*. Whether you access such articles in print or online, these are secondary sources.

USES OF PRIMARY AND SECONDARY SOURCES

Both primary and secondary sources can provide valuable information; however, they provide different kinds of information. Primary sources allow you to enter the lives and minds of the people you are studying. The documents people wrote—sermons and wills, novels and poems—and the things they made—music and movies, knife blades and buttons—bring you into direct contact with the world of the past. Secondary sources, in contrast, are written by historians who can provide a broader perspective on the events of the past than the people who actually participated in them since [historians] have more information about the context and outcome of those events, an awareness of multiple points of view, and access to more documents than any single participant. In studying nineteenth-century communes, for example, primary sources such as diaries, letters, or items that commune members produced and used can provide firsthand information about the thoughts, feelings, and daily lives of the people who lived in such communities. Primary sources would be less useful, however, in examining the larger sociological effects of communal living. To get a better understanding of those effects, secondary sources in which historians examine several such communities over time, or study the ways in which contemporary outsiders viewed communes, might prove more useful. In your own work, you will need to use both primary and secondary sources, always keeping in mind what kinds of information each of those sources can tell you about a topic.

Evaluating Sources

If primary sources always told the truth, the historian's job would be much easier—and also rather boring. But sources, like witnesses in a murder case, often lie. Sometimes they lie on purpose, telling untruths to further a specific ideological, philosophical, personal, or political agenda. Sometimes they lie by omission, leaving out bits of information that are crucial to interpreting an event. Sometimes sources mislead unintentionally because the author's facts were incomplete, incorrect, or misinterpreted. Many sources are biased, either consciously or unconsciously, and contain unstated assumptions; all reflect the interests and concerns of their authors. Moreover, primary sources often conflict. As a result, one of the challenges historians face in writing a history paper is evaluating the reliability and usefulness of their sources.

Like primary sources, secondary sources may contradict one another. Several historians can examine the same set of materials and interpret them in very different ways. Similarly, historians can try to answer the same questions by looking at different kinds of evidence or by using different methods to gather, evaluate, and interpret evidence. To get the most out of your reading of secondary sources, you will need to study a variety of interpretations of historical events and issues.

The following sections provide specific suggestions for evaluating both primary and secondary sources.

EVALUATING PRIMARY SOURCES

Since primary sources originate in the actual period under discussion, we might be inclined to trust what they say implicitly. After all, if the author is an eyewitness, why should anyone doubt his or her word? Alternatively, we might lean toward dismissing primary sources altogether on the grounds that they are too subjective; as any police investigator could tell you, eyewitnesses see different things and remember them in different ways. In fact, historians steer a middle ground between these two approaches. Although primary sources comprise the basic material with which they work, historians do not take the evidence provided by such sources simply at face value. Like good detectives, they evaluate the evidence, approaching their sources analytically and critically.

Historians have developed a variety of techniques for evaluating primary sources. One such technique is to compare sources; a fact or description contained in one source is more likely to be accepted as trustworthy if other sources support or corroborate it. Another technique is to identify the author's biases. For example, the historian Polydore Vergil asserted in his book *Anglica Historia* that King Richard III killed his nephews. Since Vergil was a contemporary of Richard III, you might accept his account at face value, unless you were also aware that the book was commissioned by King Henry VII, an enemy of Richard III who had organized a rebellion against him, killed him in battle, and seized his throne. Taking this fact into consideration, you would want to approach Vergil's work with a more critical eye, considering whether his loyalty to his employer led to any bias in his history. Historians also read their sources carefully for evidence of internal contradictions or logical inconsistencies, and they pay attention to their sources' use of language, since the adjectives and metaphors an author uses can point to hidden biases and unspoken assumptions.

Thinking about Editions and Translations. As an undergraduate, you will probably not have the opportunity that professional historians do to work with original documents in their original languages. Instead, you will likely be relying on published, translated editions of primary sources or, increasingly, on documents posted on the Internet.

Using modern editions of sources in translation is an excellent way to enter into the worldview of the people you are studying. Be aware, however, that any edited text reflects, to some extent, the interests and experiences of the editor or translator. For example, the process by which the editor of a document collection selects which documents to include and which to leave out involves interpretation: the collection, as it appears in print, reflects how the editor has understood and organized the material and what he or she sees as significant. Similarly, excerpts from long documents can be useful in introducing you to the basic content and flavor of a document, but it is important to note that in the process of choosing excerpts, the editor of a document is making a judgment about what aspects of the source are important. You should read the whole source, if possible, rather than excerpts, in order to understand the significance of the entire document and the context of any portions of the source that you wish to discuss or quote. Finally, translation always involves decisions about word choice and grammar that can range from inconsequential to very significant.

Tips for Writers: Questions for Evaluating Text-Based Primary Sources

- Who is the author?
- When was the source composed?
- Who was the intended audience?
- What is the purpose of the source? (Note that some primary sources, such as letters to the editor, have a central theme or argument and are intended to persuade; others, such as census data, are purely factual.)
- How do the author's gender and socioeconomic class compare to those of the people about whom he or she is writing?
- What is the historical context in which the source was written and read?
- What unspoken assumptions does the text contain?
- What biases are detectable in the source?
- Was the original text commissioned by anyone or published by a press with a particular viewpoint?
- How do other contemporary sources compare with this one?

SPECIAL CONSIDERATIONS FOR EDITIONS AND TRANSLATIONS

- Is the source complete? If not, does the text contain an introductory note explaining editorial decisions?
- If you are using a document in a collection, does the editor explain his or her process of selection and/or translation?
- Are there notes introducing individual documents that provide useful information about the text?
- Are there footnotes or endnotes that alert you to alternate readings or translations of the material in the text?
- Are you using an edition or translation that most accurately reflects the current state of scholarship?

Note: Often, the introduction to an edited volume, or the short headnotes that introduce individual texts in a collection, will not only provide useful background information about the text but also alert you to the editor's choices and intentions.

Primary documents require both careful and critical reading in order to be effective research sources. When you analyze a primary source, keep in mind the questions in the Tips for Writers box on page 99.

Tips for Writers: Questions for Evaluating Nonwritten Primary Sources

FOR ARTIFACTS

- When and where was the artifact made?
- Who might have used it, and what might it have been used for?
- What does the artifact tell us about the people who made and used it and the period in which it was made?

FOR ART WORKS (PAINTINGS, SCULPTURE, ETC.)

- Who is the artist and how does the work compare to his or her other works?
- When and why was the work made? Was it commissioned? If so, by whom?
- Was the work part of a larger artistic or intellectual movement?
- Where was the work first displayed? How did contemporaries respond to it? How do their responses compare to the ways in which it is understood now?

FOR PHOTOGRAPHS

- Who is the photographer? Why did he or she take this photograph?
- Where was the photograph first published or displayed? Did that publication or venue have a particular mission or point of view?
- Are there any obvious details such as angle, contrast, or cropping that suggest bias?

FOR CARTOONS

- What is the message of the cartoon? How do words and images combine to convey that message?

- In what kind of publication did it originally appear (newspaper, magazine, etc.)? Did that publication have a particular agenda or mission?
- When did the cartoon appear? How might its historical context be significant?

FOR MAPS

- What kind of map is this (topographical, political, military, etc.)?
- Where and when was the map made? What was its intended purpose?
- Does the map contain any extraneous text or images? If so, what do they add to our understanding of the map itself?

FOR SOUND RECORDINGS

- Who made the recording and what kind of recording is it (music, speech, interview, etc.)?
- Was the recording originally intended for broadcast? If so, why was it broadcast and who was the intended audience?

FOR VIDEO AND FILM

- What kind of film is this (documentary, feature, etc.)?
- Who is the director, producer, and screenwriter for the film? Have they made other films to which you can compare this one?
- Who is the intended audience? Why was the film made?
- Does the film use particular cinematic techniques that convey a particular mood or tone?

Thinking about Nonwritten Primary Sources. Although historians work mainly from written sources, they also use a wide variety of nonwritten materials, including works of art, photographs, maps, and audio and video recordings. When dealing with nonwritten primary sources, you should consider the same questions about author, audience, and context that are outlined in the Tips for Writers box on page 99, while adding some questions from the Tips for Writers box on page 100 that are specific to the type of source you are considering.

Evaluating Primary Sources: An Example. In a letter written to Sheik El-Messiri in 1798, Napoleon expresses the hope that the sheik will soon establish a government in Egypt based on the principles of the Qur'an, the sacred text of Islam. Those principles, according to Napoleon, "alone are true and capable of bringing happiness to men."[1] Should we assume, on the evidence of this letter, that Napoleon believed in the truth of Islam? A historian might ask, "Do we have any other evidence for Napoleon's attitude toward Islam? What do other primary sources tell us about Napoleon's attitude toward religions such as Catholicism, Protestantism, and Judaism? Do any other primary sources contradict the attitude toward Islam expressed in Napoleon's letter to the sheik?" In other words, "How accurately and to what extent can this source answer questions about Napoleon's religious beliefs?" In addition, historians try to understand or interpret their sources even if those sources do not offer the best or most accurate information on a certain topic. As it happens, Napoleon did not believe in Islam. This does not mean, however, that his letter to the sheik has no value. Instead, a good historian will ask, "Under what circumstances did Napoleon write this letter? Who was Sheik El-Messiri, and what was his relationship to Napoleon? What does this letter tell us about Napoleon's willingness to use religion to his political advantage?" Thus, to write about historical questions, you will need to know how to approach many different kinds of primary sources and ask appropriate questions of them.

EVALUATING SECONDARY SOURCES

Reading secondary sources helps us understand how other historians have interpreted the primary sources for the period being studied. Students sometimes hesitate to question the conclusions of established scholars; nevertheless, as with primary sources, it is important to read secondary sources critically and analytically, asking the same questions you ask of primary sources. Evaluate a secondary source by asking the critical questions listed in the Tips for Writers box on page 102. In

---

[1]Napoleon Bonaparte, "Letter to the Sheik El-Messiri," in *The Mind of Napoleon: Selection from His Written and Spoken Words*, 4th ed., trans. and ed. J. Christopher Herold (New York: Columbia University Press, 1969), 104.

Tips for Writers: Questions for Evaluating Secondary Sources

- Who is the author? What are his or her academic credentials? (You will often find information about the author in the preface of a book; journals sometimes include authors' biographies, either on the first page of the article or in a separate section.)
- When was the text written? (On the importance of publication dates, see p. 102.)
- Who is the publisher? Is the text published by a scholarly press or a popular one? (For more information on scholarly and popular presses, see p. 103.)
- Who is the intended audience for the text (scholars, students, general reading public, etc.)?
- What is the author's main argument or thesis?
- Does the author use primary sources as evidence to support his or her thesis? Is the author's interpretation of the primary sources persuasive?
- Is there primary source evidence that you are aware of that the author does not consider?
- Does the author contradict or disagree with others who have written on the subject? If so, does he or she acknowledge and effectively address opposing arguments or interpretations?
- Do the footnotes/endnotes and bibliography reference other important works on the same topic?
- Does the author build his or her argument on any unsubstantiated assumptions? (See pp. 102–3.)

addition to the critical questions listed in that box, it is especially important to do the following when you work with a secondary source:

Consider the Implications of the Publication Date. If it is important that you know the most recent theories about a historical subject, pay special attention to the publication dates of the sources you are considering. A 2000 article reviewing theories about the construction of Native American burial mounds may contain more recent ideas than a 1964 review. Do not assume, however, that newer interpretations are always better; some older works have contributed significantly to the field and may offer interpretations that are still influential. (As you become more experienced in historical research, you will be able to determine which older sources are still useful.) Moreover, older sources might offer a historical perspective on how interpretations of an issue or event have changed over time, which is particularly important if you are writing a historiographic essay.

Evaluate the Logic of the Author's Argument. Any book or article makes an argument in support of a thesis. Once you have identified the author's thesis, you should evaluate the evidence he or she uses to support it. You may not be in a position to judge the accuracy of the evidence, although you will build expertise as you continue to read about the subject. You can, however, evaluate the way in which the author uses the evidence he or she presents. You might ask yourself whether the evidence logically supports the author's point. For example, Margaret Sanger, who founded the American Birth Control League in 1921, was also involved in the U.S. eugenics movement, which advocated, among other things, for the sterilization of individuals deemed "mentally incompetent." This, however, does not justify the conclusion that *all* early-twentieth-century birth control advocates favored eugenics. Such an assertion would be a logical fallacy known as a *hasty generalization*.

You should also ask whether the same facts could be interpreted in another way to support a different thesis. For example, G. Stanley Hall, an early-twentieth-century American psychologist, amassed evidence that demonstrated a correlation between a woman's educational level and the number of children she had: Women who attended colleges and universities had fewer children than their less educated sisters. From this fact, he concluded that higher education caused sterility in women. A modern historian looking at the same evidence might conclude that education allowed women to become economically independent, freed them from the necessity of forming early marriages, and allowed them to pursue careers other than raising children.

Another consideration is whether the cause-and-effect relationships described in a source are legitimate. It may be true that event A happened before event B, but that does not necessarily mean that A caused B. For example, on July 20, 1969, Neil Armstrong became the first person to walk on the moon. The following winter was particularly harsh in the United States. We should not conclude, however, that the lunar landing caused a change in weather patterns. This would be a *post hoc* fallacy, from the Latin *post hoc, ergo propter hoc* (after this, therefore because of this).

Finally, consider how the author deals with any counterevidence.

Distinguish between Popular and Scholarly Sources. If you consult secondary sources for your paper, it is important that you use scholarly, rather than popular, sources. Scholarly sources are written by experts in the field; usually, they are peer-reviewed — evaluated by other scholars — before being published. To determine whether a secondary source is scholarly or popular, consider the following questions:

- Does the author have academic credentials?
- Does the book or article have notes, a bibliography, and other academic apparatus?
- Is the source published by an academic press?
- Does the book or article analyze and interpret primary sources or the work of other scholars?

If you are still not sure whether a book or article you want to use is an appropriate secondary source, consult your professor or a reference librarian.

Note: While popular magazines are not appropriate *secondary* sources, they can be excellent *primary* sources for certain research topics. You might, for example, consult back issues of *Time* magazine in order to explore how the news media covered the collapse of the Soviet Union, or examine the advertisements in *Good Housekeeping* for a paper on women's economic importance in the period between the two world wars.

EVALUATING ONLINE SOURCES

As noted above, the Internet provides ready access to both primary and secondary sources. Editions of a wide variety of written primary sources (letters, treatises, government publications, even whole books) are available on the Internet, as are cartoons, photographs, images of antique maps, and other nonwritten primary sources. If you are looking for secondary sources, historians may publish their research online in electronic journals like the *E-Journal of Portuguese History* (http://www.brown.edu/Departments/Portuguese_Brazilian_Studies/ejph/); in addition, digitized versions of countless scholarly articles are available in electronic databases such as *JSTOR: The Scholarly Journal Archive* (http://www.jstor.org/), which scans and archives a wide variety of scholarly print journals.

Web sites maintained by universities, museums, government agencies, and other institutions can be a gold mine for students whose access to large research libraries is limited. Making effective use of the Internet as a research tool, however, requires you to anticipate and avoid the special problems that it presents.

The most significant difficulty you may encounter when trying to evaluate a source accessed online is determining its credibility. When working with such a source, first determine if it has a print or real-life equivalent. Is it an article from a journal that is published in print? Is it an artifact that resides in a museum? If the source actually exists in physical form, you can refer to the Tips for Writers box on page 100 to help you study and evaluate it. If, however, the source exists only online, you must use extra caution in evaluating it. This is because, while articles in scholarly journals and books from academic presses are carefully reviewed by other scholars in the field, anyone with Internet access can create a Web site or a blog. You should also be aware that many popular online resources are not appropriate sources for scholarly research. For example, Wikipedia, the widely used online encyclopedia, is comprised of entries written largely by anonymous authors. The entries are not peer-reviewed; moreover, anyone can modify most Wikipedia entries. Therefore, even though many of its entries may be informative and accurate, Wikipedia cannot be considered a reliable academic source.

The questions in the Tips for Writers box on page 105 will help you determine whether an online source is reliable. In general, the most worthwhile sites with the most accurate sources will probably have a scholarly affiliation. You can find reputable sites by consulting your professor.

Tips for Writers: Questions for Evaluating Online Sources

- Is the author's identity clear? If so, what are his or her academic credentials? Does the author list an academic degree? Is he or she affiliated with a college or university? Are there other Web sites that provide additional information about the author?

- Does the author provide evidence for his or her assertions, such as citations and bibliographies? Are the sources up to date? Are the sources for statistics included?

- Is the site affiliated with an academic institution, press, or journal? The Web address — or URL — can provide some clues to such affiliations. If *.edu* or *.gov* appears in the address, it has been posted by an educational or governmental institution, which should give you a greater degree of confidence in the material it contains.

- Is the site sponsored by a particular organization? (Look for *.org* in the URL.) Do you know anything about the interests and concerns of the person or group that publishes the site? (Check the home page or click on "About" to find a mission statement.) Does the organization seem biased?

- Does the site allow users to add or change content? If so, the site cannot be relied on to provide accurate information, even if it includes notes, references to academic sources, or useful links. (This is the case, for example, with Wikipedia articles, which often include scholarly apparatus but can be altered by any user.)

- What is the purpose of the site? Is it designed to inform? Persuade? Sell a product?

- Does the information on the site coincide with what you have learned about the subject from other sources?

- Has the site been updated recently?

- Does the site contain useful links to other sites? Are the linked sites affiliated with reputable institutions or persons? If you are still unsure if an online source is reliable, it is best to consult your professor or a reference librarian.

Finding Primary Source Material in the UT Libraries

What Is a Primary Source?

As you learned earlier in the chapter, primary sources offer unique and compelling insights into history. Usually written at the time of an event, or as a direct response to an event, primary sources offer firsthand accounts of history. Primary sources include materials such as letters, diaries, speeches, and photographs. Secondary sources usually include materials such as textbooks, film reviews, book reviews, and so on; however, these are not strict rules. The genre of an item does not define the item as a primary source.

"Finding Primary Source Material in the UT Libraries" is written by Rachel Radom and Alesha Shumar, faculty members of the UT Libraries.

Determining whether or not an item is a primary source depends upon your research question. For example, textbooks are not usually categorized as primary sources because they interpret events and scientific findings well after such events and findings have occurred or have been accepted by society. A textbook's account of Sherman's March to the Sea would be a secondary source, although the textbook may include primary sources such as photographs from 1864 or quotes from newspapers of the time to support the arguments made by the textbook's authors.

Yet a textbook can be a primary source in certain circumstances. For instance, if you were writing a paper on how evolution has been taught to school children in the United States and wanted to compare how authors presented evolution in textbooks over a span of years (for example, comparing textbooks published in 1950 to those from 2005), those textbooks would be primary sources that you, as a researcher, would interpret.

Where Can You Find Primary Sources?

The University of Tennessee (UT) Libraries have a variety of collections that include primary source materials. Librarians also review and recommend a variety of highly regarded organizations' Web sites for finding additional primary sources. Here are a few of the best ways you can find primary sources.

ONLINE: PRIMARY SOURCES FROM THE UT LIBRARIES

Have you ever tried to find an article from a newspaper published in 1896? Finding such articles is nearly impossible using free online search engines, such as Google. Many private research companies digitize unique historical and scholarly materials, such as historical collections of newspapers or images, and then provide researchers access to the digital materials for a fee. In addition, libraries with unique materials often digitize their collections and make them available at no cost to researchers.

The UT Libraries subscribe to many online collections, including collections of online primary source materials. Your tuition dollars give you access to many of these proprietary collections, called databases, which are accessible from the UT Libraries' home page with your UT NetID and password. In addition, the UT Libraries are in the process of digitizing our unique materials and have made many of these materials freely accessible online.

Listed below are several places to look for primary source materials from the UT Libraries.

⌐ **Figure 4.1** From http://www.lib.utk.edu/databases, you can search for databases by name. Once you open the database you want to use, you can search for articles, letters, and so on.

Databases

The Libraries subscribe to several databases that include primary source materials. To use these collections from off-campus, you have to login using your UT network credentials (username and password). Because access to these databases is limited to subscribers, you may not be recognized as a UT subscriber if you start from the database's home page; instead, you should first authenticate your access through the UT Libraries' home page. Start at http://lib.utk.edu, then click on "databases" in the menu on the left side of the page. You can find these collections by using the "Find Databases by Name" search box; just type into the search box the name of the database you want to access in order to find the link.

Please keep in mind that the databases that include primary sources are not limited to those listed below. If you have questions about finding primary sources, talk to your instructor or ask a librarian (http://lib.utk.edu/askusnow).

Helpful Hint

When searching for primary source materials, you may need to consider what terms and words were used by authors at the time as opposed to contemporary phrasing. For example, if you were doing research on the Trail of Tears, you would not find many articles published in the 1800s that mention the Trail of Tears, because this phrase wasn't used until after the forced relocations of native peoples took place. Instead, you would want to use phrases such as "Indian Removal Act," which would lead to some articles on the legislation that caused the Trail of Tears. The narrower, or more specific, phrase "Indian Removal Act of 1830" would not be helpful, since the words "of 1830" were added in recent times. Alternatively, the broader phrase "Indian removal" would lead to many more articles on the general attitudes of non-Native Americans towards Native Americans in the nineteenth century.

- **American History in Video:** Streaming videos that may include primary source materials, such as photographs and correspondence

- **America's Historical Newspapers:** Early American newspapers, published between 1690 and 1922

- **AP Images:** Photographs and illustrations from the Associated Press, 1850s to today

- **Book Review Index Online:** Book reviews from the 1960s to today

- **Civil War: A Newspaper Perspective:** Articles from the *New York Herald*, the *Charleston Mercury*, and the *Richmond Enquirer*, published during the U.S. Civil War

- **19th-Century U.S. Newspapers:** Digitized images from hundreds of U.S. newspapers, 1800 to 1899

- **ProQuest Historical Newspapers:** Articles from a variety of historical U.S. newspapers, including:

  - *The Atlanta Constitution* (1868–1945)

  - *The Boston Globe* (1872–1979)

  - *The Chicago Tribune* (1849–1987)

  - *The Los Angeles Times* (1881–1987)

  - *The New York Times* (1851–2007)

  - *The Wall Street Journal* (1889–1993)

  - and more

- **Reader's Guide Retrospective:** Articles published in popular American magazines from 1890 to 1982

- **Times Digital Archive:** Digitized editions of the *Times* (London), 1785–1985

- **Twentieth-Century Advice Literature: North American Guides on Race, Gender, Sex, and the Family:** Digitized books related to day-to-day American life, 1859–1995

- **Women and Social Movements in the United States:** Interviews, letters, advertisements, and other materials documenting women's involvement in social movements, such as abolition or birth control

UT Libraries Digital Collections

The Special Collections of the University of Tennessee Libraries has many unique materials (see "Special Collections" under the "In Print [Hard Copies]" section on p. 110). Special Collections is digitizing some of their materials, making them available at no cost to researchers via the Internet.

The UT Libraries Digital Collections feature Tennessee history, the Great Smoky Mountains, and UT scholarly works. You can see what digital materials are available at http://www.lib.utk.edu/digitalcollections/az-list.html. Here are examples of a select few digital collections:

- **Pippitt Diaries:** Diaries kept during the Civil War by Union soldier Harry Pippitt

- **Roth (Albert "Dutch") Digital Photograph Collection:** Photographs of areas in and around the Great Smoky Mountains, taken from the 1910s through the middle of the twentieth century

- **University of Tennessee Commencements:** UT Commencement programs, 1841–2010

- **Volunteer Yearbooks:** Digital copies of UT yearbooks, 1897–2005

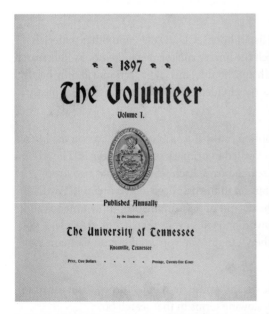

∟ Figure 4.2 The first two pages of the 1897 University of Tennessee Volunteer Yearbook.

ONLINE: PRIMARY SOURCES FROM OTHER LIBRARIES AND ORGANIZATIONS

These are sources you do not need to log into using your UT network credentials; these materials are freely available online, and have been digitized by credible, well-respected institutions.

- **American Memory:** Hosted by the Library of Congress, this site includes interviews, correspondence, diaries, and photographs related to all aspects of American life

- **Getty Research Institute Digital Collections:** A variety of materials related to art and artists, including letters written by artists

- **New York Public Library Digital Gallery:** Documents, letters, photographs, and more, on a wide range of topics, from art to society to science

- **Prints and Photographs Online Collection:** Hosted by the Library of Congress, this site is limited to images, but includes many topics, such as the history of advertising and slavery

- **Time & Life Pictures:** Photography and photojournalism from *Time* magazine and *Life* magazine

IN PRINT (HARD COPIES): PRIMARY SOURCES IN THE LIBRARY
Library Catalog: Books Plus

The UT Libraries have a searchable list of books, CDs, DVDs, and other materials available for checkout. You can search the library catalog using the Books Plus search function on the library home page (http://lib.utk.edu). This section will only briefly describe how to locate books; for more help identifying and locating books, please go to Chapter 8.

By clicking the "Advanced Search" option in the Books Plus search box on the library home page, you can specify a search limited to primary source materials. The advanced search screen gives you two search boxes. Each search box has two drop-down menus before it. The default option in the first drop-down menu is "Any." In the first search box row, maintain the default options in the drop-down menus and, in the search box, type the main keyword related to your search. For example, if you were researching a topic related to the Vietnam War, you would type "Vietnam War" in the search box.

In the second search box, change the default option in the first drop-down menu to "in subject." Then, type one of the following terms in that search box:

- Sources

- Correspondence

- Diaries

- Personal narratives

- Interviews

- Manuscripts

- Speeches

Entering one of the above words in the subject heading field will find books that are made up of collections of primary sources, such as letters, diaries, or interviews that relate to your area of research.

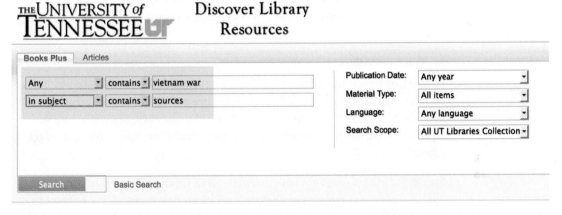

Ł Figure 4.3 An advanced search using the Books Plus search function allows you to limit results to primary sources.

After you have completed one search for primary sources, go back and do another advanced search, exchanging different words from the list above in the "in subject" search box row to find more primary source materials.

When you find a book on your topic, look at the line that says "Available" or "Checked Out." Materials that are available should be on the shelf in one of the UT Libraries (Hodges Library, DeVine Music Library, Pendergrass Ag-Vet Medical Library, or Storage Stacks). Next to the name of the library will be a series of letters and numbers—this is the call number of the book. The call number is similar to the address of the book. Call numbers relate to where the item is shelved in the library.

Helpful Hint

When using the catalog, if you find items that are print periodicals (e.g., magazines or journals), microfilm, or dissertations and theses, those materials may be in Storage. Their location would be listed as "Storage Stacks" or "Storage Microfilm." If you would like to request materials from Storage, use the links in the library catalog (the Books Plus search) for "Request: Item Pickup or Delivery" or "Request: Article or Chapter Scan." For more information about requesting items from Storage, go to http://www.lib.utk.edu/request/express_catalog.html.

The books that you may check out from Hodges Library are located in an area known as Hodges Library Stacks, which are on floors three to six of the library. If your book is available in Hodges Library Stacks, you will find the following call numbers on their respective floors:

A–GM: 3rd floor

GN–PR: 4th floor

PS–S: 5th floor

T–Z: 6th floor

For finding items at locations other than Hodges Library, please see Chapter 8, or ask a librarian for assistance (http://lib.utk.edu/askusnow).

Special Collections

Special Collections has many materials unique to the University of Tennessee Libraries. The materials in Special Collections must be specially requested and cannot leave the library. Therefore, you must plan ahead to use these materials since you will need to request them in advance and make time to use them while in Hodges Library.

Special Collections does not have materials on all topics; however, knowing what Special Collections includes can help you decide if these materials are relevant to your topic. Special Collections can prove helpful with specific research. Few people will ever have a chance to be around such unique historical files, papers, letters, books, and other materials.

- **Rare Books:** Approximately 60,000 titles primarily focused on Tennessee, Native American history, U.S. President Jackson, U.S. President Johnson, U.S. President Polk, religion in Tennessee, the Civil War and Reconstruction, the Great Smoky Mountains, and literary collections related to James Agee, William Congreve, Alex Haley, and Evelyn Scott

- **Manuscripts:** Private papers, literary manuscripts, business records, political files, broadsides, and historical records about Tennessee and the Southeast, along with significant papers related to:

  - Appalachian folklore

  - Clarence Brown, film director

  - Civil rights

  - Civil War

  - Admiral David G. Farragut

  - Great Smoky Mountains

  - Alex Haley

  - Native Americans

  - Oak Ridge and Oak Ridge National Laboratory

  - Radiation research

  - Wharton Family Papers

  - World Wars I and II

> ## Helpful Hint
>
> Plan ahead if you want to use materials from Special Collections. Manuscript and Archives collections are not stored in Hodges Library; when requested, they are pulled from an off-site storage location once a day. Materials requested before 3:00 p.m. will be available the following business day (M–F) at 9:00 a.m. Materials requested after 3:00 p.m. will be available two business days later at 9:00 a.m. Also, be aware of Special Collections Reading Room policies before you visit: http://lib.utk.edu/special/services/policies.html.
>
> To request materials from Special Collections, go to http://lib.utk.edu/special/services/request.html.

- **University Archives:** The University Archives collects and maintains the published and unpublished works of UT, including UT Press publications and materials produced by faculty, students, academic departments, administrative offices, campus organizations, and the UT Athletic Department. Significant holdings include:

  - Papers of UT Presidents

  - Minutes of the Boards of Trustees

  - Records of student organizations

  - Files from University departments and administrative offices

Special Collections materials, rare books and university publications are found in the library catalog by using the Books Plus search function. Manuscripts and University Archives are included in searchable inventory lists, or finding aids, available at http://dlc.lib.utk.edu/spc/search. Helpful information may also be found at http://lib.utk.edu/special/guides/index.html.

⌐ **Figure 4.4 A student using materials in the Special Collections Reading Room.**

✳ Questions and Activities for Chapter 4

1. A question posed in the section "Why Study History?" is "Why should we bother studying the past in our increasingly future-oriented society?" How would you answer this question?

2. Define primary and secondary sources.

3. Bring a personal artifact to class. It can be a written text, a visual text, or even an object you obtained recently, perhaps from your sorority or fraternity or during orientation. Before class, answer the questions in the appropriate "Tips for Writers" box in the section on "Working with Historical Sources" to help you begin your historical analysis of the object. In class, your instructor will ask you to get into groups of two or three and examine the artifacts you've brought, to figure out what "story" each person's artifact tells. After you've discussed the artifacts, work independently for about ten minutes to write the story of your artifact, and then share that with the class.

4. Movies that are supposedly "based upon a true story" are a common way of interpreting—or reinterpreting—history. Of course, any movie's dramatization of a "true story" tells an incomplete story at best. Select one movie you have seen or heard about recently that seems to be based on a true story (e.g., *Friday Night Lights*, *The King's Speech*, *The Social Network*, or one based upon events related to your 102 inquiry topic).

    a. If you wanted to find out how well the movie presents the "true" version of events, where would you start? Where could you learn more about the events depicted in the movie? What primary sources could you locate?

    b. Do some digging. Look for some primary sources about the events depicted in the movie, and make a list of ways that the movie producers seem to have taken liberties with history. What reasons can you think of to explain why the producers may have taken those liberties?

5. Visit the UT Libraries' home page (www.lib.utk.edu); then click on "Databases" on the left side of the screen. Using one of the primary source databases listed earlier in this chapter, find an article published in a newspaper before 1925 about Prohibition in the United States.

6. Consider the topic of the modern women's movement, or feminist movement, that began in the 1960s. What words or phrases would have been used at the time to talk about the issue? Was the phrase "women's movement" used in the late 1960s?

7. To practice doing a keyword search, find a book in the library catalog (the Books Plus search on the library home page) that includes interviews with former slaves in America.

8. Use the UT Libraries Special Collections finding aids to locate materials about former UT coach Robert Neyland. List three collection titles that have material about Neyland.

9. Construct a visual timeline of important events related to your 102 inquiry topic. (Your instructor may give you guidelines for starting and ending dates to consider as the time period.) Then, write a summary of that timeline.

10. What questions do you have about the history of your inquiry topic? Write them out so that you can refer to them as research questions. To help you imagine possible questions, refer to "Historical Questions" under "Why Study History?" and

consider issues of *advances*, *causes*, and *interesting events* that occurred during your topic's historical development.

11. Who is an important historical figure related your 102 inquiry topic? Why is this person important? Write a brief biography of this person. Focus on the "who, what, when, where, and how?" questions discussed in "Historical Questions."

12. Do a Google Web search using the phrase *history and [your 102 topic]*. What kind of information appears on the first page of "hits"? Do the same search in Google Scholar, and compare what comes up there to the regular Google Web search.

13. Locate one primary source and one secondary source on your 102 topic of inquiry (or on a narrower topic your instructor suggests). Write a paragraph that compares and contrasts the sources. Refer to the appropriate "Tips for Writers" boxes in the chapter to evaluate the sources you find. (Ask your instructor for help finding primary sources on your topic; use one of the following collections: http://memory.loc.gov, http://eudocs.lib.byu.edu, http://moa.umdl.umich.edu, http://gallica.bnf.fr, or http://yale.edu/lawweb/avalon.htm; or consult the information in "Finding Primary Source Material in the UT Libraries.")

5 Conducting Archival Research

Culture is elusive. It passes secretly, often silently, telepathically. . . . it ripens, untended, often unconsciously in dreams, suddenly unexpectedly to reveal itself in an expression or a turn of phrase . . . or, at another level, in our musical and pictorial preferences, in the narratives we construct about ourselves and others or to which we turn for understanding. It may arise by accident, from a half-remembered memory, from fingers or hands idling with instruments and tools.
— Robert Cantwell

As folklorist Robert Cantwell suggests above, culture is elusive—hard to capture and even harder to retain. One way people capture culture is by assembling archives— collections of documents and artifacts. An archive can be a shoe box full of mementos from your volleyball career, a collection of pens used by a local mayor to sign laws, an elderly neighbor's egg cup collection that attracts visitors from throughout the region, a room in your town hall showing maps and photographs tracing the town's historical development, or a city's aerospace museum. Simply, an archive contains important "stuff" so that family, ethnic, local, or national cultures and subcultures don't—to paraphrase Cantwell's words—pass secretly, silently, or untended.

One of the largest archives in the United States, the Smithsonian Institution in Washington, D.C., describes itself as "the nation's attic." In this attic, as in any archive, you will find stored a dazzling and surprising variety of artifacts, records, correspondence, historical documents, and audiovisual media. The Smithsonian has 10 separate archives, which hold an estimated 50,000 cubic feet of paper documents, 7 million still photographs, and thousands of motion picture films, videos, and audio recordings. The Smithsonian's National Museum of American History, one of its many constituent "attics," includes over 150 million items and acquires more all the time. A few of our favorite examples of its holdings:

Check out Appendix C, Work-in-Progress Research and Writing Activities, to find additional practical suggestions to help you read, research, and write successfully.

- The ruby slippers Judy Garland wore in *The Wizard of Oz*

- The Woolworth's lunch counter stools from one early civil rights sit-in

Chapter 5, "Conducting Archival Research," is taken from Bonnie Stone Sunstein and Elizabeth Chiseri-Strater, *FieldWorking: Reading and Writing Research*, Third Edition, pp. 359–88, 399–408, 412–15 (Chapter 7, "Researching Archives: Locating Culture").

- The first typewriter, from 1870, which weighs 165 pounds
- A 1918 Oldsmobile Model 37
- A urologist's surgical case from the 1830s
- A ritual circumcisionist's kit
- A piano maker's tool chest
- A shoeshine kit from the 1950s
- A computer technician's tool case from the 1990s

Online Archives

Our computer culture allows us access to many archival sources through the Internet. In fact, some exhibits are available only as "virtual tours," like the Hard Rock Cafe Web site's Memorabilia Gallery, which displays artifacts from its franchised cafes across the world. Online, you can view rock star Jim Morrison's leather pants, Eric Clapton's favorite bar stool, and the wool herringbone suit Rex Harrison wore when he played Professor Henry Higgins in the 1964 movie musical *My Fair Lady*.

The Internet allows us to tour museums all over the world. Without paying travel costs or missing much time from daily obligations, we can enter, browse, and study all kinds of collections online. From your seat at a computer, you can examine the Lincoln bedroom at the White House or scrutinize the Magna Carta in the British Library, for example. You can see images of real artifacts and also sort through enormous archives using your imagination and analytical skills.

Anyone with an Internet connection has access to an international treasure trove of public and private databases — photographs, maps, documents, works of art, manuscript collections, corporate archives, church records, and historical society records. These online collections are growing constantly. Immediate public access to such information is new in human history and represents a significant development in research and fieldwork. You can find a museum that specializes in almost any collection of artifacts or archives you can imagine: there is even a Museum of Online Museums and a Museum of Web Art. We invite you to think broadly about how you can use such archives to support your research project.

The Internet can also introduce us to museums and libraries that we might decide to visit in person. The Mount Horeb Mustard Museum, for example, in Mount Horeb, Wisconsin, displays over 3,250 types of mustards along with antique mustard pots and other mustard exhibits. After taking a virtual tour of the museum, you might take a road trip to Mount Horeb to see the actual collection. After doing some more online research, you might decide to visit the Johnson County Museum's 1950s all-electric model house in Shawnee, Kansas; or learn about African American contributions to American railroads at the A. Philip Randolph Pullman Porter Museum in Chicago, Illinois; or learn more about the history of puppets at the Ballard Institute and Museum of Puppetry in Storrs, Connecticut.

More and more archival material is available to the public every day. Even a quick Internet search can locate thousands of existing archival collections. Among many others, you can visit these American collections online or in their actual physical locations:

American Textile History Museum, Lowell, Massachusetts

Balch Institute for Ethnic Studies at the Historical Society of Pennsylvania, Philadelphia, Pennsylvania

Baltimore Streetcar Museum, Baltimore, Maryland

Bathtub Art Museum, Portland, Oregon

Bicycle Museum of America, New Bremen, Ohio

International Bowling Museum and Hall of Fame, Arlington, Texas

Corvette Hall of Fame, Cooperstown, New York

Dinosaur Journey Museum at the Museum of the West, Grand Junction, Colorado

Eric Carle Museum of Picture Book Art, Amherst, Massachusetts

Flashlight Museum, Maple Grove, Minnesota

National Cartoon Museum, New York, New York

Advertising Icon Museum, Kansas City, Missouri

Museum of Questionable Medical Devices at the Science Museum of Minnesota, St. Paul, Minnesota

National Cowboy and Western Heritage Museum, Oklahoma City, Oklahoma

Offshore Energy Center's *Ocean Star* Offshore Drilling Rig and Museum, Galveston, Texas

Spam Museum, Austin, Minnesota

Wild Turkey Center and Museum, Edgefield, South Carolina

World Kite Museum and Hall of Fame, Long Beach, Washington

Representative Artifacts

All cultures and subcultures collect representative artifacts to hand down to group members. To an outsider, those collections may appear to be mere clutter; to an insider, they are precious identity markers and artifacts of a subculture's history. These are the concrete objects of tradition—symbols of the rituals, behaviors, language, and beliefs that teach a culture about itself as it shifts and changes with time. Even when a cultural group is oppressed or exiled from its place of origin, human ingenuity prevails, finding ways to preserve old traditions and apply them in new settings.

⌐ Hmong Storycloth

Hmong embroidery, for example, is intricate and beautiful but not merely decorative. Rather, it stitches the story of the Hmongs' life for 2,000 years in Laos, Thailand, and China and later in refugee camps as they prepared for relocation in cultures very different from theirs. "Flower cloth stitching" (*paj ntaub*) is an old art form of appliqué and embroidery in geometric patterns, often depicting animals and other forms of nature. In the 1970s, after the Vietnam War, the Hmong were pushed into refugee camps in Thailand. Since they had no written language, they developed the concept of the "storycloth" (*pa ndau*) to retain and pass on their history. The storycloth was an artistic document of the Hmongs' recent history and allowed them to become small entrepreneurs in their new locations in the Western world. They used the ancestral traditions of embroidery to record the stories of their past, share their current situation, and anticipate their future lives.

In this chapter, we explore a wide range of archival materials—the stuff of collections—from private family diaries, journals, letters, and scrapbooks to the bigger institutional archives like museum holdings and the very public archive, the Internet. All archival work, including traditional library research, strengthens fieldwork through triangulation—ways to validate, check, confirm, or disconfirm data. And, of course, accumulating and analyzing multiple data sources can make fieldstudies more persuasive.

Family Archives

Digging through any archive can be as overwhelming as entering a fieldsite for the first time. Even if it's a small private archive like your grandmother's attic, you have no idea at first how to sort through and make use of it in any systematic way. The way to organize someone else's clutter does not announce itself to you; that process is the job of the fieldworker.

Tradition-bearing archives are part of almost every family's legacy. There is great joy and pleasure in knowing that you have an artifact or an archive of stuff from someone in your own family. And yet trunks full of family heirlooms often go unexplored and unexamined in attics and cellars until someone in the family is interested enough to look. Boxes of old photographs, bundles of letters, diaries, journals, daybooks, family Bibles with genealogies and notes, jumbles of mementos, and business ledgers can all open up a family's connection with the cultures that define it.

Meg Buzzi's Family Archive: The Letters of "Rad-Rad"

Every family in the United States that is able to trace its roots has some version of an "arrival narrative," even when it is the story of displacement or oppression. Our student Meg Buzzi grew up in a large Italian American family in Pittsburgh, Pennsylvania, where she is called "the main cousin" by the 17 younger ones. Meg's recorded family story begins in Naples, Italy, where, as the oral tale goes, her great-great-grandfather was a switch operator for the railroad and lost both his legs in an accident. This event somehow prompted her great-grandfather "Peep" to immigrate to the United States, where he hopped a train to Cleveland and labored on an auto assembly line there. At night he took a real estate correspondence course, and two years later he landed in Pittsburgh with a real estate license and no money. Somehow, he found a financial backer, founded a real estate company, and found himself a wife. Over the years, they prospered and had four children, the oldest of whom was Meg's grandfather, Raymond Barone, born in 1922. Raymond eventually took over Peep's business and expanded its success. He was in the right place at the right time; Pittsburgh was experiencing its urban renaissance, and real estate was a key to that renewal. So Raymond, known to his family as "Rad-Rad," completed the family's Horatio Alger story by funding the college educations of his eight children and 18 grandchildren.

But Raymond left another legacy far more valuable to his family. Feeling both proud and abandoned when his children left home for college, he began writing family letters as a way of keeping them together. For Raymond, the extended family was his most important community and his way of maintaining the traditions he wanted to pass on. His handwritten letters on yellow legal paper cover a nearly 30-year period. Each letter, about nine to 12 pages long, begins with the salutation "Dear Kiddies," and is addressed to the collective audience of children and grandchildren. Each person's name is underlined when Raymond mentions noteworthy information about them. Because these letters were an entertaining, literary accounting of family activities, they were often read aloud at family parties and holidays. In fact, on the day that the relatives were notified of Raymond's sudden death, they gathered at his home, and his children read aloud from many of the letters. Later, Meg's mother and aunts typed the letters and placed them in two large binders of 500 pages each.

Meg saw these letters as a family archive and used them in a fieldstudy incorporating family research, interviews, history, and her own reflective commentary. Her study is full of her grandfather's humor (which she inherited): "Our family uses humor because it is entertaining," she writes, "and because it teaches lessons and communicates arguments without as much hostility." She expands on the importance of family humor as it's represented in the letters: "It is our drug of choice, our solace, our subversion, and our sneak attack. This satire we employ relies on the assumption that there will always be a force above us. Always a power with whom to negotiate. Always someone to ridicule."

She loved poring through hundreds of her grandfather's letters recalling events she had been part of and many which she had not. The letters were so full of history, politics, and family details that she felt she could spend a lifetime, rather than just a semester, on her study. In the back of her mind, Meg knew that she was searching for a theme or a focus within this mass of paper. When she began telephone and in-person interviews with her relatives—Aunt Monica, her mother, brother, and cousins—she noticed that they each recalled hilarious events that featured Rad-Rad's outrageous humor. She looked back through her own personal journals to connect dates with facts in the letters and found that she too had recorded funny family stories. Then she e-mailed her brother Nathan and her cousins Ben and Bryan, asking them to add their own memories and confirm the details of the letters. As a researcher, Meg knew enough not to take personal letters on their face value alone. Any stories written down privately need confirmation from a broader, more public range of evidence. To get a feel for the times her grandfather wrote about, she familiarized herself with a 30-year period in politics and popular culture by looking at newspapers, magazines, and books. So in addition to the collection of Raymond's personal letters, Meg triangulated these other data sources and in the process discovered the theme of family humor.

In this excerpt called "The Fridge," from her larger study called "Dear Kiddies," Meg incorporates and analyzes three letters. Notice that she draws on the following data sources—her grandfather's 1979 letter about the vegetable drawer, a family photograph of vegetables that she now owns, and refrigerator notes written by her grandfather to her grandmother.

The Fridge

When our freezer section is opened, something invariably falls to the floor. . . . Of late things don't just fall straight down; they kind of leap out about 3–4 feet. Actually, the most interesting thing about our "fridge" is the various textures which can be achieved in its various sections. From your crisper sections comes your "no-noise" carrots. . . . It works for celery and radishes too. One week in the CRISPER takes all the noise out. On the other hand, the bottom shelf will put snap, crackle, and pop in cooked spaghetti, put the snap back into cooked green beans and even make stewed prunes crunchy. . . . I believe that "fridges" should be seen and not heard. (1/26/79)

⌐ **Still Life?**

After this excerpt from one of her grandfather's letters, Meg writes:

> There is a story about a photograph my grandfather took. It is a picture of rotting vegetables: carrots, onions, tomatoes, and peppers in varying degrees of decay, all carefully arranged on my grandmother's heirloom serving platter. Entitled "Still Life?" this 40" x 28" masterpiece hung in his dining room as a constant reminder to my grandmother that her produce-preservation skills were less than acceptable. Currently it graces my dining room wall in a black and gold Baroque-style frame with cream-colored matting. Previous to that, it was I who dared to remove it from the basement bowels it had been condemned to by my grandmother. His aim to satirize her treatment of the vegetable drawer had never been well received.
>
> In addition to the art projects he endeavored to torture her with, Rad-Rad also played a passive-aggressive note game with her on the front of their monster appliance: "We must get stronger magnets soon. Our messages are now three deep, and they tend to slide down the door as it's used" (2/28/79). When the magnets gave up, he bought a blackboard and hung it on the front of the basement door.

Meg could not have accomplished her study of her grandfather's humor without the collection of letters that her mother and aunts kept. The boxes you discover in your own family archives can come in all shapes and sizes. Meg's family consciously built

Box 5.1: A Box about Boxes

Purpose

Sometimes dusty boxes, even boxes that we find in our homes or that belong to people we know, are important sites for archival study. Meg Buzzi's study of family stories began with two binders full of her grandfather's letters. Looking with the eyes of a researcher can shift the way we sort through a collection of stuff, whether it comes from a family member, someone we know (like a teacher or a student), or an anonymous figure whose stuff promises the beginning of a fascinating fieldstudy.

Action

Locate a box of archival stuff — a grouping of artifacts or documents that someone has collected, even if the purpose is simply "to keep because it's important." This box could belong to you, a member of your family, or someone else. List the contents of the box. Try organizing or mapping the contents in different patterns — chronologically, by size, by type or shape, by order from beginning to end or from inside to outside. See if there are one or more overall logical shapes to the data, and determine how the organizing patterns would show different themes about the contents of the box.

Response

David Jakstas, one of our students, comes from a family that owns a hotel on a lake in a small town in Illinois, not far from Chicago. The hotel is old and stately and is known to city weekenders as "the big white building on the lake." It was built in 1884 with 100 rooms, a 240-foot porch, a ballroom, a tower, and a bar. Only the bar exists today for business, though the family is planning to restore both the bar and the hotel. David's uncle, who is planning the restoration, manages a successful marina next to the hotel. For David, the hotel itself is an archive full of information, documents, and artifacts from basement to tower. Already equipped with the family stories he's heard all his life and knowing he could listen to other family versions of them, David's early fieldwork consisted of uncovering archival material from the old hotel, much of which was in the bar. "One particular slot machine," he writes, "sits in a showcase of the bar but was found in one of the storage rooms in the hotel. The sign below the machine reads, 'a switch underneath the machine quickly makes this machine dispense candy instead of money, in case of a police raid.'" Also in the showcase is a hat with this caption: "This hat was worn by Al Capone. It was left by him in the back seat of a cab after leaving the hotel."

David's research led him to wonder what role the hotel had played in the lives of Chicago gangsters, who would "pull off a big heist in the city" and head for the lake-area hotels. His family's stories involve bullet holes in the walls, ghosts in the rafters, boating accidents, and floods. David studied a scrapbook of news articles about the hotel that had been clipped by various family members throughout the hotel's lifetime. He found an original lease, evidence that the hotel had once been a clubhouse for a Board of Trade, several old maps, menus, souvenir programs from celebrations, and news articles with pictures, details, and stories spanning a hundred years of history. David writes:

Box 5.1: *continued*

"I did not start with this topic; I literally walked into it one day. My problem was that I had never looked at the place as a place for research. . . . My dad and I went through boxes of things about the hotel in our basement before I talked to anyone at the bar. Although my mom thought we'd trashed the basement, I found plenty of information and a lot of history. I had the main material for my project."

an archive of letters by typing and binding them, but many families have more informal archives of stuff they don't quite know what to do with—a relative's diary, a scrapbook of pictures and newspaper clippings, a box or drawer full of random-looking odd items.

It is both puzzling and thrilling to find family letters, journals, and artifacts that explain—or complicate—hunches you've always had about traits you've inherited, stories you've overheard, or histories your family has witnessed. Finding personal archives can lead you into further research to confirm and expand the data. Writer Edward Ball used his extended family's personal archives as a starting point for his institutional research. Through deeds, documents, and ledgers he found at the South Carolina Historical Society, Ball continued constructing the story of his family. In his book *Slaves in the Family*, Ball rhapsodizes on the emotions he experiences as he works with old documents:

> Old papers are beautiful things. Coarse, mottled parchment containing business records sometimes has the look of white skin. The pages are veiny, with age spots, the black ink coursing down them like hair. In some places, the ink is as dark as the day it was unbottled, and the paper as blotchy as an English cheek. I read through the Ball papers, beginning with the story of the first Elias Ball, who died in 1751, at 75; his will filled four pages with script. The paper was pierced here and there by holes, signatures of bookworms. A rip had been mended on the second page, and there in the splotch of a dried glue stain, a thumb print appeared.

> The deeds were the most beguiling. They came with maps, or "plats," that showed the layout of a plantation and the location of its buildings. One plat had a red border, faded like a child's watercolor, while some pages had brown splatter marks, perhaps from ancient splashes of tea. Other papers had curled up from dryness or changes in chemistry. In the old days, each deed was folded into an envelope shape, tied shut with a strip of parchment, and sealed with red wax. The wax was crusty, with black streaks where the burning candle had dripped carbon into the seal.

> I read the papers slowly, lingering on the chatty letters, smiling at the quirks of the garrulous Balls, savoring their loopy signatures. Then I found the slave lists.

There were bundles of them, in thick sheaves, each sheaf containing a stack. When a rice planter handed out shoes, he wrote down the names of who got them. To pay taxes, he made an inventory of his human property. If he bought fabrics so people could make clothes, he noted how many yards were given to each person. When a woman gave birth, the date and the name of the child appeared. And when Mr. Ball died, his executor appraised everyone before title passed to the heir. I began to count the names on some of the bigger lists, up to a few hundred, then lost track. . . .

Shut in the vaults of the historical society's pink stucco building, I read as much as I could absorb. One family at a time, the stories surfaced, and in glimpses and parts, I began to piece together what happened.

Ball did research on his own family based on documents that were housed in institutions open to the public. In his book, he hunts down the history of his family, which includes plantation owners in South Carolina and the slaves with whom they had children. In the following excerpt from this nonfiction best seller, Ball traces his genealogy to a "mixed-blood" namesake born in 1740. Notice how, as archivist, he adopts the stance of a detective toward the records he examines to make this discovery. As you read this short selection from *Slaves in the Family*, try making a mental or a written list of all the types of documents you think Ball needed to consider in his genealogical detective work.

Slaves in the Family

EDWARD BALL

In the early 1730s, a young black woman named Dolly came to work in the Comingtee big house. Elias's second wife had three children at the time, and Dolly probably helped with the young ones, cleaned house, and cooked. A little homage to Dolly appears in the published Ball memoir. "Perhaps the name that stands out above the others is 'Dolly,'" wrote one of the Ball women at the beginning of the twentieth century. "We know little about her, but enough to show that she was well thought of in the family. Perhaps she had 'minded' the children, and been a faithful nurse in illness. The ministrations of such humble friends of the family—they were surely no less—have soothed many a bed of suffering; and in death their hands have tenderly performed the last offices."

It seems strange that the name of a slave would evoke sentimental memories in the family of her owners some 150 years after her death. Just as strange is the aside "We know little about her," which seems to contradict the familiarity of the memory.

Dolly was born in 1712, though I cannot say where and I can only fix the year of her birth from a note about her death that states her age. Dolly was evidently more than a good housekeeper. In his will, dictated in 1750, Elias devoted considerable thought to

Dolly, whom he called his "Molattoe Wench." As used then, the word "mulatto" described children of black mothers and white fathers. (In Elias's day, the children of one Native and one black parent were called "mustees" by whites.) Since the colonial legislature had already passed a law forbidding sex between white women and enslaved blacks, the white mother of a daughter of color would have been subject to prosecution. Therefore, in all likelihood, Dolly's father was white, her mother black.

It is undeniable that white men on the plantations forced and persuaded black women to have sex with them, and evidence of white-black sex appears in official records from the earliest days. In one case, from 1692, a woman named Jane LaSalle filed a petition with the Grand Council, the highest authority in Charleston. The petition involved her husband, who had left her for a black woman, probably one of the white couple's slaves. The abandoned wife appealed for help, and the Grand Council ordered the husband to return to his spouse, or else pay her a sum of money. The public nature of the case and matter-of-fact way in which it was disposed give reason to believe that interracial sex was a common part of Elias's world.

Because the earliest Ball plantation records date from 1720, and Dolly was born in 1712, it is difficult to say who her parents were. I don't believe her father was Elias Ball. I suspect, from much circumstantial evidence, he bought her as a child and later grew fond of her. During her youth Dolly seems to have gotten unusual attention. At age sixteen, according to plantation accounts, Dolly fell ill and Elias quickly summoned a doctor to the plantation to treat her. The following year, he again called a doctor for Dolly and paid a high fee for the cure. It almost never occurred, on the remote plantations, that a slave was singled out for individual medical care. Physicians were scarce, and doctors had to be enticed with large sums of money to make trips to the country, since they could easily find patients in Charleston. But thanks to Elias, Dolly received house calls, the only black person on Comingtee to warrant such attention.

The pattern of care continued throughout Dolly's young life. On one occasion Elias had special shoes made for her. Beginning in the colonial days, plantation owners hired shoemakers to sew one kind of footwear for themselves and their families and another kind, called Negro shoes, for slaves. Once, Elias hired a shoemaker from the nearby settlement of Goose Creek to sew shoes for his son, and, in the same order, to make similar high-priced footwear for Dolly. There is no evidence that other slaves ever received such treatment.

Dolly was about twenty when she went to work in the Ball house. After a year or two there, she began to have children. Her son Cupid was born April 1735. Because the slave owners often left out the name of the father in records of slave births, I cannot say who Cupid's father was. In all likelihood he was another slave on Comingtee, because Cupid went on to become a field hand, lived his entire life on Ball plantations, and died sometime after 1784.

In the 1730s, Elias and Mary were also having children. Mary gave birth to her last, a son, in 1734; he died as an infant. There is no record of Mary's death, but soon after the birth of her final child, Mary herself passed away and Elias buried her sometime around 1735, ending a marriage of fifteen years. Upon Mary's death, Elias was left with three daughters to look after—Mary, Eleanor, and Sarah—ages two to thirteen. In

1736, he turned sixty. When Elias married Mary Delamare, he had made clear his preference for younger women. Now Dolly, twenty-four, was on hand.

Mary's death seems to have made possible a liaison between Elias and Dolly. On September 16, 1740, Dolly gave birth to her second child, who was given the name Edward. Among the slaves on Comingtee, none carried English forenames. What's more, when Edward grew up, records show that the Ball family paid him respect. Edward was given his freedom and lived among the Balls, who handled his business affairs. When he died, at eighty, his will and other papers went into the Ball family collection. According to probate records, Edward was a mulatto, described in his estate papers as "a free yellow man." If Edward had been able to take the name of the man whom I believe was his father, he would have been called Edward Ball.

A few years later, while still working in the big house, Dolly had another child who received an English name, Catherine. Like her brother Edward, Catherine would also later gain freedom, evidently granted to her by the Balls. The two siblings, Catherine and Edward, were the only people owned by Elias who would ever be freed from slavery.

Around the time Dolly began to have her mulatto children, sex between whites and blacks was a topic of sharp discussion in the local newspaper. The frequency of the editorials suggests that Elias and Dolly's relationship had plenty of precedent. In July 1736, one writer for the *South Carolina Gazette* pleaded with "Certain young Men" of Charleston to hide their relationships with colored women. He called on them to "frequent less with their black Lovers the open Lots and the . . . House on the Green between old Church street and King street." If they did not keep their heads down, he added, other whites might step in "to coole their Courage and to expose them." The writer ended his cranky editorial with an appeal to white men to stay away from women slaves, if only in solidarity with other whites. White women, he maintained, were "full as capable for Service either night or day as any Africain Ladies whatsoever."

When he sat down to write his will, Elias kept young Dolly high in his mind. After declaring that his property would pass to his white children, he added this unusual clause: "I give & Bequeath the Molattoe Wench called Dolly to such of my children as she shall within three months next after my Decease make her Election for her master or mistress." Elias wanted Dolly to be able to decide her fate after he was gone: she was to choose which among Elias's white children would give her a home. It was an incomplete gesture—Dolly could select only her next master or mistress, not freedom—but in this way Elias acknowledged her humanity. The telltale clue is the phrase "within three months next after my Decease." Dolly would have a period of mourning to collect herself before deciding her next step, a graceful interval of grief.

If Dolly and Elias kept up a relationship for several years, was it rape? Or could they have cared for each other? Mockery and danger would have faced the couple on both sides. Not only would Elias have felt ostracized by some whites, but Dolly may have angered some of the other slaves at Comingtee by sleeping with the master. As for the sex itself, could Elias and Dolly both have felt desire? Or did Dolly trade sex (willingly or not) for more lenient treatment? Despite the pitiful circumstances of their attachment, could these two have, somehow, loved each other?

I imagine several of these things may simultaneously have been true.

As a researcher, writer Edward Ball used a range of institutional archives and special collections as he studied his family history to find evidence of intermarriage between his white rice-plantation owner relatives and their slaves. To make sense of how the mulatto slave Edward (Ball), son of Dolly, may have been his distant relative, he had to read family histories, plantation records, wills, and business records, as well as newspapers of the times. His primary sources were the oral histories he recorded from his relatives. To confirm (and sometimes disconfirm) parts of the oral histories, Ball relied on an interesting array of public archives—the Afro-American Historical and Genealogical Society in New York, family papers that he found in several states' historical society archives and university libraries, United States census records, warrants and deeds, mortgage records, town papers, genealogies and maps, birth records, statutes, contracts, probate records, estate inventories, wills, medical and death records, and even gravestones. He consulted books on Indian history, American slavery, economic life and rice farming in the southern United States, life in seventeenth- and eighteenth-century Africa, and more specific resources as he needed them in his research.

Not all archival research projects are this complex. Edward Ball wondered about his roots throughout his lifetime and even moved to Charleston, South Carolina, to conduct the research for his book.* Some fieldworkers—anthropologists, journalists, historians, and other writers—spend decades of their professional lives conducting in-depth studies. Your study won't demand as much time of you but will require you to examine and consider a wide range of sources.

Organizing Archival Material

When you look at historical documents—old photos, family letters (as Meg Buzzi acquired from her grandfather), maps or blueprints, a family's financial records, a handmade quilt, or an old steamer trunk full of mildewed fabrics and rusty tools—your first job is to organize what you see. There is no one way to do this. As historians and researchers have learned, there are always options for organizing archival material.

---

*Like Ball, many African Americans encounter challenges in doing genealogical research since few records of slave families exist. New archival sources are helping African Americans trace their roots. For example, a CD-ROM contains the records of the Freedman's Bank, an institution that was created for freed slaves after the Civil War and that required depositors to list all members of their families, even relatives who had been sold to others. This database will be helpful in doing research on African American families and is available from www.ldscatalog.com.

Your decision about how to organize artifacts, archives, fieldnotes, print sources, transcripts, and other data provides a framework for how you might write about your material. But even as you are collecting data, your organizational structure will help you decide what else to collect. Our colleague and graduate student Lia Schultz set out to study 15 generations of her family's education between the years 1600 and 2000. Like Edward Ball, she was studying many generations of one family and therefore had the challenge of determining how to arrange her data. Her study began with a pile of letters, her relatives' stories, and a stash of old books, many with notes in the margins.

Over four years, Lia created a detailed genealogy and a series of what she calls "educational biographies"—oral histories of each family member's education. She designed a Web site to help her envision her materials and how they all interconnected. She traveled to sites where her ancestors had lived and gone to school. In libraries and town historical societies, she found many kinds of records—including wills and estate inventories, census records, land deeds, tax records, sale bills or other indications of ownership, personal letters, journals and diaries, school assignments and records, accounting ledgers, calling cards, textbooks, Bibles, book lists, church records, published sermons, newspapers and other periodicals, photographs, and certificates (with signatures) of births, marriages, and deaths. We invited Lia to contribute a guest box to this book, based on her experiences organizing her substantial collection of archives.

Box 5.2: Framing Time: Synchronic and Diachronic Organization

Lia Schultz, Ph.D. candidate, University of Iowa, Iowa City

Purpose
Curators, archivists, archaeologists, and even the elders of our families know that there are different ways to represent events and objects in time. This box will help you think about how you can consider any historical artifact using two different orientations to time — *diachronic* (across multiple points in time) or *synchronic* (at one point in time, with a broad range of cultural information coming to bear on that one point).

Action
Choose a particular archive that you have located or created. Select one artifact from the archive. Identify the time period in which it was made or used. Try to be as accurate as you can. Is there a date imprinted somewhere on the artifact? Can you identify or estimate the date it was created based on its content? Can an antique guide, a historical reference, a curator, or a family member provide clues about the time period in which the artifact was used? After you have dated your artifact, choose an organizational method for analyzing it in relationship to time:

Box 5.2: *continued*

1. **Diachronic.** Select multiple points in time at which to investigate your artifact, or identify two or more periods that you wish to compare. Examples of time periods include four years of college, three generations in one family, the years 1906 and 2006, and points before, during, and after World War II. Consider how the uses and meanings of your artifact have changed over time. Do different generations assign different meanings or values to your artifact? What historical factors may have influenced those changes?

2. **Synchronic.** Select one point in time in which to investigate your artifact. You might identify the significance the artifact had in the year it was manufactured. Alternatively, you might consider the meaning of a document in the present or choose a significant date to investigate (for example, your grandfather's wedding day, the start of World War I, or the late 1980s).

Response

As part of my larger project on the literacy of my ancestors, many of whom were teachers, I chose to investigate the following 1890 artifact. It is a set of rules for female public school teachers at the Country School House Museum, Goewey #5, Osceola County, Sibley, Iowa:

Teachers are expected to keep the schoolroom clean and neat at all times by sweeping the floors at least once a day; scrubbing the floor once each week with hot water and lye soap; cleaning the blackboards daily; starting the fire at 7 a.m. so that the schoolroom will be warm by 8 a.m.

Teachers will not dress in bright colors. Dresses must not be more than two inches above the ankles. At least two petticoats must be worn. Their petticoats will be dried in pillowcases.

The teacher will not marry or keep company with men during the term of her employment.

She will not get into a carriage or an automobile with any man except her brother or father. Teachers will not loiter at ice cream stores.

Teachers are expected to be at home between the hours of 8 p.m. and 6 a.m. unless in attendance at a school function.

The teacher will not smoke cigarettes or play cards. She will not dye her hair under any circumstances.

It is understood the teacher will attend church each Sunday and either teach a class in Sunday school or sing in the choir.

The teacher will not leave town at any time without permission of the chairman of the school board.

There are two ways to represent this artifact in my study, depending on how I choose to write it up. Because I am examining my family's education over time but also representing various time periods in my educational portraits, I have to decide whether to present the information diachronically or synchronically. The following paragraphs show my thinking about the pros and cons of each approach.

1. **Questions for a diachronic approach.** With this approach, I need to decide what points over time might usefully frame this artifact and in what context. Should I work the artifact into the history of women in education in the United States? Or should I show how the preparation of teachers has changed over time? Should I consider the architectural and domestic features of nineteenth-century schools, like the use of soap and lye for cleaning? Or should I think about rules, manners, and etiquette during the westward expansion — proper behavior in ice cream stores, fashion trends among teachers, the rise and fall of curfews, or churchgoing habits for adults?

2. **Questions for a synchronic approach.** Thinking synchronically would lead me to research what was happening in the time and place this artifact was written. What was happening in Osceola County, Iowa, during the year 1890? What was it like to live there? Who lived there? What songs did church choirs sing? What did the townspeople read? What were their occupations? What did their homes look like? Which women in that town dried their petticoats in pillowcases? How did their lives differ from other Americans at the same time? From other Iowans? From other teachers in other states?

Either of these two choices could create an exciting description, but their results would be very different from each other. I chose the diachronic approach because in my much larger project I wanted to show one family's literacy (mine) over 15 generations — my ancestors' reading and writing habits since colonial times in the United States.

Both Lia Schultz's study and Edward Ball's book show us how we can use archives to research our own families. Historical archives (which we discuss in a moment) are generally far more organized than family archives and therefore easier to access. One important idea in any historical research, then — whether it is about a family, an institution, a period in history, or even oneself — is that we need to decide how to place our archival material within a time frame.

As Lia's box shows, we can organize materials diachronically (according to many points over a length of time) or synchronically (according to events, environmental features, or artifacts or items that exist at one period of time). We illustrate these organizational concepts with two very different kinds of historical research. The first example is both diachronic and autobiographical; in fact, we might call it "auto-ethnographic" or "autoarchival" research. The second example is a comprehensive, scholarly, synchronic study of one year in one famous man's history.

Author and comedian Amy Borkowsky chose a diachronic approach to analyze and write about a boxful of bills. In the introduction to her book *Statements: True Tales of Life, Love, and Credit Card Bills*, she writes as follows:

Not long ago, I was looking through some boxes in my closet and became nostalgic. I'm talking all-out, mascara-running, nose-blowing nostalgic.

The boxes didn't hold faded photographs.

They didn't contain love letters.

They held twelve years of credit card statements, chronicling virtually every significant event in my life as a single career woman.

While I was too busy to keep a diary, it turned out that American Express had kept one for me.

They've recorded for all eternity the fact that on July 7, 1992, I spent $89.12 at Victoria's Secret — and that on July 17, 1992, I returned the entire purchase, documenting in black and white a relationship that unraveled just before The Lingerie Phase. The $30.25 charge for my first caller ID box forever preserves the memory of my fruitless attempts to avoid my interfering mother, and I can tell just how many late nights I worked at my high-pressure ad job by tracking the charges for Chinese take-out.

This is a collection of true stories about how I, literally, spent my early years living, working, and looking for love in Manhattan when it seemed that the only knight in armor I'd find was the one on the front of my Amex card.

Borkowsky's sometimes poignant and often hilarious analysis is diachronic. By looking at her credit-card purchases and returns over 12 years and triangulating the data with memories, other artifacts, people, and knowledge of her life, she offers a view of her private life and a portrait of a single, contemporary urban woman. If she were researching this subculture as a fieldworker, she would need to gather more data.

As researchers, we can also organize our material by choosing to look synchronically at the entire culture surrounding one single moment in time. An exciting example of synchronic research is a book by Columbia University professor James Shapiro called *1599: A Year in the Life of William Shakespeare*. Shapiro chronicles one year in Shakespeare's life by looking at as much as he can see:

I've chosen to write about 1599 not only because it was an unusually fraught and exciting year but also because . . . it was a decisive one, perhaps *the* decisive one, in Shakespeare's development as a writer (and, happily, one from which a surprising amount of information about his professional life survives). My interest in this subject dates back fifteen years. At that time, though I was familiar with Shakespeare's plays and taught them regularly, I didn't know enough about the historical moment in which plays like *As You Like It* and *Hamlet* were written and which they engaged. I had no idea, for example, that England braced itself for an invasion in the summer of 1599. . . . I knew less than I should have known about how Shakespeare traveled to and from Stratford or about the bookstalls and playhouses that he frequented in London. . . . My ignorance extended beyond history. Along with other scholars, I didn't fully grasp how extensively Shakespeare revised and what these changes revealed about the kind of writer he was. And my notion of the sources of Shakespeare's inspiration was too bookish. It was one thing to know what Shakespeare was reading, another to know about what sermons he may have heard or what art he viewed in the royal palaces of Whitehall and Richmond where he regularly performed.

This work, then, grew out of frustration with how much I didn't know and frustration with scholars . . . who never quite got around to addressing the question I found most pressing: how, at age thirty-five, Shakespeare went from being an exceptionally talented writer to being one of the greatest who ever lived — put another way: how in the course of little over a year he went from writing *The Merry Wives of Windsor* to writing a play as inspired as *Hamlet*. (xxi–xxii)

Shapiro organizes his 15 chapters in four chronological sections, one for each season of the year 1599. He uses illustrations, maps, and a fascinating bibliographic essay to look ethnographically at the culture, politics, and even weather conditions of the environment in which Shakespeare spent his pivotal thirty-fifth year, one in which the Globe theater was built and Shakespeare wrote four new plays: *Henry the Fifth*, *Julius Caesar*, *As You Like It*, and a first draft of *Hamlet*. Shapiro's book is a fine example of a synchronic study that carefully draws on one particular moment in time.

Historical Archives

Researchers' passion for historical archives has been greatly helped by their increased access to all kinds of information in all kinds of places, and this access affects the kinds of documentary films, radio essays, TV series, and books that are made. As we write this book, we're particularly fond of *History Detectives*, a one-hour PBS television show in which scholars (a sociologist, an anthropologist, a museum curator, an appraiser, and a library archivist) examine an interesting artifact and reconstruct the story of the culture that surrounds the object. Another one-hour PBS show, *Secrets of the Dead*, uses forensic science and teams of researchers to investigate the past and reinterpret the details of history they find by looking at long-buried mysteries.

Perhaps the best-known public fieldworker is Ken Burns, the filmmaker. As a researcher, writer, and producer, he has given us a detailed look at American cultural history through public TV at the rate of one film per year since 1981, the year he made *Brooklyn Bridge*. Among his documentaries are *The Civil War* (1990), *Baseball* (1994), *Jazz* (2001), and *Unforgivable Blackness: The Rise and Fall of Jack Johnson* (2004). These examples of suspenseful, artful, educational entertainment are also ethnohistory. A standard definition of *ethnohistory* would imply "a study of the development of cultures," but anthropologist James Peacock reminds us that we understand history through the perspectives of the people who lived at the time. Archival historical research allows us to do just that.

Like Lia Schultz, James Shapiro, and the History Detectives, you may become fascinated by a topic or an artifact from another time. Even if most of that historical period has vanished, leaving only traces, you will be able to retrieve and re-create whole pieces of it. One of our students, Bill Polking, used an institutional archive in his study of a Catholic boarding school for Native American tribes of the Southwest United States. Bill had been a teacher and dorm counselor at the school before it closed its doors in 1998. His project posed a special challenge because the fieldsite he once knew no longer existed. It also posed an ethical challenge to him because of the way Native Americans had previously been studied and represented by other fieldworkers. He writes, "Ethnography, rightfully, has a bad name in Native America, and I didn't want to see myself as another bone collector, another collector of artifacts." And yet Bill had access to personal and historical archives as well as Internet connections with his former colleagues and students. Bill began the study with his own archives, a few boxes full of mementos from his years at this school, since, as he writes, "I am my own best and worst informant." He supplemented the study with e-mail interviews with former students and colleagues, as well as a return visit to the site of the school. In reflecting about doing this study, he catalogs the data sources, many of them archives, from which he drew:

> Obviously, my own observations are a continual source throughout the essay. But I have also "borrowed" from license plates, signs, school newspapers, city newspapers, day students, girls' dorm students, boys' dorm students, Sisters, girls' dorm staff, boys' dorm staff, the language of my informants, the official publications of the Sisters and the school, histories of Indian education, and Peshkin's book on Santa Fe Indian School.

Eventually, a visual artifact helped Bill determine his focus — a framed rectangular sign that had hung above the door of the boys' dorm and announced "Nothing But the Best for the Boys Because the Boys Are the Best." This motto became the title and controlling thesis of his fieldwork essay. Before he settled on this saying as a focus, Bill worried about how to use the archives he had at his disposal. How would he use his personal journal? What was important about the order of nuns who ran the school? What was the value of the other fieldstudies he'd read? How would he bring the voices from personal e-mails into this study? He needed to find one way to represent his complicated understanding of the school's culture. Using the motto as his thesis helped to guide his awareness of the ethics of his position, the needs and opinions of the former students and colleagues who were his informants, and the tangled cultural issues that arose at this Catholic coed boarding school for Native Americans. Based on a flood of e-mails from friends, Bill noticed that dorm life seemed to be an important theme in people's memories:

> A small school, down to just over two hundred students by the time it closed, St. Catherine prided itself on its sense of community: "Some seek St. Kate's to escape the hardships at home. We welcome them. Some come here to escape other hardships of life. We welcome them. Some come here because they belong nowhere else. We welcome them, too" (Belin Tsinnajinnie, boys' dorm student).

> "Everyone was like a family here," said day student Nicole Hernandez, and from my beginnings in 1992, as a volunteer freshly graduated and looking for a year apart from the life he had seen and the life he foresaw, to the end in 1998, when one year had drawn into six and I had become assistant director of the dorm, St. Catherine and the boys' dorm in particular were my family, my home. Home in the literal sense, as I lived in the dorm, in a small room next to the ninth graders and (unfortunately) the bathroom. And home also in the sense poet Michael Blumenthal describes, "Anywhere / that makes the relentless heart / relent, friends, can be your home."

> Others saw the boys' dorm in similar fashion: "Although it was infused with respect for the cultural/tribal traditions from which its students came, the boys' dorm seemed to form an identity, a 'culture,' quite apart from those traditions, and in this way it was able to unite students from diverse backgrounds" (Jenn Guerin, girls' dorm director).

> "I believe the main objective of the boys' dorm, aside from introducing a person to a very diverse community and making sure they did well academically, was to create an environment where a sense of brotherhood evolved and a comfortable form of reliance on one another was developed" (Oscencio Tom, boys' dorm student).

> "The thing that has stood out in my memory . . . is the respect the boys seemed to show for each other. The fact that we didn't have one fist fight all year is remarkable. . . . Even the tougher kids treated each other with dignity or indifference" (Tom McGrory, boys' dorm staff).

> "Nothing but the best for the boys because the boys are the best" (sign made by Jerry Payne, boys' dorm director).

> "The boys are spoiled" (numerous girls' dorm students).

Whether you supplement your study with archival research or identify a fieldstudy topic from personal, historical, or online sources, archives can provide the shape, texture, depth, and color that help bring a study to life. Even though institutional archives are organized more formally than family archives, the challenge of the research is still the same—finding a focus. Eventually a visual artifact—a framed rectangular sign—helped Bill figure out his focus.

Museum Archives

Many of us are unaware of the archival resources we have in our hometowns or nearby cities. Bonnie comes from the Philadelphia area, the home of some of our nation's most important museums (the Philadelphia Museum of Art, the Rodin Museum, and the Franklin Institute) as well as buildings that hold collections of historical artifacts (including the Betsy Ross House, the United States Mint, and the Independence Hall plaza with the Liberty Bell). Elizabeth grew up in a small Ohio town and as a child visited the Pioneer Historical Society, of which both her parents were members. Although Bonnie had early contact with rich metropolitan resources through her art-teacher mother, Elizabeth didn't realize that her Ohio hometown was important, historically or artistically, as a ceramic center until she moved to New York City and found that many people collected Roseville and Zanesville pottery. (Her hometown now has a modest pottery museum.)

We like to tell the story of a high school student we know in a small town in New Hampshire who was assigned a fieldwork project and complained to his teacher, "There's nothing in this town—nothing to do, nothing to research, no one to talk to. All I'm interested in is basketball."

"Okay," his teacher replied, "Why don't you try to find out about the history of basketball in this town?"

He grumbled all the way to the town archives in the small Historical Society building where he began his research. There he discovered pictures and newspaper clippings about a family basketball team formed at the turn of the twentieth century in New England, just a few decades after basketball was invented in Springfield, Massachusetts. The four boys and one girl were the town's first team and won fame because the sister helped win many contests. Our young researcher was intrigued and traced the local family until he found a living relative. He interviewed this elderly man, one of the original team members, and wrote a compelling study of the team, which became part of the school district's collective fieldproject (called "The Four Towns Museum"). Even with a skeptical attitude, this student was able to use archival research to inspire his rediscovery of a local family's sports fame long ago. Sometimes a fieldworker can overlook a small-town archive or even a small institutional archive.

Even experienced fieldworkers sometimes ignore possible archival resources. We suffered from a kind of unawareness when we visited Ball State University in Muncie, Indiana, to give a talk about doing fieldwork. Little did we know that we would find a fascinating museum that would unlock the whole culture of this interesting midwestern town. We knew we were going to be writing this chapter on archives and knew that transplanted college students often feel disconnected from the culture of their surroundings. So we wanted to see what sources might be available for a student to discover at the beginning of a fieldstudy.

From our Ball State colleagues, we learned that Muncie had a history of being studied as a typical American city. Muncie has been the subject of four separate studies—*Middletown* (1929), *Middletown in Transition* (1935), *Middletown III* (1977), and *The Other Side of Middletown* (2004). A student at Ball State who wanted to investigate the connections between the university and the town, for instance, might begin with these books or with the town's history. In the town's history, this fieldworker would discover that for over a hundred years, between 1888 and 1998, Muncie was the world headquarters of the Ball Corporation, makers of glass jars for preserving foods.

As the Muncie story goes, the region had an abundance of natural gas that attracted the glass and steel manufacturing industries, which needed the enormous amounts of heat and energy the gas produced. The five Ball brothers moved their manufacturing plant from Buffalo, New York, to Muncie, Indiana, made their fortune, and left their mark on the town. At the crest of a hill overlooking the muddy White River, the Ball brothers' impressive homes and gardens once stood watch over the town. Two of these homes are now the sites of a cultural museum and a conference center. Our fieldworker might start with a visit to Minnetrista, Muncie's cultural center, which displays rooms full of old-fashioned glass Ball jars, both utilitarian and unusual. Our favorite was a huge Ball jar of preserved pears from a nineteenth-century world's fair, claimed to still be edible.

We became fascinated with the kinds of archives and talented people who could teach us about how the culture of a town is reflected in its history. Folklorist Beth Campbell, curator and exhibits developer at Minnetrista, guided us through the exhibits and shared with us the kind of archival research projects she develops for the museum's heritage collection. We learned from Beth that her research resulted in two exhibition scripts that became part of the museum's archives. The first was written for an exhibition on the restoration of Minnetrista's gardens, and the other was a transcript from an oral history project, interviews of senior citizens who had worked in the Ball brothers' glass jar factory. To our delight, Beth shared the exhibition script and the interview transcript with us, and we realized how valuable such rich sources could be for a fieldwork project.

A full exhibition script is the curator's organizational blueprint. When you tour an exhibit, you'll see brief excerpts of this text placed near objects or pictures. But a curator must first develop a long script to focus and sharpen a huge amount of information about the exhibit. Here are three sections from the 25-page script that describes the unearthing and reconstruction of Elisabeth Ball's garden dollhouse:

3D. Rediscovering the Grounds

. . . the project team used a three-step "triangulated" analysis. During the first step, team members superimposed a fifty-foot grid over each section of the grounds, made a list of each species and its location within the grid, and noted structural remains. They then conducted archival research in order to map buildings and grounds. . . . During the fieldwork, the team made many discoveries, including old gardens and evidence of an arbor and a dollhouse. . . .

3E. Rehabilitating the Grounds

In 1990, the gardens looked wild and overgrown. Having made the decision to rehabilitate the gardens . . . thickets of invasive plants were removed so that dormant plants might find new life. . . . A sunken rock garden similar to Elisabeth's "sunk" was designed, using her notes and plant invoices as a guide . . . bellflowers, buttercups, daylilies, lamb's ear, and creeping phlox. . . .

3F. Recreating Vistas

. . . After researchers learned of Elisabeth's garden dollhouse, they tracked down the people who had purchased it at a charity auction.

Beth Campbell was interested in the factory's owners, their gardens, and their dollhouses. But she also wanted to gather data about the lives of everyone in the town, from the original gardens' owners to the factory workers. And so she offered us another document, an interview with Almeda Mullin, who had been a "stamper" (of the Ball logo on the glass jar) and "spare girl" at the Ball factory. Mullin, born in 1907, began working in the factory at age 13 and worked there for 40 years—the same years that the Ball women worked their gardens.

In the following excerpt, Almeda Mullin gives us a sense of her working conditions:

BC: What was [your boss] like to work for?

AM: (*laughs*) He was just as cocky as you'd let him be. I hated that bloody glass house with a purple passion. So one night, after I got off work at the glass house, I came out, my hands were swollen, my fingers were cut, and I was a-crying. I must have been 17, 18. I said "Sam, I can't work in that glass house." "Oh," he said, "shut up you big old baby and go on home. . . ."

BC: What was it about the glass house that people hated so much?

AM: They pushed those jars on a conveyor, and you had to stick your hands into them. . . . it just pinched pieces and cut, your hands would just bleed and be so sore. . . .

Beth Campbell's interview with Almeda Mullin will become part of an exhibition about the everyday lives of workers at the Ball factory. As museum curator, Beth was interested in collecting data about the lives of everyone in the town, from the original gardening of the Ball wives to the everyday routines of the factory workers. As a fieldworker, Beth collected materials to document the class differences in Muncie, Indiana, during the 1920s. She also consulted other sources written at that time — such as diaries, journals, letters, and newspapers — and interviewed town residents about their memories of the Ball family. But that's only one researcher's choice. There are many ways to use archival resources to develop a project. This material could be used as a backdrop for a fieldstudy of class differences in the culture of contemporary Muncie, for a historical study of the glass industry, or for a study of the history of landscaping.

You can find scripts and transcripts in many different places. We were happy to learn that Garrison Keillor devoted a segment of his radio show, *A Prairie Home Companion*, to the Ball jar connections when he visited Muncie in 1997. When Keillor visits a city to broadcast a show, he depends on local researchers to feed him background information about the culture of the place. Our colleague, Professor Joe Trimmer of Ball State University, did the research for Keillor's Muncie visit, including the following information:

> The Ball Brothers' Glass Manufacturing Company set up shop in 1886. Its glass containers and Ball jars enabled the business to dominate the local economy. . . . Most of what's distinctive in Muncie is the direct result of the generosity of the Ball family. . . . Everything in town is named Ball — there's Ball Corporation, Ball Foundation, Ball Gym, Ball Memorial Hospital, Ball Field, Ball Building, Ball Avenue, and, of course, the town's currently largest employer, Ball State University.

A seasoned storyteller, Keillor typically uses humor to engage his audience. In his 1997 Muncie broadcast, he shaped his commentary for his many radio fans across the United States as well as the local live audience of Muncie's college students, their parents, and townspeople. He also drew on Minnetrista's museum archives, Joe Trimmer's research notes, and other sources to tell the story of the Ball jar culture. We found the citation for Keillor's show online through National Public Radio's Performance Archives, ordered the tape, and transcribed it with Keillor's permission.

Keillor begins his monologue with a familiar transition — "Well, it's been a quiet week in Lake Wobegon, my hometown out here on the prairie" — which prepares his audience for a story. He uses a deadpan sense of humor to capture his audience's attention: "Winter is good for you in so many different ways. Winter cures people of self-pity." With this ironic quip he begins to discuss the world of country life, which includes hard weather, hard work, and thrift in all things — including how people

↑ A Ball jar. (Photo: Lia Schultz)

grow and store food. His monologue eventually takes us to the subject of canning and putting up produce for the winter in glass containers, in this case in Ball jars:

Now, when I was a boy, the way you combated the winter blues was very simple. You went down the basement. You went to those shelves that were behind the wash tubs, and you reached up there, and there were all of your mother's canned vegetables and jams and peaches. And there was corn, and there was applesauce and apple butter. And you reached down to the end, and you got a jar of stewed tomatoes. You took that up and took off the lid, and you put some of it in a pan. You heated it up, and you put butter on it. And in those stewed tomatoes that you yourself had picked and had helped your mother can last August: you found in those tomatoes the courage or sunshine or whatever it was you needed to buck yourself up and get on with winter and not complain about it. And, of course, those were Ball fruit jars. Those were Ball canning jars. They were always Ball jars with Kerr lids in our family.

So it always made me want to come to Muncie, Indiana—sort of the home of the mother church. Then I come here and found out that the Ball Corporation has gotten out of the fruit jar business. Which is all well and good, until I start to think that there may be children who are growing up not knowing of the existence of Ball fruit jars—not knowing about canning. The children are missing out on this. There was a time in my lifetime when everyone all across the Midwest saved their Ball jars and filled them up in the month of August. They were sealed, and they were put away. And you ate this over the next fall and winter and spring—produce from your own garden.

Keillor expands on the virtues of canning. He suggests to his college audience at Ball State University in Muncie, Indiana, that if their own parents had just taken the time to put up food in Ball jars, they might have saved enough money to send them to a really good college. Keillor says, "But because your parents don't can their own food, you may have to go to some college that is a sort of little cluster of cinder block buildings that's around a parking lot. . . . All because your parents didn't have the industry, the gumption, the wit, to grow their own tomatoes, grow their own tomatoes and put them in jars, Ball canning jars from Muncie, Indiana." Keillor uses the Ball jar as the key artifact to illustrate much about Muncie's culture.

To find radio and television transcripts, you can use the educational resources of National Public Radio, the Public Broadcasting System, and most other networks. As you probably know, most radio and TV news broadcasts, magazine shows, talk shows, and other informative presentations end their programs with information about how to request a taped or transcribed copy of the program.

Box 5.3: Sorting through Public Archives

Purpose

For the kind of fieldwork we describe, we define *public archive* as a place where collections of public and private records, as well as other historical documents and artifacts, are stored. It can be a town hall, a museum, a library's or business's special collection, a school, a club, or a church. A public archive might be as small as a scrapbook or as large as a building.

The archive's organizational patterns will probably be less than efficient—from files in chronological order to jumbles of papers in large boxes. Looking for his slave and slave owner heritage, Edward Ball reflected as he pored through wills, deeds, ledgers, and town records: "Shut in the vaults of the historical society's pink stucco building, I read as much as I could absorb. One family at a time, the stories surfaced, and in glimpses and parts, I began to piece together what happened." Working your way through a public archive can be frustrating and sometimes daunting; it

Box 5.3: *continued*

takes time and patience and offers no quick answers. But as we mention at the beginning of this chapter, you will find that the data begin to come alive as you find what you need.

Action

To see how archival material coincides with other sources of data, check out a few public archives related to your topic of interest, your site, or your informants. These archival materials can be any documents or artifacts that are part of a collection; the collection can be either organized or disorganized. List the sources you've looked at, and see what connections or correspondences turn up or what gaps you can perceive. Freewrite about the archives themselves and the ways that they relate to your topic, your site, and your informants. Try to triangulate this information with other material you might find about your topic while cruising the Internet — the giant technological archive we have at our fingertips. As you might notice, the jobs of collecting, selecting, and making sense out of archival data sources are the ones that are used in reflective critical analysis, much like the strategies used in creating a research portfolio.

Response

Brenda Boleyn prepares students to become elementary public school teachers. She writes about an archival search she did on the conflicts young men face when they choose to become elementary school teachers. Notice the range of archival material she considers:

I located several items that I felt could be viewed as archival when trying to understand from the male perspective the culture tied to becoming an elementary teacher:

1. **An article.** From the *USA Today* archive, the article is entitled "Elementary School Students Need More Male Teachers." It is relevant to my study for a couple of different reasons. It gives percentages of males who are currently in elementary education and compares today's statistics with those in 1981 and 1961. What's important to me is that the trend is downward. The article speculates about why males are choosing the field of teaching less often.

2. **A Web site address.** This Web site gives readers a forum to further discuss the topic of males and their roles in elementary education. I went to this Web site to get a glimpse of the public conversation surrounding this topic, and it proved very interesting. Everything from classroom discipline to pay/respect issues to bashing feminists surfaced in this discussion. Most seemed to agree that there is a shortage, but no one seemed surprised.

3. **A brochure.** This was among our college's collection of brochures, about education as a career. For those students who *do* decide to consider early childhood or elementary education majors, the common path is to meet with an advisor and discuss coursework, requirements, field experience options, etc. I serve as advisor

for 30 students, and one is male. Most of this is factual information, but I found the image of "teacher" in the brochure photos was definitely female. That's why this brochure is important.

4. **Two lists.** One is a list for teachers at a local elementary school where I place preservice teachers for their practicum experiences. It shows that out of 15 teachers in kindergarten through third grade, only one is male. The other is a list of students from the fall semester — all female. This document speaks to the demographics of students in our program and also to the available teacher models and classrooms we have to mentor our preservice teachers.

5. **Textbooks.** One of the first courses our students take is literacy methods. Usually after this course students have a pretty good idea if they want to remain in teaching. I looked at a stack of texts (in a sense, an archive in a book closet), books I'm considering using in my course, and made photocopies of the front of every literacy text that featured teachers and students working together on the cover. Although the representations of teachers on (and in) these texts show ethnic diversity (in both students and teachers), the gender of the teacher is always the same — female. Scary!

6. **Artifacts.** I examined and photographed some of the items various education professors had in or displayed in their offices. Although I found more gender-neutral items around the department, I looked long and hard for images of males working with young children. I was not successful in my search. The items highlighted for me the dominant image of female "teacher" and caused me to wonder about the impact that may have on prospective male teachers. Can they see themselves in the images that are portrayed? Or do they position themselves in opposition to these images, encouraging them to seek out more traditionally masculine roles in middle schools and high schools, science rooms and gymnasiums?

Brenda Boleyn's project raised more questions than she originally asked about the role of men in elementary school teaching. In her pursuit of archival sources, she found many artifacts that were relevant to her question and that she may not have originally considered. As you work, we hope that you'll collect family, historical, and institutional items to create an archive that is specific to your project.

Poet and essayist Naomi Shihab Nye shares the feelings of archival researchers in her prose poem "The Attic and Its Nails." In her attic archive, the narrator tries to decide what fits, what doesn't fit, and how to organize it.

With words like "crowded" and "dizzy" and phrases like "It's hard up there" and the "search takes on an urgent ratlike quality," Nye shows us how we can begin to make sense of the "dark" and the chaos we feel when we first confront archives.

The Attic and Its Nails (poem)

NAOMI SHIHAB NYE

It's hard up there. You dig in a box for whatever the moment requires: a sweater, wreath, the other half of the walky-talky, and find twelve things you forgot about which delay the original search, since now that you found them you have to think about them. Do I want to keep this, bring it downstairs? Of course your life feels very different from the life you had when you packed it up there. Maybe your life has another kind of room in it now, maybe it feels more crowded. Maybe you think looking at this old ceramic cup with the pocked white glaze that you made in college would uplift you in the mornings. Your search takes on an urgent ratlike quality as you rip paper out of boxes, shredding and piling it. Probably by now you've stood up too fast and speared your head on one of the nails that holds the roof shingles down. They're lined up all along the rafters, poking through aimed. Now you have to think about tetanus, rusty nails, the hearty human skull. A little dizzy for awhile, you're too occupied to remember what sent you up into the dark.

Alternative Archives

For many people—though certainly not Naomi Shihab Nye—attics, basements, garage sale tables, flea markets, backyard sheds, and professional storage containers hold junk. But for collectors and curators of both public and private archives—and for fieldworkers—someone else's junk could be the treasure needed to understand a culture or subculture. We don't often think about the artifacts that people discard, but sometimes they hold important cultural meanings. Researchers who work in schools, for example, find themselves emptying wastebaskets to read through the papers and notes that students or teachers throw away—to find clues to what matters and what doesn't matter within the culture of school. [. . .]

Electronic Archives: Using the Internet

It is difficult to imagine doing any research these days without using the Internet. It has become, among other things, a giant, decentralized, public archive, and having so much information available immediately means that we're not sure how to value what we see. As with any kind of research, it takes skill and knowledge to surf and sift through large amounts of data, make choices about what is credible, decide how it might be useful, and link your sources together with one another and with your project as a whole.

Like the kind of research you do at your actual fieldsite, conducting research with a Web site requires patience, attention to detail, selectivity, and analysis. We are careful in this section to refer to *fieldsite* or *Web site* and not to confuse you with the shorter term *site*. Web "surfing" can make people think that doing research online will be quick and easy, but it takes time, care, and rigor. Just as you might spend hours sitting and watching your fieldsite, piecing together information as you find it, you ought to spend much time simply sitting and reading information on the Web until you know what focus you need, what data seem appropriate, and how the information will fit with the other parts of your research. You may uncover a wealth of information quickly but will need time to assess it:

- Is what you've found useful to your project?

- Does it answer any questions you or your informants have raised?

- Does it supplement incomplete facts and details about people, places, histories, ideas, and artifacts you've already heard about?

- Are the sources up-to-date?

- What evidence do you have that they're believable?

These questions require your patience, attention to detail, and ability to be selective.

And then you will need to ask questions of analysis — how the details fit into your broader ideas. You will need to decide what fieldsites and Web sites are telling you:

- How can the Web sites enhance your ideas about your fieldsite and about your informants and their culture?

- How does each Web site relate to the others — and to your fieldsite?

- Is the information similar?

- If it's not, how is it different?

- Would one Web site have a different purpose for displaying itself than another?

- And is its information consistent with its purpose?

- How is that consistent with what you know or think already about your fieldsite?

What you find on the Web works in three ways. First, it is a source of basic information to supplement all that you've gathered at your fieldsite, much like library books or journal articles that offer facts, histories, and descriptions about the culture or subculture you're studying. Second, it can offer you potential contact information— telephone numbers or e-mail addresses of possible informants. As Bill Polking discovered from his online chats with former students and colleagues from the Indian school no longer in existence and Meg Buzzi found in her correspondence with relatives, e-mails from distant but involved people can be an enormously rich source of data. But probably the most important way the Internet works is that the online information itself becomes an artifact that a culture or subculture has produced. Lia Schultz, as we mentioned, made a Web site to study the interconnections of her family genealogy. We think, in fact, that these new electronic resources blur the traditional boundaries between primary and secondary sources.

When we wrote about Hmong storycloths, for example, in one short paragraph at the beginning of this chapter, we used the Internet to confirm what we'd learned from two Hmong embroiderers, a local folklorist who collects storycloths, a few presentations we've attended, and Hmong students we've known. But we wanted to be sure we had the history right, so we used the word *Hmong* as a keyword in an online search. Instantly, we found a wealth of written material, both published and unpublished, about the Hmong people, traditions, and histories. We found virtual museum exhibits displaying detailed pictures of Hmong crafts, foods, and music traditions, Web sites in which Hmong in various parts of the world can talk with one another in chat rooms, and newsletters with activities and invitations to participate. In a few hours, we had confirmed what we'd learned from informants about storycloths and felt more confident about writing the paragraph you read at the beginning of this chapter. But we also had found the connected Web sites themselves to be artifacts of the Hmong culture itself, offering us much new knowledge of the culture in the words and choices of the informants who manage the Web sites. This way, we were able to access the Hmong's perspective on their own transplanted American culture.

This all seems familiar, suspiciously, in fact, like the library work you may have done to write a report. And, of course, online research is research.

To demonstrate the process of using electronic archives, we asked our colleague Sarah Townsend how she'd search the Web as part of a research project. Sarah has had experience as a Web developer as well as a student. "Choose any topic," we urged. "And show us what you'd do." Join Sarah here as she begins forming ideas for a 10- to 20-page fieldstudy on comic books.

A Comic-Book Search

Sarah Townsend

Doing Research on the Web—and a False Start

I hardly know where to begin—so many search engines, so much information. So I begin with the beginning of my own Web browsing—the trusty Yahoo!, which I know is useful for structuring a top-down approach to organizing online research.

To get myself rolling, I do a simple search for the text string *comic books* on Yahoo!'s homepage and see what turns up. In this case, several subcategories emerge. I need to figure out which ones are relevant to my study. I decide to ignore all of the regional subcategories (for instance, *Regional>Countries>Singapore>Entertainment>Comics and Animation*) for the time being, although this may be a sign that regions have their own comic-book styles. But that's not what I'm interested in. At this stage I decide I'll start by looking in the most general of the listed categories: *Entertainment>Comics and Animation>Comic Books.*

Following this link, I see a listing of further subcategories as well as a list of Web site links. A quick glance down this page tells me that I'd better narrow my search. I'm lost already: I realize that the world of comic books is far more extensive than I could possibly treat in any 10- to 20-page essay. What I need to think about right now is what interests me and why it would make it a good subject for a fieldstudy.

Maybe I've jumped online too soon. Without a clearer idea of where I want to go, I'm going to get lost in the limitless forest of information. Like Hansel and Gretel as they followed a trail of breadcrumbs, I need to find a way to find my way. Time to step back from the computer and think about where I want to go with my online research.

Asking the "What Intrigues Me?" Question

When I was considering potential topics, why did I decide on comic books in the first place? I sit down to think, jot notes, do some freewriting, and circle in closer to the heart of what most interests me.

I think about my first associations with comic books. My older brother gave me a vintage *Spiderman* book encased in plastic, and I kept it safe in my sock drawer for years. He particularly loved Spiderman and the Hulk; there was a kind of tragic glamour to both of them, a dark side maybe shared by all superheroes—the inevitable doom of being separated from the rest of humanity. There was something in those associations that appealed to my brother and to me on his behalf.

And then there was the time when I saw my first copy of *Love and Rockets* on the coffee table at a friend's house. It was a comic book like I'd never imagined before. Instead of superheroes, it was populated by regular neighborhood people, dealing with real-life dramatic scenarios—similar to serial soap operas or reality TV but with an edge. This darkly drawn book featured strong women characters—not the whitewashed images of girls gracing the pages of *Seventeen* magazine.

But how can this topic become a fieldwork project? Where is the culture of comic-book lovers? What do I already know? And who, I wonder, reads comic books regularly? I've noticed comic-book stores tucked away in every urban center I've ever visited. I realize that I need to talk to the proprietor of the local comic-book store, but before I do that, I want to come up with a list of questions to help direct the conversation.

Continuing My Comic-Book Research Online

I've decided that what most interests me about comic books is the community around them. Who reads them? Who writes them? And who sells them? I can now return to my online research with more confidence that I have specific questions I want answered. And while I am surfing the Web for relevant material, I can be looking into other electronic resources as well.

This time I decide to start out with another big search engine: Google. Once I type in comic books, Google returns several promising links. The snippet of text indexed by this search engine can tell me a lot at a glance. As Figure 1 shows, I can see how the first site describes itself ("A Research Guide"), and I can learn from the site's URL whether it's an institutional site (like <www.nypl.org>, the New York Public Library's *org* address) or somebody's personal page (like <www.geocities.com/SoHo/55371/>). I also can read

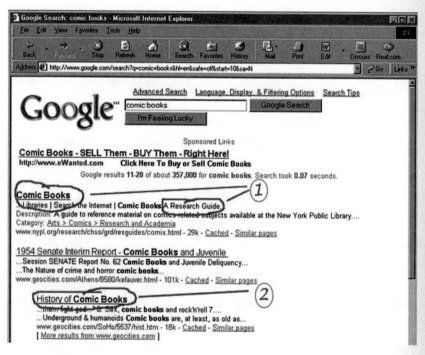

Figure 1 Result of search on Google for "comic books."

a little snippet of text from the actual site, which suggests the tone or the intention of the writing ("Comic books are, at least, as old as . . .").

The first link I pursue (labeled 1) that attracts my interest turns out to be a section of the New York Public Library's official site. The site details ways to research comic books using materials in the library. I make a note of it as a potentially helpful model to follow when I go to an actual library. Then I take a quick look around the site for any other bits that might prove useful.

Well, here's something: "Comics and comic books are one of the most pervasive and influential media forms of 20th-century popular culture." Wow. This is a pretty big validation of my topic's cultural significance, posted by the esteemed New York Public Library. I file it away for potential use as a quote for my own writing. If I do quote from this Web site, I'll be sure to use citation standards from the MLA, the APA, or the *Chicago Manual of Style*, noting the URL and the entity I took the information from— just like I would with any other published source.

This site gives me an idea for my research. In a section entitled "The Comic Book Controversy," it introduces the debate about the "moral influence of comic books" in the 1940s and 1950s. I find that I've begun to identify a point of interest in comic books from 50 years ago or more—how they serve or cut through the mainstream and how their readership accepts or rejects standards set by authorities. I think about some of the comic-book readers I've known and how they've intersected with other countersubcultures (skateboarders, computer geeks). I'll need to think about this some more and see what evidence I can turn up to support or contradict it.

The next link I follow (labeled 2) in my Google search takes me to a "history of comic books" compiled by someone who seems to be an English-speaking student in Brazil. As I cruise around the site, I decide that it's pretty well researched and responsibly constructed. The author portrays an array of comic-book types in his list of his "preferred comics," and he's careful to attribute in a bibliography page the artwork and information he uses. This impresses me. It also gives me a list of books and authors I might consult for my own research.

But what appeals to me most is Rafael's portrayal of himself as a lifelong reader of comic books. Reading his Web page is equivalent to talking with a comic-book aficionado at length. I get a kind of Web-based portrait of his history of reading comic books and a log of what he's found most appealing and influential. Rafael's overview is engaging and authoritative:

> The '50s staged the greatest witchhunt of comics ever, and a lot of prejudice from those days still remains. Psychiatrist Frederic Wertham wrote a book, *The Seduction of the Innocent*, where he accused comic books of causing youth corruption and juvenile delinquency. Among many other weird subjects, he accused comics of inciting youth to violence (what had already happened with rock 'n' roll). A Comics Code was then created destined to limit and rule on what could appear (and what could not) in the pages.

Rafael's site seems almost like formal research rather than a collection of light commentary. Even better, he's got a section entitled "Alternative Comics," which seems promising to my current working thesis that comic-book culture is alternative or countercultural:

> [In alternative comics] the scope is widened. Superhero parody, trash, futurism, ecological concern, social commentary, action, history, fantastic realism — anything can be shown in a comic page. The space for unusual issues was already opened, and the new authors used their creativity to capture the readers' attention. Even in the superhero genre, changes conquer space with new views on old characters and concepts.

Rafael's comments are so interesting that I decide to write him an e-mail, and thus my search takes me into another electronic space. In less than 24 hours, we connect:

ST: Hi Rafael. I came across your comic book site recently and wanted to tell you how much I liked it. . . . It certainly is well-presented and informative. How did you assemble the site? Who's your audience? How would you advise a student to find out more? Thank you. :-) . . . I'm working on a piece about comic books. I'm intrigued by them and don't know much. . . . Thanks again!

RL: Hi Sarah . . . Thanks for your comments. I would say that the site is the result of an assemblage of 15 years or so of information about comic books. Scott McCloud is the main scholar nowadays, and both his books are the most up-to-date sources. I'd recommend them to students, amateurs, researchers with the same enthusiasm. . . . I hope that your work will help to bring back to the comics the respectability and cultural relevance they've always deserved. . . . You are welcome.

Both Rafael and his Web site are important sources for me, as well as a great motivation to keep going. From here my online research will continue through who knows how many more layers of branching links. Each step I take will inform my next step.

My path through further layers of Web sites will grow complex, and I need to be careful to note the steps I take along the way. I know from past experience how easy it is to click from one Web page to another, following the trail farther into the forest until I finally find myself far from home with little idea of what the path looked like that took me there. This is both the wonder and the problem with doing online research. But I know that making careful notes about where I've been, what I've seen, and how it's all influenced my thinking is essential.

These notes will be my trail and will be valuable as I digest, sort, and plan with my data, but there is also the "live" fieldwork part of this project — the local comic-book store owner and the comic-book readers I'll interview, the young and the middle-aged people who were at one time "counterculture" comic readers. With a bit more research online, I'll know enough to feel confident when I'm in actual places talking to actual people.

Some Final Words on My Comic-Book Project

To be honest I'm just getting started on the electronic part of my research into comic-book culture. Before I'm done, I will visit more sites and glean much more information.

But this is a start. And I hope it helps you envision how you might start your own study online. Throughout the course of online research we'll both need to keep a few things in mind:

1. **Evaluate.** A Web site or other electronic resource is only as good as the information it provides. Be a smart researcher. Carefully gauge the value and verifiability of all information. Triangulate it using information from other kinds of data sources.

2. **Document.** Be responsible. Carefully document, cite, and attribute the text, graphics, and data you use from electronic sources the way you would any other published material, both out of respect for the author and for your readers' benefit.

3. **Research.** There is more to electronic media than the Internet. Look around the electronic world. See who's talking where — in listservs or e-mail discussion groups, chat rooms, and other online forums. And always remember to be a courteous member of the communities you join.

4. **Mark your trail (or, track your breadcrumbs).** Don't forget to make notes about the divergent paths your online search takes you on. You never know when you're going to want to go back later and check something that you barely noticed or thought was unimportant when you first saw it.

Box 5.4: Finding Your Way in the Online Forest

Purpose

Learning to navigate around the Internet is one of the first things most of us do online, but doing a focused study with the help of electronic tools requires that you use a more systematic approach to browsing online, as well as a more discerning eye about what you turn up. Because the Internet is nonlinear, as Sarah Townsend points out in the reading on pages 149–53, searches can take you in several directions in a single sitting. Keeping notes serves as a scattering of virtual bread crumbs, marking your path and allowing you to go back later and revisit information you might want.

Action

Starting with a major search engine, input a word or phrase related to your fieldwork subject, and track the links you follow. Keep a notepad beside your keyboard for jotting down notes and thoughts on each stop along your way. Limit your time to half an hour or so to cruise around different sites, and then close down your browser. Afterward, map out the path your search took, noting surprises, unpursued possibilities, and general trends you noticed.

As you look over the steps you took, consider the following questions: How many different trails did you use simultaneously in this short period of browsing? How were some of the sites you turned up more helpful than others? What details suggested a given site's authority or value from your researcher's perspective? What telltale signs made you dismiss other sites as unreliable or irrelevant? Where was the most helpful information?

Box 5.4: *continued*

Response

As she did her online research on comic books, Sarah realized it would be easy to become lost in multiple and simultaneous layers of sites. As a means of retracing her steps, she made the following brief notes in a notebook.

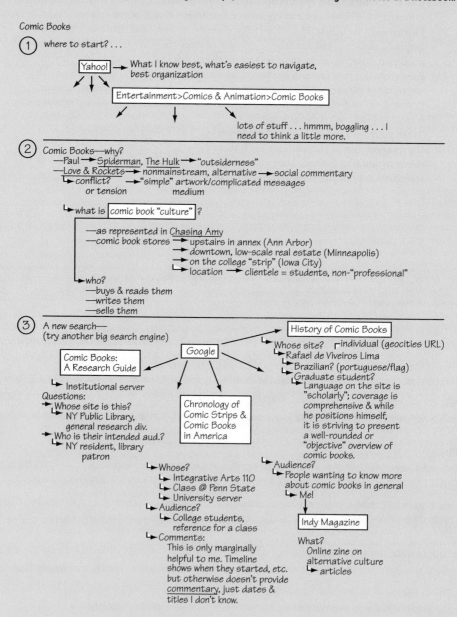

Sarah's chart about her online search of electronic archives illustrates how to use the Internet as a research tool for a possible comic-book study.

The electronic communities online can be both the source of archival information and the focus of a fieldstudy. Our students have studied many electronic subcultures, including buying and selling musical instruments on eBay, DIY ("do it yourself") band relationships, and a chat room of fans devoted to one singer. In other studies, the Internet becomes an important research source. Our students have used the Web creatively to support their fieldsites, such as Renaissance festivals (eventually one of our students held her wedding at one) and reenactments of military events (one student focused, for instance, on women who pose as men). Bilingual students have the advantage of being able to compare Web sites in different languages—finding surprisingly different perspectives (for example, a study of birthing rituals in Korea and in the United States).

We'd like to share an essay by Michelle Hanson, a student of our colleague Donna Qualley at Western Washington University in Bellingham, Washington, who was using *FieldWorking* in her class. Michelle studied an online gaming culture, a MUD (multiuser dimension), from the perspective of a "newbie" (or novice) with the guidance of her own special informant. A virtual culture like this one is literally made up of archives—lists and lists of contingencies, descriptors for characters, rules of behavior, methods of travel, even rituals for different kinds of deaths. As she grows to understand this subculture, which exists only online, Michelle's sub-headings—"I Am Born," "MUDding School," "My First Words," "Learning to Walk," "Death and Resurrection," and "Cleaning Up"—take us through her experiences as a player in this MUD. You can read Michelle's complete essay online at **bedfordstmartins.com/fieldworking**. As we've worked with Michelle's essay, we can see that this online game is a virtual archive that actually *creates* a culture. [...]

The Research Portfolio: Representing the Unflat Stuff

Whether archives belong to families or to local or international institutions, whether they're in dusty boxes or posted on the Internet, it's hard to know how to use them and what references to include as "stuff" in your research portfolio. What "stuff" can you call yours? How do you represent something that was important to your project when it doesn't fit into a paper portfolio? Why should you include what you decide to include? What does each item mean to your overall research project? We've heard teachers and students puzzle over the value of portfolios as a research tool for researchers to document their learning to themselves and to others who might need to assess and evaluate their work.

A high school teacher in a portfolio workshop once asked Bonnie, "What's the difference between a portfolio and a garage sale?" Although at first the question rattled her, she knew the teacher was saying that from his perspective, a portfolio looked like random items of junk sitting in a pile, waiting to be discarded. She eventually thought, "Hmmmm, looking over the array of items at a garage sale and trying to piece together stories of the past is, in fact, *very much* like the reflective work of a portfolio."

Lots of people puzzle over portfolios, wondering how to organize what might appear to someone else as junk. And sometimes the most important "junk" comes in inconvenient sizes and shapes. Perhaps the most provocative question we've ever heard about portfolios came from a high school student: "What do we do with the unflat stuff?" A portfolio, because it usually incorporates only two-dimensional materials, most often cannot include "unflat stuff" like performances, audio or videotapes, an informant's one-of-a-kind artifacts or photos, songs or important sounds, and original documents that are critical parts of your research. Nor can a portfolio house every piece of data you've collected: it would be heavy and unwieldy and wouldn't allow you to arrange and rearrange categories as you continue to work with it. In short, a "portfolio of everything" would simply show the "collection" process—and leave no room for the important processes of selection, reflection, and projection.

A well-designed portfolio is all about representation. It is anything but "flat," even if it fits into a three-ring binder with plastic document covers and stick-on notes. Like a well-designed Web page, it displays the items and connections ("links") you've selected to represent the categories of your research, the data you've collected, and the ways your thinking develops as you look it over, plan more research, and then perhaps recategorize further. A high-tech portfolio using Web technology can—despite a flat, two-dimensional screen—combine even more data than a paper portfolio, show connections and links even better, incorporate sound and motion, and reorganize itself as you shift your understandings and click your mouse.

A portfolio offers you the chance to sift through the chaos of piles of data and select representations that will enable you to see what you have more easily. Sometimes, with new thinking and lots of data, researchers need something concrete to help them understand abstract ideas. We think portfolios—whether on paper or online—are an important way to bring the process of analysis into a clear and concrete form.

We weren't able to explain our own experience in Muncie, Indiana (see pages 138–43 earlier in this chapter), until we laid out all the representative items and tried to understand the relationships they had with one another. At the time we were visiting, we just grabbed everything we could. It all looked interesting, and we weren't sure what was going to be important. But later we studied what we had. We didn't need everything (all our notes, all our e-mails, all the books, or the jars, buildings, landscapes, and talk we'd seen and heard). We already knew that data well. Rather, to tell our story efficiently to you, we needed a way to represent those items.

Here is a list describing some representative items we would include in a portfolio for our Ball jar project, with some of our thoughts about their significance:

1. An image of a Ball jar. A glass jar is far from flat but represents the industry and craft that defines the history and culture we discovered in Muncie. We might take a snapshot (like the one on page 142 from Bonnie's Kitchen), photocopy a picture from a book, or use a commercial postcard.

2. A section from the exhibition's background script, with a photo of the building and grounds. Although we'd be tempted to include brochures describing many interesting things from the museum (for instance, the hundred-year-old preserved pears), they are not relevant to the focus we took for our project. We did, though, learn a lot about the life of the Ball family from the script about the rehabilitation of the grounds and the dollhouse and from looking at the grounds themselves.

3. An excerpt from the transcript of the interview with Almeda Mullin. Curator Beth Campell's interview with Mullin gave us an exciting and detailed window into the life of one glass factory worker in the early part of the twentieth century. It wasn't until we had these two items together (the information about Elisabeth Ball's dollhouse and the interview with Almeda Mullin) that we realized we had evidence of the lives of two very different young women who lived in the culture of this town at about the same time in history. By putting these items together in our portfolio, we represent connections we might otherwise have overlooked.

4. A photocopy of the cover of the tape from Garrison Keillor's radio program, which we ordered from Minnesota Public Radio over the Internet. We'd accompany it by a section of our transcript. The tape isn't flat either. But our job for the portfolio is simply to represent the tape, not to play it. It comes from a two-cassette audio collection of Keillor's monologues called *Mother, Father, Uncle, Aunt: Stories from Lake Wobegon.*

5. A photocopy of the cover of one of the Middletown books to illustrate Muncie's history of being a sociological spot known as a "typical" American town, driven by the ingenuity of one family, a rich underground natural gas resource, and a supply of ready workers. Although we didn't read all four books, one was very helpful to us, and we found it important to know that four were written over a 75-year period.

6. A few snippets from our notes, correspondences, and e-mails with Professor Joe Trimmer, who originally invited us to Ball State University, and Beth Campbell, who spent an afternoon with us at Minnetrista, the cultural center. Without the help of these people, who were both our contacts and our references, we wouldn't have been able to conduct this short bit of fieldwork.

When you create a portfolio of representative items, you can organize and reorganize, label each item with a sticky note explaining what you think it means, and reflect on what you have selected. As you go through this process, the themes of your project will become clearer. As you discover more connections, as the themes begin to emerge, as you have more items with which to triangulate, you will learn much about your data, yourself in relationship to it, and what you want to share with your readers. Portfolios are wonderful tools for representation and analysis, whether the "stuff" is flat or not.

FieldWriting: Annotated Bibliographies

One useful way to represent the source materials for your fieldwork is to create an *annotated bibliography*, which provides your reader with more information about the published sources you've used than just the basics of author, title, date, and place of publication. Many researchers, writers, and scholars rely on annotated bibliographies to help them sort through masses of material without having to read each and every source. Each bibliographic citation summarizes a large amount of material into just the key concepts of the book, article, or electronic source. To do that well, the researcher must have a good understanding of the original material and its overall importance. Here are some sample entries of annotated sources relevant to ideas of material culture in this chapter:

Ball, Edward. *Slaves in the Family*. New York: Ballantine, 1998. Print. This research into the writer's white and black plantation ancestors employs 200-year-old archival documents and oral histories. Ball is a skilled writer who presents a vivid and detailed picture of how the history and devastating legacy of the institution of slavery affected millions of American lives for centuries.

Belanus, Betty J., and Cathy Kerst. "Everyone Eats Bread." *FieldWorking Online.* Field-Working Community, 2006. Web. 14 Mar. 2006. Betty J. Belanus of the Smithsonian Center for Folklife and Cultural Heritage and Cathy Kerst of the Library of Congress's American Folklife Center developed this lesson plan unit for primary schoolers in Wheaton, Maryland. The unit teaches the importance of bread—its forms, its ingredients, and the reasons that people eat it in different cultures.

Hanson, Michelle. "Playing in the MUD: A Newbie's Experience with Online Gaming." 2004. TS. Western Washington University, Bellingham. College student Michelle Hanson conducted an online fieldstudy of one MUD, an online game called Sojourn. As a participant-observer, she learns to play the game, interviews more experienced players, and reflects on its human cultural dimensions.

Keillor, Garrison. "Ball Jars." *Mother, Father, Uncle, Aunt: Stories from Lake Wobegon.* Rec. 15 Mar. 1997. HighBridge Audio, 1997. Audiocassette. In this radio show taped in Muncie, Indiana, Garrison Keillor muses in historical and humorous ways on the importance of Ball jars. Originally presented before a live audience, Keillor's monologue connects American folk humor about Ball canning jars with other features of living in the Midwest. This transcription was prepared by Bonnie Stone Sunstein, Elizabeth Chiseri-Strater, and Beth McCabe.

Smith, Bruce R. "Shakespeare in an Age of Visual Culture." *Folger Shakespeare Library.* Folger Institute, 1998–1999. Web. Oct. 2005. <http://www.folger.edu/html/folger_institute/visual/index.htm>. Accessed October 2005. Scholar Bruce R. Smith's essay on the Folger Institute's virtual museum Web site discusses the conventions of various media that have interpreted Shakespeare's plays. The essay has four sections—digital media, film and video, stage production, and printed media.

WORKS CITED

Ball, Edward. *Slaves in the Family.* New York: Ballantine, 1998. Print.

Borkowsky, Amy. *Statements: True Tales of Life, Love, and Credit Card Bills.* New York: Penguin, 2005. Print.

Cantwell, Robert. *Ethnomimesis: Folklore and the Representation of Culture.* Chapel Hill: U of North Carolina P, 1993. Print.

Keillor, Garrison. "Ball Jars." *Mother, Father, Uncle, Aunt: Stories from Lake Wobegon.* Rec. 15. Mar. 1997. HighBridge Audio, 1997. Audiocassette.

Nye, Naomi Shihab. "The Attic and Its Nails." *Red Suitcase, Poems.* Rochester: BOA Editions, 1994. Print.

Shapiro, James. *1599: A Year in the Life of William Shakespeare.* New York: Harper-Collins, 2005. Print.

Sample Student Transcription of a Letter from a UT Archive

Following is a letter from the Harry Cushing Collection in the UT Special Collections archives that a English 102 student transcribed. The instructor, Teresa Hooper, explains the process for doing a transcription:

How to Make a Transcription

The purpose of transcribing a document is to make a piece of difficult primary information much easier to use for the purposes of research. Here are the basics:

1. Always transcribe in pencil. Keep an eraser in your hand for mistakes.

2. Work with only one line of the document at a time, and number the lines of your transcription. If you can, cover up everything except the line you're writing down.

3. Across the top or the side of your paper, make note of how the handwritten letters are formed. This will help you to recognize strange letters.

4. You *will* run into things you can't read. Don't get frustrated! Here are some pointers for deciphering:

    • Use context to help. You can narrow down the possible meanings of a word by what the rest of the sentence implies.

    • Use your finger to trace how the letters are written. If you can figure out how a letter is written, often you can decipher what letter it is.

    • If you're stuck, just move on and come back to the word later. Just mark off a space for the word with brackets like this: [ ].

5. Here are some conventions you can use:

    • Use brackets [ ] to mark off things that are there but you can't read. Write down letters you're fairly sure of. If you can count letters, put dots in the brackets to show the number of letters: [. . .em. . .]

    • Use left- and right-angle brackets to insert things that are lost by damage: D‹ece›mber.

    • Write out abbreviations, and underline the letters you supply: D<u>ecember</u>

Transcription Sheet

MS collection/item #: _____

Box #: _____

Folder #: _____

Page #: _____

1. _____

2. _____

3. _____

4. _____

5. _____

6. _____

7. _____

8. _____

9. _____

10. _____

11. _____

12. _____

13. _____

14. _____

15. _____

16. _____

17. _____

18. _____

19. _____

20. _____

Sample Student-Transcribed Letter Harry Cushing to his friend Ned Atwater

Letter transcribed by Beth-Ann Duncan, 102 Student

Harry Cushing

Map 301

Shasting, Virginia March 30 1863

Dear Ned

I write to let you know that I have got you a Secesh musket one which was picked from a dead rest at the battlefield of Winchester. It was found lying beside the re[ ] as if it had fallen out of his hand where he fell and was picked up by a man who was in the fight who sold it to me—as I wished to send one home to you, at first he wasn't going to sell it deeming it quite a trophy but with persuasive eloquence and still more persuasive cash I got it from him and you will have as good as I can and it—the mace who had was evidently killed before he had a chance to find in and I had some idea of firing it off and catching the fall [ ] my hand to send also but our conclusion

[page 2]

thoughts I wouldn't. As you have probably had descriptions of the fight I will not weary you and myself in a new description but will only tell you how the field looked after the battle was over as I wasn't over it the next day. I have already described one battle to you but from "reasons kept known to myself" I had not opportunity to describe the battlefield after the fight but will now endeavor to exhibit a field after a fight. As you leave the town of Winchester about 2 miles out there is a slight ascent and on the farther side of this the ground slopes gently down in a long gradual descent till it spreads out in one broad stretch of fields as the farther side of which the ground r<i>ses in golden heights then the other. These latter are coursed with thick woods except in two spots—one on your extreme right as you gain the top of the

[page 3]

hill and directly to your front along the edges of their fields runs a heavy stone wall. Behind this was the enemy in position and in the open spot to the front were parted their artillery which some of it was placed in shelter of the woods. Our troops formed line of battle on the hill mentioned as about two miles from town the distance between the two positions as first was about a mile and a half gradually as the battle grew hotter reducing to about a thousand or eight hundred yards for the artillery and close quarters for the infantry. The first thing which strikes you as you enter upon our position is the rails all scattered around the fences torn down and the trampled appearance of the ground. And all over the hill are the marks of the crossing and recrossing of artillery as they dashed madly around bunkering and unl<im>bering the ground presented eversure

[page 4]

of the severe fire by its torn up, broken appearance. All around lay pieces of shell, round shot. And limbs of trees torn off by the shower or iron power upon them. As you advance towards the scene of the infantry conflict the scene of destruction assumes a more fearful cast. Every fence was riddled with balls. Splinters of wood broken musket stocks cartridge bones torn in fragments lay around and every bush appeared as if some strong reaper with an immense scuttle had been engaged in cutting them to pieces. But in this copse of wood is the most horrible sight of all. Amid the rotten branches, broken twigs, roots, rocks, and stones lie thirty human beings flung out in every imaginable shape. Dead. The blood is splattered over the rocks and incarndining the mossy tunnels up the trees. Their mattered hands clotted with great floods of gore lawlessly

[page 5]

over the dead leaves and their brains ooze out of their mutilated foreheads and mingle with the dust of the earth. Here is one with great staring eyes glazed and motionless — his tongue protruding from his mouth — his rigid limbs and clenched hands stretched over the sharp stones while he stares — stares — stares — at the blue heaven above this young man presses his hand against his heart where the remorseless ball has entered while this one writhing in his agony expires with a ghastly smile on his face and a bloody froth on his mouth. Under this silver leaved birch his foot caught in a vine he's a poor fellow who fell upon his face and the sharp cute stone has cut to the bone. Still his clenched hand shakes defiantly at the foe. You turn in horror from [page 6]

the sight and new horrors await you. This hand has evidently been torn open with a shell and the broken fragments blood bones and [ ] show the terrible execution of the missile.

It was a memorable scene we are now very quiet here although we are having little skirmishes with calvary artillery and infantry every day but they don't amount to shucks.

Our company was thirty miles from the scene of battle but as are ready now to fight for the Union. As was our luck we got up after it was all done and had no chance to shell them at all. Give my love to all inquiring friends and send on that photograph card to your [ ] friend.

H.C. Cushing

2nd Lt.: 4th Artillery

Chief of Artillery

William Division

Banks 5th Army Corp.

Via Yhasburg Virginia

✳ Questions and Activities for Chapter 5

1. Review the information about "Finding Primary Source Material in the UT Libraries" in Chapter 4, including how to find materials in Special Collections. Using an archival database, find a primary text related to your course topic that you can access either electronically via a UT Libraries database or physical archive.

2. Visit the McClung Museum on UT's campus, and examine an exhibit in just one area of the museum.

   a. Briefly describe four historical artifacts in the area of the museum you've selected.

   b. How do these artifacts work together to show us the history of the time period upon which the exhibit focuses? Be sure to take all four artifacts into account.

   c. Are the artifacts in this exhibit arranged *synchronically*, *diachronically*, or both? Why do you think they are arranged this way?

   d. Examine the captions for two of the artifacts in your selected area. What might the museum curator have had to research in order to write these brief captions/explanations for these artifacts?

3. Examine an historical diary or collection of letters. (You can find some of these in the UT Library's Special Collections; search for materials at http://dlc.lib.utk.edu/spc/search. Be sure to review the policies—http://www.lib.utk.edu/special/services/policies.html—for using the archives before you go there.) Select one letter or diary, and write out your answers to the questions below.

   a. What is the physical size of the manuscript, measured in inches?

   b. Is the manuscript in the shape of a book, or are loose leaves joined together in some other way? Is the paper folded or gathered together?

   c. What is the quality of the paper like (i.e., is it brittle, rough, etc.?)

   d. What do you notice about the handwriting or typeface?

   e. What do you notice about the author's use of language, such as grammar?

   f. What markers of the author's identity do you find in the manuscript?

   g. What things are important to the person whose life you are reading about?

h. What do you learn about the author's experience in the given time period?

i. What do you learn about gender in the given time period?

j. Do extraneous documents (such as quotations or newspaper clippings) provide additional context for understanding the author?

k. What do you learn about history by reading the manuscript?

l. What do you learn about specific events in the given time period?

m. What do you learn about a specific place by reading the manuscript?

n. How does your understanding of genre (i.e., your ideas about what a letter is or what a diary is) affect how you interpret this manuscript?

o. How would you describe your experience of digging through the box to find the manuscript?

4. **The library stacks as archive.** Using the online catalog, find the oldest print version of a magazine or journal that Hodges Library carries related to your course topic. Briefly describe the issue (perhaps including a discussion of the editor's note or introduction—if one exists—or one of the articles), and explain how the views expressed in the issue relate to what people today (your class; your instructor; what you've seen, heard, or read) seem to think. Copy a short excerpt of the writing, and discuss its style.

5. **Digital archives.** Using either America's Historical Newspapers or the Archive of Americana database (http://www.lib.utk.edu/databases/) or another suggested by your instructor, search for two items or stories related to your course topic. Print out copies and bring them with you to class. Be prepared to discuss how the items you've found connect to the course topic.

6. **Visual archives.** Visit the McClung Museum, and be prepared to discuss in class the way one of the permanent exhibits (Archaeology & Native Peoples of Tennessee, Ancient Egypt, Geology & Fossil History of Tennessee, The Decorative Experience, Tennessee Freshwater Mussels, Human Origins, or The Civil War in Knoxville) uses historical documents or artifacts to explain its subject.

7. **Family archives.** If possible, locate a collection of old family letters or a photo album of old family pictures. What do you learn about your family history from these artifacts? What insight do you get into the cultural context of the artifacts?

8. Museum archives. Choose a site from the list of "East Tennessee and Regional Resources for Historical Research," which appears below. Visit a site of your choosing from the list, and write a one-page report on a historical fact or event that you learned about through your visit to the site.

East Tennessee and Regional Resources for Historical Research

- **Beck Cultural Exchange Center.** 1927 Dandridge Avenue, Knoxville, TN 37915-1997. Phone: 865-524-8461. Web: http://www.beckcenter.net

- **Blount Mansion.** 200 W. Hill Avenue, Knoxville, TN 37902. Phone: 865-525-2375. E-mail: blountmansion@hotmail.com. Web: http://www.blountmansion.org

- **East Tennessee History Center/Historical Society.** 601 S. Gay Street, Knoxville, TN 37901-1629. Phone: 865-215-8824. E-mail: eths@east-tennessee-history.org. Web: http://www.east-tennessee-history.org

- **James White's Fort.** 205 East Hill Avenue, Knoxville, TN 37915. Phone: 865-525-6514. E-mail: jameswhitefort@aol.com. Web: http://www.jameswhitesfort.org

- **Frank H. McClung Museum** (UT Campus). 1327 Circle Park Drive, Knoxville, TN 37996. Phone: 865-974-2144. E-mail: museum@utk.edu. Web: http://mcclungmuseum.utk.edu

- **Fort Loudoun State Historical Area** (visitor center/museum and reconstructed fort). 338 Fort Loudoun Road, Vonore, TN 37885. Phone: 423-884-6217. E-mail: FortLoudoun@tds.net. Web: http://www.fortloudoun.com

- **Highlander Research and Education Center.** 1959 Highlander Way, New Market, TN 37820. Phone: 865-933-3443. E-mail: hrec@highlandercenter.org. Web: http://www.highlandercenter.org

- **Marble Springs State Historic Homestead.** 1220 West Gov. John Sevier Highway, Knoxville, TN 37920. Phone: 865-573-5508. E-mail: marblesprings@hotmail.com. Web: http://www.marblesprings.net

- **Museum of Appalachia.** P.O. Box 1189, Norris, TN 37828. Phone: 865-494-7680. E-mail: museumappalachia@bellsouth.net. Web: http://museumofappalachia.org

- **Museum of the Cherokee Indian.** 589 Tsali Boulevard, Cherokee, NC 28719. Phone: 828-497-3481. E-mail: infocwy@cherokeemuseum.org. Web: http://www.cherokeemuseum.org

- **National Civil Rights Museum.** 450 Mulberry Street, Memphis, TN 38103. Phone: 901-521-9699. E-mail: contact@civilrightsmuseum.org. Web: http://www.civilrightsmuseum.org

- **Ramsey House Plantation.** 2614 Thorngrove Pike, Knoxville, TN 37914. Phone: 865-546-0745. E-mail: info@ramseyhouse.org. Web: http://www.ramseyhouse.org

9. A number of subject bibliographies relating to a wide array of academic programs (American cultural history, women's studies, religion, native Americans, literature and journalism, education, Tennessee history, arts and architecture) are available on the University of Tennessee Special Collections Web site (http://www.lib.utk.edu/spcoll/guides/index.html). Consult a "Special Collections Research Guide" that is relevant to your 102 course topic, and locate an archival document or documents from the special collections. Write a one-page report on what you discovered, and be prepared to share your findings with your classmates.

10. After reading one of the Sample Student Papers in the Historical Research section of Appendix D, summarize the writer's thesis or main idea. Identify the writer's supporting points. What evidence does the writer use to support the claims? Analyze sources used beyond the letters themselves—how does the writer use these sources in the paper?

PART THREE Qualitative Research

 In the academic coursework you have done so far (in high school and college), has most of your research involved reading books and articles—written texts—to find out what has been said about a subject? That is the usual research background for most first-year college students. However, there is another type of research with which you may be less familiar—"qualitative" research, the field or hands-on methods introduced in Chapters 6 and 7.

A defining feature of field or hands-on research—terms you're likely to hear in English 102 to describe qualitative research—is that its purpose is to gain a rich, deep understanding of people's actions, opinions, and attitudes about particular activities, events, situations, or issues that affect them. This type of research is common in a variety of courses you may take as an undergraduate, such as sociology, political science, child and family studies, social work, anthropology, and more.

Since many first-year students are unfamiliar with what qualitative research is and how to do it, Chapter 6, "An Introduction to Qualitative Research," provides an overview of the major concepts and practices associated with it. Following that, Chapter 7, "Conducting Interviews, Observations, and Surveys," provides practical, how-to information to guide your research projects from settling on a research question, to collecting your data, to analyzing and interpreting your research materials and writing them up successfully. Also included are examples of student-written work from research projects conducted at UT: a summary of field observations and interviews, and a transcript of an interview.

6 An Introduction to Qualitative Research

What Is Qualitative Research?

As Beverley Hancock explains in her research report *An Introduction to Qualitative Research*,

> Qualitative research is concerned with developing explanations of social phenomena. That is to say, it aims to help us to understand the world in which we live and why things are the way they are. It is concerned with the social aspects of our world and seeks to answer questions about:
>
> - Why people behave the way they do
> - How opinions and attitudes are formed
> - How people are affected by the events that go on around them
> - How and why cultures have developed in the way they have
> - The differences between social groups
>
> Qualitative research is concerned with finding the answers to questions which begin with: why? how? in what way? Quantitative research, on the other hand, is more concerned with questions about: how much? how many? how often? to what extent?
>
> — Beverley Hancock, "Trent Focus for Research and Development in Primary Health Care: An Introduction to Qualitative Research." [Research Report.] Nottingham, U.K.: Trent Focus, 1998. 14 June 2008. http://www.trentrdsu.org.uk/cms/uploads/Qualitative%20Research.pdf.

Like all types of research, qualitative or field research starts with the assumption that you don't already know what you need in order to answer the question that is driving your inquiry. That is, you do not already possess the rich, complex, and thorough understanding of how the people involved in the particular situation or issue you're investigating think, feel, and act. Research questions about how people think and act are best answered by talking with those people and observing their actions within a particular setting—that is, by using the qualitative research methods of fieldwork observations, interviews, and surveys.

Check out Appendix C, Work-in-Progress Research and Writing Activities, to find additional practical suggestions to help you read, research, and write successfully.

For example, suppose your class topic involves a social issue—let's say you're discussing current debates about public schooling in the United States—and one of the things you notice in your initial reading and discussion is that the written texts about this debate don't take into account the perspective of one important group: parents. You do some more reading and discover that many people write *about* parents, but very few actual parents' words, opinions, and experiences are presented directly. You suspect that parents' opinions may offer an important point of view that could affect the overall debate about public schooling. You might then frame the question, "What do parents think about their children's educational experiences?"

This is the type of research question that can best be answered by using qualitative or hands-on research, using methods such as fieldwork observations, interviews, and surveys, which seek to gather information directly from the people involved in a particular issue, situation, or event.

Here is another example, also related to a topic about schooling, that illustrates a research problem and questions that call for the use of field or qualitative research methods. Suppose you are talking in a class about a debate in higher education involving the supposedly decreasing competitiveness of U.S. students in science disciplines. Let's imagine the discussion turns to how students' knowledge in chemistry, a notoriously difficult course for most university students, could be increased. Later, in your subsequent reading, you find articles that refer to many professors' and administrators' belief that the best way to increase students' knowledge is to give them more homework. According to these professors and administrators, students need to spend much more time on chemistry than is available in class so that they will learn the greatest amount of information possible. Then, perhaps more alarmingly, you find out that a movement on this campus is developing to propose increasing student homework by 50 percent—not just in chemistry but in *all* courses.

However, suppose you also discover in the articles you read that nowhere in the presentation of the professors' and administrators' position is an acknowledgment that they've considered *students'* actual practices of doing homework or *students'* attitudes and ideas about it. Moreover, based upon your own experience with homework and that of your peers, you may think that the proposal to increase homework won't lead to the increased knowledge the professors seem to think it will. *This*, then, is your "research problem": You want to find out how more students than just you do homework and what they think about it, because you think that a presentation of the students' perspective could contribute productively to the conversation about this proposed policy.

Therefore, one of your research questions might be, "How do students actually *do* homework?" The corresponding research method might be to conduct a field observation of students' homework behavior in The Commons.

Another research question might be, "What are students' attitudes and opinions about the helpfulness of homework to them?" The corresponding research method might be to conduct personal interviews with or surveys of students. If no one had done such research before, an important body of knowledge would have been left out of the discussion of this issue.

A Model of the Process of Conducting Qualitative Research and Data Analysis

In general, you should follow the model below to design and carry out your hands-on research projects. The model was created by British researchers Celia Taylor and Graham R. Gibbs, and the material we present below is an excerpt from their work on the Web site *Online QDA*, a resource you may find helpful when conducting qualitative research projects.* Various steps of this research model are explained in greater detail in Chapter 7, including how to collect data through interviews and surveys.

About Your Project and Research Questions

WHY ARE YOU RESEARCHING THIS AREA?

The reasons you are researching a topic area could be because you have chosen an area that interests you or you have been [assigned] to conduct a project chosen by someone else. [. . .] The answer to this question will help you preserve your motivation at difficult times in the project and might even help you think about different ways the knowledge you discover could be used.

WHAT ARE THE GAPS IN CURRENT KNOWLEDGE/RESEARCH?

It is essential to be familiar with current research in order to identify an area that has not yet been explored or an area that needs further investigation. This will not only help you determine your research question(s) but will also focus your analysis so

*Taylor, Celia, and Graham R. Gibbs, "Complete Beginner." *Online QDA*. 14 June 2008 http://onlineqda.hud.ac.uk/ Introduction/complete_beginner.php. Used by permission. (Brackets indicate changes we have made to present the information most relevant to English 102 research projects. In most places we have retained the British spellings and punctuation from the original source.)

that you can pull out from your data what you have found but no one else has—yet. Being aware of the research literature will also make you aware of how what you have discovered fits in with the existing knowledge about the topic. This background research will also help you to think about the kinds of [. . .] methodological approaches you need to adopt or that you will choose to take.

WHAT ARE YOUR RESEARCH QUESTIONS?

What questions are you trying to answer during your research project? You may also identify new questions as your research progresses. In a qualitative project it usually make[s] most sense to have a broad research question or a small set of related research questions. This is a very important stage in developing your research as it is all too easy to set out to address a research question that is far too broad and vague.

(The above questions are based on those raised by Jennifer Mason in her book, *Qualitative Researching*, London: Sage, 1996.)

Collecting the Data

WHAT TYPE OF DATA WILL YOU COLLECT?

The most common way to collect qualitative data is by interviews. These can be conducted face-to-face, over the telephone or via email. Other methods of collecting qualitative data include [surveys], observations, focus groups, field work and through the collection of documents, images, video and other cultural artefacts.

WHAT FORMAT DO YOU NEED THE DATA TO BE IN?

When you collect data it could be in the form of audio recordings, video, photographs, and hand-written notes. These data then need to be put into a format suitable for analysis, for example, by transcribing the audio or video recording.

WILL YOU BE COLLECTING ALONE OR IN A TEAM?

Collecting data takes a considerable amount of time. You will probably need to contact individuals to take part in your research. If they agree you may need to travel to their location to conduct the research.

ETHICAL APPROVAL

All research projects involving people require ethical approval before they can commence. The nature of the project will determine the type of ethical approval required. Ethical procedures vary between institutions so it is important to find out what they are where you are working. [See Appendix C, "Obtaining Permission to Conduct Research with People" and "Sample Informed Consent Form," pp. 342–46.]

ETHICAL ISSUES

This will include an assessment of the risk to participants and researchers (if any) and how you intend to deal with those risks. It is normal to protect the identity of participants, organizations and situations, usually by some form of anonymizations. You should also make arrangements to keep your data secure and confidential.

WHAT INFORMATION DO YOU NEED TO PROVIDE TO [RESEARCH PARTICIPANTS]?

Volunteers need to be provided with a Participant Information Sheet and Informed Consent Form. The Participant Information Sheet includes such things as details of the purpose of the study, why the individual has been invited to take part, and who is conducting the research. The Informed Consent Form is signed by individuals that agree to take part in the research stating they have understood the purpose of the study, how the information they provided will be used and have decided of their own free will to take part.

HOW WILL YOU SAMPLE?

You may not think this is an issue if you are undertaking participant observation or ethnographic work and you have already chosen or have no choice about your setting. You just keep field notes whenever you are in the field setting. However, even here you may have choices about when you go into the field, who you talk to and which part of the setting you will spend your time in. More commonly, qualitative research involves a number of interviews with participants. You will need to decide which participants and how many and the sampling method you will use to select them. In some qualitative research sampling is intended to produce a representative sample, but usually other sampling strategies are used, e.g., convenience sampling, purposive sampling, snowball sampling and theoretical sampling. Similar considerations will apply to the selection of settings, organisations, institutions etc. for your data collection.

HOW WILL YOU CONTACT YOUR SAMPLE?

You need to decide how you will contact individuals to invite them to take part in your research project, e.g., by letter or telephone. You may need to approach people through a third party such as a company or institution. In these cases, the role of gatekeepers and inside contacts can be very important.

HOW ARE YOU GOING TO COLLECT THE DATA?

It depends on the type of data needed for your project and the budget you have available. You can interview people face-to-face, over the telephone or via email. You will need to think about the technology needed for this, such as voice recorders (consider new technologies such as mini-disk and MP3 recorders) and telephone recorders. Alternatively you might want to take field notes (again consider the technology you might need such as dictation machines, laptop computers, etc.) or video sessions (best if you can use digital video recorders).

HOW LONG WILL IT TAKE TO COLLECT THE DATA AND THEN FORMAT IT?
You need to estimate how long it will take to select your sample, undertake fieldwork and/or interview individuals and then transcribe your notes and interviews. This needs to be planned into the schedule of your research project. If you find you are over-running the time you had allocated you need to decide how this will affect the rest of the research project and therefore what action to take.

Analyzing the Data

Analyzing your data also needs to be planned into your project schedule. There is a great range of approaches you can take, but some may be predetermined as a result of your choice of methodology. [See "How and What to Code" in Chapter 7 of this textbook for more information on data analysis. That section gives] some details of the more common approaches used by several methodologies. This includes coding the data, [. . .] making comparisons, and moving to more analytic and theoretical [concepts].

Presenting the Findings

Depending on the type of research project you are conducting you are likely to have to report on the research in a specified format such as a research report. [. . .] Consider the structure of your final report and write it as you go along to help your thinking during the research. Also take into account the likely audience of your report to decide how much detail to include on various aspects.

Introduction to Primary Research:
Observations, Surveys, and Interviews

DANA LYNN DRISCOLL

Primary Research: Definitions and Overview

How research is defined varies widely from field to field, and as you progress through your college career, your coursework will teach you much more about what it means to be a researcher within your field. For example, engineers, who focus on applying scientific knowledge to develop designs, processes, and objects, conduct research using simulations, mathematical models, and a variety of tests to see how well their designs work. Sociologists conduct research using surveys, interviews, observations, and statistical analysis to better understand people, societies, and cultures. Graphic designers conduct research through locating images for reference for their artwork and engaging in background research on clients and companies to best serve their needs. Historians conduct research by examining archival materials—newspapers, journals, letters, and other surviving texts—and through conducting oral history interviews. Research is not limited to what has already been written or found at the library, also known as secondary research. Rather, individuals conducting research are *producing* the articles and reports found in a library database or in a book. Primary research, the focus of this essay, is research that is collected firsthand rather than found in a book, database, or journal.

Primary research is often based on principles of the scientific method, a theory of investigation first developed by John Stuart Mill in the nineteenth century in his book *Philosophy of the Scientific Method*. Although the application of the scientific method varies from field to field, the general principles of the scientific method allow researchers to learn more about the world and observable phenomena. Using the scientific method, researchers develop research questions or hypotheses and collect data on events, objects, or people that is measurable, observable, and replicable. The ultimate goal in conducting primary research is to learn about something new that can be confirmed by others and to eliminate our own biases in the process.

ESSAY OVERVIEW AND STUDENT EXAMPLES

The essay begins by providing an overview of ethical considerations when conducting primary research, and then covers the stages that you will go through in your primary research: planning, collecting, analyzing, and writing. After the four stages comes an introduction to three common ways of conducting primary research in first year writing classes:

- **Observations.** Observing and measuring the world around you, including observations of people and other measurable events.

- **Interviews.** Asking participants questions in a one-on-one or small group setting.

- **Surveys.** Asking participants about their opinions and behaviors through a short questionnaire.

Dana Lynn Driscoll, "Introduction to Primary Research: Observations, Surveys, and Interviews." From *Writing Spaces: Readings on Writing*, Volume 2, pp. 153–74.

In addition, we will be examining two student projects that used substantial portions of primary research:

Derek Laan, a nutrition major at Purdue University, wanted to learn more about student eating habits on campus. His primary research included observations of the campus food courts, student behavior while in the food courts, and a survey of students' daily food intake. His secondary research included looking at national student eating trends on college campuses, information from the United States Food and Drug Administration, and books on healthy eating.

Jared Schwab, an agricultural and biological engineering major at Purdue, was interested in learning more about how writing and communication took place in his field. His primary research included interviewing a professional engineer and a student who was a senior majoring in engineering. His secondary research included examining journals, books, professional organizations, and writing guides within the field of engineering.

Ethics of Primary Research

Both projects listed above included primary research on human participants; therefore, Derek and Jared both had to consider research ethics throughout their primary research process. As Earl Babbie writes in *The Practice of Social Research*, throughout the early and middle parts of the twentieth century researchers took advantage of participants and treated them unethically. During World War II, Nazi doctors performed heinous experiments on prisoners without their consent, while in the United States, a number of medical and psychological experiments on patients caused undue mental and physical trauma and, in some cases, death. Because of these and other similar events, many nations have established ethical laws and guidelines for researchers who work with human participants. In the United States, the guidelines for the ethical treatment of human research participants are described in *The Belmont Report*, released in 1979. Today, universities have Institutional Review Boards (or IRBs) that oversee research. Students conducting research as part of a class may not need permission from the university's IRB, although they still need to ensure that they follow ethical guidelines in research. The following provides a brief overview of ethical considerations:

- **Voluntary participation.** *The Belmont Report* suggests that, in most cases, you need to get permission from people before you involve them in any primary research you are conducting. If you are doing a survey or interview, your participants must first agree to fill out your survey or to be interviewed. Consent for observations can be more complicated, and is discussed later in the essay.

- **Confidentiality and anonymity.** Your participants may reveal embarrassing or potentially damaging information such as racist comments or unconventional behavior. In these cases, you should keep your participants' identities anonymous when writing your results. An easy way to do this is to create a "pseudonym" (or false name) for them so that their identity is protected.

- **Researcher bias.** There is little point in collecting data and learning about something if you already think you know the answer! Bias might be present in the way you ask questions, the way you take notes, or the conclusions you draw from the data you collect.

The above are only three of many considerations when involving human participants in your primary research. For a complete understanding of ethical considerations please refer to *The Belmont Report.*

Now that we have considered the ethical implications of research, we will examine how to formulate research questions and plan your primary research project.

Planning Your Primary Research Project

The primary research process is quite similar to the writing process, and you can draw upon your knowledge of the writing process to understand the steps involved in a primary research project. Just like in the writing process, a successful primary research project begins with careful planning and background research. This section first describes how to create a research timeline to help plan your research. It then walks you through the planning stages by examining when primary research is useful or appropriate for your first year composition course, narrowing down a topic, and developing research questions.

THE RESEARCH TIMELINE

When you begin to conduct any kind of primary research, creating a timeline will help keep you on task. Because students conducting primary research usually focus on the collection of data itself, they often overlook the equally important areas of planning (invention), analyzing data, and writing. To help manage your time, you should create a research timeline, such as the sample timeline presented here.

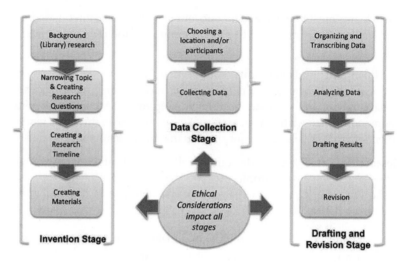

⌐ Figure 6.1 The Research Process

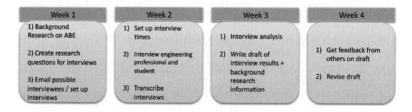

⌐ Figure 6.2 A sample timeline for Jared's research project.

WHEN PRIMARY RESEARCH IS USEFUL OR APPROPRIATE

In *Evaluating Scientific Research: Separating Fact from Fiction*, Fred Leavitt explains that primary research is useful for questions that can be answered through asking others and direct observation. For first year writing courses, primary research is particularly useful when you want to learn about a problem that does not have a wealth of published information. This may be because the problem is a recent event or it is something not commonly studied. For example, if you are writing a paper on a new political issue, such as changes in tax laws or healthcare, you might not be able to find a wealth of peer-reviewed research because the issue is only several weeks old. You may find it necessary to collect some of your own data on the issue to supplement what you found at the library. Primary research is also useful when you are studying a local problem or learning how a larger issue plays out at the local level. Although you might be able to find information on national statistics for healthy eating, whether or not those statistics are representative of your college campus is something that you can learn through primary research.

However, not all research questions and topics are appropriate for primary research. As Fred Leavitt writes, questions of an ethical, philosophical, or metaphysical nature are not appropriate because these questions are not testable or observable. For example, the question "Does an afterlife exist?" is not a question that can be answered with primary research. However, the question "How many people in my community believe in an afterlife?" is something that primary research can answer.

NARROWING YOUR TOPIC

Just like the writing process, you should start your primary research process with secondary (library) research to learn more about what is already known and what gaps you need to fill with your own data. As you learn more about the topic, you can narrow down your interest area and eventually develop a research question or hypothesis, just as you would with a secondary research paper.

DEVELOPING RESEARCH QUESTIONS OR HYPOTHESES

As John Stuart Mill describes, primary research can use both *inductive* and *deductive* approaches, and the type approach is usually based on the field of inquiry. Some fields use *deductive reasoning*, where researchers start with a hypothesis or general conclusion and then collect specific data to support or refute their hypothesis. Other fields use *inductive reasoning*, where researchers start with a question and collect information that eventually leads to a conclusion.

Once you have spent some time reviewing the secondary research on your topic, you are ready to write a primary research question or hypothesis. A research question or hypothesis should be something that is specific, narrow, and discoverable through primary research methods. Just like a thesis statement for a paper, if your research question or hypothesis is too broad, your research will be unfocused and your data will be difficult to analyze and write about. Here is a set of sample research questions:

Poor Research Question
What do college students think of politics and the economy?

Revised Research Question
What do students at Purdue University believe about the current economic crisis in terms of economic recoverability?

The poor research question is unspecific as to what group of students the researcher is interested in—i.e. students in the United States? In a particular state? At their university? The poor research question was also too broad; terms like "politics" and the "economy" cover too much ground for a single project. The revised question narrows down the topic to students at a particular university and focuses on a specific issue related to the economy: economic recoverability. The research question could also be rephrased as a testable hypothesis using deductive reasoning: "Purdue University college students are well informed about economic recoverability plans." Because they were approaching their projects in an exploratory, inductive manner, both Derek and Jared chose to ask research questions:

> Derek: Are students' eating habits at Purdue University healthy or unhealthy? What are the causes of students' eating behavior?

> Jared: What are the major features of writing and communication in agricultural and biological engineering? What are the major controversies?

A final step in working with a research question or hypothesis is determining what key terms you are using and how you will define them. Before conducting his research, Derek had to define the terms "healthy" and "unhealthy"; for this, he used the USDA's Food Pyramid as a guide. Similarly, part of what Jared focused on in his interviews was learning more about how agricultural and biological engineers defined terms like "writing" and "communication." Derek and Jared thought carefully about the terms within their research questions and how these terms might be measured.

CHOOSING A DATA COLLECTION METHOD

Once you have formulated a research question or hypothesis, you will need to make decisions about what kind of data you can collect that will best address your research topic. Derek chose to examine eating habits by observing both what students ate at lunch and surveying students about eating behavior. Jared decided that in-depth interviews with experienced individuals in his field would provide him with the best information.

To choose a data collection method for your research question, read through the next sections on observations, interviews, and surveys.

Observations

Observations have lead to some of the most important scientific discoveries in human history. Charles Darwin used observations of the animal and marine life at the Galapagos Islands to help him formulate his theory of evolution that he describes in *On the Origin of Species*. Today, social scientists, natural scientists, engineers, computer scientists, educational researchers, and many others use observations as a primary research method.

Observations can be conducted on nearly any subject matter, and the kinds of observations you will do depend on your research question. You might observe traffic or parking patterns on campus to get a sense of what improvements could be made. You might observe clouds, plants, or other natural phenomena. If you choose to observe people, you will have several additional considerations including the manner in which you will observe them and gain their consent.

If you are observing people, you can choose between two common ways to observe: participant observation and unobtrusive observation. Participant observation is a common method within ethnographic research in sociology and anthropology. In this kind of observation, a researcher may interact with participants and become part of their community. Margaret Mead, a famous anthropologist, spent extended periods of time living in, and interacting with, communities that she studied. Conversely, in unobtrusive observation, you do not interact with participants but rather simply record their behavior. Although in most circumstances people must volunteer to be participants in research, in some cases it is acceptable to not let participants know you are observing them. In places that people perceive as public, such as a campus food court or a shopping mall, people do not expect privacy, and so it is generally acceptable to observe without participant consent. In places that people perceive as private, which can include a church, home, classroom, or even an intimate conversation at a restaurant, participant consent should be sought.

The second issue about participant consent in terms of unobtrusive observation is whether or not getting consent is feasible for the study. If you are observing people in a busy airport, bus station, or campus food court, getting participant consent may be next to impossible. In Derek's study of student eating habits on campus, he went to the campus food courts during meal times and observed students purchasing food. Obtaining participant consent for his observations would have been next to impossible because hundreds of students were coming through the food court during meal times. Since Derek's research was in a place that participants would perceive as public, it was not practical to get their consent, and since his data was anonymous, he did not violate their privacy.

ELIMINATING BIAS IN YOUR OBSERVATION NOTES

The ethical concern of being unbiased is important in recording your observations. You need to be aware of the difference between an observation (recording exactly what you see) and an interpretation (making assumptions and judgments about what you see). When you observe, you should focus first on only the events that are directly observable. Consider the following two example entries in an observation log:

1. The student sitting in the dining hall enjoys his greasy, oil-soaked pizza. He is clearly oblivious of the calorie content and damage it may do to his body.

2. The student sits in the dining hall. As he eats his piece of pizza, which drips oil, he says to a friend, "This pizza is good."

The first entry is biased and demonstrates judgment about the event. First, the observer makes assumptions about the internal state of the student when she writes "enjoys" and "clearly oblivious to the calorie content." From an observer's standpoint, there is no way of ascertaining what the student may or may not know about pizza's nutritional value nor how much the student enjoys the pizza. The second entry provides only the details and facts that are observable.

To avoid bias in your observations, you can use something called a "double-entry notebook." This is a type of observation log that encourages you to separate your observations (the facts) from your feelings and judgments about the facts.

Observations	Thoughts
The student sits in the dining hall. As he eats his piece of pizza, which drips oil, he says to a friend, "This pizza is good."	It seems like the student really enjoys the high-calorie content pizza.
I observed cash register #1 for 15 minutes. During that time 22 students paid for meals. Of those 22 students, 15 grabbed a candy bar or granola bar. 3 of the 22 students had a piece of fruit on their plate.	Fruit is less accessible than candy bars (it is further back in the dining court). Is this why more students are reaching for candy bars?

ㄴ Figure 6.3 Two sample entries from a double-entry notebook.

Observations are only one strategy in collecting primary research. You may also want to ask people directly about their behaviors, beliefs, or attitudes—and for this you will need to use surveys or interviews.

Surveys and Interviews: Question Creation

Sometimes it is very difficult for a researcher to gain all of the necessary information through observations alone. Along with his observations of the dining halls, Derek wanted to know what students ate in a typical day, and so he used a survey to have them keep track of their eating habits. Likewise, Jared wanted to learn about writing and communication in engineering and decided to draw upon expert knowledge by asking experienced individuals within the field.

Interviews and surveys are two ways that you can gather information about people's beliefs or behaviors. With these methods, the information you collect is not first-hand (like an observation) but rather "self-reported" data, or data collected in an indirect manner. William Shadish, Thomas Cook, and Donald Campbell argued that people are inherently biased about how they see the world and may report their own actions in a more favorable way than they may actually behave. Despite the issues in self-reported data, surveys and interviews are an excellent way to gather data for your primary research project.

SURVEY OR INTERVIEW?

How do you choose between conducting a survey or an interview? It depends on what kind of information you are looking for. You should use surveys if you want to learn about a general trend in people's opinions, experiences, and behavior. Surveys are particularly useful to find small amounts of information from a wider selection of people in the hopes of making a general claim. Interviews are best used when you want to learn detailed information from a few specific people. Interviews are also particularly useful if you want to interview experts about their opinions, as Jared did. In sum, use interviews to gain details from a few people, and surveys to learn general patterns from many people.

WRITING GOOD QUESTIONS

One of the greatest challenges in conducting surveys and interviews is writing good questions. As a researcher, you are always trying to eliminate bias, and the questions you ask need to be unbiased and clear. Here are some suggestions on writing good questions:

Ask about One Thing at a Time. A poorly written question can contain multiple questions, which can confuse participants or lead them to answer only part of the question you are asking. This is called a "double-barreled question" in journalism. The following questions are taken from Jared's research:

> **Poor Question**
> What kinds of problems are being faced in the field today and where do you see the search for solutions to these problems going?
>
> **Revised Question #1**
> What kinds of problems are being faced in the field today?
>
> **Revised Question #2**
> Where do you see the search for solutions to these problems going?

Avoid Leading Questions. A leading question is one where you prompt the participant to respond in a particular way, which can create bias in the answers given:

> **Leading Question**
> The economy is clearly in a crisis, wouldn't you agree?
>
> **Revised Question**
> Do you believe the economy is currently in a crisis? Why or why not?

Understand When to Use Open and Closed Questions. Closed questions, or questions that have yes/no or other limited responses, should be used in surveys. However, avoid these kinds of questions in interviews because they discourage the interviewee from going into depth. The question sample above, "Do you believe the economy currently is in a crisis?" could be answered with a simple yes or no, which could keep a participant from talking more about the issue. The "why or why not?" portion of the question asks the participant to elaborate. On a survey, the question "Do you believe the economy currently is in a crisis?" is a useful question because you can easily count the number of yes and no answers and make a general claim about participant responses.

Write Clear Questions. When you write questions, make sure they are clear, concise, and to the point. Questions that are too long, use unfamiliar vocabulary, or are unclear may confuse participants and you will not get quality responses.

Now that question creation has been addressed, we will next examine specific considerations for interviews and surveys.

Interviews

Interviews, or question and answer sessions with one or more people, are an excellent way to learn in-depth information from a person for your primary research project. This section presents information on how to conduct a successful interview, including choosing the right person, ways of interviewing, recording your interview, interview locations, and transcribing your interview.

CHOOSING THE RIGHT PERSON

One of the keys to a successful interview is choosing the right person to interview. Think about whom you would like to interview and whom you might know. Do not be afraid to ask people you do not know for interviews. When asking, simply tell them what the interview will be about, what the interview is for, and how much time it will take. Jared used his Purdue University connection to locate both of the individuals that he ended up interviewing—an advanced Purdue student and a Purdue alum working in an Engineering firm.

FACE-TO-FACE AND VIRTUAL INTERVIEWS

When interviewing, you have a choice of conducting a traditional, face-to-face interview or an interview using technology over the Internet. Face-to-face interviews have the strength that you can ask follow-up questions and use nonverbal communication to your advantage. Individuals are able to say much more in a face-to-face interview than in an email, so you will get more information from a face-to-face interview. However, the Internet provides a host of new possibilities when it comes to interviewing people at a distance. You may choose to do an email interview, where you send questions and ask the person to respond. You may also choose to use a video or audio conferencing program to talk with the person virtually. If you are choosing any Internet-based option, make sure you have a way of recording the interview. You may also use a chat or instant messaging program to interview your participant—the benefit of this is that you can ask follow-up questions during the interview and the interview is already transcribed for you. Because one of his interviewees lived several hours away, Jared chose to interview the Purdue student face-to-face and the Purdue alum via email.

FINDING A SUITABLE LOCATION

If you are conducting an in-person interview, it is essential that you find a quiet place for your interview. Many universities have quiet study rooms that can be reserved (often found in the university library). Do not try to interview someone in a coffee shop, dining hall, or other loud area, as it is difficult to focus and get a clear recording.

RECORDING INTERVIEWS

One way of eliminating bias in your research is to record your interviews rather than rely on your memory. Recording interviews allows you to directly quote the individual and re-read the interview when you are writing. It is recommended that you have two recording devices for the interview in case one recording device fails. Most computers, MP3 players, and even cell phones come with recording equipment built in. Many universities also offer equipment that students can check out and use, including computers and recorders. Before you record any interview, be sure that you have permission from your participant.

TRANSCRIBING YOUR INTERVIEW

Once your interview is over, you will need to transcribe your interview to prepare it for analysis. The term transcribing means creating a written record that is exactly what was said—that is, typing up your interviews. If you have conducted an email or chat interview, you already have a transcription and can move on to your analysis stage.

Surveys

Other than the fact that they both involve asking people questions, interviews and surveys are quite different data collection methods. Creating a survey may seem easy at first, but developing a quality survey can be quite challenging. When conducting a survey, you need to focus on the following areas: survey creation, survey testing, survey sampling, and distributing your survey.

SURVEY CREATION: LENGTH AND TYPES OF QUESTIONS

One of the keys to creating a successful survey is to keep your survey short and focused. Participants are unlikely to fill out a survey that is lengthy, and you'll have a more difficult time during your analysis if your survey contains too many questions. In most cases, you want your survey to be something that can be filled out within a few minutes. The target length of the survey also depends on how you will distribute the survey. If you are giving your survey to other students in your dorm or classes, they will have more time to complete the survey. Therefore, five to ten minutes to complete the survey is reasonable. If you are asking students as they are walking to class to fill out your survey, keep it limited to several questions that can be answered in thirty seconds or less. Derek's survey took about ten minutes and asked students to describe what they ate for a day, along with some demographic information like class level and gender.

Use closed questions to your advantage when creating your survey. A closed question is any set of questions that gives a limited amount of choices (yes/no, a 1–5 scale, choose the statement that best describes you). When creating closed questions, be sure that you are accounting for all reasonable answers in your question creation. For example, asking someone "Do you believe you eat healthy?" and providing them only "yes" and "no" options means that a "neutral" or "undecided" option does not exist, even though the survey respondent may not feel strongly either way. Therefore, on closed questions you may find it helpful to include an "other" category where participants can fill in an answer. It is also a good idea to have a few open-ended questions where participants can elaborate on certain points or earlier responses. However, open-ended questions take much longer to fill out than closed questions.

SURVEY CREATION: TESTING YOUR SURVEY

To make sure your survey is an appropriate length and that your questions are clear, you can "pilot test" your survey. Prior to administering your survey on a larger scale, ask several classmates or friends to fill it out and give you feedback on the survey. Keep track of how long the survey takes to complete. Ask them if the questions are clear and make sense. Look at their answers to see if the answers match what you wanted to learn. You can revise your survey questions and the length of your survey as necessary.

SAMPLING AND ACCESS TO SURVEY POPULATIONS

"Sampling" is a term used within survey research to describe the subset of people that are included in your study. Derek's first research question was: "Are students' eating habits at Purdue University healthy or unhealthy?" Because it was impossible for Derek to survey all 38,000 students on Purdue's campus, he had to choose a representative sample of students. Derek chose to survey students who lived in the dorms because of the wide variety of student class levels and majors in the dorms and his easy access to this group. By making this choice, however, he did not account for commuter students, graduate students, or those who live off campus. As Derek's case demonstrates, it is very challenging to get a truly representative sample.

Part of the reason that sampling is a challenge is that you may find difficulty in finding enough people to take your survey. In thinking about how get people to take your survey, consider both your everyday surroundings and also technological solutions. Derek had access to many students in the dorms, but he also considered surveying students in his classes in order to reach as many people as possible. Another possibility is to conduct an online survey. Online surveys greatly increase your access to different kinds of people from across the globe, but may decrease your chances of having a high survey response rate. An email or private message survey request is more likely to be ignored due to the impersonal quality and high volume of emails most people receive.

Analyzing and Writing about Primary Research

Once you collect primary research data, you will need to analyze what you have found so that you can write about it. The purpose of analyzing your data is to look at what you collected (survey responses, interview answers to questions, observations) and to create a cohesive, systematic interpretation to help answer your research question or examine the validity of your hypothesis.

When you are analyzing and presenting your findings, remember to work to eliminate bias by being truthful and as accurate as possible about what you found, even if it differs from what you expected to find. You should see your data as sources of information, just like sources you find in the library, and you should work to represent them accurately.

The following are suggestions for analyzing different types of data.

OBSERVATIONS

If you've counted anything you were observing, you can simply add up what you counted and report the results. If you've collected descriptions using a double-entry notebook, you might work to write thick descriptions of what you observed into your writing. This could include descriptions of the scene, behaviors you observed, and your overall conclusions about events. Be sure that your readers are clear on what were your actual observations versus your thoughts or interpretations of those observations.

INTERVIEWS

If you've interviewed one or two people, then you can use your summary, paraphrasing, and quotation skills to help you accurately describe what was said in the interview. Just like in secondary research when working with sources, you should introduce your interviewees and choose clear and relevant quotes from the interviews to use in your writing. An easy way to find the important information in an interview is to print out your transcription and take a highlighter and mark the important parts that you might use in your paper. If you have conducted a large number of interviews, it will be helpful for you to create a spreadsheet of responses to each question and compare the responses, choosing representative answers for each area you want to describe.

SURVEYS

Surveys can contain quantitative (numerical) and qualitative (written answers/descriptions) data. Quantitative data can be analyzed using a spreadsheet program like Microsoft Excel to calculate the mean (average) answer or to calculate the percentage of people who responded in a certain way. You can display this information in a chart or a graph and also describe it in writing in your paper. If you have qualitative responses, you might choose to group them into categories and/or you may choose to quote several representative responses.

Writing about Primary Research

In formal research writing in a variety of fields, it is common for research to be presented in the following format: introduction/background; methods; results; discussions; conclusion. Not all first year writing classes will require such an organizational structure, although it is likely that you will be required to present many of these elements in your paper. Because of this, the next section examines each of these in depth.

INTRODUCTION (REVIEW OF LITERATURE)

The purpose of an introduction and review of literature in a research paper is to provide readers with information that helps them understand the context, purpose, and relevancy of your research. The introduction is where you provide most of your background (library) research that you did earlier in the process. You can include articles, statistics, research studies, and quotes that are pertinent to the issues at hand. A second purpose in an introduction is to establish your own credibility (ethos) as a writer by showing that you have researched your topic thoroughly. This kind of background discussion is required in nearly every field of inquiry when presenting research in oral or written formats.

Derek provided information from the Food and Drug Administration on healthy eating and national statistics about eating habits as part of his background information. He also made the case for healthy eating on campus to show relevancy:

> Currently Americans are more overweight than ever. This is coming at a huge cost to the economy and government. If current trends in increasing rates of overweight and obesity continue it is likely that this generation will be the first one to live shorter lives than their parents did. Looking at the habits of university students is a good way to see how a new generation behaves when they are living out on their own for the first time.

DESCRIBING WHAT YOU DID (METHODS)

When writing, you need to provide enough information to your readers about your primary research process for them to understand what you collected and how you collected it. In formal research papers, this is often called a methods section. Providing information on your study methods also adds to your credibility as a writer. For surveys, your methods would include describing who you surveyed, how many surveys you collected, decisions you made about your survey sample, and relevant demographic information about your participants (age, class level, major). For interviews, introduce whom you interviewed and any other relevant information about interviewees such as their career or expertise area. For observations, list the locations and times you observed and how you recorded your observations (i.e., double-entry notebook). For all data types, you should describe how you analyzed your data.

The following is a sample from Jared about his participants:

> In order to gain a better understanding of the discourse community in environmental and resource engineering, I interviewed Anne Dare, a senior in environmental and natural resource engineering, and Alyson Keaton an alumnus of Purdue University. Alyson is a current employee of the Natural Resource Conservation Service (NRCS), which is a division of the United States Department of Agriculture (USDA).

Here is a sample from Derek's methods section:

> I conducted a survey so that I could find out what students at Purdue actually eat on a typical day. I handed out surveys asking students to record what they ate for a day . . . I received 29 back and averaged the results based on average number of servings from each food group on the old food guide pyramid. The group included students from the freshman to the graduate level and had 8 women and 21 men respond.

DESCRIBING YOUR STUDY FINDINGS (RESULTS)

In a formal research paper, the results section is where you describe what you found. The results section can include charts, graphs, lists, direct quotes, and overviews of findings. Readers find it helpful if you are able to provide the information in different formats. For example, if you have any kind of numbers or percentages, you can talk about them in your written description and then present a graph or chart showing them visually. You should provide specific details as supporting evidence to back up your findings. These details can be in the form of direct quotations, numbers, or observations.

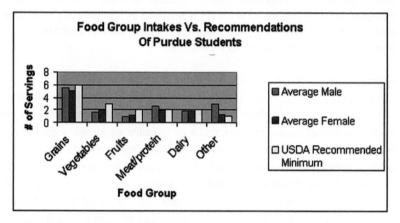

⌐ **Figure 6.4 Graphic from Derek's results section.**

Jared describes some of his interview results:

> Alyson also mentioned the need for phone conversation. She stated, "The phone is a large part of my job. I am communicating with other NRCS offices daily to find out the status of our jobs." She needs to be in constant contact in order to insure that everything is running smoothly. This is common with those overseeing projects. In these cases, the wait for a response to an email or a memo can be too long to be effective.

INTERPRETING WHAT YOU LEARNED (DISCUSSION)

In formal research papers, the discussion section presents your own interpretation of your results. This may include what you think the results mean or how they are useful to your larger argument. If you are making a proposal for change or a call to action, this is where you make it. For example, in Derek's project about healthy eating on campus, Derek used his primary research on students' unhealthy eating and observations of the food courts to argue that the campus food courts needed serious changes. Derek writes, "Make healthy food options the most accessible in every dining hall while making unhealthy foods the least. Put nutrition facts for everything that is served in the dining halls near the food so that students can make more informed decisions on what to eat."

Jared used the individuals he interviewed as informants that helped him learn more about writing in agricultural and biological engineering. He integrated the interviews he conducted with secondary research to form a complete picture of writing and communication in agricultural and biological engineering. He concludes:

> Writing takes so many forms, and it is important to know about all these forms in one way or another. The more forms of writing you can achieve, the more flexible you can be. This ability to be flexible can make all the difference in writing when you are dealing with a field as complex as engineering.

PRIMARY RESEARCH AND WORKS CITED OR REFERENCES PAGES

The last part of presenting your primary research project is a works cited or references page. In general, since you are working with data you collected yourself, there is no source to cite an external source. Your methods section should describe in detail to the readers how and where the data presented was obtained. However, if you are working with interviews, you can cite these as "personal communication." The MLA and APA handbooks both provide clear listings of how to cite personal communication in a works cited/references page.

Conclusion

This essay has presented an overview to three commonly used methods of primary research in first year writing courses: observations, interviews, and surveys. By using these methods, you can learn more about the world around you and craft meaningful written discussions of your findings.

Discussion

1. Primary research techniques show up in more places than just first year writing courses. Where else might interviews, surveys, or observations be used? Where have you seen them used?

2. The chapter provides a brief discussion of the ethical considerations of research. Can you think of any additional ethical considerations when conducting primary research? Can you think of ethical considerations unique to your own research project?

3. Primary research is most useful for first year writing students if it is based in your local community or campus. What are some current issues on your campus or in your community that could be investigated using primary research methods?

4. In groups or as a class, make a list of potential primary research topics. After each topic on the list, consider what method of inquiry (observation, interview, or survey) you would use to study the topic and answer why that method is a good choice.

Suggested Resources

For more information on the primary methods of inquiry described here, please see the following sources:

Babbie, Earl. *The Practice of Social Research.* 10th edition. Wadsworth Publishing, 2003. Print.

Creswell, John. *Research Design: Qualitative, Quantitative, and Mixed Methods Approaches.* 3rd ed. Thousand Oaks, CA: Sage Publications, 2008. Print.

Rubin, Herbert and Irene Rubin. *Qualitative Interviewing: The Art of Hearing Data.* 2nd edition. Thousand Oaks, CA: Sage Publications, 2004. Print.

Fink, Arlene. *How to Conduct Surveys: A Step-by-Step Guide.* 4th ed. Thousand Oaks, CA: Sage Publications, 2008. Print.

Sanger, Jack. *Compleat Observer? A Field Research Guide to Observation.* New York: Routledge, 1996. Print.

The National Commission for the Protection of Human Subjects of Biomedical and Behavioral Research. *The Belmont Report.* 18 April 1979. Web. http://ohsr .od.nih.gov/guidelines/belmont.html.

Works Cited

Babbie, Earl. *The Practice of Social Research.* 10th ed. Belmont, CA: Wadsworth Publishing, 2003. Print.

Creswell, John. *Research Design: Qualitative, Quantitative, and Mixed Methods Approaches.* 3rd ed. Thousand Oaks, CA: Sage Publications, 2008. Print.

Shadish, William, Thomas, Cook and Donald Campbell. *Quasi-Experimentation: Design and Analysis Issues.* Boston, MA: Houghton Mifflin Company, 1979. Print.

Darwin, Charles. *On the Origin of Species by Means of Natural Selection.* New York: L Hurst and Company, No date. Print.

Lauer, Janice and William Asher. *Composition Research: Empirical Designs.* Oxford: Oxford University Press, 1988. Print.

Leavitt, Fred. *Evaluating Scientific Research: Separating Fact from Fiction.* Long Grove, IL: Waveland Press, 2004. Print.

Mead, Margaret. *Growing Up in New Guinea: A Comparative Study of Primitive Education.* New York: Morrow, 1930. Print.

Mill, John Stuart. *John Stuart Mill's Philosophy of Scientific Method.* Ernest Nagel, Ed. New York: Hafner Publishing Co, 1950. Print.

Rubin, Herbert and Irene Rubin. *Qualitative Interviewing: The Art of Hearing Data.* 2nd ed. Thousand Oaks, CA: Sage, 2004. Print.

✳ Questions and Activities for Chapter 6

1. In what ways are qualitative research methods, which are used to gain an understanding of people, different from quantitative research methods? When is it more advisable to use qualitative or field methods instead of quantitative methods?

2. According to researchers Bonnie Stone Sunstein and Elizabeth Chiseri-Strater, in their book *FieldWorking: Reading and Writing Research*, in qualitative research "we shed hypotheses that close down study" and instead "step into the worldview of others" (p. 237). In your own words, explain what this means and why this is an important frame of mind to adopt when conducting field or hands-on research.

3. When you conduct qualitative research, you will sometimes need to have the participants in your research sign an Informed Consent form. Look at "Obtaining Permission to Conduct Research with People and Sample Informed Consent Form" in Appendix C. What information do participants need to have in order to provide informed consent to participate in your research? When might it be appropriate not to secure informed consent from the people involved in your research? Compare your answers to the discussion of informed consent in *The Belmont Report*: http://www.hhs.gov/ohrp/humansubjects/guidance/belmont.html#xinform.

4. As you saw in Chapter 2, the first step of any project is to do as much reading as possible to educate yourself about your subject, so you must do a literature review

to explore relevant published material and to find gaps in current knowledge. (A literature review, despite its name, doesn't refer to literary works but rather to the articles and information already published about a particular topic.) Using your instructor's suggestions and those at http://www.unc.edu/depts/wcweb/handouts/ literature_review.html, get started on a literature review for your upcoming hands-on research project.

5. To prepare for the hands-on or field research project, many instructors will ask you to create an annotated bibliography—a report of the background reading you've already done. See Chapter 3 and Appendix C for information about annotated bibliographies, and get started on writing a first draft of yours.

6. Once your instructor has assigned a hands-on or field research project, develop a detailed plan for your research. Since a plan for a qualitative research study differs in certain ways from that of a traditional research proposal, review "A Model of the Process of Conducting Qualitative Research and Data Analysis" in this chapter, and answer each of the bulleted questions posed in the model. (Answer "Not Applicable" [N/A] to any question that does not apply to your project.) By the time you are finished with this activity, you will have a well thought-out research plan for your instructor to review.

7 Conducting Interviews, Observations, and Surveys

Published documents aren't the only source of information for a research project. Nor are they always the best. Publications — such as books, articles, Web sites, or television reports — offer someone else's interpretation of an event or an issue. By relying on another person's interpretation, you're looking through that person's eyes rather than through your own.

Experienced research writers know that you don't have to use published reports to find out how an event or issue has affected people — you can ask the people yourself. You don't have to view television or radio coverage of an event — you can go to the event yourself. And you don't have to rely on someone else's survey of public opinion — you can conduct your own.

What's My Purpose?

Your preparations for using field research methods will be most effective if you clearly understand your purpose for carrying out your research project and your purpose for using field research. Before committing yourself to designing and administering a survey, for example, ask yourself what kind of results you can expect to gain and what role those results will play in your project. Ask as well whether a certain field research method is the best technique for gaining that information, or whether you might gain it more effectively and efficiently in another way.

How Can I Use Interviews to Collect Information?

Interviews — in which one person seeks information from another — can provide firsthand accounts of an event, authoritative interpretations of events and issues, and reactions to an event or issue from the people who have been affected by it. Most interviews follow a question-and-answer format, but some more closely resemble a free-flowing discussion. You can conduct interviews face to face, over the telephone, via email, and even through an instant messaging program.

Decide Whether to Conduct an Interview

Thinking carefully about the role an interview might play in your research project can help you decide whether and how to conduct it.

Check out Appendix C, Work-in-Progress Research and Writing Activities, to find additional practical suggestions to help you read, research, and write successfully.

Chapter 7, "Conducting Interviews, Observations, and Surveys," is taken from Mike Palmquist, *The Bedford Researcher*, Third Edition, pp. 150–61 (Chapter 11, "Searching for Information with Field Research Models").

Sometimes the decision to interview is a natural extension of the kind of work you're doing. For example, although student writer Alexis Alvarez was able to find plenty of information from other sources about the pressures that would lead adolescent female athletes to use performance-enhancing drugs, she decided to interview friends and family members who had played competitive sports because she knew that firsthand reports would strengthen her argument. Sometimes interviews are conducted because an issue is so current that little authoritative information is available to a writer. Conducting an interview can provide needed information about the issue.

Sometimes the decision to conduct an interview isn't so much the result of careful planning as it is the recognition of an available opportunity. Pete Jacquez, a student who created a Web site about wind-generated electrical power, learned that one of his friends had recently signed up for a wind power program offered by his university. His interviews produced a personal perspective about wind power that he wouldn't have been able to find through print or electronic sources.

Plan Your Interview

The most important things to consider as you plan your interview are whom to interview and what to ask.

Deciding Whom to Interview. Your decisions about whom to interview should be based on the kind of information you want for your research project.

- If you're trying to better understand a specific aspect of a conversation, interview an expert in the field.

- If you want to learn what people in general think about an issue, interview a number of people who are affected by the issue.

- If you're hoping to collect quotations from people who are authorities on a subject, interview someone who will be recognized as an authority.

Once you've decided what sorts of people you want to interview, you'll need to identify and contact interview candidates. If you're working on a research project for a class, ask your instructor and classmates for suggestions. Then ask whether they can introduce you to the people they suggest. Before you call to set up an interview, make some preparations.

1. Write a script to help you remember what to say.

2. Prepare a list of dates and times that work for you.

3. Estimate how much time you'll need to complete the interview.

4. Be ready to suggest a location for the interview.

5. Leave your phone number or email address so that your interview candidate can get in touch with you if a conflict arises.

Deciding What You Should Ask. Your interview questions should focus on the issue you want to address in your project. As you prepare your questions, keep the following principles in mind.

1. *Consider your research question, the role you are adopting, and the kind of information you want to collect.* Are you seeking background information, or do you want someone's opinion? An answer to the question, "How did this situation come about?" will be quite different from an answer to the question, "What do you think about this situation?"

2. *Ask questions that require more than a yes or no answer.* You'll learn much more from an answer to a question such as, "What factors will affect your vote on referendum X?" than from an answer to, "Will you vote for referendum X?"

3. *Prepare a limited number of main questions and many follow-up questions.* Good interviews seldom involve more than eight to ten main questions, but experienced interviewers know that each question can lead to several follow-up questions.

4. *Be flexible.* Be prepared to tailor your follow-up questions to the interviewee's responses.

Conduct Your Interview

Consult the following checklist before you conduct your interview.

✔ **Arrive early and review your questions.** If you are conducting your interview over the phone, set time aside before the call to review your questions and then call the person you are interviewing at the agreed-upon time.

✔ **Introduce yourself and ask for permission to record the interview.** Explain why you are conducting the interview. Ask for permission to record and use quotes from the interview.

Checklist for Conducting Interviews

@ Find a list of Web sites about conducting interviews at **bedfordresearcher.com**. Click on **Links > Resources for Conducting Field Research**.

✔ **Set up and test your recording equipment.** Ideally, use an audio or video recorder to make a complete record of your interview. At a later time, you can review what was said and carefully transcribe exact quotations from the tape.

✔ **Ask your questions clearly and be ready to respond with follow-up questions.** Allow the person you are interviewing a chance to answer your questions fully. Don't insist on strictly following your list of interview questions; if discussion naturally flows in another, useful direction, be prepared to shift your line of questioning.

✔ **Take notes, even if you are using a video or audio recorder.** A set of handwritten notes will serve as a backup if there are technical glitches and will help you remember ideas you had during the interview. You should write down key points made during the interview as well as any important ideas that come to mind.

✔ **Be alert for related sources mentioned in the interview.** If specific sources that might be relevant to your research writing project are mentioned during the interview, ask for copies of those sources, or for the exact titles and where you might find them.

✔ **Leave your contact information when the interview is over.** Provide a way for the person you interviewed to reach you to change or add anything to his or her comments.

✔ **Send a thank-you note.** Let the person you interviewed know how much you appreciated the opportunity to learn from him or her.

How Can I Use Observation to Collect Information?

Like interviewing, observing a setting can provide you with valuable information you would not be able to find in other sources. Although some observations can involve a significant amount of time and effort, an observation need not be complicated to be useful.

Decide Whether to Conduct an Observation

The most important decision you'll make regarding an observation is whether to conduct it in the first place. Some topics are more suited for observation than others. For example, before writing his multimodal essay on the resurgence of metal music, student writer Chris Norris observed musicians and fans at two concerts. Observing gave Chris insights that he couldn't have gained simply by reading about metal music or interviewing musicians and fans.

Plan Your Observation

As you plan your observation, determine the following:

What You Should Observe and How Often You Should Observe It. If, for example, you've decided to observe children in a day-care center, you'll quickly learn that there are not only many day-care providers in your community but also several different kinds of providers. Clearly, observing a large day-care center won't tell you much about what happens in a small center operated out of a home. In addition, there's no guarantee that what you'll see in one day-care center on any given day will be typical. Should you conduct multiple observations? Should you observe multiple types of day-care providers?

The answers to these questions will depend largely on what role the information you collect during your observations will play in your research writing project. If you want to learn more about the topic but don't plan to use anything you observe as a source of evidence in your project, then you might want to conduct a fairly limited observation. If you decide to use evidence from your observations throughout your project, then you will need to conduct multiple observations, possibly in more than one setting.

What to Look For. The biggest limitation of observation is that you can see only one thing at a time. Experienced observers focus their observations on activities that are most relevant to their research projects. As a result, their observations are somewhat selective. Spreading yourself too thin will result in fairly "thin" results. Then again, narrowing in too quickly can mean that you miss important aspects of the setting. Your reasons for conducting an observation and what you hope to gain from it are probably your best guide to what to focus on.

Whether You Need Permission to Observe. Seeking permission to observe someone can be complicated. People have expectations about privacy, but people can (and often do) change their behavior when they know they are being observed. As you consider whether to ask for permission, imagine yourself in the position of someone who is being observed. If you are still uncertain, ask your instructor for advice.

> @ Find a list of Web sites about conducting observations at **bedfordresearcher.com**. Click on **Links > Resources for Conducting Field Research**.

Conduct Your Observation

You'll find a number of similarities between collecting information in an interview and collecting information during an observation. The checklist that follows will help you conduct your observation.

Checklist for Conducting Observations

✔ **Arrive early.** Give yourself time to get prepared.

✔ **Review your planning notes.** Remind yourself what you're looking for and how you will record your observations.

✔ **Introduce yourself.** If you have asked for permission to observe a setting (such as a class or a day-care center), introduce yourself before you begin your observation. Use your introduction as an opportunity to obtain signatures or consent forms if you need them.

✔ **Set up your recording equipment.** You'll certainly want to make sure you've got a notepad and pens or pencils. You might also have an audio or video recorder, a laptop computer, or a handheld, such as a Palm or Pocket PC. Test whatever you've brought with you to make sure it's working properly.

✔ **Take notes.** As with interviews, take notes during your observation even if you're using an audio or video recorder. Noting your impressions and ideas while conducting an observation can help you keep track of critical events. In addition, if your recorder doesn't work as expected, a set of notes can mean the difference between salvaging something from the observation and having to do it all over again. If you find yourself in a situation where you can't take notes—such as at a swimming lesson, when you're taking part in the lesson—try to write down your thoughts about what you've observed immediately after the session.

✔ **Leave contact information and send thank-you notes.** If you have asked someone for permission to observe the setting, give the person a way to contact you, and send a thank-you note after you have completed the observation.

How Can I Use Surveys to Collect Information?

Surveys allow you to collect information about beliefs, attitudes, and behaviors from a group of people. Typically, surveys help you answer *what* or *who* questions—such as "Who will you vote for in the next election?" Surveys are less useful in obtaining the answers to *why* questions. In an interview, for instance, you can ask, "Why did you vote the way you did in the last election?" and expect to get a reasonably well-thought-out answer. In a survey, however, people often neglect to write lengthy, careful responses. If you conduct a survey, remember to include a copy of your survey questions in an appendix to your project document.

Decide Whether to Conduct a Survey

Your decision about whether to conduct a survey should be based on the role it will play in your research project, the amount of work required to do a good job, and the kind of information you are seeking. In many cases, you'll find that other field research methods are more appropriate than surveys. Surveys are useful if you want to collect information about the attitudes and behaviors of a large group of people (more than five or ten). If you simply want opinions from a handful of people, you can gain that information more efficiently by interviewing or corresponding with them.

Plan Your Survey

As you plan your survey, determine the following:

Whom to Survey. You must decide whom and how many people to survey. For instance, if you're interested in what students in a specific class think about an issue, survey all of them. Even if the class is fairly large (say, one hundred students), you probably won't have too much trouble tabulating the results of a brief survey. Keep in mind, however, that most surveys aren't given to everyone in a group. National polls, for instance, seldom survey more than one thousand people, yet they are used to assess the opinions of everyone in the country. So how will you select your representative sample? One way is to choose people from the group at random. You could open your school's telephone book and then pick, say, every twentieth name. Another option is to stratify your sample. For example, you could randomly select a specific number of first-year, second-year, third-year, and fourth-year students—and you could make sure that the number of men and women in each group is proportional to their enrollment at the school.

@ Find a list of Web sites about conducting surveys at **bedfordresearcher.com**. Click on Links > Resources for Conducting Field Research.

What to Ask and How to Ask It. Designing effective surveys can be challenging. Understanding the strengths and weaknesses of the kinds of questions that are frequently asked on surveys is a good way to get started. Figure 7.1 illustrates the main types of questions found on surveys.

Election Survey

Thank you for completing this survey.

A 1. Did you vote in the last presidential election? ☐ Yes ☐ No

2. I vote:

In every election	In most elections	In about half of the elections	Rarely	Never
☐	☐	☐	☐	☐

B 3. I have voted in the following types of elections (check all that apply):
☐ Regular local elections
☐ Special local elections
☐ Regular statewide elections
☐ National elections

C 4. Voting is a civic duty: ☐ True ☐ False

D 5. All eligible voters should participate in local, state, and national elections:

Strongly Agree	Agree	Not Sure	Disagree	Strongly Disagree
☐	☐	☐	☐	☐

6. Please rate the following reasons for voting on a 1-to-5 scale, in which 5 indicates very important and 1 indicates not at all important:

	1	2	3	4	5
To be a good citizen	☐	☐	☐	☐	☐
To have a say in how government affects my life	☐	☐	☐	☐	☐
To support a particular cause	☐	☐	☐	☐	☐
To vote against particular candidates	☐	☐	☐	☐	☐

E 7. Please rank the following types of elections from most important (4) to least important (1):
_____ Presidential elections
_____ Statewide elections
_____ Local (city and county) elections
_____ Student government elections

F 8. Please tell us what influenced your decision to vote or not vote in the last election.

↳ **Figure 7.1 Sample Survey**

A Yes/no items divide respondents into two groups.

B Multiple-choice items indicate whether a respondent knows something or engages in specific behaviors. Because they seldom include every possible answer, be careful when including them.

C True/false items more often deal with attitudes or beliefs than with behaviors or events.

D Likert scales measure respondents' level of agreement with a statement, their assessment of something's importance, or how frequently they engage in a behavior.

E Ranking forces respondents to place items along a continuum.

F Short-answer items allow greater freedom of response, but can be difficult to tabulate.

How Do I Write a Good Survey Question?

Developing a good survey question is challenging. The process is similar to writing an essay. The first drafts of survey questions serve to express your thoughts. Subsequent revisions help clarify questions for survey respondents. Keep your purpose in mind to be sure your question will elicit the information you need.

In this example, Chris Norris devised a survey question to find out how fellow students view heavy metal music.

1 Write a first draft of the question:

Do you listen to heavy metal music and why or why not?

2 Simplify the question:

Why do you listen — or not listen — to heavy metal music?

3 Consider alternative ways of asking a question — including whether it should be a question:

What are your reasons for listening — or not listening — to music by heavy metal bands like Slayer and Pantera?

4 Identify and then clarify key words and phrases:

List five words to describe music by heavy metal bands like Slayer and Pantera.

5 Ask for feedback from potential respondents. Review and clarify key words and phrases. Consider potential reactions to phrasing:

Please describe your reaction when you hear a song by heavy metal bands like Slayer or Pantera.

Review another example and work on refining survey questions at **bedfordresearcher.com**. Click on Interactive Exercises.

Whether You Are Asking Your Questions Clearly. Test your survey items before administering your survey by asking your classmates or family members to read your questions. A question that seems perfectly clear to you might cause confusion to someone else. Try to rewrite the questions that confuse your "testers" and then test them again. Doing so will help you improve the clarity of your survey. Consider the evolution of the following question.

Original Question
What can be done about voter turnout among younger voters?

Revised Question
In your opinion, what can be done to increase turnout among 18- to 24-year-old voters?

> Does "about voter turnout" mean increasing voter turnout, decreasing voter turnout, or encouraging younger voters to be better informed about candidates? Does the phrase "younger voters" mean 18-year-olds or 30-year-olds?

Conduct Your Survey

The sheer number of surveys people are asked to complete these days has reduced the public's willingness to respond to them. In fact, a "good" response rate for a survey is 60 percent, and many professional pollsters find lower response rates acceptable. The checklist that follows can help you achieve a reasonable response rate.

Checklist for Conducting Surveys

✔ **Keep it short.** Surveys are most effective when they are brief. Don't exceed one page.

✔ **Format and distribute your survey appropriately.** If your survey is on paper, make sure the text is readable, there is plenty of room to write, and the page isn't crowded with questions. If you are distributing your survey through email, you can either insert the survey questions into the body of your email message or attach the survey as a word processing file. If you are distributing your survey on the Web, you can

- code your survey so that survey responses are added to a database (if you can create Web pages of this kind or know someone who can).

- ask respondents to copy the text on the page and paste it into an email message that they then send to you.

- link a word processing file containing your survey to a Web page and ask respondents to fill it out and return it to you as an email attachment.

- ask respondents to print the survey and fax or mail it back to you.

✔ **Explain the purpose of your survey.** Explaining who you are and how you will use the results of the survey in your research writing project can help increase a respondent's willingness to complete and return your survey.

✔ **Treat survey respondents with respect.** People respond more favorably when they think you are treating them as individuals rather than simply as part of a mailing list. When possible, use first-class stamps on surveys sent through the mail and, when appropriate, address potential respondents by name in cover letters or email messages.

✔ **Make it easy to return the survey.** If you are conducting a survey through the mail, be sure to include a stamped, self-addressed envelope. If you are conducting your survey on the Web or via email, be sure to provide directions for returning completed surveys.

Analyze Your Results

Once you've collected your surveys, you must tabulate your responses. It's usually best to tabulate survey responses using a spreadsheet program, which provides flexibility when you want to analyze your results. You can also organize the results in a table in a word processing program. Once you've tabulated the responses, spend time analyzing the results. You should look for trends in your data. For example, ask whether groups respond differently on particular questions, or whether age or experience seems to predict responses. Look as well for surprising results, such as unexpectedly high levels of agreement or disagreement with Likert-scale items or striking differences in the responses to short-answer questions.

How Can I Use Correspondence to Collect Information?

Correspondence includes any textual communication, such as letters, faxes, and email. Correspondence can also take place through real-time communication using chat or instant messaging. If you use chat or instant messaging, be sure to save a record—or transcript—of the exchange.

Although many research writers benefit from corresponding with experts, correspondence need not be sent only to experts. If you are writing an article about the effects of recent flooding in the Midwest, you could correspond with relatives, friends, or even strangers to ask them about their experiences with the floods. You can use their responses to illustrate the impact of the flood on average folks. You can also correspond with staff at government agencies, corporations, and organizations. Many of these institutions hire public relations personnel to respond to inquiries from the public.

Courtesy is essential when corresponding. Introduce yourself and explain the goals of your research project. Make sure that you are clear and ask specific questions.

Thank your reader and indicate that you look forward to hearing from him or her. If you decide to send a letter via regular mail, include a self-addressed, stamped envelope to increase your chances of getting a response.

How Can I Use Public Events and Broadcast Media to Collect Information?

Public events, such as lectures, conferences, and public meetings and hearings, often provide research writers with useful information. As with observations, you can record many public events by taking notes or bringing an audio or video recorder. Be aware, however, that it is unethical to record events that specifically ask that you not do so. If you are asked not to record an event, find out whether a transcript, podcast, or video recording of the event will be available.

Radio and television are sources of information that research writers frequently overlook. News and information programs on television, such as *Nightline* and *60 Minutes*, might provide useful information about the conversation you plan to join. You may want to record the programs in order to examine them in detail. In addition, check the Web for radio programs and transcripts. National Public Radio's news information program *All Things Considered*, for instance, has audio archives going back to January 1996 that you can listen to on the Web (visit npr.org and search the program's archives). You can also record local public events that are broadcast on public access cable channels or streamed over the Web.

In Summary: Conducting Interviews, Observations, and Surveys

+ **Plan and conduct interviews (p. 197).**

+ **Plan and conduct observations (p. 200).**

+ **Design, conduct, and analyze a survey (p. 202).**

+ **Use correspondence to collect information (p. 207).**

+ **Attend public events and view broadcast media to gather information about your issue (p. 208).**

Analyzing Qualitative Research Data

As mentioned in the Chapter 6 section "A Model of the Process of Conducting Qualitative Research and Data Analysis," any qualitative or hands-on research project cannot be complete without analyzing the information or data that is gathered. After all, there isn't any way to answer a research question without looking at the information collected from field observations, interviews, or surveys and drawing some conclusions from it.

David Thomas (2003, p. 2),[1] a social science researcher, describes the purposes of qualitative data analysis as follows:

1. To condense extensive and varied raw text data into a brief, summary format.

2. To establish clear links between the research objectives and the summary findings derived from the raw data and to ensure these links are both transparent (able to be demonstrated to others) and defensible (justifiable given the objectives of the research).

3. To develop a model or theory about the underlying structure of experiences or processes which are evident in the text (raw data).

The information that follows in the remainder of this chapter is an excerpt from the work of British researchers Celia Taylor and Graham Gibbs (2005).[2] They discuss how to categorize or code data gathered from field research in order to come to reliable conclusions that address a research question.

How and What to Code

CODING

Coding is the process of combing the data for themes, ideas, and categories and then marking similar passages of text with a code label so that they can easily be retrieved at a later stage for further comparison and analysis. Coding makes it easier to search the data, to make comparisons, and to identify any patterns that require further investigation.

---

[1]Thomas, D. R. (2003). A general inductive approach for qualitative data analysis. Retrieved June 14, 2008, from http://www.health.auckland.ac.nz/hrmas/resources/Inductive2003.pdf. (We have used APA reference style throughout this chapter because it is the standard format used by social sciences researchers who conduct qualitative research. Also, the original spellings have been retained.)

[2]Taylor, C., & Gibbs, G. R. (2005). Complete beginner. *Online QDA*. Retrieved June 14, 2008, from http://onlineqda.hud.ac.uk/Intro_QDA/how_what_to_code.php. Used by permission. (Minor changes, deletions, and adaptations have been made to the original to achieve consistency with this textbook.)

Codes can be based on:

- Themes, Topics,
- Ideas, Concepts,
- Terms, Phrases, or
- Keywords found in the data.

Usually it is passages of text that are coded, but it can be sections of an audio or video recording or parts of images. All passages and chunks that are coded the same way—that is, given the same label—have been judged (by the researcher) to be about the same topic, theme, or concept.

The codes are given meaningful names that give an indication of the idea or concept that underpins the theme or category. Any parts of the data that relate to a code topic are identified with the appropriate label. This process of coding (associating labels with the text, images, or the like) involves close reading or inspection of the text, video, or images. If a theme is identified from the data that does not quite fit codes already established, then a new code is created.

As the researcher reads through the data, the number of codes he or she has established will evolve and grow as more topics or themes become apparent. The list of codes thus will help to identify the issues contained in the data set.

APPROACHES TO STARTING CODING

It is possible to start coding with themes identified from *a priori* ideas such as pre-existing theories, or you can just simply let new codes emerge from your data as you read it (grounded codes).

A Priori Codes. These can be identified from a range of sources:

- Previous research or theory
- Research or evaluation questions you are addressing
- Questions and topics from your interview schedule
- Your gut feeling about the data or the setting

Grounded Codes. Grounded codes emerge from the data because you put aside your prejudices, presuppositions, and previous knowledge of the subject area and concentrate instead on finding new themes in your data.

WHAT TO LOOK FOR WHEN YOU ARE CODING

Most typically, when coding, researchers have some codes already in mind and are also looking for other ideas that seem to arise out of the data. When coding in this second, open-minded manner, Charmaz (2003, pp. 94–95) suggests you ask the following questions about the data:

- What is going on?
- What are people doing?
- What is the person saying?
- What do these actions and statements take for granted?
- How do structure and context serve to support, maintain, impede, or change these actions and statements?

A more detailed list of the kinds of things that can be coded is in the chart below:

\ Types of Phenomena That Can Be Coded		
No.	**What Can Be Coded**	**Examples from Data**
1.	Behaviours, specific acts	Seeking reassurance; bragging
2.	Events — short, once-in-a-lifetime events or things people have done that are often told as a story	Wedding day; day moved out of home for university; starting first job
3.	Activities — these are of a longer duration, involve other people within a particular setting	Going clubbing; attending a night course; doing conservation work
4.	Strategies, practice, or tactics	Being nasty to get dumped; staying late at work to get promotion
5.	States — general conditions experienced by people or found in organizations	Hopelessness: "I'll never meet anyone better at my age"; settling for someone who is not really suitable
6.	Meanings — A wide range of phenomena at the core of much qualitative analysis.	
	Meanings and interpretations are important parts of what directs participants' actions.	
	a. What concepts do participants use to understand their world? What norms, values, and rules guide their actions?	The term "chilling out" is used by young people to mean relaxing and not doing very much
	b. What meaning or significance [something] has for participants: how do they construe events; what are their feelings?	Jealousy: "I just felt, why did she get him?"
	c. What symbols do people use to understand their situation? What names do they use for objects, events, persons, roles, setting, and equipment?	A Ph.D. is referred to as "a test of endurance" (because finishing a Ph.D. is a challenge)

7.	Participation — adaptation to a new setting or involvement	About new neighbors: "In my new house I have to keep my music down at night as the neighbors have young children."
8.	Relationships or interaction	Seeing family: "Now my sister lives in the next road; she visits more and we've become much closer."
9.	Conditions or constraints	Loss of job (before financial difficulties); moving away (before lost contact with old friends)
10.	Consequences	Confidence gets dates; positive attitude attracts opportunities
11.	Settings — the entire context of the events under study	University; workplace; housing estate
12.	Reflexive — researcher's role in the process, how intervention generated the data	Probing question: "How did you feel when he said that?"

Adapted from Bogdan & Biklen, 1992; Strauss, 1987; Mason, 1996; and Gibbs, 2006.

THE "CONSTANT COMPARISON" METHOD

Many writers make suggestions about the ways you can approach your data so that you remain open-minded about what can be coded and start to notice significant patterns in the data. Perhaps the most famous are those made by the grounded theorists.

The most common procedure they recommend is **constant comparison**. What this means is that every time you select a passage of text (or its equivalent in video or other data) and code it, you should compare it with all those passages you have already coded that way. [. . .] This ensures that your coding is consistent and allows you to consider the possibility either that some of the passages coded that way don't fit as well (and might therefore be better coded as something else), or that there are dimensions or phenomena in the passages that might well be coded another way. [. . .]

OTHER TECHNIQUES TO IDENTIFY THEMES AND CODES

Ryan and Bernard (2003) suggest a number of ways in which researchers coding interview transcripts or field notes can discover new themes in their data. Drawing heavily on Strauss and Corbin (1990), their strategies include:

- **Word repetitions.** Look for commonly used words and words whose close repetition may indicate emotions.

- **Key-words-in-context.** Look for the range of uses of key terms in the phrases and sentences in which they occur.

- **Compare and contrast.** This is essentially the grounded theory idea of constant comparison. Ask, "What is this about?" and "How does it differ from the preceding or following statements?"

- **Social science queries.** Introduce social science explanations and theories, for example, to explain the conditions, actions, interaction, and consequences of phenomena.

- **Searching for missing information.** Try to get an idea of what is not being done or talked about but which you would have expected to find.

- **Metaphors and analogies.** People often use metaphor to indicate something about their key, central beliefs about things, and these may indicate the way they feel about things too. [. . .]

- **Unmarked text.** Examine the text that has not been coded as a theme or even not at all.

- **Pawing (i.e., handling).** Eyeball or scan the text. Circle words, underline, use colored highlighters, or run colored lines down the margins to indicate different meanings and coding. Then look for patterns and significances.

- **Cutting and sorting.** Use the traditional technique of cutting up transcripts and collecting everything coded the same way into piles, envelopes, or folders or pasting them onto cards. Laying out all these scraps and re-reading them, together, is an essential part of the process of analysis. [. . .]

ORGANIZING CODES INTO A "CODING FRAME" OR "CODING LIST"

As well as marking the transcript or field notes to show what is coded as what, you should keep a separate list of the codes you have constructed, and beside each one write a short definition. Next time you find a passage you think can be coded with an existing code, you can see if it exists in your frame or list, and if it does, check with the definition to be sure that it does fit there. If you can't find an appropriate code (there isn't one or the text doesn't fit with the definitions) then you can create a new one.

Eventually, you will have a large number of codes, and you will find it necessary to sort them into some sort of order or into groups. One way to do this is using a hierarchy. You may find several codes group together as types or kinds of something. In that case move them together and put them in a list of their own. [. . .]

APPLYING NEW CODES

As you code the data you are likely to create new codes, so you therefore need to go back and check the units of data you coded previously. This is to check if there are any more data that should be coded under a newly created code.

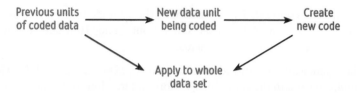

⌐ **Diagram to show how new codes should be applied to previously coded data.**

It is important to apply all your codes to the whole data set because:

- Something you come across later on may change how you want to code the data; or

- You may not notice a new pattern in the data until you have coded a number of interviews. [. . .]

MEMOS AND CODES

It is important to keep written notes that are meaningful to you during your coding process. These notes are often called memos. A major use for memos is to record longer definitions of the codes and to note any analytic thoughts you have about the significance and relationship to others of the code in question.

Typically, information you could incorporate into the memo about a code will include:

- Why you have created the code

- Some detail of what the code is about and what the coded text reveals

- Why you have changed a code (for instance, re-named it)

- Thoughts and questions about the analysis that occur to you as you code. [. . .]

SUMMARY

- Coding involves categorizing and indexing sections or chunks of your data.

- Codes can come from theory and explanations "outside the data" and/or "emerge from the data."

- Coding often starts by being descriptive but needs to become analytical.

- Any new codes created should be applied to the whole data set (previously coded units of data).

- Memos should be used to record your thoughts and ideas about your codes during the process.

REFERENCES[3]

Bogdan, R., & Biklen, S. K. (1992). *Qualitative research for education.* Boston: Allyn and Bacon.

Charmaz, K. (2003). Grounded theory. In J. A. Smith (Ed.), *Qualitative psychology: A practical guide to research methods* (pp. 81–110). London: Sage.

Gibbs, G. (2006). *Analyzing qualitative data.* London: Sage.

Mason, J. (1996). *Qualitative researching.* London: Sage.

Ryan, G. W., & Bernard, H. R. (2003). Techniques to identify themes. *Field Methods, 15*(30), 85–109.

Strauss, A. (1987). *Qualitative analysis for social scientists.* Cambridge: Cambridge UP.

Strauss, A., & J. Corbin. (1990). *Basics of qualitative research: Grounded theory procedures and techniques.* Newbury Park, CA: Sage.

[3]Note again that APA style is used here because it is the standard reference format for social science research.

✱ Sample Student Summary of Field Observations and Interviews

Marcos Loe

Ms. Fedukovich

English 102

27 Sept. 2010

While at college, students learn so much in their specific fields of study. More important, they also learn about themselves and how to deal with responsibilities, stress, time management, pressures, and social networking. One way in which they might cope is to ignore pressures, and become detached. Some individuals escape with music and a pair of headphones. These "Pod People" are those who listen to the iPod portable media player in public. They are often found involved in any activity that does not need one's undivided attention, such as walking, working, lifting weights, and studying. Why must they have a soundtrack to their life? What makes them special?

To learn more about the "Pod People," I observed students walking between classes during one of the busiest times of the day. At the University of Tennessee, I staked out the Pedestrian Mall during the lunch rush. Among the hundreds of students walking, I observed on average about one Pod Person to seven other students. While watching the Pod People, I noticed an obvious characteristic: they typically do not engage socially. The Pod Person is a loner. I tried to determine whether there was a dominant gender of Pod People but found there was not. While my observation notes show there were more males than females using iPods, the number was not significant enough to conclude there is any gender dominance. I wonder if the slightly higher number of male

Loe 2

iPod users is because males are stereotypically categorized as "gear heads" and are more interested in technological gadgets than females. Yet, my actual observations don't support the idea that females don't appreciate technology, as many could be observed talking on their cell phones. Perhaps this suggests females are more social than males, which may be why they are either on the phone or talking with others as opposed to hooking into an iPod.

After observing, analyzing, and thinking about the obvious characteristics of the Pod People, I was left wondering why people insist on listening to the iPod in public. To explore this question, I interviewed random Pod People in search of an answer and simply asked them "Why do you listen to your iPod?" The Pod People say they usually listen to music between classes and while walking around campus and on average listen for about one to two hours daily. Most of them say they listen to get away from the stresses and pressures of school. For example, one student, David Robinson,[1] said "It keeps me chill," a response that most people can relate to. Some also say they listen while working out, to pump up their adrenaline. I interviewed Dennis Canter, a music performance/education major, and asked why he listens in public, and he answered, "Why not? Music is amazing. It is a great way to release emotions."

The college-student Pod People are an interesting subculture. They believe in trends and follow the new tech-gadgets, which they use to escape the stress of college life. The population of Pod People is as vast and dynamic as the music it plays. The Pod People are not a traditional subculture. They say they simply enjoy music and just try to get through the day like everybody else. The interesting aspect of this subculture is what is playing through their heads and why. Try not to ask them, though, as they will probably not hear you!

[1]Pseudonyms are used throughout.

✳ Sample Student Interview Transcript

Karen Wolf, Interviewer, with Multiple Interview Participants

1   **Interviewer:** How does language differ in the workplace?

2   **Sam:** My language at work is exceptional. At work you have to sound like you know

3   something, but at home they already know that you do. I have to be professional.

4   **Interviewer:** Do you change your language for different people?

5   **Sam:** It all depends. It depends on who I'm talking to and what I'm talking

6   about. I do talk on different levels. It's just like teaching a second grader a

7   math problem compared to teaching a high schooler. For a second grader, I

8   would use popsicle sticks to show what three plus three equals. If I speak to

9   another accountant I don't have to clarify. When I'm talking to a co-worker

10   about accounting, I have to break it up so they can easily understand.

11   **Interviewer:** How does language differ in the workplace?

12   **Carolyn:** At work I talk more grammatically correct. I want to impress the pub-

13   lic by sounding professional and knowledgeable about the company. When

14   someone calls I want to sound like I know exactly what I'm doing. I'm sup-

15   posed to speak with a smile on my face so that the customers won't know if

16   I'm having a bad day. At home I'm more relaxed.

17   **Interviewer:** How does language change in the workplace?

18   **John:** During the meeting we have to be professional. We have to speak formally

19   and conduct ourselves appropriately. Our respectful manner toward the auditor

20   is for the sole purpose that she takes us and the whole company seriously. Now

21   that we have spoken with meeting jargon, let's get back to men jargon.

22   **Interviewer:** Why is it important to alter your language at work?

23   **Tom:** The significance of altering language is to blend in better. My goal at

24   work is to make others feel accepted. Whether I change my dialect, my diction,

25   or my tone, it is for the intention of making others feel comfortable in a pro-

26   fessional atmosphere. I speak to their (employees') same level.

✱ Questions and Activities for Chapter 7

1. During a class period, you and your classmates will formulate a research question and then take a short "field trip" to a nearby campus site to collect some data to answer your question. Your instructor may have already selected a site to visit, or you may determine the site during a class discussion before you go. The place you select should be easily accessible, and there should be people at the site doing something that anyone may observe.

a. Before you leave your classroom, read and discuss with your classmates the passage below. The teacher of a 200-level sociology class at the University of Wisconsin–Madison gives this to her students when they are about to do field research. She says,

> When I say you should talk about and analyze a social setting, I mean tell me about the physical setting, the people and more specifically the roles that are being played by the actors in the setting. Who is in charge, who tells whom what to do, what are the ages, genders, races of these players, and do you see any patterns in these structured role relationships? Tell me what things are surprising or unexpected, but (more difficult) tell me "obvious" things that are going on. Include people's non-verbal communication, use of body language, clothing, everything. One of the tasks of doing field research is to discover interesting patterns in the "taken for granted" of everyday life.
>
> — J. A. Piliavin. "Writing a Journal and Taking Field Notes." *The Social Science Computing Cooperative.* 14 June 2008 http://www.ssc.wisc.edu/~jpiliavi/236/JOURNAL_FIELDNOTES.htm

Briefly discuss what one is looking for when the research question is so broadly stated: "What's happening in this setting?" What do you think the sociology teacher means when she says that it is "more difficult" to take field notes about the "obvious things"?

b. At the top of a piece of notebook paper, write down the following open-ended research questions, "What's happening in [the selected setting]?" and "What's important about what's going on in [the selected setting]?" These questions will guide your collection of field data, and you'll return to them when you analyze your field notes.

c. Now, with your class, go to your selected site, and spend about fifteen minutes writing down what you see. The key is to be as specific and detailed in your note-taking as possible. (For example, what does the setting look like? Describe the place; you may want to sketch a map of its layout. What are the people in the setting doing? Write down what you observe: the way people look, their actions, what they are saying, and the like. Take note of people's nonverbal communication, body language, and gestures also. What other sounds or sights do you notice?)

d. When you return to your classroom, the first thing to do is label your field notes—identify the site and the date. Keep these original notes separate from any additional notes you may make and analysis you may do about this site. Your field notes are primary data and should be preserved so that you always have the original observations you made.

e. In class, share the details of what you observed. Your instructor may write some of these on the board. You should write each detail mentioned by others in *your* notebook as well, on a separate page—not on your original field notes— since those details may help with the process of analyzing and coding the data later.

f. Write a summary of the situation, events, and actions you observed. That is, tell the story of what happened in the site. Connect your observations with the research question, "What's important about what is happening in this setting?" (See "How to Take Field Notes" in Appendix C and the "Sample Student Summary of Field Observations and Interviews" on p. 216 for more information.)

2. Conduct a field observation by visiting "The Rock." Start with the research question "How is the Rock used on UTK's campus?" Go to the Rock one, two, or three times. (If you're not able to visit the Rock in person, you can see several pictures of it at http://www.utk.edu/therock/.) Take descriptive field notes of what you observe. Pay particular attention to the Rock's location, what it looks like, what is written on it, what materials are used to write/mark on it. Also, observe the people who look at the Rock and note their actions and reactions. After conducting one or more field observations, write a summary of your observations that answers the original research question. (See "How to Take Field Notes" in Appendix C and the "Sample Student Summary of Field Observations and Interviews" on p. 216 for more information.)

3. Conduct a field observation by riding the KAT bus. Start with the research question "What are the characteristics of the people who ride one of the West Knoxville bus routes?" Go to the bus stop on the corner of James Agee and Cumberland Avenue (on the north side of Cumberland Avenue). Take Bus #10 and ride until it returns to campus. You'll need to have correct bus fare ($1.50); you can find more

information about schedules, routes, and fares at the KAT Web site: http://www.katbus.com/ADA/index.php. While on the bus, record your observations in your notebook. Pay particular attention to people — their general appearance, dress, behavior, overheard public conversations. When you are finished, write a summary of your observations that answers the original research question. (See "How to Take Field Notes" in Appendix C and the "Sample Student Summary of Field Observations and Interviews" on p. 216 for more information.)

4. To create an online survey, try using one of the links below. Be sure to consider the issues outlined in the section "How Can I Use Surveys to Collect Information?" (p. 202) and "How to Create a Survey" and "Revise Your Interview or Survey Questions" in Appendix C before you distribute your survey.

http://freeonlinesurveys.com

http://tjshome.com/survey/createsurvey.php

5. Run a pilot test of your survey. This exercise asks you to discuss a draft of your survey with a classmate — to pilot-test it before you ask others to complete it. See Appendix C, "How to Create a Survey" and "Revise Your Interview or Survey Questions."

a. In your own words, summarize your research question, explaining your research to your classmate. Your research question is the main question you hope to answer with your survey.

b. Ask your classmate to read your survey to see if it seems it will provide the feedback needed to answer your research question. Make note of your classmate's responses.

c. Ask your classmate if all the questions/survey items are clear. Could any questions be misread or misunderstood? How might you revise those questions?

d. Based on your conversation with your classmate and your own developing understanding of your research, make revisions to your survey.

6. Interview a member of your class whom you do not know well, and write a brief portrait of that person based on your interview.

a. You might want to start by asking where that person is from, what her or his initial experiences of UT have been like, why that person has come to college, what her or his major is, and so forth. Make notes, paying attention to both physical and verbal details.

b. Based on your interview, write a brief portrait of the person (no more than two pages).

c. Exchange portraits with the person you interviewed so that each interview respondent has a chance to see how she or he was represented and to change any details if needed.

d. Reflect on your experience of interviewing and writing about someone. What worked? What was interesting or fun about the interview? What was hard? What did you find out about note-taking? How did you record your observations? What was it like to work with the information from your respondent? What was it like to write about someone knowing that she or he will read it?

7. Before you conduct a research interview, print out copies of your interview questions. Then, sit down with another member of your class and exchange copies of your interview questions. Explain to each other what your research questions are. Then answer the following questions about each other's interview questions. (Also see Appendix C for several activities related to creating and evaluating interview questions.)

a. Do all of the questions relate to the research question? Which ones might need to be left out or changed? If some need to be changed, what suggestions do you have for revising them?

b. Consider whether the questions use language that seems clear and the interview participants can understand. Suggest revisions if you think any are needed.

c. If any of the questions are closed-ended, suggest revisions to turn those into open-ended questions.

d. Do all of the questions use neutral language? If there are any leading questions, how can you revise them?

e. Are the questions in a good order? How might you rearrange the questions?

f. What questions might you add to the list? Come up with at least two questions your partner might consider using.

8. Define qualitative data analysis and coding. Why must researchers go through a data analysis process? In your own words, how does qualitative data analysis or coding of data compare with other types of analysis you've done, such as literary or rhetorical analysis? Describe the "constant comparison" method of coding data.

9. Once you have observed a situation or setting and collected some field notes in the effort to answer a research question, your job is to code the details from your notes—that is, to find some patterns or themes in the data in order to come to some answers to your research question(s). Be aware, though, that it may take a while to determine some groupings, categories, or themes from your data. Your instructor may ask you to do this exercise in class, in groups, or on your own.

a. Take out the original field notes you wrote while observing a setting. Make sure you also have your original research question(s).

b. Now, using some of the categories in the column "What Can Be Coded" from the chart in this chapter—or categories that you create on your own—look through your notes in order to code or analyze them. You would create your own categories by finding *repeated* activities, events, or actions that you observed in the setting.

c. On a separate piece of paper, make a chart like the one shown in the chapter, listing the categories, or codes, and the details from your field notes. This process could take some time—it's not easy to find patterns in field data!

d. Once you have coded your data and categorized the information into a chart, the next step is to answer the question: What categories of data, and the details within those categories, provide answers to your research question?

e. Write a research report in which you present your answer(s) to your research question(s), and in which you refer to specific details from your field note data to defend or support your answer. (See the "Sample Student Summary of Field Observations and Interviews" on p. 216 or "A Template for Writing Up Qualitative Research" in Appendix C.)

10. To do a thorough analysis of interview data, complete the following steps to assign codes to an interview transcript.

a. Transcribe a passage (up to one page) from an interview you conducted. (See the "Sample Student Interview Transcript" on p. 218 and "How to Transcribe an Interview" in Appendix C.)

b. Moving line by line through your transcript, identify codes. It may not have been possible to transcribe all of your data, but if you recorded it, you should listen to the interview several times, stopping and starting as you need to when you recognize a code or theme. In your notes, be sure to mark down the time (minute/seconds) in the interview tape where each coded detail is mentioned.

c. From this preliminary coding, what patterns seem to be emerging from your interview data? Write a summary of your preliminary findings. (See the "Sample Student Summary of Field Observations and Interviews" on p. 216 for one way to summarize initial findings.)

11. Colorado State University maintains an excellent Web site that helps students with writing. One part of their site discusses "Content Analysis" of research data and offers a step-by-step process for coding textual data. This could be especially useful for coding interview transcripts.

a. Go to http://writing.colostate.edu/guides/research/content/.

b. Read the introduction to "Content Analysis," and then scroll down to "Methods of Conceptual Analysis." Now, remind yourself of your research question, reread the transcript, and then complete the eight steps described.

c. If you are able, you may also want to try a "relational analysis," the next item on the Writing@CS site.

d. Also, we recommend that you take a look at the sample analyses that are featured on the site.

12. Analyze survey data you collected for a qualitative research project. Once you've collected the completed surveys, tabulate all the responses according to the item and the number of responses under each. (You may want to use a spreadsheet program such as Excel, which will help you make charts of the responses.) Once you've tabulated your data, look over the responses to determine how they offer answers to your research question. To do this, make sure you don't simply count and report responses; you must try to draw conclusions about what the responses mean in terms of your research problem and research question. (See "Create a Visual Presentation of Survey Data" in Appendix C for suggestions for creating charts that present data.)

13. In your final write-up of your research, be sure to explain your data analysis methods. In his article "A General Inductive Model for Qualitative Data Analysis," David Thomas (2003, p. 5, cited earlier) provides a few examples of how researchers write about the methods they used to analyze their data. Use any of his examples, which follow, as models when you write about your research methods in your hands-on research paper.

The transcripts were read several times to identify themes and categories. [. . .] In particular, all the transcripts were read by AJ and a subsample was read by JO. After discussion a coding frame was developed and the transcripts coded by AJ. If new codes emerged the coding frame was changed and the transcripts were reread according to the new structure. This process was used to develop categories, which were then conceptualized into broad themes after further discussion. The themes were categorized into three stages: initial impact, conflict, and resolution.

> —Jain, A., & Ogden, J. (1999). General practitioners' experiences of patients' complaints: A qualitative study. *British Medical Journal, 318*, 1596–1599.

Emerging themes (or categories) were developed by studying the transcripts repeatedly and considering possible meanings and how these fitted with developing themes. Diagrams were used to focus on what was emerging and to link patient and doctor themes into major barriers to referral. Transcripts were also read "horizontally," which involved grouping segments of text by theme. Towards the end of the study no new themes emerged, which suggested that major themes had been identified.

> —Marshall, M. N. (1999). Improving quality in general practice: A qualitative case study of barriers faced by health authorities. *British Medical Journal, 319*, 164–167.

A rigorous and systematic reading and coding of the transcripts allowed major themes to emerge. Segments of interview text were coded, enabling an analysis of interview segments on a particular theme, the documentation of relationships between themes and the identification of themes important to participants. Similarities and differences across sub-groups (e.g., service providers vs. individuals, recent vs. long-term migrants) were also explored.

> —Elliott, S. J., & Gillie, J. (1998). Moving experiences: A qualitative analysis of health and migration. *Health & Place, 4(4)*, 327–339.

PART FOUR

Research Using Secondary Sources

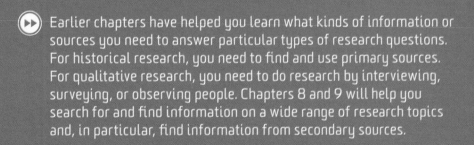 Earlier chapters have helped you learn what kinds of information or sources you need to answer particular types of research questions. For historical research, you need to find and use primary sources. For qualitative research, you need to do research by interviewing, surveying, or observing people. Chapters 8 and 9 will help you search for and find information on a wide range of research topics and, in particular, find information from secondary sources.

In Chapter 8, "An Introduction to Research Using Secondary Sources," Randall McClure's essay "Googlepedia: Turning Information Behaviors into Research Skills" gives examples of how you can take the search behaviors you use in Google and Wikipedia and then apply those behaviors (with a few adjustments) to search for scholarly materials in the library. Chapter 9, "Conducting Secondary Source Research," will help you learn some of the search modifications you will need in order to use library resources successfully and efficiently.

8 An Introduction to Research Using Secondary Sources

Knowing how to identify the sources you need and then how to find those sources are vital research skills, part of a concept known as "information literacy." As this chapter explains, people who are information literate know what kinds of information they need to answer a question and can efficiently search for and find information, evaluate information to determine credibility and relevance to the question, and answer their question using the credible information they found. Information-literate people also recognize the need to use information ethically and legally (for example, by citing their sources).

Before you read the rest of the chapter to learn why secondary source research is important and how best to do it, there are a few terms that are helpful to know. First, it is important to know the definition of *secondary sources*: materials that analyze and interpret primary sources. Scientists conducting experiments use the data they gather as primary source material; then they report their methods, discussions, and conclusions in scholarly articles. The scholarly articles in which they report their findings are secondary sources. Historians also write secondary sources. Books and scholarly articles that interpret diaries, photographs, newspaper articles, and other historical records (primary sources) are secondary sources.

Secondary sources make up the majority of published works. There are many types of secondary sources, and the following information should help you distinguish among different kinds of secondary sources that you might use in your research projects and that you will find in the UT Libraries' online and print collections.

Types of Secondary Sources

Scholarly Sources

Books. Of course, not all books are scholarly; however, if the author is a researcher at a university or research institute, the material is probably scholarly. Look at the name of the publisher—a university press is often a good indication that the material is scholarly.

> **Check out Appendix C, Work-in-Progress Research and Writing Activities,** to find additional practical suggestions to help you read, research, and write successfully.

Peer-Reviewed Articles from Scholarly/Academic Journals. Articles appear in periodicals, which are published at fixed intervals throughout the year and include newspapers, magazines, and scholarly journals. The articles that are published in scholarly journals (sometimes known as academic journals) are called "peer-reviewed." This means that the author—a scholar or academic at a university or research institute—has submitted his or her work to a group of peers (other scholars and academics) who have vetted the work. Peer-reviewed articles undergo more rigorous scrutiny and examination than popular articles, which are published in magazines and newspapers.

Popular Sources

Books. Books that express opinions or are not written by a scholar or academic are popular sources.

Magazine Articles. Examples of magazines include *Time*, *Sports Illustrated*, *Ladies' Home Journal*, *National Geographic*, the *New Yorker*, the *Nation*, and many others. Magazines are popular sources that you can easily find in bookstores.

Newspaper Articles. Examples of newspapers include the *Knoxville News Sentinel*, the *Daily Beacon*, the *Chicago Tribune*, the *Atlanta Journal Constitution*, and the *New York Times*. Newspapers are popular sources, and some are more credible and authoritative than others.

Reviews (Book Reviews and Film Reviews). Both scholarly and popular sources include book reviews; however, the reviews published in academic journals may still be considered popular sources because these reviews are sometimes not vetted as thoroughly as peer-reviewed articles.

Editorials and Letters to the Editor. Opinion pieces are written by the publication staff of a periodical, or written to the publication staff, about a particular topic.

Knowing which types of sources are appropriate for an assignment and being able to quickly find these sources are signs of a good researcher. However, as the rest of the chapter discusses, the process of becoming a good researcher has changed over time.

Googlepedia: Turning Information Behaviors into Research Skills

RANDALL MCCLURE

Introduction

The ways in which most writers find, evaluate, and use information have changed significantly over the past ten years. A recent study, for example, has shown that as many as nine out of every ten students begin the process of searching for information on the Web, either using a search engine, particularly Google, or an online encyclopedia, notably Wikipedia (Nicholas, Rowlands, and Huntington 7). I believe this finding is true of most writers, not just students like you; the Web is our research home.

To illustrate for you how the Web has changed the nature of research and, as a result, the shape of research-based writing, I trace in this chapter the early research decisions of two first year composition students, Susan and Edward, one who begins research in Google and another who starts in Wikipedia. Part narrative, part analysis, part reflection, and part instruction, this chapter blends the voices of the student researchers with me, in the process of seeking a new way to research.

Please understand that I do not plan to dismiss the use of what I call "Googlepedia" in seeking information. As James P. Purdy writes in his essay on Wikipedia in Volume 1 of *Writing Spaces*, "[Y]ou are going to use [Google and] Wikipedia as a source for writing assignments regardless of cautions against [them], so it is more helpful to address ways to use [them] than to ignore [them]" (205). Therefore, my goal in this chapter is to suggest a blended research process that begins with the initial tendency to use Google and Wikipedia and ends in the university library. While Susan and Edward find Googlepedia to be "good enough" for conducting research, this chapter shows you why that's not true and why the resources provided by your school library are still much more effective for conducting research. In doing so, I include comments from Susan and Edward on developing their existing information behaviors into academic research skills, and I offer questions to help you consider your own information behaviors and research skills.

Randall McClure, "Googlepedia: Turning Information Behaviors into Research Skills." From *Writing Spaces: Readings on Writing*, Volume 2, pp. 221–41.

Understanding Information Literacy

Before I work with you to move your information behaviors inside the online academic library, you need to understand the concept of information literacy. The American Library Association (ALA) and the Association of College and Research Libraries (ACRL) define information literacy as "a set of abilities requiring individuals to recognize when information is needed and have the ability to locate, evaluate, and use effectively the needed information" (American Library Association). The ACRL further acknowledges that information literacy is "increasingly important in the contemporary environment of rapid technological change and proliferating information resources. Because of the escalating complexity of this environment, individuals are faced with diverse, abundant information choices" (Association of College and Research Libraries). In short, information literacy is a set of skills you need to understand, find, and use information.

I am certain that you are already familiar with conducting research on the Web, and I admit that finding information quickly and effortlessly is certainly alluring. But what about the reliability of the information you find? Do you ever question if the information you find is really accurate or true? If you have, then please know that you are not alone in your questions. You might even find some comfort in my belief that conducting sound academic research is more challenging now than at any other time in the history of the modern university.

Writing in a Googlepedia World

Teachers Tiffany J. Hunt and Bud Hunt explain that the Web-based encyclopedia Wikipedia is not just a collection of Web pages built on *wiki* technology,[1] it is a Web-based community of readers and writers, and a trusted one at that. Whereas most student users of Wikipedia trust the community of writers that contribute to the development of its pages of information, many teachers still criticize or disregard Wikipedia because of its open participation in the writing process, possible unreliability, and at times shallow coverage (Purdy 209), since "anyone, at any time, can modify by simply clicking on an 'edit this page' button found at the top of every Web entry" (Hunt and Hunt 91). However, the disregard for Wikipedia appears to be on the decline, and more and more users each day believe the "information is trustworthy and useful because, over time, many, many people have contributed their ideas, thoughts, passions, and the facts they learned both in school and in the world" (91). Wikipedia and Google are so much a part of the research process for writers today that to ignore their role and refuse to work with these tools seems ludicrous.

Still, the accuracy and verifiability of information are not as clear and consistent in many sources identified through Wikipedia and Google as they are with sources found in most libraries. For this reason, I am sure you have been steered away at least once from information obtained from search engines like Yahoo and Google as well as online encyclopedias like Answers.com and Wikipedia. Despite the resistance that's out there, Alison J. Head and Michael Eisenberg from *Project Information Literacy* report from their interviews with groups of students on six college campuses that "Wikipedia was a unique and indispensible research source for students . . . there was a strong consensus among students that their research process began with [it]" (11). The suggestion by Head and Eisenberg that many students go to Google and Wikipedia first, and that many of them go to these Web sites in order to get a sense of the big picture (11), is confirmed in the advice offered by Purdy when he writes that Wikipedia allows you to "get a sense of the multiple aspects or angles" on a topic (209). Wikipedia brings ideas together on a single page as well as provides an accompanying narrative or summary that writers are often looking for during their research, particularly in the early stages of it. Head and Eisenberg term this Googlepedia-based information behavior "presearch," specifically preresearching a topic before moving onto more focused, serious, and often library-based research.

The concept of presearch is an important one for this chapter; Edward's reliance on Wikipedia and Susan's reliance on Google are not research crutches, but useful presearch tools. However, Edward and Susan admit they would not have made the research move into the virtual library to conduct database-oriented research without my intervention in the research process. Both students originally viewed this move like many students do, as simply unnecessary for most writing situations.

TALKIN' BOUT THIS GENERATION

Wikipedia might be the starting point for some writers; however, Google remains the starting point for most students I know. In fact, one group of researchers believes this information behavior—students' affinity for all things "search engine"—is so prominent that it has dubbed the current generation of students "the Google Generation." Citing not only a 2006 article from *EDUCAUSE Review* but also, interestingly enough, the Wikipedia discussion of the term, a group of researchers from University College London (UCL) note the "first port of call for knowledge [for the Google Generation] is the [I]nternet and a search engine, Google being the most popular" (Nicholas, Rowlands, and Huntington 7). In other words, the UCL researchers argue that "students have already developed an ingrained coping behavior: they have learned to 'get by' with Google" (23). I believe we all are immersed and comfortable in the information world created by Googlepedia, yet there is much more to research than this.

Despite the fact that it would be easy and understandable to dismiss your information behaviors or to just tell you never to use Google or Wikipedia, I agree with teacher and author Troy Swanson when he argues, "We [teachers] need to recognize that our students enter our[college] classrooms with their own experiences as users of information" (265). In my attempt though to show you that research is more than just a five-minute stroll through Googlepedia, I first acknowledge what you already do when conducting research. I then use these behaviors as part of a process that is still quick, but much more efficient. By mirroring what writers do with Googlepedia and building on that process, this essay will significantly improve your research skills and assist you with writing projects in college and your professional career.

THE WIKIPEDIA HOAX

At this point in the chapter, let me pause to provide an example of why learning to be information literate and research savvy is so important. In his discussion of the "Wikipedia Hoax," Associated Press writer Shawn Pogatchnik tells the story of University College Dublin student Shane Fitzgerald who "posted a poetic but phony" quote supposedly by French composer Maurice Jarre in order to test how the "Internet-dependent media was upholding accuracy and accountability." Fitzgerald posted his fake quote on Wikipedia within hours of the composer's death, and later found that several newspaper outlets had picked up and published the quote, even though the administrators of Wikipedia recognized and removed the bogus post. The administrators removed it quickly, "but not quickly enough to keep some journalists from cutting and pasting it first."

It can safely be assumed these journalists exhibited nearly all of the information behaviors that most teachers and librarians find disconcerting:

- searching in Wikipedia or Google

- power browsing quickly through Web sites for ideas and quotes

- cutting-and-pasting information from the Web into one's own writing without providing proper attribution for it

- viewing information as free, accurate, and trustworthy

- treating online information as equal to print information

Of course, it is impossible to actually prove the journalists used these behaviors without direct observation of their research processes, but it seems likely. In the end, their Googlepedia research hurt not only their writing, but also their credibility as journalists.

Edward, Susan, and Googlepedia

Edward and Susan are two students comfortable in the world of Googlepedia, begin-ning and, in most cases, ending their research with a search engine (both students claimed to use Google over any other search engine) or online encyclopedia (both were only aware of Wikipedia). Interestingly, Edward and Susan often move between Google and Wikipedia in the process of conducting their research, switching back and forth between the two sources of information when they believe the need exists.

For an upcoming research writing project on the topic of outsourcing American jobs, Susan chooses to begin her preliminary research with Google while Edward chooses to start with Wikipedia. The students engage in preliminary research, re-search at the beginning of the research writing process; yet, they work with a limited amount of information about the assignment, a situation still common in many college courses. The students know they have to write an argumentative essay of several pages and use at least five sources of information, sources they are required to find on their own. The students know the research-based essay is a major assign-ment for a college course, and they begin their searches in Googlepedia despite the sources available to them through the university library.

EDWARD

Edward begins his research in Wikipedia, spending less than one minute to find and skim the summary paragraph on the main page for "outsourcing." After reading the summary paragraph[2] to, in Edward's words, "make sure I had a good understanding of the topic," and scanning the rest of the main page (interestingly) from bottom to top, Edward focuses his reading on the page section titled "criticism." Edward explains his focus,

> Since I am writing an argumentative paper, I first skimmed the whole page for ideas that stood out. I then looked at the references for a clearly opinionated essay to see what other people are talking about and to compare my ideas [on the subject] to theirs, preferably if they have an opposing view.

This search for public opinion leads Edward to examine polls as well as skim related Web pages linked to the Wikipedia page on outsourcing, and Edward quickly settles on the "reasons for outsourcing" in the criticism section of the Wikipedia page. Edward explains, "I am examining the pros of outsourcing as I am against it, and it seems that companies do not want to take responsibility for [outsourcing]."

It is at this point, barely fifteen minutes into his research, that Edward returns to the top of the Wikipedia main page on outsourcing to reread the opening summary on the topic, as I stop him to discuss the thesis he is developing on corporate responsibility for the outsourcing problem. We discuss what I make of Edward's early research; Edward relies on Wikipedia for a broad overview, to verify his understanding on a subject.

Presearch into Research

Analysis: Some teachers and librarians might argue against it, but I believe starting a search for information in Wikipedia has its benefits. It is difficult enough to write a college-level argumentative essay on a topic you know well. For a topic you know little about, you need to first learn more about it. Getting a basic understanding of the topic or issue through an encyclopedia, even an online one, has been a recommended practice for decades. Some librarians and teachers question the reliability of online encyclopedias like Wikipedia, but this is not the point of the instruction I am offering to you. I want you to keep going, to not stop your search after consulting Wikipedia. To use it as a starting point, not a final destination.

Recommendation: Deepen your understanding. Formulate a working thesis. Reread the pages as Edward has done here. This is recursive preliminary research, a process that will strengthen your research and your writing.

After our brief discussion to flush out his process in conducting research for an argumentative essay, I ask Edward to continue his research. Though he seems to identify a research focus, corporate responsibility, and working thesis — that American corporations should be held responsible for jobs they ship overseas — Edward still chooses to stay on the outsourcing page in Wikipedia to search for additional information.

He then searches the Wikipedia page for what he believes are links to expert opinions along with more specific sources that interest him and, in his approach to argumentative writing, contradict his opinion on the subject. Unlike Susan who later chooses to side with the majority opinion, Edward wants to turn his essay into a debate, regardless of where his ideas fall on the spectrum of public opinion.

Research and Critical/Creative Thinking

Analysis: Edward's reliance on Wikipedia at this point is still not a concern. He is starting to link out to other resources, just as you should do. I, however, suggest that you spend more time at this point in your research to build your knowledge foundation. Your position on the issue should become clearer with the more you read, the more you talk to teachers and peers, and the more you explore the library and the open Web.

Recommendation: Keep exploring and branching out. Don't focus your research at this point. Let your research help focus your thinking.

Staying in Wikipedia leads Edward to texts such as "Outsourcing Bogeyman" and "Outsourcing Job Killer." Edward explains that his choices are largely based on the titles of the texts (clearly evident from these examples), not the authors, their credentials, the Web sites or sources that contain the texts, the URLs, or perhaps their domain names (e.g., .org, .edu, .net, .com)—characteristics of Web-based sources that most academic researchers consider. Even though Edward acknowledges that the source of the "Bogeyman" text is the journal *Business Week*, for example, he admits selecting the text based on the title alone, claiming "I don't read [*Business Week*], so I can't judge the source's quality."

Research and Credibility

Analysis: Understanding the credentials of the author or source is particularly important in conducting sound academic research and especially during the age of the open Web. We live in a world where most anyone with an Internet connection can post ideas and information to the Web. Therefore, it is always a good idea to understand and verify the sources of the information you use in your writing. Would you want to use, even unintentionally, incorrect information for a report you were writing at your job? Of course not. Understanding the credibility of a source is a habit of mind that should be practiced in your first year composition course and has value way beyond it.

Recommendation: Take a few minutes to establish the credibility of your sources. Knowing who said or wrote it, what credentials he or she has, what respect the publication, Web site, or source has where you found the ideas and information, and discussing these concepts with your peers, librarian, and writing teacher should dramatically improve the essays and reports that result from your research.

What Edward trusts are the ideas contained in the text, believing the writer uses trustworthy information, thereby deferring source evaluation to the author of the text. For example, Edward comments on the "Job Killer" text, "After reading the first three paragraphs, I knew I was going to use this source." Edward adds that the convincing factor is the author's apparent reliance on two studies conducted at Duke University, each attempting to validate a different side of the outsourcing debate and the roles of corporations in it. From Edward's statement, it is clear he needs help to better understand the criteria most scholars use for evaluating and selecting Web-based sources:

- Check the purpose of the Web site (the extension ".edu," ".org," ".gov," or ".com" can often indicate the orientation or purpose of the site).

- Locate and consider the author's credentials to establish credibility.

- Look for recent updates to establish currency or relevancy.

- Examine the visual elements of the site such as links to establish relationships with other sources of information. (Clines and Cobb 2)

A Text's Credibility Is Your Credibility

Analysis: Viewed one way, Edward is trying to establish the credibility of his source. However, he doesn't dig deep enough or perhaps is too easily convinced. What if the studies at Duke, for instance, were conducted by undergraduate students and not faculty members? Would that influence the quality of the research projects and their findings?

Recommendation: Know as much as you can about your source and do your best to present his or her credentials in your writing. As I tell my own students, give "props" to your sources when and where you can in the text of your essays and reports that incorporate source material. Lead-ins such as "Joe Smith, Professor of Art at Syracuse University, writes that . . ." are especially helpful in giving props. Ask your teacher for more strategies to acknowledge your sources.

Edward's next step in his research process reveals more understanding than you might think. Interested in the Duke University studies cited in the "Job Killer" text, Edward moves from Wikipedia to Google in an attempt to find, in his words, "the original source and all its facts." This research move is not for the reason that I would have searched for the original text (I would be looking to verify the studies and validate their findings); still, Edward indicates that he always searches for and uses the original texts, what many teachers would agree is a wise decision. Finding the original studies in his initial Google query, Edward's research move here also reminds us of a new research reality: many original sources previously, and often only, available through campus libraries are now available through search engines like Google and Google Scholar.

After only thirty minutes into his preliminary research, it's the appropriate time for Edward to move his Googlepedia-based approach significantly into the academic world, specifically to the online library.

Before working with Edward to bring his Googlepedia-based research process together with a more traditional academic one, I ask Edward about library-based sources, particularly online databases. His response is the following: "I am more familiar with the Internet, so there is no reason [to use the library databases]. It is not that the library and databases are a hassle or the library is an uncomfortable space, but I can get this research done in bed." Edward's response is interesting here as it conflicts with the many reports that students often find the college library to be an intimidating place. Edward doesn't find the library to be overwhelming or intimidating; he finds the information in it *unnecessary* given the amount of information available via Googlepedia.

But what if researching in the online library could be a more reliable and more efficient way to do research?

SUSAN

Susan begins her research where most students do, on Google. Interestingly, Susan does not start with the general topic of outsourcing, opting instead to let the search engine recommend related search terms. As Susan types in the term "outsourcing," Google as a search engine builds on character recognition software providing several "suggestions" or related search terms, terms that Susan expects to be provided for her, and one—"outsourcing pros and cons"—quickly catches her attention. Commenting on this choice instead of searching by the general concept of outsourcing, Susan notes, "I would have to sort through too much stuff [on Google] before deciding what to do." She selects "pros and cons" from the many related and limiting search terms suggested to her; Susan states, "I want both sides of the story because I don't know much about it."

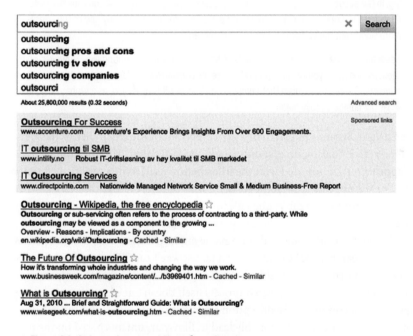

∟ Figure 8.1 Outsourcing suggestions from Google.

Susan next moves into examining the top ten returns provided on the first page of her Google search for outsourcing pros and cons. Doing what is now common practice for most Web users, Susan immediately selects the link for the first item returned in the query. I believe most search engine users are wired this way, even though they are likely familiar with the emphasis given to commercial sites on

Google and other search engines. Quickly unsatisfied with this source, Susan jumps around on the first page of returns, stopping on the first visual she encounters on a linked page: a table illustrating pros and cons. Asked why she likes the visual, Susan responds that she is trying to find out how many arguments exist for and against outsourcing. On this page, Susan notes the author provides seven pros and four cons for outsourcing. This finding leads Susan to believe that more pros likely exist and that her essay should be in support of outsourcing.

"Visual" Research

Analysis: There are at least two points worthy of your attention here. First, Susan's information behavior shows how attracted we all are to visuals (maps, charts, tables, diagrams, photos, images, etc.), particularly when they appear on a printed page or screen. Second, she fails to acknowledge a basic fact of research — that visual information of most any kind can be misleading. In the above example, Susan quickly deduces that more (7 pros vs. 4 cons) means more important or more convincing. Couldn't it be possible that all or even any one of the cons is more significant than all of the pros taken together?

Recommendation: Consider using visuals as both researching and writing aids. However, analyze them as closely as you would a printed source. Also, examine the data for more than just the numbers. It might be a truism that numbers don't lie, but it is up to you, as a writer, to explain what the numbers really mean.

Like Edward, Susan is not (initially) concerned about the credibility of the text (author's credentials, source, sponsoring/hosting Web site, URL or domain, etc.); she appears only concerned with the information itself. When prodded, Susan mentions the text appears to be some form of press release, the URL seems legitimate, and the site appears credible. She fails to mention that the author's information is not included on the text, but Susan quickly dismisses this: "The lack of author doesn't bother me. It would only be a name anyway." Susan adds that her goal is to get the research done "the easiest and fastest way I can." These attitudes — there is so much information available in the Googlepedia world that the information stands on its own and the research process itself doesn't need to take much time — appear to be a common misconception among students today, and the behaviors that result from them could possibly lead to flimsy arguments based on the multiplicity rather than the quality of information.

Research and CRAAP

Analysis: I have referenced criteria for evaluating sources throughout this chapter. If you do not fully understand them, you should consult the resources below and talk with your teacher or a reference librarian.

Recommendation: Learn to put your sources to the CRAAP test (easy to remember, huh?):

- "Currency: The timeliness of the information."
- "Relevance: The importance of the information for your needs."
- "Authority: The source of the information."
- "Accuracy: The reliability, truthfulness, and correctness of the informational content."
- "Purpose: The reason the information exists." (Meriam Library)

For specific questions to pose of your sources to evaluate each of these, visit the Web site for the developers of the CRAAP test at http://www.csuchico.edu/lins/handouts/evalsites.html. Another useful site is http://www.gettysburg.edu/library/research/tips/webeval/index.dot.

Unlike Edward, Susan is not concerned with engaging in a debate on the subject of outsourcing, regardless of her opinions on it. Susan views the assignment as I think many students would, another "get it done" research paper. Further, she believes the majority opinion, at least as it is discussed in the initial source she locates, should be *her* opinion in her essay. Susan explains, "I tend to take the side that I think I can make the stronger argument for . . . If it was a personal issue or an issue I was really interested in, like abortion, I wouldn't do this. This topic doesn't affect me though."

Good Search Terms = Good Research Options

Analysis: Susan needs to understand why being overly reliant on sources uncovered early on in the research process is a problem (particularly here where the search term pros comes before the search term cons likely leading to the results Susan has received). I hope you also share my concerns with the working thesis she appears to be constructing, though I recognize that many students approach research papers just this way.

Recommendation: Improve your research by attempting at least a handful of Web searches using different key terms. If necessary, work with the search phrases and terms provided by the search engine. Also, place your search terms inside quotes on occasion to help vary and focus your search returns. Looking at the subject from different perspectives should help you gain a better sense of the topic and should lead you to a thesis and the development of an essay that is more convincing to your readers.

To her credit, Susan understands the need to validate the information provided by her first source, and she examines the original ten search returns for another text that might indicate the number of advantages and disadvantages to outsourcing. This search behavior of relying on the first page of returns provided by a search engine query has been widely documented, if nowhere else but in the experience of nearly every computer user. When was the last time you went to say the fourth or fifth page of returns on Google? Such a research move contradicts the power browsing nature of most of today's computer users, teachers and students alike. As Susan (perhaps, to some degree, rightly) explains, "The farther away from the first page, the less topic appropriate the articles become." I would contend this might be true of the thirty-seventh page of returns; yet, please understand that you should explore beyond the first page of returns when seeking out information via a search engine. Google your own name (last name first as well) some day to see just how curiously search returns are prioritized.

Next, Susan identifies a subsequent source, www.outsource2india. com. This Web site provides the confirmation that Susan is looking for, noting sixteen pros and only twelve cons for outsourcing. At this point, Susan confirms her process for gathering source material for argumentative essays: she looks for two to three Web-based articles that share similar views, particularly views that provide her with arguments, counterarguments, and rebuttals. Once she has an adequate list of points and has determined which side of a debate can be more effectively supported, Susan refines her Google search to focus on only that side of the debate.

Don't Rush to Argument

Analysis: There are two concerns with Susan's research at this point: (1) her rush to research and (2) her rush to judgment.

Recommendation: In addition to reworking your research process with the help of the ideas presented in this chapter, consider building your understanding of writing academic arguments. In addition to your writing teacher and composition textbook, two sources to consult are http://www. dartmouth.edu/~writing/materials/student/ac_paper/what. shtml#argument and http://www.unc.edu/depts/wcweb/handouts/argument.html#2.

Similar to the way she began searching for information only fifteen minutes earlier, Susan uses Google's "suggestions" to help her identify additional sources that support the side of the debate she has chosen to argue. As she types in "pros outsourcing," Susan identifies and selects "pro outsourcing statistics" from the recommended list of searches provided by Google in a drop-down menu. Like Edward, Susan is interested in validating the points she wants to use in her essay with research studies and scientific findings. Susan comments, "Statistics. Data. Science. They all make an argument stronger and not just opinion." Susan again relies on the first page of search results and focuses on title and URL to make her selections. As she finds information, she copies and pastes it along with the URL to a Word document, noting once she has her five sources with a blend of ideas and statistics together in a Word file that she will stop her research and start her writing.

Track Your Research/Give Props

Analysis: Susan demonstrates here the common information behavior of cutting-and-pasting text or visuals from Web pages. She also demonstrates some understanding of the value of quantitative research and scientific proof. She also appears to use Word to create a working bibliography. These behaviors are far from perfect, but they can be of some help to you.

Recommendation: Learn to use an annotated bibliography. This type of research document will help you with both remembering and citing your sources. For more information on building an annotated bibliography, visit http://www.ehow.com/ how_4806881_construct-annotated-bibliography.html. There are also many software and online applications such as Zotero and RefWorks that can help you collect and cite your sources. Next, make sure to do more than just cut-and-paste the ideas of others and the information you find on the Web into an essay or report of yours.[3] Learn to use paraphrases and summaries in addition to word-for-word passages and quotes. The Purdue OWL, a great resource for all things research and writing, explains options for incorporating research into your own writing: http://owl.english.purdue.edu/owl/resource/563/1/. Finally, realize the value and limitations of statistics/numerical data and scientific findings. This type of research can be quite convincing as support for an argument, but it takes your explanations of the numbers and findings to make it so. You need to explain how the ideas of others relate to your thesis (and don't forget to give props).

EDWARD AND SUSAN: REMIX

As you know by now, I certainly have concerns with Susan's and Edward's research process; however, I recognize that the process used by each of these students is not uncommon for many student researchers. More importantly, each process includes strategies which could be easily reworked in the digital library.

Yes, I am concerned that Susan doesn't recognize that you can find two or three sources on the Web that agree on just about anything, no matter how crazy that thing might be. Yes, I am concerned that Susan opts out of forming an argument that she truly believes in. Yes, I am concerned that both Susan and Edward trust information so quickly and fail to see a need to question their sources. Despite my concerns, and perhaps your own, their Googlepedia-based research process can provide the terms they need to complete the research in more sound and productive ways, and the process can be easily replicated in an online library.

Based on their Googlepedia research to this point, I suggest to Edward that he construct his essay as a rebuttal argument and that he use the search terms "outsourcing" and "corporate responsibility" to explore sources available to him from the library. For Susan, I suggest that she too construct a rebuttal argument and that she use the search string "outsourcing statistics" to explore sources in the university's virtual library. (For more information on writing rebuttal arguments, visit http://www.engl.niu.edu/wac/rebuttal.html.)

Given the influence and value of using search engines like Google and online encyclopedias like Wikipedia in the research process, I recommend the following eight-step research process to move from relying on instinctive information behaviors to acquiring solid research skills:

1. Use Wikipedia to get a sense of the topic and identify additional search terms.

2. Use Google to get a broader sense of the topic as well as verify information and test out search terms you found in Wikipedia.

3. Search Google again using quotation marks around your "search terms" to manage the number of results and identify more useful search terms.

4. Search Google Scholar (scholar.google.com) to apply the search terms in an environment of mostly academic and professional resources.

5. Do a limited search of "recent results or "since 2000" on Google Scholar to manage the number of results and identify the most current resources.

6. Search your college's library research databases using your college library's Web portal to apply the search terms in an environment of the most trusted academic and professional resources.

7. Focus your search within at least one general academic database such as Academic Search Premier, Proquest Complete, Lexis/Nexis Academic Universe, or CQ Researcher to apply the search terms in a trusted environment and manage the number of results.

8. Do a limited search by year and "full text" returns using the same general academic database(s) you used in step 7 to reduce the number of results and identify the most current resources.

I admit that this process will certainly seem like a lot of work to you, but I want to emphasize that Edward and Susan completed this sequence in less than thirty minutes. After doing so, Edward even commented, "If someone had shown me this in high school, I wouldn't be going to Wikipedia and Google like I do." Susan added that even with her search terms, Google still presented challenges in terms of the number of potential sources: "Google had thousands of hits while Galileo might have less than 100." For students who value speed and ease, this remixed process resonated with them, and I believe it will with you.

More importantly, the remixed process addresses some of the concerns that could have hindered the research and writing of both students if they only worked with Googlepedia. By remixing and sequencing research this way, they worked with issues of currency, credibility, accuracy and bias among others, criteria vital to conducting sound research. This is not to say that Susan and Edward failed to understand or could not apply these concepts, particularly given that our research time was limited to sixty minutes total (thirty minutes researching alone plus thirty minutes for cooperative research). However, any student who makes this research move will find a more viable and valuable research path. As Edward said, "[The library sources] produced a narrowed search pattern and created less results based on a more reliable pool from which to pull the information."

The research approach I am suggesting can be quick and easy, and it can also be more connected to the values of researchers and the skills of adept information users. Don't take just my word for it though. Consider Susan's closing comment from the questionnaire she completed after our research session:

> I really hadn't ever thought of using library sources in looking up information because I've always used open Web resources. I now know the benefits of using library sources and how they can simplify my search. I found being able to categorize articles by date and relevancy very helpful . . . I am inclined to change the way I research papers from using the open Web to using library sources because they are more valid and it's as easy to use as Google.

In just a single one-hour-long preliminary research session, Susan and Edward were able to utilize the research behaviors they were comfortable with, were encouraged to continue starting their research in Googlepedia, and learned to remix their behaviors inside the online library. Working on your own or with a teacher or librarian to make the research move from Googlepedia to the library, as I suggest in this chapter, should help to improve the quality of your research and your writing based upon it.

Conclusion

Susan Blum notes that "if we want to teach students to comply with academic norms of [research], it may be helpful to contrast their ordinary textual practices—rich, varied, intersecting, constant, ephemeral, speedy—with the slower and more careful practices required in the academy" (16). Working through the research process as we have in this chapter, we are moving away from *the* research process to a combination of *our* process, as librarians and teachers, with *your* process—a process that blends technological comfort and savvy with academic standards and rigor. I believe this combination makes for an intellectual, real, and honest approach for researching in the digital age. Blum comments, "By the time we punish students, we have failed. So let's talk. These text-savvy students may surprise us" (16). Susan and Edward have done just that for me, and I hope you have learned a little from them, too.

Discussion

1. In the discussion of Edward's preliminary research, several characteristics of a Web-based source that most academic researchers consider are mentioned including the title of the webtext, the author, his or her credentials, the Web site

or source that contains the Web text, the URL, and the domain name (e.g., .org, .edu, .net, .com). What characteristic or characteristics do you examine if any? Which ones do you believe are the most important? Why?

2. Susan mentions that she "would have to sift through too much stuff" when searching for information on Google. Do you agree that Google provides too much information to examine? Why or why not? In addition to Susan's approach of using a search term suggested by Google, what strategies do you have for limiting the information returned to you when seeking information using a search engine?

3. Type your name or your favorite subject into a search engine, such as Google or Yahoo. What do you notice about the search returns? How do the returns appear to be prioritized? From the results you see, consider how the rankings of returns could help and hurt your research for an academic paper if you relied only on a search engine for your information. Discuss your response with a group of classmates.

4. Try working with Susan's search terms in reverse—the "cons" and "pros" of outsourcing. Use a search engine like Google or Yahoo to compare the results when you switch the order of search terms. How are the results for the "cons and pros of outsourcing" similar to and different from the results for the search for the "pros and cons of outsourcing"? Discuss your findings with a group of classmates.

Notes

1. Wikis are Web sites that allow a user to add new Web pages or edit any page and have the changes he or she makes integrated into that page.

2. See pages 209–211 in Purdy for more discussion on the value of Wikipedia in preliminary research.

3. See pages 217–218 in Purdy for an example of a student engaging in written conversation with her sources rather than just "parroting" them.

Works Cited

American Library Association. Presidential Committee on Information Literacy. Chicago: ALA, 1989. Print.

Association of College and Research Libraries. *Information Literacy Competency Standards for Higher Education.* 2000. Web. 17 May 2010.

Blum, Susan D. "Swimming in a Sea of Texts: Attribution in the Age of the Internet." *On Campus.* 29.1 (Sept/Oct 2009): 16. Print.

Clines, Raymond H., and Elizabeth R. Cobb. *Research Writing Simplified: A Documentation Guide.* 6th ed. NY: Pearson, 2010. Print.

Head, Alison J., and Michael B. Eisenberg. *Lessons Learned: How College Students Seek Information in the Digital Age.* U of Washington: Project Information Literacy Progress Report. 1 Dec 2009. Print.

Hunt, Tiffany J., and Bud Hunt. "Research and Authority in an Online World: Who Knows? Who Decides?" *English Journal.* 95.4 (Mar 2006): 89–92. Print.

Meriam Library. "Evaluating Information—Applying the CRAAP Test." California State U, Chico. 29 Sept 2009. Web. 9 Sept 2010.

Nicholas, David, Ian Rowlands, and Paul Huntington. *Information Behaviour of the Researcher of the Future.* 2008. Web. 4 Apr 2009.

Pogatchnik, Shawn. "Student Hoaxes World's Media on Wikipedia." *msnbc. com.* 12 May 2009. Web. 13 May 2009.

Purdy, James P. "Wikipedia Is Good for You!?" *Writing Spaces: Readings on Writing.* Vol. 1. West Lafayette, IN: Parlor P, 2010. 205–224. Print.

Swanson, Troy. "A Radical Step: Implementing a Critical Information Literacy Model." *portal: Libraries and the Academy.* 4.2 (2004): 259–273. Print.

✳ Questions and Activities for Chapter 8

1. Discuss the ethics of using Google and Wikipedia in academic research. In what ways can you use these responsibly? What would be irresponsible ways of using them?

2. Define "information literacy." Describe both the strengths and the gaps in your own information literacy.

3. Why is conducting "sound academic research" so challenging in our times? Discuss the common misconception that research doesn't take much time since information is so readily available.

4. What is "presearch," and why is it valuable?

5. Make a "double-entry notebook" entry (see Appendix C, "Create a Double-Entry Reading Notebook") about the account of Edward and Susan's research process described in the chapter. Write down what their research practices were and also what you think about these practices. Do you agree or disagree with the way they conducted research? What should they have done differently?

6. Once you have collected some sources for a project you're currently working on, put them to the CRAAP test described in the chapter (currency, relevance, authority, accuracy, and purpose). (See the handout at http://www.csuchico.edu/lins/handouts/evalsites.html and the details offered at http://www.gettysburg.edu/library/research/tips/webeval/index.dot for more information on the CRAAP test and evaluating sources.)

7. What's wrong with the "cut-and-paste" method of including source material in a research paper? How can you avoid doing that? (See the Web page suggested in the chapter, http://owl.english.purdue.edu/owl/resource/563/1/, for suggestions on better methods.)

8. For your next research paper, follow the eight steps outlined in the chapter for how to find good sources from the library and Internet for your investigation. As the chapter mentions, starting with Wikipedia or Google is not necessarily a bad thing—it's what comes after that counts! Write out your process in a research log.

9 Conducting Secondary Source Research

How Can I Locate Sources Using Electronic Resources?

Writers can turn to four general sets of electronic resources to locate information about their subjects: library catalogs, databases, the Web, and media search sites. You can search these resources using techniques ranging from simple to advanced searches.

Generate Search Terms and Strategies

Regardless of your choice of electronic resource, the results of your searches will be only as good as your search terms. Even the best search tools can produce poor results—and all too often that's exactly what happens. To increase your chances of obtaining good results, spend time identifying search terms related to your subject and learning about the types of searches you might conduct.

IDENTIFY KEYWORDS AND PHRASES

You can identify useful search terms by building on your research question or thesis statement or by using a range of idea-generating techniques, such as brainstorming, freewriting, looping, and clustering. Student writer Dwight Haynes, for example, used freewriting to generate ideas for his searches. Then he highlighted promising keywords and phrases.

> I'm most interested in finding sources that can help me understand why some approaches to reducing college drinking—and binge drinking in particular, although it's not the only problem (date rape, drunk driving, and falling out of windows or trees, for example, are related to too much drinking)—work better than others. What's been done by schools with successful programs? How much do those programs cost? And why haven't schools made more progress on this problem? Is it just something that college students have to go through? But if that's the case, why do so many students swear off drinking all together—or maybe it's just a case of extremes all around, with some people drinking too much and some people swearing off it even though they wouldn't mind having a beer now and then?

Check out Appendix C, Work-in-Progress Research and Writing Activities, to find additional practical suggestions to help you read, research, and write successfully.

Chapter 9, "Conducting Secondary Source Research," is taken from Mike Palmquist, *Joining the Conversation*, pp. 480–506, 510 (Chapter 12, "Locating Sources").

249

You can also generate search terms by using your research question or thesis statement as a starting point. Student writer Hannah Steiner, for example, typed her research question in a word-processing program, formatted the most important words and phrases in color, and then brainstormed a list of related words and phrases.

What barriers **stand in the way of** widespread use **of** hydrogen fuel **in the** United States?

limits	adoption	"fuel cells"	U.S.
limitations	utilization	"clean energy"	America
obstacles	usage	"hydrogen power"	American
hurdles		"clean power"	
difficulties			
impediment			
expense			

PLAN SIMPLE SEARCHES

Simple searches consist of entering one or more keywords or phrases in a search field and clicking on the search button. A simple search allows to you look for documents that contain a single word or phrase in the subject, title, text, or, in the case of databases, in other parts of a database record (see p. 257 for more information about databases). When you enter one or two words in the search field on Google or in your library catalog, for example, you are conducting a simple search.

Simple searches can return large sets of results. To increase the odds that your results will be relevant to your subject, consider adding keywords, using exact phrases, and using wildcards.

Adding Keywords. In most cases, using several keywords together will limit the number of results returned by your search. This strategy is especially helpful when searching the Web, which can produce thousands (sometimes millions) of hits for individual words or phrases. For example, adding *college* to a search for the keywords *binge* and *drinking* on Google will reduce the number of results by roughly 70 percent. Adding *students* to a search for *binge*, *drinking*, and *college* will reduce it even further. To find out how the search tool you are using treats multiple keywords, consult its help page—or conduct some test searches and review your results.

Searching for Exact Phrases. Sometimes the best way to locate information is to search for an exact phrase. To further refine your search, you might use *binge drinking* and *college students* as phrases. This would eliminate sources in which the words *binge* and *drinking* appear but are separated by other words. The simple search format in

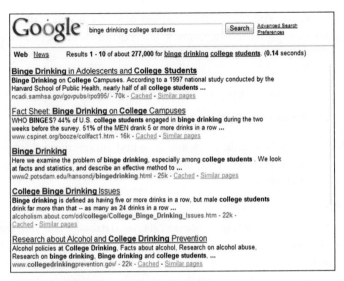

⌐ A Simple Search with Keywords on Google

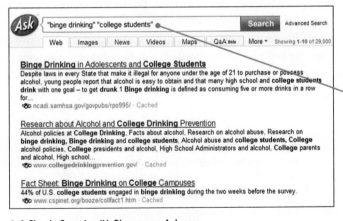

Quotation marks indicate that the words between them should be treated as a phrase.

⌐ A Simple Search with Phrases on Ask.com

many catalogs, databases, and Web search sites permits you to specify phrases using quotation marks.

Using Wildcards. Sometimes you might not be sure what form of a word is most likely to occur. Rather than conducting several searches for *drink, drinking, drinkers, drunk,* and *drunken,* for example, you can combine keywords into a single wildcard search. Wildcards are symbols that take the place of letters or strings of letters. By standing in for multiple letters, they allow you to expand the scope of your search.

The following are the most commonly used wildcard symbols:

* usually takes the place of one or more characters, such as *drink**

? usually takes the place of a single character, such as *dr?nk*

Other wildcard symbols include !, +, #, and $. To find out whether wildcard symbols are supported, consult the help section in a catalog or database or the advanced search page of a Web search engine.

PLAN ADVANCED SEARCHES

In addition to simple searches, most library catalogs, databases, and Web search sites provide an advanced search page. These pages allow you to focus your searches in powerful ways using Boolean operators (which are used to search for all, some, or none of the words in a search box) and search limits (such as publication date and document characteristics).

Focusing Searches with Boolean Operators. Boolean operators let you focus a search by specifying whether keywords or phrases *can, must,* or *must not* appear in the results. Some Boolean operators also allow you to search for keywords or phrases that appear next to, before or after, or within a certain distance from one another in a document. Here is a list of commonly used Boolean operators and their functions.

Boolean Operator	Function	Example
AND/+ (plus)	Finds sources that include both search terms (either keywords or phrases)	hydrogen AND economy
OR	Finds sources that include either search term	energy OR power
NOT/– (minus)	Finds sources that include one search term but not the other	gasoline NOT oil
ADJ (adjacent)	Finds sources in which the search terms appear next to each other	fuel ADJ cells
NEAR	Finds sources in which the search terms appear within a certain number of words of each other (usually twenty-five; depending on the database or search engine, you might be able to change the default setting)	alternative NEAR energy
BEFORE	Finds sources in which search terms appear in a particular order	clean BEFORE power
Parentheses ( )	Although not strictly a Boolean operator, parentheses are used to group search terms and Boolean operators	hydrogen AND (fuel OR energy) AND (economy NOT economics)

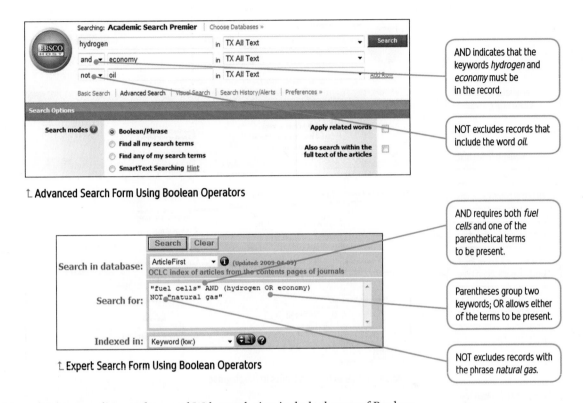

AND indicates that the keywords *hydrogen* and *economy* must be in the record.

NOT excludes records that include the word *oil*.

⌐ Advanced Search Form Using Boolean Operators

AND requires both *fuel cells* and one of the parenthetical terms to be present.

Parentheses group two keywords; OR allows either of the terms to be present.

NOT excludes records with the phrase *natural gas*.

⌐ Expert Search Form Using Boolean Operators

Many databases, online catalogs, and Web search sites include the use of Boolean search terms—typically AND, OR, and NOT or plus (+) and minus (–) signs—in their advanced search forms or in expert search forms.

Limiting Searches. Search limits allow you to limit your searches to documents that have particular characteristics, such as publication date and document type. Although the specific limits that are available in an advanced search form vary across databases, library catalogs, and Web search sites, common limits include publication date (or, in the case of Web pages, the date on which a page was last updated), type of document, and the availability of full text (for databases).

Search Library Catalogs

Library catalogs provide information about the materials in a library's collection. Most libraries provide access to their catalogs through the Web, although some smaller libraries rely on traditional print catalogs. At a minimum, an online catalog will provide information about the author(s), title, publication date, subject heading, and call number for each source in the library's collection. Often it will also indicate the location of the source in the library and whether the source is available for checkout.

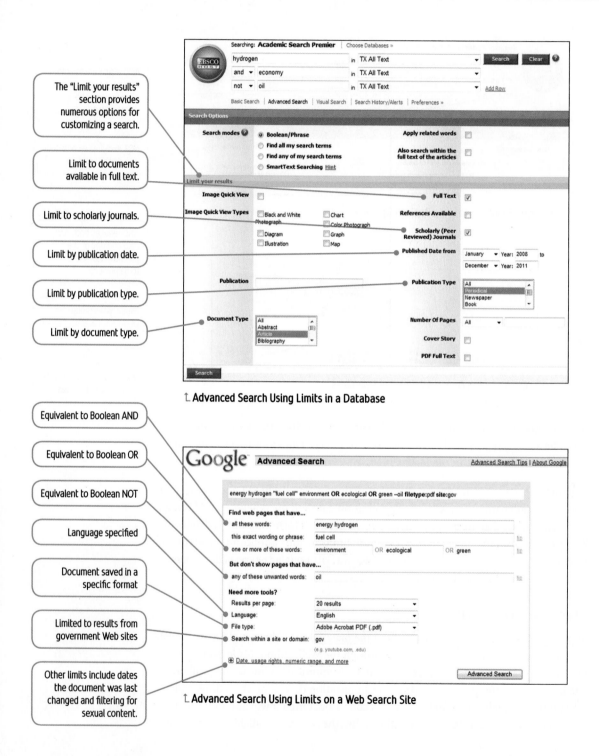

The "Limit your results" section provides numerous options for customizing a search.

Limit to documents available in full text.

Limit to scholarly journals.

Limit by publication date.

Limit by publication type.

Limit by document type.

Advanced Search Using Limits in a Database

Equivalent to Boolean AND

Equivalent to Boolean OR

Equivalent to Boolean NOT

Language specified

Document saved in a specific format

Limited to results from government Web sites

Other limits include dates the document was last changed and filtering for sexual content.

Advanced Search Using Limits on a Web Search Site

Online catalogs typically help you locate

- books

- journals owned by the library (although not individual articles)

- newspapers and magazines owned by the library (although not individual articles)

- documents stored on microfilm or microfiche

- videotapes, audiotapes, and other multimedia items owned by the library

- maps

- theses and dissertations completed by college or university graduate students

Although you can limit your search to the online library catalog at your college or university, you can benefit from searching other catalogs available on the Web. The Library of Congress online catalog (catalog.loc.gov), for example, presents a comprehensive list of publications on a particular subject or by a particular author. Some sites, such as WorldCat (www.worldcat.org), allow you to locate or search multiple online library catalogs. If your library doesn't have a listed publication in its collection, you can request it through interlibrary loan.

Most online library catalogs allow you to search or browse for sources by keywords and phrases, author(s), title, subject, and call number. The following examples illustrate common library catalog searches.

Search by Keyword. You can search for a specific keyword or phrase.

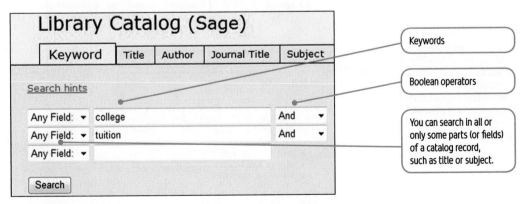

ㄴ **Searching by Keyword**

Search by Author. If you search by author, you can find sources written by a particular person or organization.

Most library catalogs assume that you will enter the last name of the author first, followed by a first name or initial.

Some catalogs allow you to search for sources by entering all or part of a last name. You might be able to use wildcard symbols, such as * or ? (see p. 251).

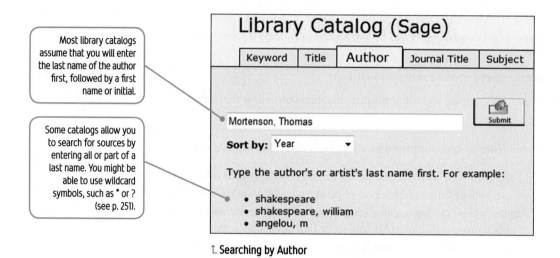

> # Library Catalog (Sage)
>
> | Keyword | Title | **Author** | Journal Title | Subject |
>
> Submit
>
> Mortenson, Thomas
>
> **Sort by:** Year ▾
>
> Type the author's or artist's last name first. For example:
>
> - shakespeare
> - shakespeare, william
> - angelou, m

L Searching by Author

Search by Title. If you know either the exact title of a source or some of the words in the title, you can search by title to find sources.

You can search for a complete or a partial title. Searching for partial titles produces a list of sources whose titles begin with the phrase or word you enter.

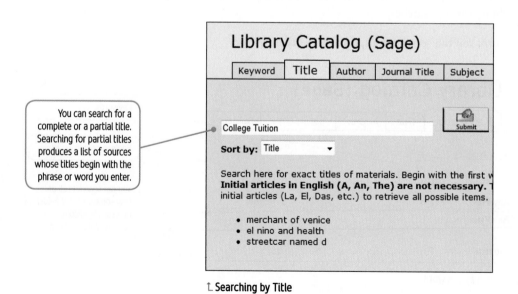

> # Library Catalog (Sage)
>
> | Keyword | **Title** | Author | Journal Title | Subject |
>
> Submit
>
> College Tuition
>
> **Sort by:** Title ▾
>
> Search here for exact titles of materials. Begin with the first w
> **Initial articles in English (A, An, The) are not necessary.**
> initial articles (La, El, Das, etc.) to retrieve all possible items.
>
> - merchant of venice
> - el nino and health
> - streetcar named d

L Searching by Title

Browse by Subject Heading. To locate sources related to a promising result, search by either call number or subject heading.

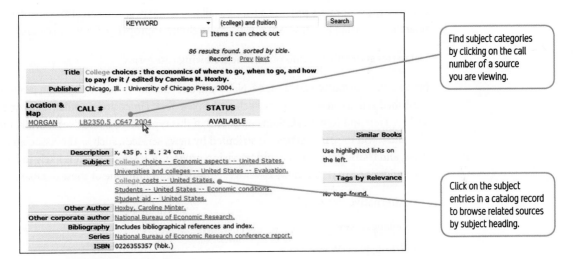

ㄴ Searching by Call Number or Subject Heading

Search Databases

Databases operate much like online library catalogs, although they focus on a different collection of sources. Whereas an online catalog allows you to search for publications owned by the library, a database allows you to search for sources that have been published on a particular topic or in a particular discipline regardless of whether the library owns the sources. Although some databases, such as ERIC (eric.ed.gov), can be accessed publicly through the Web, most are available only through library computers or a library Web site.

Databases supply publication information and brief descriptions of the information in a source; some—but not all—provide electronic copies of the source. Using the citation information provided by the database, you can check your library's online catalog for the title of the publication in which it appears. If your library does not own the publication, you can request it through interlibrary loan.

IDENTIFY RELEVANT DATABASES
Databases tend to specialize in particular subject areas and types of sources. To focus your search, try to identify the databases that will be most relevant to the subject you are addressing. Your decisions about which databases to search will be affected by your

library's holdings, although some databases, such as ERIC, MedLine, and Science Direct, are available publically via the Web (see p. 260). Large research libraries often subscribe to hundreds of databases, while smaller libraries might subscribe to only a handful. Most libraries provide a list of available databases. You can also consult a reference librarian about which databases might be appropriate for your search.

Databases generally fall into one of the following categories.

News and Information Databases. News and information databases focus on recently published articles in newspapers, such as the *New York Times*, and popular magazines, such as *Time* and *Newsweek*. Some databases of this type, such as LexisNexis Academic, also allow you to search articles distributed by news services, such as the Associated Press, and transcripts of radio and television programs. If your subject is likely to have been addressed in recent news coverage, consider searching one of these databases:

- Alternative Press Index
- Business News
- Ethnic NewsWatch
- LexisNexis Academic
- Newsbank
- Newspaper Source
- ProQuest Newspapers

Subject Databases. These databases provide information and abstracts (brief summaries) on sources about a broad subject area, such as education, business, or government. If your subject is related to a broad area of interest, consider searching databases that focus on general subjects, such as the following:

- Academic Search Premier
- ArticleFirst
- Business Search Premier
- Catalog of U.S. Government Publications
- Communication & Mass Media Complete
- Education Abstracts
- Health Source
- Humanities International Index

Bibliographies. Bibliographies provide information about publications in a specific discipline or profession, such as literary studies, computational linguistics, or the social sciences. The MLA Bibliography, for instance, provides information about sources dealing with English literature. On their database pages, many libraries provide guidance about the resources that are relevant to a particular profession or discipline. For example, if you are interested in a subject related to sociology, you might search the following databases:

- Family and Society Studies Worldwide
- Social Science Abstracts
- Sociological Abstracts

Citation Indexes. These indexes provide publication information and abstracts on sources that have referenced a specific publication. A list of these citations can lead you to other relevant sources on your subject, and they can expand your understanding of the conversation you are joining. If you have already located sources on your subject, you can search a citation database for articles that cite your sources. Depending on your topic, you might search the following databases:

- Arts & Humanities Citation Index
- Science Citation Index
- Social Sciences Citation Index

Full-Text Databases. A growing number of databases allow you to view or download the complete text of a source, either as exact replicas of the original or in a plain-text format. These files cut out the middle step of tracking down a physical copy of the periodical that published an article. If you don't know whether your library owns the sources returned by a search, or if you'd simply like to locate them more quickly, consider using full-text databases. Databases that offer some or all of their sources in full text include the following:

- Academic Search Premier
- ERIC
- IEEE Xplore
- JStor
- LexisNexis Academic
- ScienceDirect

Web-Based Databases. Libraries purchase access to most databases in a manner similar to subscribing to a journal or magazine, and they typically restrict access to the databases to library patrons, such as students, staff, and faculty. If your school library does not subscribe to databases that meet your needs, check whether another library in your area offers Web-based access to its databases (you might need to obtain a library card). Also consider using Deep Web search sites such as Academic Info (academicinfo.net) and Complete Planet (aip.completeplanet.com), which offer access to Web-based databases and specialized directories (see p. 263).

SEARCH WITHIN DATABASE FIELDS

To search for sources using a database, type keywords and phrases in the database's search fields. If you are conducting a basic search, the process will be similar to a search on a Web search site (see p. 262). The following illustrations show a simple search that student writer Donovan Mikrot conducted on the basic search page of ArticleFirst and the results that were returned.

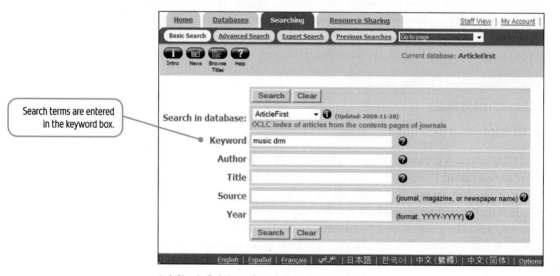

Search terms are entered in the keyword box.

⌐ **A Simple Database Search Using Keywords**

Just as you can in searches of online library catalogs, you can also focus a database search on specific fields, including

- Author

- Title

- Abstract

- Publication in which an article appears

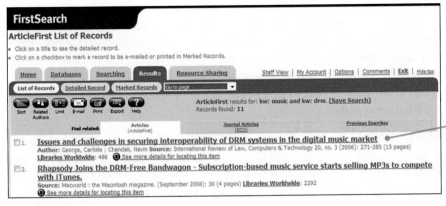

L Database Search Results

Most databases also allow you to search all fields of a database record, much as you would search the Web (see the next section). EBSCO databases, for example, allow you to search "all text," while OCLC databases use the term *keyword* to refer to searches of all fields.

Search the Web

The Web has become the largest and most accessible "library" in the world. In addition to content developed for online use, the Web is home to a great deal of material that was once available only in print. For example, many magazines and journals are placing their back issues on the Web, and others are moving completely to online publication. Similarly, a growing number of books are now available online through sites such as Google Books (books.google.com) and Project Gutenberg (www.gutenberg.org).

Unfortunately, the Web is also the most disorganized library in the world because it's being built by millions of people without a common plan or much communication among them. Thus, to locate sources, you'll need to turn to Web search sites. Like online library catalogs and databases, Web search sites help you to locate information quickly and easily. However, while library catalogs and databases provide results that have been carefully selected by librarians and editors, the pages returned by Web searches can be uneven in quality, ranging from peer-reviewed articles in scholarly journals to home pages created by fifth graders.

As you search the Web, consider the types of search sites that are available and the types of searches you'll conduct on them.

@ Find a list of additional Web search engines, search sites, and other links at **bedfordstmartins.com/ conversation**.

IDENTIFY RELEVANT WEB SEARCH SITES

A surprisingly large number of Web search sites can help you locate sources about the conversation you've decided to join. Established sites, such as Ask, Google, Bing, and Yahoo!, constantly compete with newer sites, each hoping that you'll turn to them when you wish to conduct a search. To determine which ones might be best suited to the needs of your writing situation, learn about the types of Web search sites that are available.

Web Search Engines. When you use a Web search engine, you obtain information about Web pages and other forms of information on the Internet, including PDF files, PowerPoint files, Word files, blogs (see p. 266), and newsgroup posts (see p. 267). Web search engines typically allow you to search for Web pages, news, images, and video, among other options. They keep track of these sources by locating documents on Web sites and entering them in a searchable database.

Keep two cautions in mind as you use Web search engines. First, because most of them index only a portion of the Web—sometimes as much as 50 percent and sometimes as little as 5 percent—you should use more than one. Even if you don't find what you're looking for in your first choice, you might find it in another. Second, because Web pages can be moved, deleted, or revised, you might find that a search engine's results are inaccurate.

Leading Web search engines include the following:

- AltaVista: www.altavista.com
- Ask: www.ask.com
- Excite: www.excite.com
- Gigablast: www.gigablast.com
- Google: www.google.com
- Bing: www.bing.com
- Yahoo! Search: search.yahoo.com

Web Directories. Unlike search engines, Web directories employ human editors to organize information about Web pages into categories and subcategories. Directories allow you to browse lists of Web sites by clicking on general topics, such as health or education, and then successively narrow your search by clicking on subtopics. Many directories also permit you to conduct keyword searches within specific categories.

This enables you to search within a collection of Web sites that the editors have judged to be relevant to your topic. The following are some leading Web directories:

- About.com: about.com

- Best of the Web: botw.org

- Internet Public Library: www.ipl.org

- Librarians' Index to the Internet: lii.org

- Open Directory Project: dmoz.org

- WWW Virtual Library: vlib.org

- Yahoo! Directory: dir.yahoo.com

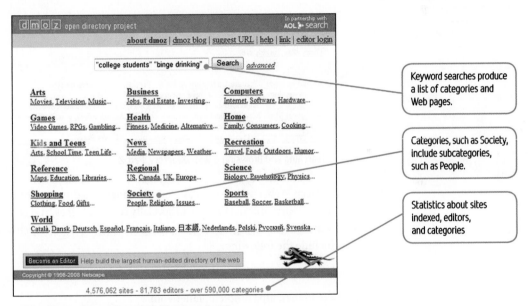

⌐ **Searching and Browsing a Web Directory, Part 1**

Deep Web Search Sites and Directories. Many specialized topics are addressed through databases or database-supported Web sites that, although accessible through the Web, are not indexed by conventional Web search sites such as Google or Yahoo!. These sites are referred to collectively as the Deep Web or the Invisible Web because they are not easily found by the search technologies used by leading search engines.

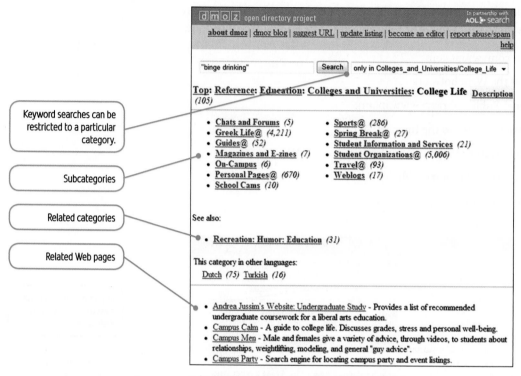

Keyword searches can be restricted to a particular category.

Subcategories

Related categories

Related Web pages

↳ Searching and Browsing a Web Directory, Part 2

To search the Deep Web, try sites such as Complete Planet, a directory of more than seventy thousand searchable databases and specialty search engines, and Scirus.com, a specialized search site focusing on the sciences. Leading Deep Web search sites and directories include the following:

- Academic Info: www.academicinfo.net

- Complete Planet: aip.completeplanet.com

- Deep Peep: www.deeppeep.org

- Internet Archive: www.archive.org

- Scirus: www.scirus.com

Meta Search Sites. On a meta search site, you can conduct a search on several Web search engines or Web directories at the same time. These sites typically search the major search engines and directories and then present a limited number of results on a single page.

Use a meta search site early in your search for information on the Web. You might use a meta search site to do a side-by-side comparison of various search sites and directories. When student writer Donovan Mikrot searched for the phrase *digital rights management* on SRCHR.com, for example, he found that Google and Yahoo! produced more useful sets of results than did Live Search. Leading meta search sites include the following:

- Yippy: yippy.com
- Dogpile: www.dogpile.com
- ixquick: ixquick.com
- Mamma: www.mamma.com
- Metacrawler: www.metacrawler.com
- Search.com: www.search.com
- SurfWax: www.surfwax.com
- Zuula: www.zuula.com

Reference Search Sites. A reference search site allows you to search for information that has been collected in encyclopedias, almanacs, atlases, dictionaries, and other reference resources. Some reference sites, such as MSN Encarta and Encyclopedia Britannica Online, offer limited access to information from their encyclopedias at no charge and complete access for a fee. Other sites, such as Information Please and Bartleby.com, allow unrestricted access to recently published reference works, including the *Columbia Encyclopedia*, *The Encyclopedia of World History*, and *The World Factbook*.

One widely used reference site is Wikipedia, whose articles are collaboratively written by its readers. Because of its comprehensiveness, Wikipedia can serve as a useful starting point for research on a topic. However, because any reader can make changes to the site, it's best to double-check any information you find there.

Leading reference search sites include the following:

- Bartleby.com Reference: www.bartleby.com/reference
- Encyclopedia.com: www.encyclopedia.com
- Encyclopedia Britannica Online: www.britannica.com
- Google Knol: knol.google.com

- Information Please: www.infoplease.com
- Wikipedia: en.wikipedia.org

Government Documents Search Sites and Directories. Many government agencies and institutions have turned to the Web as the primary means of distributing their publications. USASearch.gov, sponsored by the U.S. government, allows you to search the federal government's network of online resources. Government Printing Office Access provides publication information about print documents and links to those publications that are available online. Sites such as FedStats and FedWorld give access to a wide range of government-related materials. In addition to these specialized sites, you can locate government publications through many Web directories, such as Yahoo!. Leading government documents sites include the following:

- About.com's U.S. Government Information Directory: usgovinfo.about.com
- FedWorld: www.fedworld.gov
- Government Printing Office Access: www.gpoaccess.gov
- GovSpot.com: www.govspot.com
- SearchGov.com: www.searchgov.com
- State and Local Government Directory: www.statelocalgov.net
- USASearch.gov: usasearch.gov

Blog Search Sites. Blogs—short for Weblogs—consist of chronologically ordered entries on a Web site and most closely resemble entries in a diary or journal. Blog entries usually include a title and a text message and can also incorporate images, audio, video, and other types of media. Many entries provide links to other pages on the Web.

The purposes of blogs vary.

- Some blogs report on events and issues. The bloggers who provided daily—sometimes hourly—reports on the 2008 political conventions offered valuable, firsthand insights into aspects of the conventions that were not addressed through the mainstream media. Similarly, the bloggers who reported on the Iraq War offered a perspective on events in Iraq and elsewhere that would not have been available otherwise.
- Some blogs alert readers to information elsewhere on the Web. These blogs cite recently published news reports and articles, the latest developments in a par-

ticular discipline, and new contributions to an ongoing debate — and provide commentary on that information.

- Some blogs serve as public relations spaces for institutions and organizations, such as corporations, government agencies, and colleges. These blogs typically focus on services or activities associated with the institution or organization.

- Some blogs serve largely as a space for personal reflection and expression. A blogger might share his or her thoughts about daily life, current events, or other issues with friends and family.

Writers can use blogs as sources of information and commentary on an issue and as sources of firsthand accounts by people affected by an issue. If you find blogs by experts in the field, you can begin a discussion with people involved in or knowledgeable about your topic. To locate blogs that are relevant to your research question, use the following blog search sites and directories:

- Ask.com Blogs: www.ask.com/?tool=bls

- Best of the Web Blogs: blogs.botw.org

- BlogCatalog: www.blogcatalog.com

- Blogdigger: www.blogdigger.com

- Google Blogsearch: blogsearch.google.com

- IceRocket: www.icerocket.com

- Technorati: technorati.com

Discussion Search Sites. Electronic mailing lists, newsgroups, and Web discussion forums support conversations among people who share an interest in a subject or belong to a particular community. You can read a message sent to a mailing list, sometimes referred to as a listserv, in the same way that you read other e-mail messages. Messages posted to newsgroups and Web discussion forums can be read using most Web browsers.

In addition to reading messages, you can post your own. Although there is no guarantee that you'll receive helpful responses, experts in a particular area often read and contribute to these forums. If you are fortunate enough to get into a discussion with one or more knowledgeable people, you might obtain useful information.

Mailing lists, newsgroups, and discussion forums can be located through the following search engines and directories:

- Catalist: www.lsoft.com/lists/listref.html

- CyberFiber: www.cyberfiber.com

- Google Groups: groups.google.com

- Tile.net: tile.net/lists

Search Media Sites

@ Find a list of additional media search sites and directories at **bedfordstmartins .com/conversation.**

The Web is home not only to textual information, such as articles and books, but also to a growing collection of other types of media, such as photographs, podcasts, and streaming video. Image search sites have been available on the Web for a number of years. More recently, search sites have turned their attention to audio and video as well. You can locate useful information about your subject by searching for recordings of radio broadcasts, television shows, documentaries, podcasts, and other media.

You can search for media using established search sites, such as Ask, Google, and Yahoo!, as well as a growing number of newer media search sites.

USE IMAGE SEARCH SITES AND DIRECTORIES

Image searches have long been among the search tools available to writers. Using Google's image search, for example, you can search for images using keywords and phrases, and you can conduct advanced searches by specifying the size and kind of image you desire. The following search sites and directories allow you to locate images:

- Bing Image Search: www.bing.com/images

- Google Image Search: images.google.com

- Picsearch: www.picsearch.com

- Yahoo! Image Search: images.search.yahoo.com

USE AUDIO SEARCH SITES

Thinking of the Web as the first place to visit for new music has become second nature for many of us. But the audio content available through the Web includes more than just music. You can also find radio broadcasts, recordings of speeches, recordings of natural phenomena, and other forms of sound. Sites such as FindSounds allow you to search for sounds and listen to them before downloading. Leading audio search sites include the following:

- FindSounds: www.findsounds.com

- Internet Archive: www.archive.org/details/audio

USE VIDEO SEARCH SITES

Through sites such as YouTube and Yahoo! Video, Web-based video has become one of the fastest-growing parts of the Web. You can view everything from news reports on CNN.com, to a video about the effects of a recent earthquake, to documentaries about the Iraq War. Of course, much of the material will be of little use in a writing project. With careful selection and evaluation, however, you might find video that will help you better understand and contribute to the discussion of your subject. The following are some leading video search sites:

- Bing Video Search: www.bing.com/videos

- Blinkx: www.blinkx.com

- ClipBlast: www.clipblast.com

- Google Video: video.google.com

- Hulu: www.hulu.com

- Yahoo! Video Search: video.search.yahoo.com

- YouTube: www.youtube.com

Keep Track of Your Searches

One of the most important strategies you can use as you collect information is keeping track of your searches. Note the keywords or phrases and the search strategies you used with them (wildcards, Boolean search, author search, and so on), as well as how many sources the search turned up and whether those sources were relevant to your writing project. Keeping track of your searches will help you identify promising approaches; it will also ensure that you don't repeat your efforts.

In your writer's notebook, record the following information for each source you search:

Checklist for Recording Search Terms

✔ Resource that was searched

✔ Search terms used (keywords, phrases, names)

✔ Search strategies used (simple search, exact-phrase search, wildcard search, Boolean search)

✔ Date the search was conducted

✔ Number of results produced by the search

✔ Relevance of the results

✔ Notes about the search

How Can I Locate Sources Using Print Resources?

Contrary to recent claims, there is life (and information) beyond the World Wide Web. The print resources available in a library can help you locate a wealth of relevant material that you won't find online. If you are working on a writing project that has a historical component, for example, you'll find that bibliographies and indexes can point you toward sources that cannot be located using a database or a Web search engine. By relying on the careful selections librarians make when adding to a collection, you will be able to find useful, credible sources that reflect your purpose and address your subject.

To locate information using print resources, discuss your search plan with a librarian, visit the library stacks, browse periodicals, and check reference works.

Discuss Your Search Plan with a Librarian

As you begin collecting information about your subject, think about how your search plan can capitalize on your library's print resources. If you are uncertain about how you might use these resources, discuss your project with a reference librarian. Given the wide range of specialized print resources that are available, a few minutes of discussion with a knowledgeable librarian could save you a great deal of time or point you to key resources you might have overlooked.

Visit the Library Stacks

The library stacks—or shelves—house the library's collection of bound publications. By browsing the stacks and checking publications' works cited pages, you can locate related sources. Once you've decided that a source is relevant to your project, you can check it out or request it through interlibrary loan.

BROWSE THE STACKS

One of the advantages of the classification systems used by most libraries—typically the Library of Congress or Dewey decimal classification system—is that they are subject-based. Because books on similar subjects are shelved together, you can browse the stacks to look for sources on a topic. For example, if your research takes you to the stacks for books about alcohol abuse, you're likely to find books about drug abuse, treatment programs, and codependency nearby. When you find a publication that seems useful, check the works cited list for related works. The combination of browsing the stacks for sources and checking those sources' works-cited lists can lead you to publications relevant to your subject.

CHECK OUT RELEVANT ITEMS

You can usually take library books—and some periodicals and media items—home with you to read or view at your own pace. In some cases, a publication you want might not be available because it has been checked out, reserved for a course, or placed in off-site storage. If a publication has been checked out, you might be able to recall it— that is, ask that it be returned to the library and held for you. If it has been placed on reserve, ask whether you can photocopy or take notes on it. If it has been placed in off-site storage, you can usually request it at the circulation desk.

USE INTERLIBRARY LOAN

If you can't obtain a particular book, periodical, or media item from your library, use interlibrary loan to borrow it from another library. Most libraries allow you to request materials in person or on the Web. Some libraries let you check the status of your interlibrary loan request or renew interlibrary loan materials through the Web. To learn how to use interlibrary loan, consult your library's Web site or ask a librarian.

Browse Periodicals

Periodicals include newspapers, magazines, and academic and professional journals. A periodicals room—or journals room—contains recent issues that library visitors may browse. Many libraries also have a separate room for newspapers published in the last few weeks or months. To ensure everyone's access to recently published issues, most libraries don't allow you to check out periodicals published within the last year, and they usually don't allow newspapers to be checked out at all.

Older periodicals are sometimes placed in bound volumes in the stacks. Few libraries, however, keep back issues of newspapers in paper form. Instead, you can often find back issues of leading newspapers in full-text databases or in microform. *Microform* is a generic name for both microfilm, a strip of film containing greatly reduced images of printed pages, and microfiche, film roughly the size of an index card containing the same kinds of miniaturized images. You view these images using a microform reader, a projection unit that looks something like a large computer monitor. Many microform readers allow you to print full-size copies of the pages.

To help you locate articles in periodicals, most periodicals rooms provide access to electronic databases, which are more likely than print indexes and bibliographies to contain listings of recent publications. Once you've identified an article you want to review, you'll need to find the periodical in which it appears. Most online library catalogs allow you to conduct a title search for a periodical, in the same way you conduct a title search for a book. The online catalog will tell you the call number of the periodical and usually will give information about its location in the library. In addition, some libraries provide a printed list that identifies where periodicals are located. If you have difficulty finding a periodical or judging which publications are likely to contain articles relevant to your writing project, ask a librarian for assistance.

Check Reference Works

Reference rooms contain reliable print resources on a range of topics, from government to finance to philosophy to science. Although many of these reference books serve the same purposes as electronic databases, others offer information not available in databases. Using reference books to locate print resources has several advantages over using databases.

- **Most databases have short memories.** Databases typically index sources only as far back as the mid-1980s and seldom index anything published before 1970. Depending on your subject, a database might not allow you to locate important sources. If you use a reference book, however, you might be able locate print resources dating back a century or more.

- **Most databases focus on short works.** In contrast, many of the print resources in library reference rooms will refer you to books and longer publications as well as to articles in periodicals.

- **Many library reference resources are unavailable in electronic form.** For instance, the *Encyclopedia of Creativity*, which offers more than two hundred articles, is available only in print form.

- **Entries in print indexes are easier to browse.** Despite efforts to aid browsing, databases support searching far better than they do browsing.

Some of the most important print resources you can consult in a reference room include bibliographies, indexes, biographies, general and specialized encyclopedias, handbooks, almanacs, and atlases.

BIBLIOGRAPHIES

Bibliographies list books, articles, and other publications that have been judged relevant to a topic. Some bibliographies provide only citations, while others include abstracts—brief descriptions—of listed sources. Complete bibliographies attempt to list all of the sources published about a topic, while selective bibliographies attempt to list only the best sources on a topic. Some bibliographies limit their inclusion of sources by time period, often focusing on sources published during a given year.

You're likely to find several types of bibliographies in your library's reference room or stacks.

- **Trade bibliographies** allow you to locate books published about a particular topic. Leading trade bibliographies include *The Subject Guide to Books in Print*, *Books in Print*, and *Cumulative Book Index*.

- **General bibliographies** cover a wide range of topics, usually in selective lists. For sources on humanities topics, consult *The Humanities: A Selective Guide to Information Sources*. For sources on social science topics, see *Social Science Reference Sources: A Practical Guide*. For sources on science topics, go to bibliographies such as *Information Sources in Science and Technology*, *Guide to Information Sources in the Botanical Sciences*, and *Guide to Information Sources in the Physical Sciences*.

- **Specialized bibliographies** typically provide lists of sources—often annotated—about a topic. For example, *Bibliography of Modern American Philosophers* focuses on sources about important American philosophers.

Although most general and trade bibliographies can be found in the library reference room, specialized bibliographies are usually shelved in the library's stacks. To locate them, start by consulting a cumulative bibliography, such as *The Bibliographic Index: A Cumulative Bibliography of Bibliographies*, which identifies bibliographies on a wide range of topics and is updated annually. You might also search your library's online catalog using keywords related to your subject plus the keyword *bibliography*. If you need help finding bibliographies that are relevant to your subject, ask a reference librarian.

INDEXES

Indexes provide citation information for sources found in a particular set of publications. Many indexes also include abstracts—brief descriptions—that can help you determine whether a source is worth locating and reviewing. The following types of indexes can be found in libraries:

- **Periodical indexes** list sources published in magazines, trade journals, scholarly journals, and newspapers. Some periodical indexes, such as *The Reader's Guide to Periodical Literature*, cover a wide range of general-interest publications. Others, like *Art Index*, focus on periodicals that address a single subject. Still others focus on a small set or even an individual periodical; *The New York Times Index*, for example, lists articles published only in that newspaper and organizes entries by subject, geography, organization, and references to individuals.

- **Indexes of materials in books** can help you locate articles in edited books. Turn to resources such as the *Essay and General Literature Index*, which indexes nearly five thousand book-length collections of articles and essays in the arts, humanities, and social sciences. You might also find subject-specific indexes. *The Cumulative Bibliography of Asian Studies*, for example, covers articles in edited books.

- **Pamphlet indexes** list the pamphlets that libraries frequently collect. If your subject is likely to be addressed in pamphlets, ask a reference librarian whether your library has a pamphlet index. You can also consult the *Vertical File Index*, which lists roughly three thousand brief sources on ten to fifteen newsworthy topics each month.

- **Government documents indexes** list publications from federal, state, and local governments. The most useful indexes include *Monthly Catalog of United States Government Publications*, *CIS Index to Publications of the United States Congress*, *Congressional Record* (for daily proceedings of the House of Representatives and the Senate), *United States Reports* (for Supreme Court documents), and *Statistical Abstract of the United States* (for census data and other statistical records). These types of indexes might be found in either the reference room or a separate government documents collection in your library. Ask a reference librarian for help.

- **Citation indexes** allow you to determine which sources make reference to other publications, a useful strategy for finding sources that are engaged in the same conversation. For example, to learn which sources refer to an article published in a scientific journal, consult the *Science Citation Index*.

BIOGRAPHIES

Biographies cover key figures in a field, time period, or geographic region. *Who's Who in America*, for instance, provides brief biographies of important figures in the United States during a given year, while *Great Lives from History* takes a broader view, offering biographies of key figures in world history.

ENCYCLOPEDIAS

General encyclopedias attempt to provide a little knowledge about a lot of subjects. The purpose of a general encyclopedia, such as the *New Encyclopaedia Britannica*, is to present enough information about a subject to get you started on a more detailed search. Specialized encyclopedias, such as *The MIT Encyclopedia of the Cognitive Sciences*, take a narrower focus, usually covering a field of study or a historical period. Articles in specialized encyclopedias are typically longer than articles in general encyclopedias and offer more detailed coverage of subjects.

HANDBOOKS

Like encyclopedias, handbooks provide useful background information about a subject in a compact form. Unlike encyclopedias, most handbooks, such as *The Engineering Handbook* and the *International Handbook of Psychology*, cover a specific topic area. The entries in handbooks are also much shorter than the articles found in encyclopedias.

ALMANACS

Almanacs contain lists, charts, and tables of information of various types. You might be familiar with *The Old Farmer's Almanac*, which is known for its accuracy in predicting weather over the course of a year. Information in almanacs can range from the average rainfall in Australia to the batting averages of the 1927 Yankees to the average income of Germans and Poles before World War II.

ATLASES

Atlases provide maps and related information about a region or country. Some atlases take a historical perspective, while others take a topical perspective.

In Summary: Conducting Secondary Source Research

+ **Generate search terms and choose search strategies (p. 249).**

+ **Search your library's online catalog (p. 253).**

+ **Search relevant databases (p. 257).**

+ **Use appropriate Web search sites (p. 262) and media search sites (p. 268).**

+ **Browse the library stacks (p. 271).**

+ **Examine periodicals (p. 271).**

+ **Use the reference room (p. 272).**

How Can I Locate Secondary Sources Using UT Libraries' Resources?

The University of Tennessee (UT) Libraries have large collections of secondary and scholarly sources. As with primary sources, many of the Libraries' scholarly collections are online. Therefore, it is important to become familiar not only with library buildings — UT has several libraries on campus, including Hodges Library, DeVine Music Library, and Pendergrass Agriculture and Veterinary Medicine Library — but also with the UT Libraries' Web site. This discussion will help you find library resources, both in print (hard copies) and online.

Search Strategies: A Step-by-Step Guide

As was explained earlier in this chapter, searches in library collections work differently than Google searches in a number of ways. For example, the items found in a Google search are often very different from the items found in a library search. Searching library collections often results in a list of reputable popular sources, such as articles from the *New York Times* or books published by Random House, in addition to scholarly, peer-reviewed articles from academic journals such as the *New England Journal of Medicine*.

Furthermore, the way that you probably search with Google is different from the way that you should search library collections. The search strategies below will help you use library resources and save time in your research by leading you to a number of relevant and reputable sources.

1. BRAINSTORM POSSIBLE RESEARCH QUESTIONS

When you are first presented with a topic for a paper, your first task should be to come up with a list of possible research questions. Depending on the scope of the assignment, the length of the paper, and other parameters set by your instructor, brainstorming gives you a chance to consider which questions would be suitable for your project.

Helpful Hint

For more information about what makes something a popular source (e.g., a newspaper article) or a scholarly source (e.g., a peer-reviewed journal), watch these short tutorial videos at

- http://www.youtube.com/watch?v=VeyR3OYq1tA, or

- http://www.youtube.com/watch?v=w9rSkYwOCKA.

"How Can I Locate Secondary Sources Using UT Libraries' Resources?" is written by Rachel Radom, faculty member of the UT Libraries.

For example, if you were given the assignment to write a paper on *technology and society*, you might begin with a list of narrower topics, and then think of potential research questions for each narrower topic.

Narrower Topics	Possible Research Questions
Facebook/Online social networking sites	What do Facebook users think about online privacy?
Online banking	What are banks doing about replacing credit cards and debit cards with smart phones?
File sharing and music recording	Is online music sharing changing the recording industry's business model? What are the effects on musicians?
Cell phones	Is there a correlation between cell phone use while driving and traffic accidents?
Online dating	Who uses online dating sites? Are there any social stigmas associated with their use?
Cyberbullying	What effect does cyberbullying have on school children? What are schools doing about it?

2. DO PRELIMINARY SEARCHES

When you have identified a few possible research questions that are of interest to you, then do several quick searches using Google, Wikipedia, and online library search engines. Search for both books and articles, and see if you find enough sources on the topic to complete your project. As part of this preliminary research, think about whether the research question is too broad and should be more specific, or whether the question is too focused and should be broadened.

3. REFINE THE RESEARCH QUESTION

Once you have done a preliminary search and determined that there are enough sources you could use to develop or support your own argument, look at your research question more carefully and review it in light of the project requirements. Can your research question be fully examined given the page requirement for the paper? Is your research question clear?

4. IDENTIFY KEYWORDS IN THE QUESTION

When you have an appropriate research question, you are ready to think about how you will search for appropriate sources. Unlike the preliminary search for any available sources in Step 2 above, you now want to search for the best, most relevant sources related to your question.

To do that, you need to identify the keywords in your research question. Keywords do not include words such as *the, of, it,* or *an*. Keywords also do not include words such as *effects*, *benefits*, *disadvantages*, or *results*. Keywords *do* include only the most significant words in your research question. Let's identify keywords using this sample research question:

What are <u>schools</u> doing to minimize the effects of <u>cyberbullying</u> on <u>children</u>?

The keywords in this question are *schools, cyberbullying,* and *children*. The word "effects" is not a keyword, because any source that examines cyberbullying and children will naturally talk about effects, although the author may not use the exact word "effects" to describe the relationship between the two.

5. RELATED TERMS

Now that you have identified keywords in your research question, it is important to think about related terms for each keyword. Why are related terms important? If you search for articles on *schools, cyberbullying,* and *children*, you will find a list of articles that match those words exactly. Perhaps an article was published last year and the author wrote about schools, cyberbullying, and students. This article has many statistics and interviews that would be helpful in your research, but the author never mentioned the word "children," only "students." Your search for *schools, cyberbullying,* and *children* would probably have missed the article because your search used the word "children" instead of "students."

Authors use different words to describe the same ideas. Online search engines match only the exact words you enter in the search box; therefore, it is often valuable to search for resources using a variety of related keywords.

Using our example research question, the table below lists words related to the main question's keywords. Since the word "cyberbullying" is a compound word, it may be useful to separate the word and find related terms for each concept.

schools	cyberbullying	cyber	bullying	children
School administration	Cyber harassment	Online	Threats	Students
School administrators	Online bullying	Texting	Harassment	Adolescents
School boards	Cyber stalking	Text messages	Humiliation	Juveniles
Teachers		Social networking	Aggression	Young adults
Principals		Cell phones	Victimization	Youth
Elementary schools		Email	Violence	
Middle schools		Instant messaging	Intimidation	
High schools		Chat rooms	Embarrassment	

Using a different word for each concept in multiple searches will help you find a variety of sources, no matter what words different authors use to refer to the same concept.

6. USING "AND" TO CREATE SEARCHES

In Google, you can enter nearly any combination of words into the search box and find results. In library search engines, it is best to use keywords only, with "and" between the keywords. So, once you have identified your keywords and created a list of related terms, create a main search and other optional searches by combining different, related keywords, using "and" between keywords.

Using our example from Step 5, each search should include one related term for "schools," one related term for "cyberbullying," and one related term for "children." Alternatively, because cyberbullying is a compound word, you could also create a search with one related term for "schools," one related term for "cyber," one related term for "bullying," and one related term for "children."

Good Searches

✓ schools and cyberbullying and children

✓ schools and cell phones and bullying and students

✓ schools and online and bullying and students

✓ school boards and cyberbullying and adolescents

Ineffective Searches

✕ how are schools minimizing cyberbullying

✕ cyberbullying and students and children and adolescents

✕ online, bullying, students

✕ online + harassment + school administration

✕ "preventing cyberbullying in schools"

Helpful Hint

Subject librarians at the UT Libraries have created Research Guides that highlight the most important online search engines in specific research areas. These guides often refer to online search engines used to find materials in databases (see "Articles" on page 283 for more information on databases). Visit http://libguides.utk.edu/ to see Research Guides in a variety of subjects.

7. MULTIPLE SEARCHES IN APPROPRIATE COLLECTIONS

Each search with an online search engine will bring back different results; therefore, it is important to use each online search engine more than once with a different combination of keywords each time. It is also important to know that there is more than one online search engine to use. The sections on the following pages highlight some particularly useful search engines available via the UT Libraries' Web site.

Find Resources in the UT Libraries

BOOKS

To find books in the UT Libraries, there are two steps:

1. Search for books that are relevant to your topic.

2. Locate each book on the appropriate library shelf.

To search for books, use the Libraries' online catalog, choosing the *Books Plus* search box on the Libraries' home page (http://lib.utk.edu). A search will bring back a list of books, CDs, and DVDs that match your search terms (see Figure 9.1). You will find more information about the items on the lines below each title. Most important for locating each item is the line that begins with green or red text—green text will say "Available" if the item is available on the shelf for checkout, while red text will say "Checked Out" if the item is not available.

Next to the availability is the "location" of the item. If the item location is Hodges Library Stacks, then the letter and number combination in parentheses next to it will help you locate the item in Hodges Library. The letter and number combination is the call number for the item. Call numbers are arranged in Hodges Library Stacks in the following manner:

A–GM: 3rd floor

GN–PR: 4th floor

PS–S: 5th floor

T–Z: 6th floor

Call numbers organize materials on related subjects near one another on the shelf. For example, all materials on medicine are shelved in the "R" section, and materials on sport and recreation are in the "G" section. The majority of the Hodges Library stacks are organized using the alphanumeric Library of Congress Classification system, in which books are arranged alphabetically by the letter(s) that begins the call number.

☆ **Cyber bullying : protecting kids and adults from online bullies**
Samuel C. McQuade James P Colt; Nancy B. B Meyer
Westport, Conn. : Praeger Publishers 2009
Available - Hodges Library Stacks (HV6773 .M395 2009) - Check Locations tab for other copies

Book

Locations   Details   Items 🗗 Reviews & Tags   Additional services

☆ **Confronting Cyber-bullying : what schools need to know to control misconduct and avoid legal consequences**
Shaheen Shariff
New York : Cambridge University Press 2009
Available - Hodges Library Stacks (K5210 .S53 2009) - Check Locations tab for other copies

Book

Locations   Details   Items 🗗 Reviews & Tags   Additional services

☆ **More bullies in more books**
C. J. Bott (Christie Jo), 1947-
Lanham, Md. : Scarecrow Press 2009
Available - Hodges Library Stacks (LB3013.3 .B685 2009) - Check Locations tab for other copies

Book

Locations   Details   Items 🗗 Reviews & Tags   Additional services

↥ Figure 9.1 A search for *cyberbullying* using the Books Plus search function on the UT Libraries' home page returns several matches, including *Confronting Cyber-bullying* by Shaheen Shariff.

How to Find a Book by Call Number in Hodges Library

Hodges Library Stacks (K5210 .S53 2009)

K   4th floor of Hodges Library (K = books about law)

5210   Subdivision of "K" section; could be any number from 1 to 9999. All numbers are arranged 1, 2, 3, 4, 5 . . . 9999. For this book, look for the 5210 section in the "K" shelving range

.S53   Once you have found the "K" shelves and are in the 5210s, then look for the K5210 .S section. The number 53 that follows the ".S" (and, for any other book, the second set of numbers in the call number) is read as a decimal, even if the decimal point is not present.

2009   The year of publication

Searching the library catalog using the Books Plus search function on the UT Libraries' home page will sometimes find materials that are not in Hodges Library Stacks. Materials may be located in one of several other UT Libraries locations:

- **AgVet Med Library:** Pendergrass Agriculture & Veterinary Medicine Library. Located on campus at the UT College of Veterinary Medicine.

- **Hodges Library Children's and Young Adult Collection:** 3rd floor of Hodges Library. This collection uses a different call number arrangement (Dewey Decimal Classification system) than the rest of Hodges Library (Library of Congress Classification system).

- **Hodges Library Leisure Reading:** 1st floor galleria of Hodges Library.

- **Hodges Media Center:** At the circulation desk on the 2nd floor of Hodges Library. This location is usually used in reference to DVDs.

- **Hodges Reference:** 1st floor of Hodges Library.

- **Music Library:** George F. DeVine Music Library (currently under construction—temporarily located in the Humanities and Social Science [HSS] building). This location holds CDs, books, sheet music, scores, or other music-related formats.

- **Online access:** Under the item's title and author information, click on the blue text that says "online resources" to access the digital copy of the item.

- **Special Collections Rare Books:** 1st floor of Hodges Library. Use of Special Collections requires scheduling an appointment. See "Special Collections" in Chapter 4 for more information.

- **Storage Stacks:** Off-site storage of low-use and duplicate material for the Libraries. Materials requested from Storage will be available within two days of the request, Monday through Friday. Request materials using the link on the Libraries' home page (in the Books Plus search function) or the Web form at http://www.lib.utk.edu/request/storage.html.

Helpful Hint

If you are unable to find books on your topic, consider broadening your search. If you have three keywords, try a search using just the single most significant keyword. For example, a search for *cyberbullying* using the Books Plus search function returns more than ten matching books. A search for *cyberbullying and schools and children* returns only four matching books.

When you search for articles, using more keywords will be more useful, as it will narrow your results from many matches to a smaller number of more highly relevant matches.

Please note that books on law, music, and agriculture are not usually found in Hodges Library. If you are looking for materials on one of these topics, try the UT College of Law Library or one of the branch UT Libraries (DeVine Music Library or Pendergrass AgVet Med Library). Each of these libraries has a

Web site with more information. You are allowed to check out materials from any of these libraries, though there may be some restrictions on particular collections (e.g., materials from Special Collections do not leave the library).

ARTICLES

The UT Libraries have many collections of online articles in library databases. These databases often include materials other than articles, such as statistics, polls, reports, editorials, book reviews, film reviews, and other items. Therefore, you should think of databases as search engines for both articles and other nonbook materials.

You read earlier that databases usually focus on particular subject areas or sources. A database you might use to find sources for a paper in a business class would be different from the database you would use to find sources for a paper in a cinema studies class. General topic databases, such as *Academic Search Premier,* are good databases to start searching, no matter your topic. Keep in mind that the UT Libraries have hundreds of databases, each of which include different materials from different sources. One database may focus on industry data, another may primarily include peer-reviewed articles from medical journals, and yet another may index historical photographs and images. If you aren't sure which databases to use for your research, don't hesitate to ask a librarian (http://lib.utk.edu/askusnow).

When you are on campus, you will be able to access library databases automatically. When you are off campus, you will need to log in to the databases using your UT username and password. This is because the library databases are not freely available. Although library databases are accessible via the Web, they are subscription sites, and your tuition gives you access to these online collections. For help with access, you can find more information here: http://www.lib.utk.edu/databases/remoteaccess.html.

One other search engine that you should be aware of is Google Scholar, which searches only scholarly publications. Google Scholar is not as comprehensive

Helpful Hint

Most library databases have applications that give you suggestions for formatting a source in MLA or APA citation style. Look for a link that includes words such as "cite this" or "how to cite this item" within the database. If you have trouble finding the citation link in a database, ask a librarian (http://lib.utk.edu/askusnow).

Helpful Hint

When you are using Google Scholar from your own computer, make sure that you set Google Scholar to recognize you as a student at UT. Google Scholar will give you links to access articles that the library has a subscription to, but only if you tell Google Scholar that you are a student at UT. Not all people have access to the UT Libraries' online collections, but you do have access with your UT NetID and password. From scholar.google.com, go to the gear icon next to the "Sign in" link at the top right, choose "Scholar Preferences" (see Figure 9.2), and then enter "University of Tennessee" into the "Library Links" section. Choose "University of Tennessee–FullText@UTLibraries" and then save your preferences.

as library subscription databases, and many of its results are links to books that you will need to check for in the library, but it is another resource that may be of help during your research.

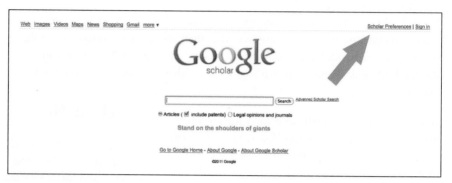

⌐ **Figure 9.2**

To find . . .	Use this search engine . . .
Articles	Library databases, Google Scholar
Books	Catalog (Books Plus search)
Reports, Statistics	Library Databases, Google Advanced Search
Web sites	Google, Google Advanced Search

Information about the UT Libraries

- **Get research help:** Librarians are available to help you with your research. Chat with, email, or call a librarian for help by visiting http://www.lib.utk. edu/askusnow. You can also stop by the Research Assistance desk (North Commons in Hodges Library on the 2nd floor) to talk with a librarian in person.

- **The Commons in Hodges Library:** Computer labs, printers, loaner laptops, OIT help, research help, the Writing Center, the Stat Lab, the Student Success Center, and more—all are in one convenient location—on the 2nd floor of Hodges Library.

- **Get library information for undergraduate students:** http://lib.utk.edu/ undergrad

- **Find maps of Hodges Library:** http://www.lib.utk.edu/aboutlibs/libmaps.html

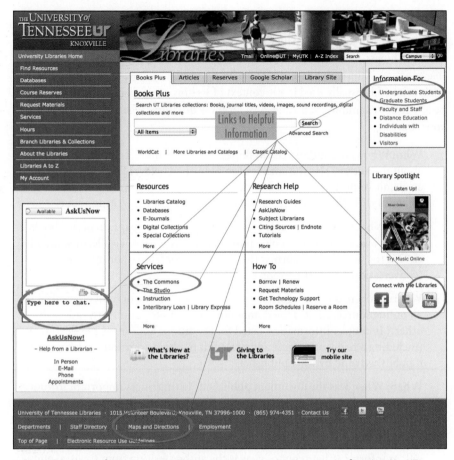

⌐ Figure 9.3 More information about library services and collections can be found on the UT Libraries' home page: http://www.lib.utk.edu.

- **The UT Libraries YouTube channel:** How-to videos to help with your research can be found at http://www.youtube.com/user/utkinstruct.

- **Research guides:** For helpful guides to finding the most important online search engines for specific research areas, visit http://libguides.utk.edu.

- **Quiet floors:** 1st, 4th, and 5th floors in Hodges Library

- **Group study floors:** 2nd, 3rd, and 6th floors in Hodges Library

- **Branch Libraries:** http://lib.utk.edu/branches

Evaluate the Sources You Find

Before using any source in a paper, you will want to consider the validity, reliability, trustworthiness, bias, and other qualities of your source. One method that can assist in evaluation is to recall the "5 Ws": who, what, where, when, why, and how. The 5 Ws method is usually used in the context of writing a paper; however, it can also be applied to examining sources. Consider these questions when you are evaluating your sources:

- **Who:** Who is the author? Use Wikipedia or Amazon to find information about the author. Has the author been published before? Does the author have academic or professional credentials (i.e., has he or she studied or worked at a university)? Is the author an expert on what he or she is writing about?

- **What:** What is the document? Is it a magazine or newspaper article, a book, a book review, an editorial, a blog post, a scholarly journal article, or something else? Is the writing style formal (technical and/or factual) or informal (conversational and/or opinionated)?

- **Where:** Where did the information come from (online or hard copy)? If it is an online source, what is the domain of the Web site (.com, .org, .gov, .edu, other)? Is contact information listed for the author and/or the publication (including a real world street address)? If it is a hard copy source, where was it published (and by what publisher)?

- **When:** When was the document published? Is timeliness important to your research; that is, do you need only recent publications, or is your research topic one in which historical documents are required?

- **Why:** Why did the author write this document—to convince, entertain, sell, or inform? What point of view is the author writing from (neutral and presents both sides, or opinionated, emotional, and only presents one side)? What type of audience is your author addressing (scholars or the general public)?

- **How:** How is the document organized—and does it contain an abstract, methodology, graphs and charts, and references? How did the author get his or her information—are there references cited throughout the document and listed in footnotes, endnotes, or a bibliography, or are no references identified?

It takes a few minutes to skim a source and investigate the author or institution he or she is affiliated with before you can evaluate the overall quality of your source. Feel free to use Wikipedia, Amazon, and Google to find more information on your author, the author's employer, and the author's publisher. While skimming your source, also look for evidence of bias or one-sidedness and think about whom the author talked to, interviewed, or observed, and whom the author left out of the analysis.

Keep in mind that biased articles, editorials, or books that only look at one side of an issue or focus on one group of people can sometimes be more appropriate to cite in certain papers than others. For example, when you are writing a paper on a controversial topic, you may want to include highly opinionated sources in your paper in order to highlight what each side says about the issue. You should identify which sources are highly opinionated, and then attempt to find other sources that are less opinionated. Additionally, you might want to make sure that you are using a variety of highly opinionated sources that represent different views from across the spectrum.

It is also useful to examine the methodology an author used to conduct his or her research. Is the author interviewing a random sample of people, or is the author targeting only one source for his or her interviews or tests? Is the sample size large enough to be statistically significant, or is the author making generalizations based on limited data? Critical analysis requires you to think about the material you are reading not as fact, but as the work of people who may have used flawed research methods, observations, or analysis.

For more information about how to use sources successfully in your paper, see Appendix B, "Using Sources Effectively in Your Written Draft."

✳ Questions and Activities for Chapter 9

1. What are the four types of electronic resources that writers can turn to?

2. Describe some successes and some frustrations you've had in the past with trying to locate sources. After reading this chapter, what did you do "right" in your searches, and what could you have done differently to avoid frustrations?

3. Do a "Deep Web" search on your topic, and write a one-page summary of what you find.

4. Visit the Hodges Library, locate some of the reference materials and indexes mentioned in the chapter, and look up information related to your topic. Write a one-page summary of what you find.

5. You have two articles from a database. One author identifies herself as working at the Heritage Foundation and another identifies himself as working at the Center for American Progress. What do you think this means for each author's biases? Use Google and Wikipedia to help you determine your answer.

6. Imagine you have to write a paper about the following topic: modern issues in education in the United States. Using the seven strategies listed in "Search Strategies," outline the steps you would take to develop a research question, and begin research towards answering that question.

7. Look at the Web site globalwarming.com. Use the 5 Ws to evaluate the site. Would you use globalwarming.com as a source in a college paper about the causes of global warming?

8. Look at a Web site your instructor suggests (or one you've discovered through your initial search). Use the 5 Ws to evaluate the site.

9. The chapter mentions using "and" in your keyword searches in library search engines, where it is best to use keywords only, with *and* between the keywords. Once you have identified your keywords and created a list of related terms, create a main search and other optional searches by combining different, related keywords, using *and* between keywords. Write a list of the promising results you gathered from your keyword search.

10. Go to http://libguides.utk.edu/eng102, and watch one or both of the video guides (Finding Articles and Finding Books). When you are done viewing the video(s), write a short summary of the process of finding materials in the UT Libraries.

11. Go to http://libguides.utk.edu/ to find a Research Guide that is relevant to your secondary source research paper assignment. When you've explored one or more of the guides, write a short summary of your process of searching and of what information you discovered.

12. After reading the sample student secondary source research paper in Appendix D, "Millennial Finance: Budgeting Is the New Saving," describe the main thesis or claim of the paper, and identify the different types of sources used to support and develop the claim. What primary sources are used? What secondary sources? What does each type of source contribute to the overall argument the writer is making? Write out your evaluation of the effectiveness of the way the writer uses secondary sources.

APPENDIXES

 The appendixes that follow offer information and activities to help you during the research and writing process. Since most of the information may apply to any of the 102 research papers — historical, qualitative, and secondary source research — it is collected here to make it easier to browse and use as needed.

Appendix A includes advice about how to pull together all your research material and create a good draft of a research paper.

Appendix B includes advice about how to write about and integrate source material correctly; it provides information about how to paraphrase and quote properly to avoid plagiarism.

Appendix C includes a variety of activities to support you during any stage of your research and writing projects. There are detailed instructions and additional resources that will help you conduct and write successful historical, qualitative, and secondary source research projects.

Appendix D provides annotated model student papers for each of the three research units in English 102. Even if the papers here are not written in response to the particular assignment you've been given, it is still a good idea to read the samples to gain an idea about "best practices" for researched writing. Each of the papers includes short comments that point out its successful features.

A Drafting Your Research Paper

Research writing isn't so much the act of putting words to paper or screen as it is the process of identifying and learning about an issue, reflecting on what you've learned, and contributing to the conversation about your issue.

How Can I Use My Outline to Draft My Document?

Your outline provides a framework you can use to draft your document. Your outline likely includes your plans for:

- the points you will include in your document
- the order in which you will make your points
- the amount of space you plan to devote to each point

If you created an informal outline, it can be the skeleton of your document, and you can now begin fleshing out sections. Translate a bulleted list of items, for instance, into a series of brief sentences, or write paragraphs based on the key points in the outline. If you created a formal outline, such as a topical outline or a sentence outline, you can use each main point in the outline as a topic sentence for a paragraph. For example, you can form supporting sentences from the subpoints under each main point.

What's My Purpose?

Review your purpose and your outline. Check whether you have organized your points in a way that will allow you to achieve your purpose and whether you are addressing the needs, interests, values, and beliefs of your readers. If you have listed information about the sources you will use to support your points, you can check whether you are

- providing enough evidence to support your points
- relying too heavily on a limited number of sources
- relying too heavily on support from sources that favor one side of the conversation

As you prepare to draft your document, you might find it necessary to reorganize your ideas to achieve your purpose.

If your outline contains references to specific notes or sources, make sure that you use those notes in your draft. Take advantage of the time you spent thinking about which sources are most appropriate for a particular section of your document.

As you work on your document, you might find it necessary to reorganize your ideas. Think of your outline as a flexible guide rather than a rigid blueprint.

Appendix A, "Drafting Your Research Paper" is taken from Mike Palmquist, *The Bedford Researcher*, Third Edition, pp. 203–21 (Chapter 14, "Drafting").

How do I use an outline to draft my document?

Use your outline as the "skeleton" of the first draft of your document. In this example, student writer Alexis Alvarez expands her outline into a rough draft.

1 Save your outline with a new name, such as Draft1.doc.

2 Turn major headings in your outline into headings and subheadings in your draft.

3 Convert lower-level entries into topic sentences for paragraphs.

4 Use lists of items as sentences in each paragraph.

5 Locate evidence to support your points. Quote, paraphrase, and summarize sources identified in your outline.

---

1. Benefits of Sports for Girls
   a. Physical Health Benefits
      i. Reduces risks of adult-onset coronary disease and some cancers (Kane & Larkin, 1997)
      ii. Enhances immune system, posture, strength, flexibility, and heart-lung endurance (Kane & Larkin, 1997; "Sports in America," 1994)
   b. Mental Health Benefits (Kane & Larkin, 1997; Orozco interview)
      i. Positive body image
      ii. Confidence and self-esteem
      iii. Sense of control
   c. Social benefits (Orozco and Alvarez interviews)
2. Problems Caused by Sports for Girls
   a. Physical side effects

Girls and Sports: The Upside

According to Kane and Larkin (1997), adolescent girls who exercise regularly can lessen their risks for adult-onset coronary disease and certain cancers. Girls' involvement in sports and exercise also tends to improve immune functioning, posture, strength, flexibility, and heart-lung endurance (Kane & Larkin, 1997; "Sports in America," 1994).

In addition, competitive athletics can enhance mental health by offering adolescent girls positive feelings about body image; tangible experiences of competency, control, and success; improved self-esteem and self-confidence; and a way to reduce anxiety (Kane & Larkin, 1997). Juan Orozco, who has coached competitive soccer for nine years at the adolescent female level, confirmed that making a competitive sports team is a privilege that many girls work toward with determination and longing and that being picked to participate encourages these young athletes to believe in themselves and their abilities (personal interview, Sept. 22, 2004).

A final benefit is that sports expand social boundaries and teach many of the personal and social skills girls will need throughout their lives. According to Orozco, through competitive athletics girls learn a crucial lesson in how to

---

Review another example and work on using your outline to draft your document at **bedfordresearcher.com**. Click on Interactive Exercises.

How Can I Draft Effective Paragraphs?

Writers use paragraphs to present and develop a central idea. Depending on the complexity of your argument and the type of document you are writing, a single paragraph might be all you need to present a supporting point and its associated reasoning and evidence, or it might play only a small role in conveying your thinking about an issue. You can create effective paragraphs by ensuring that they are focused, organized, and well developed. You can enhance the effectiveness of your document by creating transitions that clearly convey the relationships between paragraphs.

Focus on a Central Idea

Each of your paragraphs should focus on a single idea. Paragraphs often have a topic sentence in which the writer makes an assertion, offers an observation, or asks a question. The rest of the sentences in the paragraph elaborate on the topic. Consider the following paragraph, drawn from student writer Patrick Crossland's research essay:

> Of course, one of the greatest monsters applicants must slay before they can enter college is taking an entrance exam or standardized test, such as the SAT and ACT. These tests are used by many colleges to assess student aptitude and academic capability. According to Joel Levine and Lawrence May, authors of *Getting In*, entrance exams are an extremely important part of a student's college application and carry a great deal of weight. In fact, they claim that a college entrance examination is "one of the two most significant factors" (116) in getting into college (the other, unsurprisingly, being high school grades).

The central idea of the paragraph is provided in the first sentence, following the transitional phrase *of course*.

The second sentence explains the purpose of entrance exams.

The third and fourth sentences use evidence from a source to convey the importance of entrance exams.

Follow an Organizational Pattern

Effective paragraphs follow an organizational pattern, often the same one that the document as a whole follows, such as:

- chronology: identifying the sequence in which events occur over time
- definition: explaining an idea, concept, or event
- description: presenting the distinguishing features of an idea, concept, or event
- categorization: classifying information and ideas

- cause/effect: identifying factors that lead to (cause) an outcome (effect)

- problem/solution: defining a problem and presenting a solution

- comparison/contrast: exploring similarities and differences

- analogy: suggesting that one thing is like another

- pro/con: presenting reasons and evidence in favor of and against an idea

- costs/benefits: presenting the tradeoffs involved in a choice

- strengths/weaknesses: using a set of criteria to make judgments about an idea, concept, event, or individual

- advantages/disadvantages: contrasting the positive and negative aspects of an idea, concept, event, or individual

These common patterns help readers anticipate what you'll say. Readers who recognize a pattern, such as problem/solution, will find it easier to focus on your ideas and argument if they understand how you are organizing your paragraph. Note how the following paragraph, drawn from Alexis Alvarez, uses the problem/solution organizing pattern.

> The paragraph begins by restating the problem.

> The central idea of the paragraph is provided in the third sentence.

> One part of the solution to the larger problem is provided.

What can we do to help adolescent female athletes avoid illicit drug use? How can we help them avoid the pitfalls of competitive athletics? Parents, coaches, and the athletes themselves all play a crucial role in averting bad choices. First, parents and coaches need to be aware that performance-enhancing drugs are a problem. Some adults believe that steroid use is either minimal or nonexistent among teenagers, but one study concluded that "over half the teens who use steroids start before age 16, sometimes with the encouragement of their parents. . . . Seven percent said they first took 'juice' by age ten" (Dudley, 1994, p. 235).

> The fifth sentence provides evidence from a source to illustrate the nature of the problem.

Use Details to Capture Your Readers' Attention

An effective paragraph does more than simply convey information—it provides details that bring an issue to life. Consider the differences between the following paragraphs:

Example 1: Minimal Details

In fact, pollution from power plants may worsen as the demand for electric power continues to increase. Despite plans to build new power plants fueled by renewable energy and nuclear power, the U.S. Department of Energy projects that use of fossil fuels in power plants will actually increase. Moreover, Clayton (2004) notes that developing nations will also increase their reliance on fossil fuels. All of this is likely to lead to increased air pollution.

Example 2: Extensive, Concrete Details
In fact, pollution from power plants may worsen as the demand for electric power continues to increase. The U.S. Department of Energy (2005b) predicts that, despite ongoing efforts to build power plants powered by renewable and nuclear energy, U.S. demand for power generated by fossil fuels will keep growing. Moreover, demand in developing nations is expected to increase even more dramatically. China and India are poised to build a total of 775 new conventional power plants by 2012 (Clayton, 2004). The addition of so many new plants will almost certainly lead to more global air pollution in the near term.

Both examples, drawn from student writer Pete Jacquez's Web site on wind energy, convey the same main point. The first example, however, does little more than state the facts. The second example provides details from a U.S. Department of Energy report about demand for power in the United States and offers statistics about the number of conventional power plants that are projected to be built in China and India in the next few years. These details allow readers to gain a more complete, and more concrete, understanding of the issue.

Integrate Information from Sources Effectively

Information from sources can be used to introduce an important concept, establish the strength of a writer's argument, and elaborate on the central idea of a paragraph. Writers frequently state a point, offer a reason to accept it, and support their reasoning with evidence from a source, typically in the form of quotations, paraphrases, and summaries. In the following example, drawn from Pete Jacquez's Web site, a quotation and a paraphrase are used to support a point introduced in the first sentence of the paragraph:

In fact, pollution from power plants may worsen as the demand for electric power continues to increase. The U.S. Department of Energy (2005b) notes that "it is likely that the nation's reliance on fossil fuels to power an expanding economy will actually increase over at least the next two decades even with aggressive development and deployment of new renewable and nuclear technologies" (para. 1). Moreover, demand in developing nations is expected to increase even more dramatically. China and India are poised to build a total of 775 new conventional power plants by 2012 (Clayton, 2004). The addition of so many new plants will almost certainly lead to more global air pollution in the near term.

By quoting an authority on the issue, the U.S. Department of Energy, Pete strengthens his argument. The quotation, along with a subsequent paraphrase of a passage from another source, provides evidence to support his point. He follows the quotation and paraphrase with a sentence that restates the main point of the paragraph—and an important supporting point for his argument.

Create Transitions Within and Between Paragraphs

Transitions are words and phrases, such as *however* and *on the other hand*, that show the relationships between paragraphs and sentences. Transitions help readers understand how one sentence builds on another and how a new paragraph is related to the one that came before it. By signaling these relationships, they help readers anticipate how the information and ideas they are about to read are related to the information and ideas they've just read. Here are some common transitions and their functions.

To Help Readers Follow a Sequence

Furthermore

In addition

Moreover

Next

First . . . Second . . . Third

To Elaborate or Provide Examples

For example

For instance

Such as

In fact

Indeed

To illustrate

To Compare

Similarly

In the same manner

Like

As in

To Contrast

However

On the other hand

Nevertheless

Nonetheless

Despite

Although

To Signal a Concession

I admit that

Of course

Granted

To Introduce a Conclusion

As a result

As a consequence

Therefore

Thus

For this reason

As you create effective transitions, pay attention to the order in which you introduce new information and ideas in your paragraphs. In general, it is best to begin a sentence with a reference to information and ideas that have already been introduced and to introduce new information and ideas at the end of a sentence. For example, consider the following examples, which begin a new paragraph:

Introducing New Information First

Admissions staff look at the kind of courses students are taking, in addition to looking at grades.

Building on Information That Has Already Been Introduced

And it's not just grades that matter; admissions staff also look at the kind of courses students are taking.

The second example, by referring to information that has been introduced in the previous paragraph, provides an effective transition to a new paragraph, even as it introduces new information about additional college admissions criteria. In contrast, readers of the first example would not have the benefit of seeing how the new information fits into what they've already read.

How Can I Draft My Introduction?

All readers expect documents to include some sort of introduction. Whether they are reading a home page on a Web site or an opening paragraph in a research report, readers want to learn quickly what a document is about. Drafting an introduction involves framing your main point and choosing a strategy to begin your document.

Frame the Issue

Your introduction provides a framework within which your readers can understand and interpret your information, ideas, and argument. By calling attention to a specific situation, by asking a particular question, or by conveying a carefully chosen set of details, you can help your readers view your issue in a particular way. Consider, for example, the differences between two introductions to an essay about low turnout among younger voters.

Introduction 1

Ever since 1972, when 18-year-olds gained the right to vote, voter turnout among America's youth has been significantly lower than that of older Americans. Following an initial turnout of 52 percent of younger registered voters in 1972, the percentage declined to an all-time low of only 32 percent in the 1996 presidential election (Capuano 221). And despite gains in the 2000 and 2004 elections, the youth vote has continued to trail that of older Americans by roughly 20 percentage points (Lopez 2). The causes of this problem are complex and varied: lack of investment in government institutions, lack of attention to issues of concern to younger voters, and the idea that not voting sends a message to government.

Introduction 2

Americans between the ages of 18 and 24 are in danger of losing the most important privilege granted to U.S. citizens: the right to vote. Since 1972, when 18-year-olds first gained the right to vote, turnout among younger voters significantly lagged behind that of older Americans, with an average gap of roughly 20 percent in presidential elections since 1972 (Capuano 221, Lopez 2). While apologists are quick to point out that low turnout among younger voters results from their lack of knowledge of the importance of voting or their belief that not voting provides an effective protest against politicians who do not recognize them as important members of the populace, younger voters may soon find out that their failure to exercise their right to vote will carry a heavy price. Unless they begin participating in the democratic process, they may lose the right to do so — at least until they reach their early twenties.

The first introduction frames the issue as an explanation of the causes of low turnout among younger voters. The second introduction frames the issue as a warning that the voting age might be raised. While each introduction draws on the same basic information about voting rates, and while both will do a good job of introducing an essay, they ask readers to focus their attention on different aspects of the issue.

The ability to frame your readers' understanding of an issue is a powerful tool. By directing readers' attention to one aspect of an issue, rather than to others, you can influence their beliefs and, potentially, their willingness to take action.

You can frame your discussion by calling attention to specific aspects of a topic, including

- agent: a person, organization, or thing that is acting in a particular way
- action: what is being done by the agent
- goal: why the agent carried out the action
- result: the outcome of the action

Introduction 2

■ Agent
■ Action
■ Goal
■ Result

Americans between the ages of 18 and 24 are in danger of losing the most important privilege granted to U.S. citizens: the right to vote. Since 1972, when 18-year-olds first gained the right to vote, turnout among younger voters significantly lagged that of older Americans, with an average gap of roughly 20 percent in presidential elections since 1972 (Capuano 221, Lopez 2). While apologists are quick to point out that low turnout among younger voters results from their lack of knowledge of the importance of voting or their belief that not voting provides an effective protest against politicians who do not recognize them as important members of the populace, younger voters may soon find out that their failure to exercise their right to vote will carry a heavy price. Unless they begin participating in the democratic process, they may lose the right to do so — at least until they reach their early twenties.

Select a Strategy for Your Introduction

You can introduce your document using one of several strategies.

State the Topic. Tell your readers what your issue is, what conversation you are focusing on, and what your document will tell them about it, as in the following introduction:

> Artists and their artwork do not exist in a vacuum. The images artists create help shape and in turn are shaped by the society and culture in which they are created. The artists and artworks in the Dutch Baroque period are no exception.

Define Your Argument. If your research document presents an argument, use your introduction to get right to your main point — the point you are trying to persuade your readers to accept. In other words, lead with a thesis statement, as in the following introduction:

> While the private tragedies of its central characters have public implications, William Shakespeare's *Julius Caesar* is more about personal struggles than political ambition. It is easy to see the play as one whose focus is the political action of public events. The title character, after all, is at the height of political power. However, the interior lives of Julius Caesar, Marcus Brutus, and their wives offer a more engaging storyline. Shakespeare alternates between public and private scenes throughout the play to emphasize the conflict between duties of the Roman citizenry and the feelings and needs of the individual, but it is the "private mind and heart of the individual" (Edwards 105) that the reader is compelled to examine.

Define a Problem. If your research has led you to propose a solution to a problem, you might begin your document by defining the problem. Alexis Alvarez used this strategy to introduce her essay:

> Almost daily, headlines and newscasters tell us about athletes' use of performance-enhancing drugs. Indeed, stories of such drug use seem to increase each year, with investigations of possible steroid use by college football players, by major league baseball players, and even by Olympic gold medalists. It is easy to gain the impression that many adult athletes, particularly males, may be using drugs in order to improve their performance and physical appearance. What may be surprising and even shocking to most of us, however, is that these drugs, especially anabolic steroids, are increasingly used by adolescent athletes and that girls are just as likely as boys to be users.

Ask a Question. Asking a question invites your readers to become participants in the conversation. At the end of her introduction, Alexis Alvarez encouraged her readers to take an interest in the problem of steroid use by adolescent female athletes by asking a question:

> What role is competitive sports playing in this dangerous trend? Why are some girls feeling the need to ingest performance-enhancing drugs?

Tell a Story. Everyone loves a story, assuming it's told well and has a point. Patrick Crossland began his research project with a story about his brother, Caleb, a high school student and a star athlete who was applying to colleges and universities:

> Caleb is a junior in high school. Last night his mom attended his varsity wrestling match, cheering him on as he once again defeated his competitors. On the way home, they discussed his busy schedule, in which he balances both schoolwork and a job at his father's company. Caleb manages to get good grades in his classes while at the same time he learns a trade in the woodworking industry. . . .

Provide a Historical Account. Historical accounts can help your readers understand the origins of a situation and how the situation has changed over time. A Web site focusing on relations between the People's Republic of China and Taiwan used this historical account:

> On February 21, 2000, the People's Republic of China (PRC) shocked the world with its release of the white paper "The One-China Principle and the Taiwan Issue." In this 18-page document, the Chinese government outlined its case that, in keeping with the "One China" principle to which the United States and Taiwan had allegedly agreed, Taiwan is the rightful property of the People's Republic of China, and revealed that it intended to use force if Taiwan did not move to reunite with the mainland.

Make a Contrast. Setting up a contrast asks your readers to begin making a comparison. Student writer Elizabeth Leontiev began her essay by contrasting what the word *cocaine* means to U.S. citizens and South American coca farmers:

> To most Americans, the word *cocaine* evokes images of the illegal white powder and those who abuse it, yet the word has a completely different meaning to the coca farmers of South America.

Lead with a Quotation. A quotation allows your readers to learn about the issue from someone who knows it well or has been affected by it, as in the following introduction:

> "Without a few lucky breaks, we'd still be bagging groceries at Albertsons," says lead singer Rickie Jackson of the recent Grammy winning band, Soft Affections.

How Can I Present Evidence to Support My Points?

Using sources to support your points is the essence of research writing. Whether you are making your main point or a supporting point, readers will expect evidence to back it up. Depending on the point you want to make, some types of evidence might be more effective than others. The key is how your readers will react to the evidence you provide. In some cases, for example, statistical evidence might lend better support for a point than a quotation. The following are some of the most effective ways to support your points.

Direct Quotation. Quotations from experts or authorities can lend weight to your argument, and quotations from people who have been affected by an issue can provide concrete evidence of the impact of the issue. Patrick Crossland used a quotation from an admissions expert to support his point about the competitiveness of the college admissions process:

> Duke University Director of Undergraduate Admissions Christoph Guttentag uses a baseball analogy in describing how students advance in the admission process. "Think of it as a baseball game. Everybody gets [his] time at bat. The quality of [students'] academic work that we can measure through test scores and analysis of high school courses gets about 10 percent of the applicants to third base, 50 percent to second base, and about 30 percent to first base. And 10 percent strike out" (qtd. in "College Admissions").

Statistical and Other Numerical Evidence. Much of the support you'll use in your document is textual, typically presented in the form of quotations, paraphrases, and summaries. But your topic may lend itself to numerical evidence. Alexis Alvarez used statistical evidence throughout her essay:

> In May 2004, the Centers for Disease Control and Prevention (CDC) published its latest figures on self-reported drug use among young people in grades 9 through 12. The CDC study, "Youth Risk Surveillance Study — December 2003," found that 6.1% of its survey participants reported using steroids at least once, up from 2.2% in 1993. The report also showed that use of steroids appears to be increasing among younger girls: While only 3.3% of twelfth-grade girls reported using steroids, 7.3% of ninth-grade girls reported using them.

Example. It's often better to *show* with an example than to *tell* with a general description. Examples provide concrete evidence in your document. Student writer Kevin Fahey used an example to illustrate a point in his essay about Hemingway's depiction of his character Nick Adams:

> "The End of Something," one of the only stories in which Hemingway depicts Nick alone with a female companion for an extended scene (Flora 55), provides a convincing portrayal of Nick as the Everyman. As the story opens, Nick and his girlfriend row to a beach on Horton's Bay, a once-bustling mill town that is now deserted. Hemingway's description of the town's demise heralds catastrophe for the couple's relationship. While the two fish, Marjorie asks Nick what has been bothering him. Revealing his lack of self-understanding, Nick replies, " 'I don't know. . . . It isn't fun any more. . . . I don't know, Marge. I don't know what to say' " (Hemingway 204).

Definition. Definitions explain what something is, how a process works, or what you mean by a statement. Elizabeth Leontiev used a definition to help her readers understand the uses of the coca plant:

> According to Arthur C. Gibson, an economic botanist at UCLA, *Erythroxylum coca*, or the tropical coca plant, has been grown in the mountainous regions of Colombia, Bolivia, and Peru since 3000 B.C. (Gibson).

Qualification. You can use qualifications to make your meaning more precise and reduce the possibility that your readers might misunderstand your point. Qualifications allow you to narrow the scope of a statement. In the following example, a research writer uses a qualification to clarify the relationship between painting and culture in seventeenth-century Dutch society:

> Because of their faithful depiction of the world and their painstaking attention to detail, seventeenth-century Dutch paintings of domestic scenes can be called realistic. However, it is important to remember that these images do not always simply depict the people and their world exactly as they were. Instead, these works served multiple purposes — to spread and promote ideas about domestic virtue, to instruct viewers about women's roles, and, finally, to entertain viewers (Franits, *Paragons* 9).

Amplification. Amplification expands the scope of your point. Patrick Crossland used amplification to broaden his discussion of the criteria used in college admissions decisions:

> And it's not just the grades that matter — admissions staff also look at the *kind* of courses students are taking.

Analogy. One of the most common ways to support a point is to describe similarities between one thing and another. Here's an example: "Drafting a research document is similar to cooking. Without the proper tools, ingredients, and knowledge, the document won't turn out as well as you'd like."

Association. If you remember the advertising slogan "I want to be like Mike," you're already familiar with association. Through association you can support a point by connecting it with something or someone else. When you support your argument using a quotation from an expert, you're using a form of association. It's as if you're saying, "Look, this intelligent person agrees with me."

Contrast. Contrasts are similar to association, but in reverse. You can use contrasts to show that something is not like something else.

Illustration. Visual elements can help your readers understand your points more clearly. In print documents, illustrations are usually photos, drawings, or charts. Elizabeth Leontiev, for example, included a chart tracking the historical impact of the U.S. war on drugs on wholesale and retail cocaine prices.

How Can I Make Sure My Document Is Easy to Follow?

In addition to expecting that you'll support your points, readers expect you to organize your document in a sensible way that allows them to understand it easily. Fortunately, you've already spent time organizing your document. It's also likely that you've continued to refine your organization as you've prepared to draft your document.

A well-organized document allows a reader to anticipate—or predict—what will come next, which helps readers understand your goals more easily. The test of good organization is whether your readers can move smoothly through your document without wondering, "Where did that come from?" As you draft, check whether your document is organized consistently and predictably. You might find the following techniques useful.

Provide a Map. The most direct way of signaling the organization of your document is to provide a map in your introduction. You might write something like "This report will cover three approaches to treating cancer of the bladder: chemotherapy, a combination of chemotherapy and radiation, and surgical removal of the organ."

Use a Table of Contents, a Home Page, or a Menu. Tables of contents, home pages, and menus are similar to maps. If you are writing a print document, decide whether your document is long enough to justify using a table of contents. While academic essays seldom use a table of contents, a report prepared for a course might use a table of contents if the length runs to 20 or more pages and the report contains several sections. If you are writing an electronic document such as a Web site, you can lay out the key elements of your document on a home page. Similarly, you can add a menu on the side, top, or bottom of your pages that readers can see as they work through your site. Pete Jacquez provided a menu on every page of his site (see Figure A.1).

Learn More
Fossil Fuel Economics
Fossil Fuel & the Environment
Wind Power Economics
Wind Power & the Environment
Bibliography
Related Links

Take Action
Local Efforts
State-Wide Efforts
National Efforts

About This Site
Written by Pedro Jacquez
References

⌐ Figure A.1 Menu on Pete Jacquez's Web Site. The menu helps readers understand the organization of the site and move to pages within it.

Use Headings and Subheadings. You can help your readers keep their place in your document by using headings and subheadings. Your formatting should distinguish between headings (major sections) and subheadings (subsections).

Provide Forecasts and Cross-References. Forecasts prepare your readers for a shift in your document, such as the boundary between one section and the next. A forecast at the end of a major section might say, "In the next section, you can read about. . . ." Cross-references tell your readers that they can find related information in another section of the document or let them know that a particular issue will be addressed in greater detail elsewhere. On a Web site, forecasts and cross-references might take the form of small images, flags, or statements such as "Continue to next section" or "Follow this link for more information."

How Can I Make My Document More Readable?

Even a thoughtful, well-researched document will be ineffective if it's difficult to read. As you draft your document, give attention to paragraphing and paragraph structure, transitions between sentences and paragraphs, tone and style, and economy. These issues are discussed briefly in this section.

Vary Sentence and Paragraph Structure

Although each of your sentences and paragraphs, when read by itself, might be well written, grammatically correct, and engaging, you run the risk of boring—and even losing—your readers if you fail to vary the structure. To ensure variety in the structure of your paragraphs, use different organizational patterns. Relying on a mix of organizational patterns, such as definition, cause/effect, comparison /contrast, and chronology, for example, can help keep your document lively, interesting, and readable. To ensure variety in the structure of your sentences, use different types of sentences, rely on a mix of independent and dependent clauses, and create a mix of longer and shorter sentences.

Create Effective Transitions

Good writers provide clear directions to their readers in the form of transitions between sections and paragraphs. Effective transitions smooth readers' movement from one idea to another. Some transitions might be sentences, such as "A sudden job loss creates not only a financial burden but a psychological one as well." By referring to an idea already discussed in the document—in this case, the financial burden created by the sudden loss of a job—the author connects what readers have already read with what they are about to read—in this case, the psychological burden associated with the loss of a job. Other types of transitions come in the form of headings and subheadings, which explicitly signal a change in topic. Still others are signal words or phrases, such as *however, on the other hand, in addition,* and *first.*

Use Appropriate and Consistent Tone and Style

In many cases, readers and writers never meet, so your document might be the only point of contact between you and your readers. As a result, your readers will judge you and what you have to say based not only on what you say but on how you say it. Ensure that you are presenting your ideas clearly and effectively by paying attention to the following:

- **Word choice.** Make sure that your readers understand your words, and use technical language appropriate for your audience. How will your readers react to slang? Also ask yourself whether they will find your words too stiff and formal.

- **Sentence length and complexity.** A sentence that is too complex will make your readers work overtime to figure out what it means. Can a complicated concept be more simply stated?

- **Variety.** A steady stream of sentences written in exactly the same way will have the same effect as a lecture delivered in a monotone. Vary your sentence length and structure.

- **Reader expectations.** Consider not only what you say, but also your readers' expectations about how you should say it. If you are writing a blog entry about the local music scene and you know your readers will expect a casual, down-to-earth report on the show you attended over the weekend, it would be fine to write, "The sound quality was lousy." If, however, you are writing a report about the show for one of your courses, you might want to use a more formal tone, such as "The sound quality was poor," or perhaps "The quality of sound produced by the band's equipment was inadequate."

Strive for Economy

An effective document says enough to meet the writer's goals, and no more. As you draft your document, ask yourself whether you've written enough to make your point. Then ask whether you could make your point more economically without compromising your ability to meet your goals.

Create an Effective Design

As you write your document, pay attention to its design. Using a readable body font that is clearly different from the font used for headings and subheadings, for example, can improve readability significantly. Similarly, breaking out information using bulleted and numbered lists, providing descriptive page headers or footers, and integrating illustrations effectively into your text can greatly enhance readability.

How Can I Draft My Conclusion?

Your conclusion provides an opportunity to reinforce your message. It offers one last chance to achieve your purpose as a writer and to share your final thoughts about the issue with your readers.

You've probably read conclusions that simply summarize the document. These summaries can be effective, especially when the document has presented complex concepts. A conclusion can do more, though, than simply summarize your points. It can also give your readers an incentive to continue thinking about what they've read, to take action about the issue, or to read more about it.

As you draft, think about what you want to accomplish. You can choose from a range of strategies to draft an effective conclusion.

Summarize Your Argument. Sum up the argument you've made in your document. Elizabeth Leontiev concluded her analysis of the impact of Evo Morales' vision for South American coca farmers by using this technique.

> Through his bold program of "zero cocaine, not zero coca," Morales aims to improve the lives of Andean farmers and the economies of South American countries, while still remaining committed to controlling the illegal drug trade. Morales' example illustrates that it is time to work *with* coca farmers, rather than against them.

Offer Additional Analysis. Extend your analysis of the issue by supplying additional insights. In his Web site about wind-generated electrical power, Pete Jacquez concluded his discussion of wind power and the environment by linking wind power to the production of hydrogen gas.

> Another promising area — in terms of wind power's contribution to clean energy — is the role it can play in a "hydrogen economy." Because hydrogen gas, when burned, does not produce carbon dioxide (its only emission is water vapor), some legislators and environmentalists are looking to hydrogen as a replacement for fossil fuels. Generating hydrogen gas, however, requires

power, and a number of plans to generate it rely on coal-powered plants. Wind-power advocates argue, instead, that wind turbines can supply the power needed to produce hydrogen gas. Recent government studies support this approach ("Wind Power Facts," 2004).

Speculate about the Future. Reflect on what might happen next. An essay about younger voters, for example, might speculate on the consequences of their historically low turnout and what will be required to increase it.

> While a repeal of voting rights for 18- to 21-year-olds might be unlikely, other effects will certainly be felt: younger people's interests will not be properly evaluated, and the "cycle of mutual neglect" will continue. Clearly, the demographic group of 18- to 24-year-olds in America has shown less of an interest in participating in the political process than everyone else. This will remain true until younger voters feel they have trustworthy sources of information as well as candidates to choose from who they feel listen to them. Finally, they must understand the importance of their vote, and why it is not just a right, but a civic duty.

Close with a Quotation. Select a quotation that does one of the following:

- sums up the points you've made in your document
- points to the future of the issue
- suggests a solution to a problem
- illustrates what you would like to see happen
- makes a further observation about the issue

Alexis Alvarez used a quotation from a personal interview to underscore her main point about the use of steroids among adolescents girls involved in competitive sports.

> In short, these athletes have not lost sight of the true objective of participating in sports — they know that their success is due to their efforts and not to the effects of a performance-enhancing drug. When asked what she would say to athletes considering steroid use, Melissa Alvarez said:
>
> > If you are training and doing your best, you should not have to use steroids. At the end of the day, it is just a game. You should never put your health at risk for anything, or anyone. It should be your top priority. (personal communication, September 26, 2004)

Close with a Story. Tell a story about the issue you've discussed in your document. The story might suggest a potential solution to the problem, offer hope about a desired outcome, or illustrate what might happen if a desired outcome isn't realized. Patrick Crossland continued the story he used to introduce his research paper.

> Thus, in the midst of Caleb Crossland's busy schedule, he applies to various colleges he wants to attend. He continues to get good grades, studies for the SAT, and stays involved in extracurricular

activities. He researches schools and plans to apply early. And with the support of his family, Caleb should have an edge over the many other students competing against him for a spot at the nation's top colleges.

Link to Your Introduction. This technique is sometimes called a "bookends" approach because it positions your introduction and conclusion as related ends of your document. The basic idea is to turn your conclusion into an extension of your introduction.

- If your introduction used a quotation, end with a related quotation or respond to the quotation.
- If your introduction used a story, extend that story or retell it with a different ending.
- If your introduction asked a question, answer the question, restate the question, or ask a new question.
- If your introduction defined a problem, provide a solution to the problem, restate the problem, or suggest that readers need to move on to a new problem.

How Should I Document My Sources?

You should document your sources in the body of your document and at the end of it — in a works cited or reference list. Documenting sources acknowledges the contributions of the writers whose work you've used in your project. Documenting sources also helps your readers locate the sources you cited. For guidelines on the MLA, APA, and other documentation systems, see your grammar handbook.

In Summary: Drafting Your Research Essay

+ **Use your outline to begin drafting your document.** (p. 291)

+ **Develop effective paragraphs.** (p. 293)

+ **Draft your introduction.** (p. 297)

+ **Support your points with evidence.** (p. 300)

+ **Use an appropriate organizational pattern.** (p. 303)

+ **Pay attention to paragraph and sentence structure, transitions, tone, style, economy, and design.** (p. 304)

+ **Draft your conclusion.** (p. 306)

+ **Document your sources.** (p. 308)

B Using Sources Effectively in Your Written Draft

How Can I Use Sources to Accomplish My Purposes as a Writer?

Your sources can help you introduce ideas, contrast the ideas of other authors with your own, provide evidence for your points, define concepts, illustrate processes, clarify statements, set a mood, provide examples, and qualify or amplify a point. You can present information from sources in several ways:

- as a quotation, paraphrase, or summary
- as numerical information
- as illustrations such as images, audio, video, and animations

Depending on the point you want to make, some types of evidence might be more effective than others. Be sure to consider how your readers will react to the information you provide. In some cases, for example, numerical evidence might lend better support for a point than a quotation would.

As you draft your document, identify what you want the information from your sources to accomplish. Consider how quotations, paraphrases, summaries, numerical information, and various types of illustrations from your sources might lead your readers to see the subject you are addressing in terms that are most favorable to your purposes. By selecting source information carefully, you can present ideas that are more pointed than you might want to make on your own. Calling opponents of a proposal "inflexible" and "pig-headed," for example, might signal your biases too strongly. Quoting someone who uses those terms, however, allows you to get the point across without undermining an otherwise even and balanced tone.

The following are some of the most effective ways to use information, ideas, and arguments from sources as you contribute to a written conversation about a subject.

Appendix B, "Using Sources Effectively in Your Written Draft," is taken from Mike Palmquist, *Joining the Conversation*, pp. 572–94 (Chapter 17, "Using Sources Effectively").

Introduce a Point

You can use a quotation, paraphrase, or summary to introduce a point to your readers.

Quotation Used to Introduce a Point

"When I came around the corner, a black bear was standing in the middle of the trail," said Joan Gibson, an avid hiker. "We stared at each other for a moment, wondering who would make the first move. Then the bear looked off to the right and shambled up the mountain. I guess I wasn't worth the trouble." Joan Gibson's story, like those of most hikers who encounter bears in the woods, ends happily. But the growing encroachment of humans on rural areas once left largely to wildlife is causing difficulties not only for people who enjoy spending time in the wide-open spaces but also for the animals that make those spaces their home.

Paraphrase Used to Introduce a Point

A *New York Times* article recently reported that human-bear encounters in Yosemite National Park, which had been on the decline during most of the last decade, has more than doubled in the past year (Spiegel A4). Although no humans have been injured and only one incident resulted in a decision to destroy a bear, park officials point to the uptick in encounters as a warning sign that . . .

Your choice of a quotation or paraphrase will frame the point you want to make, calling your readers' attention to a specific aspect of an idea or argument and laying the groundwork for a response. Think about how the following quotation leads readers to view a public debate about education reform as a battle between reformers and an entrenched teachers union.

> Phrases such as "balked at even the most reasonable proposals" and "their obstructionist behaviors" place the blame for the problem on the teachers union.

"The teachers union has balked at even the most reasonable proposals for school reform," said Mary Sweeney, press secretary for Save Our Schools, which has sponsored a referendum on the November ballot calling for funding for their voucher plan. "We believe the November election will send a wake-up call about the need to rethink their obstructionist behaviors."

If Sweeney and supporters of Referendum D are successful, the educational landscape in . . .

In contrast, note how the following quotation frames the debate as a question of how best to spend scarce education funds.

"In the past decade, state and local funding of public education in real dollars has declined by 7.2 percent," said Jeffrey Allister, state chair of the governor's Special Commission on Education Reform. "Referendum D, if passed, would further erode that funding by shifting state dollars to private schools." As the state considers the merits of Referendum D, which would institute the first statewide voucher program in the United States, opponents of the measure have . . .

> Phrases such as "funding of public education in real dollars has declined" and "further erode that funding" call attention to the financial challenges faced by schools.

Contrast Ideas

When you want to indicate that disagreement exists on a subject, you can use source information to illustrate the nature and intensity of the disagreement. The following example uses partial quotations (see p. 317) to highlight differences in proposed solutions to a problem.

Solutions to the state's higher education funding shortfall range from traditional approaches, such as raising taxes, to more radical solutions, among them privatizing state colleges and universities. Advocates of increased taxes, such as Page Richards of the Higher Education Coalition, argue that declines in state funding of higher education "must be reversed immediately or we will find ourselves in a situation where we are closing rural community colleges and only the wealthiest among us will have access to the best education" (A4). Those in favor of privatizing higher education suggest, however, that free-market approaches will ultimately bring about "a fairer situation in which the poor, many of whom have no interest in higher education, are no longer asked to subsidize higher and higher faculty salaries and larger football stadiums" (Pieters 23).

Base your choices about how to contrast ideas on the clarity and length of your sources and on the effects you hope to achieve. If you want to express complex ideas as concisely as possible, you might use paraphrase and summary. If you want to convey the emotional qualities of an author's position on a subject, use quotations.

Provide Evidence

Documents that consist of a series of unsupported assertions amount to little more than a request for the reader's trust. Even when the writer is eminently trustworthy, most readers find such documents easy to dismiss. In contrast, providing evidence to support your assertions increases the likelihood that your readers will accept your main point. Note the differences between the following passages.

Unsupported Assertion

> No evidence is provided to support the writer's assertion.

Given a choice between two products of comparable quality, reputation, and cost, American consumers are far more likely to purchase goods that use environmentally friendly packaging. Encouraging the use of such packaging is a good idea for America.

Supported Assertion

> Summaries of the results of two studies provide evidence for the assertion made in the first sentence.

Given a choice between two products of comparable quality, reputation, and cost, American consumers are far more likely to purchase goods that use environmentally friendly packaging. A recent study by the High Plains Research Institute found that the shelf life of several biodegradable plastics not only exceeded the shelf life of the products they were used to package but also cost less to produce (Chen and Lohann 33). In addition, a study by the Consumer Products Institute found that, when made aware that products were packaged in environmentally friendly materials, consumers were more likely to buy those products.

Similarly, visual sources can lend support to an assertion. An assertion about the unintended consequences of military action, for example, might be accompanied by a photograph of a war-torn street or a wounded child.

Align Yourself with an Authority

Aligning yourself with an authority shows your readers that your points are supported by a leader in that area—such as a subject-matter expert, a scientist, a politician, or a religious figure—and that you are not alone in your convictions. Essentially, this technique allows you to borrow the credibility and status of someone who has compiled a strong record of accomplishment. Start by making an assertion, and follow it with supporting information from a source, such as a quotation, paraphrase, or summary.

Although voice recognition appears to be a promising technology, challenges associated with vocabulary, homonyms, and accents have slowed its widespread implementation. "The computer right now can do a very good job of voice recognition," said Bill Gates, co-founder and chairman of Microsoft Corporation (59). "Demonstrations are good but whenever you get it out and start working with it, it has a hard time, particularly if you are working with a very large vocabulary. It certainly will re-define the way we think of the machines when we have that voice input" (Gates 59).

Define a Concept, Illustrate a Process, or Clarify a Statement

Writers commonly turn to information from sources to define concepts, illustrate processes, or clarify statements when the information is clearer and more concise than what they might write themselves. For example, to define a concept, you might quote or paraphrase a dictionary or an encyclopedia. To help readers understand a complex process, such as the steps involved in cellular respiration, you might use an illustration.

Writers also use information from sources to clarify their statements. A writer might explain a point by providing examples from sources or by using quotations or paraphrases to back up an assertion.

> Studies have found connections between weight loss and coffee intake. This doesn't mean that drinking a couple of cups of coffee each day leads to weight loss. However, three recent studies reported that individuals who increased their coffee intake from fewer than three cups to more than eight cups of coffee per day experienced weight losses of up to 7% over a two-month period (Chang; Johnson and Salazar; Neiman). "It may be that increased caffeine intake led to a higher metabolic level, which in turn led to weight loss," noted John Chang, a senior researcher at the Centers for Disease Control. "Or it might be that drinking so much coffee depressed participants' appetites" (232).

Set a Mood

You can also choose quotations and illustrations with an eye toward establishing an overall mood for your readers. The emotional impact of images of a celebration at a sporting event, an expression of grief at a funeral, or a calming mountain vista can lead your readers to react in specific ways to your document. Similarly, a striking quote, such as "The screams of pain coming out of that room will stay with me as long as I live," can evoke a particular mood in your readers.

Provide an Example

It's often better to *show* with an example than to *tell* with a general description. Examples provide concrete evidence in your document. Student writer Caitlin Guariglia uses an example from a well-known film to illustrate a point in her essay about her family's relationship with food.

And the obsession with eating! My grandmother feeds us constantly. My dad and I always laugh at that scene in *Goodfellas* where the mobsters show up at two in the morning after killing someone, and one mobster's mother whips up a full pasta meal for them. We know that my grandmother would do the same thing: "Are you hungry? Here, sit, eat!" Grandma holds interventions over pasta. If she is unhappy with something someone in the family is doing, she invites everyone over for pasta, and we hash it out together. Was this something all Italians do? Or was my idea of a typical Italian person all wrong? Our time in Rome clarified some of these questions for me.

Amplify or Qualify a Point

You can use amplification to expand the scope of a point. In her analytical essay, student writer Ali Bizzul uses information from a source to broaden her discussion of the dangers football players face when they add bulk.

> NFL offensive linemen who weigh less than 300 pounds are often described as "undersized," so it's no surprise that young football players are getting the message that bigger is better — and bulking up. A recent study of high school linemen in Iowa showed that 45% were overweight and 9% were severely obese, while only 18% of other young males were overweight; even more troubling, a study in Michigan revealed that among football players from ages 9 to 14, 45% could be considered overweight or obese (as cited in Longman, 2007).

Qualifications, in contrast, allow you to narrow the scope of a statement. You can use qualifications to present a point more precisely, reducing the possibility that your readers might misunderstand your meaning. Ali Bizzul makes it clear that deaths related to weight gain are a rare occurrence in football.

> Although such fatalities are unusual, a growing number of doctors believe that use of dietary supplements increases the risk of heatstroke among football players.

How Can I Integrate Sources into My Draft?

Source material can be used to introduce important concepts, establish a main idea, and support or elaborate on a point. Writers use a range of strategies, such as quoting, paraphrasing, and summarizing, to integrate information, ideas, and arguments from sources into their documents. In the following example, the evidence takes the form of a quotation and a paraphrase, both of which support a point introduced in the first sentence of the paragraph.

> One way colleges should use tuition money to benefit students is by redesigning their financial aid systems. Although colleges have reportedly increased their need-based financial aid, most of these precious funds go to boost tuition aid for middle-class students. Tamar Lewin from the *New York Times* writes, "Student borrowing has more than doubled in the last decade, and students from lower-income families, on average, get smaller grants from the colleges they attend than students from more affluent families." Basing more award decisions on financial need instead of merit would allow more students from lower-income families to attend college. As hard economic times continue to affect family finances, some colleges are even offering emergency aid and loans, particularly in cases where parents have lost jobs (Young). More colleges must take similar steps to ensure that students from all economic backgrounds have a fighting chance at affording an education.

By quoting a recent *New York Times* article on the issue, student writer Jennie Tillson strengthens her argument about the burden of student loans on lower-income families. The quotation, along with a subsequent paraphrase of a passage from another source, provides evidence to support her point that colleges should rethink how they award financial aid. Finally, she follows the quotation and paraphrase with a sentence that restates the main point of the paragraph—and an important supporting point for her argument.

You can integrate sources by quoting, paraphrasing, summarizing, presenting numerical information, and using illustrations. When you do so, be sure to distinguish your ideas and information from those found in your sources.

Identify Your Sources

You should identify the sources of information in your document for several reasons. First, doing so fulfills your obligation to document your sources. Second, it allows you (and your readers) to recognize the boundaries between your ideas and those borrowed from sources. Third, it can help you strengthen your document by calling attention to the qualifications or experiences of the person whose ideas you are incorporating.

USE ATTRIBUTIONS AND IN-TEXT CITATIONS

Whenever you quote, paraphrase, or summarize, distinguish between your ideas and the information you obtained from your sources by using attributions—brief comments such as "according to" or "as the author points out"—to alert your readers that the point is not your own.

Writers who use the MLA or APA documentation system also provide citations— or acknowledgments of source information—within the text of their document to indicate where borrowed material ends. These citations, in turn, refer readers to a list of works cited or a list of references at the end of the document.

Note the following examples, which use attributions and in-text citations.

> Attributions identify the author of the quotations.

MLA Style

Pamela Coke argues, "Education reform is the best solution for fixing our public schools" (22).

> MLA-style in-text citations include the author's name and exact page reference.

"Education reform is the best solution for fixing our public schools" (Coke 22).

APA Style

Pamela Coke (2008) has argued, "Education reform is the best solution for fixing our public schools" (p. 22).

> APA-style in-text citations include the author's name, publication date, and exact page reference.

"Education reform is the best solution for fixing our public schools" (Coke, 2008, p. 22).

When you acknowledge material you've borrowed from sources, try to vary the wording of your attributions. Be aware, however, that the verbs in attributions can convey important shades of meaning. For example, saying that someone "alleged" something is quite different from saying that someone "confirmed" something. The form your attributions take will depend on your use of citation style. MLA recommends present tense ("the author points out"), while APA recommends past tense ("the author pointed out").

Some Common Attributions

according to	claims	expresses	reports
acknowledges	comments	inquires	says
affirms	confirms	interprets	states
alleges	declares	muses	suggests
asserts	denies	notes	thinks
assumes	describes	observes	wonders
asks	disputes	points out	writes
believes	emphasizes	remarks	

PROVIDE A CONTEXT

Skilled writers know the importance of providing a context for the source information they include in their documents. It's not enough to simply put text within two quotation marks and move on. Such "orphan quotations"—quotations dropped into a paragraph without any introduction—are confusing. Worse, paraphrases and summaries inserted without context can easily be mistaken for plagiarism.

To provide a clear context for your source information, establish why the quotation, paraphrase, or summary is reliable by identifying the source's credentials. In addition, indicate how it relates to your main idea and what it contributes to the point you are making. If you don't, readers will wonder why it's there.

However, Wechsler et al. (2003) analyzed trends at schools using social norms marketing and revealed that the campaigns did not necessarily decrease student drinking; in some cases, schools even reported higher alcohol consumption, according to seven criteria that measured whether students drank, how much, and how often. The team, from the Harvard School of Public Health's College Alcohol Study, suggested that because social norms marketing was first developed at a small school that wasn't very diverse, it might not be as suitable for schools with many different kinds of people. As the researchers explained, "Individual students' drinking behaviors align more closely to the drinking behaviors of their immediate social group rather than to the overall student population at a given school" (p. 492).

> Description of the findings

> Attribution identifies the source as experts.

> The writer follows APA style; parenthetical citation identifies the page number where the quotation was found.

Quote Strategically

A well-chosen quotation can have a powerful impact on your readers' perception of your main point and on the overall quality of your document. Quotations can also add a sense of immediacy by bringing in the voice of someone who has been affected by a subject or lend a sense of authority to your document by conveying the words of an expert. Quotations can range in form from brief partial quotations to extended block quotations. As you integrate quotations, you might need to modify them to suit your purpose and to fit the flow of your sentences. When you do, be careful to punctuate them properly.

USE PARTIAL, COMPLETE, OR BLOCK QUOTATIONS

Quotations can be parts of sentences (partial), whole sentences (complete), or long passages (block). When you choose one type of quotation over another, consider the length and complexity of the passage as well as the obligation to convey ideas and information fairly.

Partial quotations can be a single word, a phrase, or most of a sentence. They are often used to convey a well-turned phrase or to complete a sentence using important words from a source, as in the following example.

> Quotation marks indicate the borrowed phrase.

> Weitzman (2004) notes that by changing the "contextual forces," such as the availability of alcohol, that encourage students to drink, this approach more strongly emphasizes policies that directly put a stop to excessive drinking—unlike the social norms marketing approach, which relies on influencing individual behavior (p. 187).

> Source information, including the page number containing the quotation, is clearly identified.

Complete quotations are typically one or more full sentences and are most often used when the meaning of the passage cannot be conveyed adequately by a few well-chosen words, as in the following example.

> I smiled when I read Elizabeth Gilbert's memoir *Eat, Pray, Love*. Gilbert writes, "The Neapolitan women in particular are such a gang of tough-voiced, loud-mouthed, generous, nosy dames, all bossy and annoyed and right up in your face just trying to friggin' *help* you for chrissake, you dope—*why they gotta do everything around here?*" (78).

Block quotations are extended quotations (usually more than four typed lines) that are set off in a block from the rest of the text. In general, use a colon to introduce the quotation, indent the entire quotation one inch from the left margin, and include source information according to the documentation system you are using (such as MLA or APA). Since the blocked text indicates that you are quoting directly, you do not need to include quotation marks.

> Instead of cutting education funding, states should provide more money for schools, especially now when jobs are scarce and even trained workers are eager to return to school. Patrick Callan, president of the National Center for Public Policy and Higher Education, observes:

> Parenthetical citation indicates that this material was quoted in another source. In block quotations, the citation information is placed after the period.

> > When the economy is good, and state universities are somewhat better funded, we raise tuition as little as possible. When the economy is bad, we raise tuition and sock it to families, when people can least afford it. That's exactly the opposite of what we need. (qtd. in Lewin)

MODIFY QUOTATIONS AS APPROPRIATE

You can modify quotations to fit your draft. It is acceptable, for example, to delete unnecessary words or to change the tense of a word in a partial quotation so that it fits your sentence. Keep in mind, however, that writers have an obligation to quote sources accurately and fairly. You should indicate when you have added or deleted words, and you should not modify quotations in a way that distorts their meaning.

The most useful strategies for modifying quotations include using ellipses (. . .) to indicate deleted words, using brackets ([ ]) to clarify meaning, and using "sic" to note errors in a source.

The following example shows the use of brackets to change the tense of a verb in a partial quotation.

Original Quotation

"They treated us like family and refused to accept a tip."

Modified Quotation

It's a place where the staff treats you "like family and refuse[s] to accept a tip," said travel writer Melissa Ancomi.

> Brackets indicate that the tense of a word has been changed.

PUNCTUATE QUOTATIONS CORRECTLY

Use the following rules for punctuating quotations:

- Use double quotation marks (" ") around partial or complete quotations. Do not use quotation marks for block quotations.

- Use single quotation marks (' ') to indicate quoted material within a quotation.

  "The hotel manager told the guests to 'make yourselves at home.'"

- Place commas and periods inside quotation marks.

- Place question marks and exclamation points outside quotation marks if the punctuation pertains to the entire sentence rather than the quotation. In the following example, the original quotation is not a question, so the question mark should be placed after the quotation mark.

  But what can be gained from following the committee's recommendation that the state should "avoid, without exceptions, any proposed tax hike"?

- Place question marks and exclamation points inside quotation marks if the punctuation pertains to the quotation itself.

> Dawn Smith asked an important question: "Do college students understand the importance of avoiding running up the debt on their credit cards?"

- Place colons and semicolons outside quotation marks.

> Many college students consider themselves "free at last"; all too often, however, they find that freedom has its costs.

- When citation information is provided after a partial or complete quotation, place the punctuation mark (comma, period, semicolon, colon, or question mark) after the parenthetical citation.

> "Preliminary reports have been consistent," Yates notes. "Without immediate changes to current practices, we will deplete known oil supplies by midcentury" (335).

- At the end of a block quotation, place the final punctuation before the parenthetical citation.

- Use three spaced periods (ellipsis) to indicate an omission within a sentence.

> According to critic Joe Robinson, Americans are overworked: "Ask Americans how things are really going and you'll hear stories of . . . fifty- and sixty-hour weeks with no letup in sight" (467).

- Place a period after the ellipsis to indicate an omission at the end of a sentence.

> The most recent information indicates, says Chen, that "we can expect a significant increase in costs by the end of the decade. . . . Those costs, however, should ramp up slowly" (35).

Paraphrase Information, Ideas, and Arguments

A paraphrase is a restatement, in your own words, of a passage from a source. Paraphrases can be used to illustrate or support a point you make in your document or to illustrate another author's argument about a subject.

Your notes are likely to include a number of paraphrases of information, ideas, and arguments from your sources. Before you integrate a paraphrase into your document, make sure that it is an accurate and fair representation of the source. Reread the source, and double-check your paraphrase against it. Then revise the paraphrase as necessary so that it fits the context and tone of your document. Use attributions and citations to ensure a smooth transition between your ideas and ideas from the source.

In the following example, note how student writer Donovan Mikrot lets readers know where his statement ends and where the support for his statement, in the form of a paraphrase, begins.

> As digital music and video gained popularity, inventors assumed that the same rules would apply to the new hardware and software they developed for digital files. Instead, the DMCA lets music, computer, gaming, and other companies restrict technology and research that could potentially be used to get around their DRM — including research that would help address computer security issues (EFF).

The writer's idea

Source of paraphrase (in this case, a Web document) is cited per MLA style.

Summarize Sources

A summary is a concise statement, written in your own words, of the information, ideas, and arguments found in a source. When you integrate a summary into your draft, review the source to make sure your summary is an accurate and fair representation. In addition, be sure to identify the source and include a citation.

You can summarize an entire source, parts of a particular source, or a group of sources to support your ideas.

SUMMARIZE AN ENTIRE SOURCE

Writers frequently summarize an entire work. In some cases, the summary might occupy one or more paragraphs or be integrated into a discussion contained in one or more paragraphs. In other cases, the summary might be as brief as a single sentence.

In her analytical essay about the health risks faced by overweight athletes, student writer Ali Bizzul provides a detailed summary of a scholarly article published in the *Journal of the American Medical Association.*

> According to Harp and Hecht (2005), two researchers at the University of North Carolina who conducted a study of 2,168 professional football players competing in the 2003–2004 season, 97% of NFL players would be considered "overweight" and 56% "obese" under the Body Mass Index (BMI) guidelines published by the National Institutes of Health for men in their twenties (see Fig. 1). The researchers noted that the group of football players with the highest rates of obesity — the linemen — also

According to APA style, the authors are identified in an attribution and the publication year is provided parenthetically.

The main point of the article

Additional information from the article

had higher blood pressure readings and higher incidences of sleep-disordered breathing than any other group of football players.

In contrast, Ali offers a much briefer, "nutshell" summary of another source.

The entire source is summarized; because it is a summary, not a direct quotation, page numbers are not necessary.

In an editorial in the medical journal *Neurosurgery*, three sports-medicine specialists noted that after a 1994 federal law exempted dietary supplements from regulation by the Food and Drug Administration, heat-related injuries among football players began to rise (Bailes, Cantu, & Day, 2002).

SUMMARIZE SPECIFIC INFORMATION AND IDEAS FROM A SOURCE

You can also use summaries to convey key information or ideas from a source. In the following example, the writer of an essay summarizes a section of a book about college admissions. His summary is highlighted in yellow.

Summary is introduced with the author of the book, title, and specific source of the ideas.

Bill Paul, author of *Getting In: Inside the College Admissions Process*, a book that tells the stories of several students applying to an elite Ivy League institution, shares three suggestions for students who want to get into a college. Paul bases these suggestions on his discussions with Fred Hargadon, who in 1995 was dean of admissions at Princeton. Hargadon suggested that the best way students can enhance their chances for acceptance into the college of their choice is to read widely, learn to speak a second language, and engage in activities that interest and excite them and that also help them develop their confidence and creativity (235–49).

Per MLA style, exact pages are cited.

SUMMARIZE A GROUP OF SOURCES

In addition to summarizing a single source, writers often summarize groups of sources. Such collective summaries (often introduced by phrases such as "Numerous authors argue . . ." or "The research in this area seems to indicate that . . .") allow you to establish a point briefly and with authority. They are particularly effective at the beginning of a document, when you are establishing the nature of the conversation you are joining, and can serve as a transitional device when you move from one major section of the document to another.

When you summarize a group of sources, separate the citations with a semicolon. MLA guidelines require including author and page information, as in the following example.

Several critics argue that the Hemingway code hero is not always male (Graulich 217; Sherman 78; Watters 33).

In APA style, the author and the date of publication must be included.

> The benefits of early detection of breast cancer have been well documented (Page, 2007; Richards, 2007; Vincent, 2008).

Present Numerical Information

If it suits your subject, you might use numerical information, such as statistics, in your document. You can present this information within sentences, or you might use tables, charts, or graphs, as student writer Jennie Tillson did in her problem-solving essay about college tuition costs.

If you use tables, charts, or graphs, you still need to accurately and fairly present the numerical information in your document and clearly identify the source of the data, just as you would for textual information.

Use Images, Audio, and Video

Including images in your print document or adding images, audio, or video files to your electronic document can enhance its effectiveness. Use caution, however, when taking images and audio or video files from other sources. Simply copying a photograph or an audio or video file into your document might be a form of plagiarism.

Student writer Hannah Steiner carefully documented the source of the image she used in her informative essay. Because she was writing an academic essay—rather than a document intended for publication and wide distribution—she did not seek permission to use it. (In contrast, the publisher of this book sought and received permission to publish that image.)

If you are creating an electronic document, such as a Web page or a multimedia presentation, use the following guidelines to integrating digital illustrations:

- Make a link between your document and a document that contains an image, a sound clip, or a video clip—rather than copying the image and placing it in your document.

- If it isn't possible or appropriate to create a link to another document, contact the owner of the image, sound clip, or video clip for permission to use it.

- If you cannot contact the owner, consult the Fair Use Guidelines on the UT Libraries' Web page at http://www.lib.utk.edu/copyright/fairuse.html.

As you would for any sources you cite in your document, make sure you fairly present images, audio, or video and identify the author or creator.

Only by investing in educating their citizens during hard economic times will states see the benefits of having educated workers and business owners—and higher-earning taxpayers—in the state during better times. For this reason, higher education should be a top priority in even trimmed-down state budgets so that students and their families won't face drastic increases in tuition.

At the same time, students still ultimately bear the responsibility for finding the best path to an affordable college education. Students and their families are a necessary part of the solution. They should be willing to apply to a variety of schools, including those they can afford more easily without financial aid. Many students and their families are now considering less expensive routes to a college degree, such as enrolling in public universities or community colleges in their home states (Young). Out of eighty-seven college freshmen surveyed at Colorado State University, 80% were likely to recommend community college to a sibling or friend concerned about tuition costs (Tillson). When asked about the benefits of attending community college, students responded that they saw it as "easier to afford" and appreciated that it "makes it easier to work and attend school at the same time" (see fig. 1). The survey shows that students today are giving community colleges serious thought as an alternative to a four-year university.

A parenthetical reference to the figure is provided.

The figure is located immediately below where it is mentioned in the text.

The figure summarizes key findings from a survey.

A caption provides information about the source of the data.

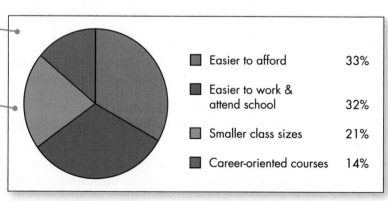

■	Easier to afford	33%
■	Easier to work & attend school	32%
■	Smaller class sizes	21%
■	Career-oriented courses	14%

Fig. 1: The perceived benefits of choosing a community college. Based on survey data from Tillson

⌐ A Chart Presenting Information in an Essay

the most promising alternatives in development is hydrogen — an abundant fuel that is environmentally safe, is far more versatile than gasoline or diesel, can be used to create electricity and fuel internal combustion engines, and produces no waste. Because of these attributes, some experts have argued that a hydrogen economy — an energy system that uses only a hydrogen-oxygen reaction to create energy and electricity — could solve many fuel-related problems, from global warming to America's dependence on foreign oil (Crabtree, Dresselhause, and Buchanan 39). At first glance, hydrogen appears to be the perfect choice. However, three barriers stand in the way of widespread hydrogen usage: as a fuel, it is expensive to produce, difficult to store, and complicated to distribute.

The key to a hydrogen economy is the fuel cell, which uses hydrogen gas and oxygen to produce electricity. In a way, a fuel cell is like a battery, but it never requires charging and it produces only electricity, heat, and water vapor (see Fig. 1). The U.S. Department of Energy (DOE) explains that hydrogen fuel cells use electrode plates to separate hydrogen's protons and electrons, diverting the stream of electrons to

Fig. 1: Simplified model of a fuel cell. United States Department of Energy, "Hydrogen Fuel Cells."

> The figure is located next to where it is referred to in the text.

> A parenthetical reference to the figure is provided.

> Text is "wrapped" around the figure and caption.

> The figure illustrates a complex process that would be too difficult to describe using text alone.

> A caption provides information about the source of the figure.

create electricity. A "stack" of fuel cells is scalable, so the same basic structure has many different uses ("Hydrogen Fuel"). In theory, stacks of hydrogen fuel

ꞁ An Image Providing an Overview of a Complex Process

How Can I Ensure I've Avoided Plagiarism?

Because plagiarized material will often differ in style, tone, and word choice from the rest of your document, your readers are likely to notice these differences and wonder whether you've plagiarized the material—or, if not, why you've written a document that has so many stylistic inconsistencies. If your readers react negatively, it's unlikely that your document will be successful.

You can avoid plagiarism by quoting, paraphrasing, and summarizing accurately and appropriately; distinguishing between your ideas and ideas in your sources; and identifying sources in your document.

Quote, Paraphrase, and Summarize Accurately and Appropriately

Unintentional plagiarism usually occurs when a writer takes poor notes and then uses the information from those notes in a document. As you draft, do the following:

- Look for notes that differ from your usual style of writing. More often than not, if a note doesn't sound like your own writing, it isn't.

- Place quotation marks around any direct quotations, use ellipses and brackets appropriately, and identify the source and the page or paragraph number of the quotation.

- Make sure that paraphrases differ significantly in word choice and sentence structure from the passage being paraphrased, and identify the source and page or paragraph number from which you took the paraphrase.

- Make sure that summaries are not just a series of passages or close paraphrases copied from the source.

Distinguish between Your Ideas and Ideas in Your Sources

Failing to distinguish between your ideas and ideas drawn from your sources can lead readers to think other writers' ideas are yours. Examine how the following writer might have failed to distinguish his ideas from those of Joel Levine and Lawrence May, authors of a source he used in his essay.

Failing to Credit Ideas to a Source

According to Joel Levine and Lawrence May, authors of *Getting In*, entrance exams are an extremely important part of a student's college application and carry a great

deal of weight. In fact, a college entrance examination is one of the two most significant factors in getting into college. The other, unsurprisingly, is high school
grades.

Because the second and third sentences fail to identify Levine and May as the source of
the information about the second important factor affecting admissions decisions—
high school grades—the passage implies that the writer is the source of that
information.

As it turns out, the writer actually included the necessary attribution in his essay.

Giving Credit to the Source

According to Joel Levine and Lawrence May, authors of *Getting In*, entrance exams
are an extremely important part of a student's college application and carry a great
deal of weight. In fact, they claim that a college entrance examination is "one of the
two most significant factors" in getting into college (the other, unsurprisingly, is
high school grades).

> The attribution "they claim" credits the source of the information to Levine and May.

> Quotation marks are used to indicate a partial quotation.

You can use attributions to distinguish between your ideas and those obtained from
your sources. As you draft your document, use the name of an author or the title of
the source you're drawing from each time you introduce ideas from a source.

Examples of Attribution

According to Scott McPherson . . .

Jill Bedard writes . . .

Tom Huckin reports . . .

Kate Kiefer observes . . .

Bob Phelps suggests . . .

In the words of Pamela Coke . . .

As Ellen Page tells it . . .

Reid Vincent indicates . . .

Jessica Richards calls our attention to . . .

Check for Unattributed Sources in Your Document

Writers sometimes neglect to identify the sources from which they have drawn their
information. You should include a complete citation for each source you refer to in

your document. The citation should appear in the text of the document (as an in-text citation, footnote, or endnote) or in a works cited list, references list, or bibliography.

The following examples use MLA style for citing sources; more detailed information about the sources appears in a list of works cited at the end of the document. In the first example, the writer uses a combination of attribution and parenthetical information; in the second example, the writer provides only a parenthetical citation.

> MLA-style in-text citations include the author's name and exact page reference.

Reid Vincent argues, "We must explore emerging energy technologies before we reach a peak oil crisis" (322).

"We must explore emerging energy technologies before we reach a peak oil crisis" (Vincent 322).

If you are using MLA format, be sure to cite page or paragraph numbers not only for direct quotations but also for paraphrased and summarized information. (If no page or paragraph numbers are provided, such as in a Web source, cite the author only.) The following paraphrase of Reid Vincent's comments about energy needs includes the page number of the original passage in parentheses.

Reid Vincent argues that we need to investigate new energy technologies now, instead of while we are facing a critical oil shortage (322).

To learn more about identifying sources in your document, see page 315.

How Should I Document My Sources?

In addition to citing your sources within the text of your document, you should provide complete publication information for each source you've used. Fully documenting your sources helps you avoid plagiarism, gives credit to others who have written about a subject, and creates a record of their work that your readers can follow and build on. By documenting your sources, you show that you are aware that other writers have contributed to the conversation about your subject and that you respect them enough to acknowledge their contributions.

Documenting your sources can help you achieve your purposes as a writer, such as establishing your authority and persuading your readers. If your readers find that you haven't documented your sources, either they'll suspect that you're careless or they'll decide that you're dishonest. In either case, they won't trust what you have to say.

Choose a Documentation System

Many professional organizations and publications have developed their own rules for formatting documents and citing sources. As a result, writers in various disciplines know how to cite their sources clearly and consistently, and their readers know what to expect. For example, a psychologist writing an article for the *Journal of Counseling Psychology* knows that submissions to the journal go through a rigorous review for substance and style before being accepted for publication. The journal requires that writers use the documentation system created by the American Psychological Association (APA). Given the high level of competition for space in the journal, the writer knows that even if the article is substantive and compelling, it will not be accepted for publication if it does not use APA style appropriately. After ensuring that the article is clearly written and well argued, the writer will double-check the article to be certain it follows the APA's formatting and source citation guidelines.

The documentation systems most commonly used in academic disciplines are the following:

- **MLA**. This style, developed by the Modern Language Association, is used primarily in the humanities—English, philosophy, linguistics, world languages, and so on.

- **APA**. Developed by the American Psychological Association, this style is used mainly in the social sciences—psychology, sociology, anthropology, political science, economics, education, and so on.

- ***Chicago***. Developed by the University of Chicago Press, this style is used primarily in history, journalism, and the humanities.

- **CSE**. This style, developed by the Council of Science Editors (formerly the Council of Biology Editors), is used mainly in the physical and life sciences—chemistry, geology, biology, botany, and so on—and in mathematics.

Your choice of documentation system will be guided by the discipline or field within which you are writing and by any documentation requirements associated with your writing project. If your project has been assigned to you, ask the person who assigned it or someone who has written a similar document which documentation system you should use. If you are working on a project for a writing class, your instructor will usually tell you which documentation system to follow.

You should also consider the genre you have chosen for your document. The manner in which sources are cited can vary widely from one type of document to another. For example, while academic essays and articles appearing in scholarly journals typically use a documentation system such as MLA or APA, newspaper and magazine articles often do not; instead they identify sources in the main text of the document rather than in a works cited or references list. If you write an electronic document that cites other online sources, you might simply link to those sources.

Provide In-Text References and Publication Information

How you document sources will depend on your writing situation. Most often, you will (1) provide a reference to your source within the text and (2) provide a complete set of citations for your sources in a works cited or references list.

The specific format of your in-text citations will depend on the documentation system you are following. If you use MLA or APA style, you will refer to sources in the text of your document using a combination of attributions and parenthetical information and include a list of sources at the end of your document. The works cited list (MLA) or references list (APA) includes the following key publication information about each source:

- author(s) and/or editor(s)
- title
- publication date
- publisher and city of publication (for books)
- periodical name, volume, issue, and page numbers (for articles)
- URL and access date (for online publications)

Each documentation system creates an association between in-text citations and the works cited or references list.

In Summary: Using Sources Effectively in Your Written Draft

- ✦ Use sources to support your points (p. 309).

- ✦ Indicate the boundaries between source material and your own ideas (p. 314).

- ✦ Modify direct quotations carefully (p. 319).

- ✦ Revise paraphrases to fit your style (p. 320).

- ✦ Summarize entire sources, parts of sources, or groups of sources (p. 321).

- ✦ Integrate numerical information appropriately (p. 323).

- ✦ Integrate images, audio, and video responsibly (p. 323).

- ✦ Check for unintentional plagiarism (p. 326).

- ✦ Document your sources (p. 328).

C Work-in-Progress Research and Writing Activities

Understand Your Paper Assignment

Read and Reread Your Assignment.

Reading your assignment multiple times before you begin writing (and while you are writing your first draft) will give you a clearer idea of what the assignment is asking you to do. It's a good idea to underline, circle, or highlight key words or phrases in the assignment.

Identify the Paper's Purpose.

Most of the papers you write in first-year composition courses have the purpose of persuasion—perhaps of **informing readers** by telling them new information, **changing the minds of readers** who do not share your point of view, and/or **prompting readers to take some action**.

Identify the Question to Answer or Issue Requiring Your Response.

Usually, your paper assignment will tell you to answer a particular question or to examine a specific issue. (You even may find it helpful to phrase the issue in the form of a question.)

Use the Questions below to Understand Your Paper Assignment.

Answer these questions after you have completed the readings that accompany your paper assignment:

1. What is the purpose of the paper you need to write? (Do you need to inform, change someone's mind, or prompt someone to take action?)

2. What specific question(s) have you been asked to answer?

3. What specific issue(s) have you been asked to respond to?

4. What type of paper have you been asked to write? That is, do you need to write an argument paper, a research report, or some other type of paper?

5. Name the readings you must complete and/or further research you must do *before* you can start your paper.

Fill in the following:

In this paper, I am going to write an essay about the topic of _____

_____ after I read the following texts _____

_____

and/or do the following research _____

_____.

My thesis should make a claim about the issue of _____

_____ or answer the following

research question(s) _____

_____. The intended reader for my paper is _____

_____.

If you do not have a good idea about what you are supposed to do for your paper, talk with your instructor or a Writing Center tutor.

Create a Double-Entry Reading Notebook

Try using a helpful approach to reading called a **double-entry notebook**.

Get a notebook and draw a line down the middle of each page. (Most people find a spiral-bound notebook best for this purpose.)

On one side of the page, write down the information you most often need to know when completing an assigned reading, some of which is referred to in Chapter 2. Common information includes the answers to such questions as: Who is the author? What do I know about the reason this text was written—the context and purpose? What is the main point, and where is it located in the text? What evidence does the author give to support that point? These are just the basics, of course—and you should add your own.

On the other side of the page, jot down your own notes, questions, and opinions as you read—a kind of running commentary on the information you find out from the author and the text. Using this method, you gain a clearer sense of what the author is saying (and why and how), and also you get a chance to start questioning and making connections to things you already know or want to know. Plus, you get a chance to voice your own opinions about what is being said and how it's being presented.

For an example, see http://writingcommons.com/research/textual-research/critical-reading/double-entry-response-format.

Go ahead and try this on your own—in English and any other class!

Use the SQ3R Approach to Better Understand an Assigned Reading

A popular method of reading called **SQ3R** refers to the process of **surveying**, **questioning**, **reading**, **reciting**, and **reviewing**.

To use the SQ3R method, you first survey (or skim) the material you're reading pretty quickly and then try to jot down some questions that come to mind about it. Next you read the material more carefully, looking for answers to your questions and also, of course, for the main points of the text. Once you're done, you recite to yourself, a classmate, or your instructor what those main points are. Finally, you go back and review the text.

You may be surprised at how helpful the SQ3R method is for preparing for class discussions about your topic and for getting through the mountains of research material you find!

Your instructor may ask you to try this out in class or to do it for homework:

1. Skim the assigned reading.

2. Write down two or three questions.

3. Read the text more carefully, and answer your questions.

4. Create a bulleted list that "recites" on paper the main points of the text.

5. Review the text again, and write down what you now know about its content.

Read a Scholarly Source as a Believer— and as a Doubter

Try this technique, made popular by the rhetorician Peter Elbow, to help you understand scholarly essays. For this activity, you will need to read a text **twice**—first as a **believer**, and then as a **doubter**.

When you read as a believer, you discard your own opinions and get into the writer's argument. Reading as a believer involves trying to see the world as the writer does. Empathize with the writer's beliefs and values, and put aside your skepticism and biases while you listen to what he or she has to say. This can be a difficult task if you already have strong opinions about an issue. If you are struggling to believe the writer's position, think about experiences from your own life that might support that position or beliefs and values that you and the writer share.

Reading as a doubter involves questioning what the writer has to say. Be skeptical, challenge assumptions, and demand proof as you read. Raise objections based on your doubts. Reading as a doubter seems easier for most people, but it still requires a lot of work. If this type of reading proves difficult because you agree with the writer's argument, imagine what objections might be raised by someone who doesn't share the same beliefs and values. You might even picture yourself as a lawyer cross-examining a witness in a courtroom.

1. Based on your reading as a **believer**, write a brief summary of the essay.

2. When you read as a believer, which of the writer's arguments were you best able to connect with? Why?

3. Describe the experience of reading this essay as a believer. Was it easy? Difficult? Did any of your views on the issue discussed in the essay change? Could you connect any of your beliefs and values with the writer's?

4. Based on your reading as a **doubter**, write a brief summary of the essay.

5. When you read as a doubter, what were your objections to the essay? What questions did you raise?

6. Describe the experience of reading this essay as a doubter. Was it easy? Difficult? Did any of your views on the issue discussed in the essay change?

7. Having read as both a believer and a doubter, what is your position now on the issue discussed in the essay?

How to Write an Abstract

Your instructor may ask you to write an **abstract** of a research report. An abstract is a short summary—a "capsule" of the paper. It is used to help other researchers know quickly the most basic information about your work so that they can decide whether it's relevant to their interests. People also read abstracts to gain a "digest" form of what a particular research study did and what its conclusions were.

The following Web pages provide details about how to write a good abstract and include multiple examples:

http://owl.english.purdue.edu/owl/resource/656/1

http://owl.english.purdue.edu/archive/oldfiles/angela/originalfiles/e%20abstract.html

http://research.berkeley.edu/ucday/abstract.html

Read the information and instructions on the above sites, and then write a draft of the abstract your instructor asked you to write.

If possible, ask a classmate, your instructor, or a Writing Center tutor to review your draft once it's done.

How to Write a Research Proposal

Use the following activity to create a formal **research proposal** for any of your research projects. See Chapter 3 for more information on writing a research proposal.

1. Provide the working title for your project.

2. Describe your issue.

3. Describe your purpose for working on this project.

4. Describe your readers' needs and interests.

5. State your research question.

6. Briefly review key findings about your issue from the sources you found as you explored your topic.

7. Indicate how you'll locate additional arguments, ideas, and information about your issue.

8. Include your project timeline.

9. Include your working bibliography.

10. Discuss the key challenges you face (optional).

11. Identify specific funding requests (optional).

You can download or print this activity at **bedfordresearcher.com**. Click on **Activities > Create a Research Proposal**.

If possible, ask a classmate, your instructor, or a Writing Center tutor to review your draft once it's done.

How to Write an Annotated Bibliography

Creating an **annotated bibliography** is more than an exercise in research. When you make an annotated bibliography with several entries that address the same subject, you create a "map" of the current written conversation in the area in which you're reading. When it's time to write your essay, it is much easier to position other voices in relation to your own, because you'll be on top of your research!

An **annotated bibliography entry** consists of a **works cited** bibliographic entry and a **short paragraph that both summarizes and comments upon the information and usefulness of a given source**. In addition to reading the information about creating an annotated bibliography in Chapter 3 and reviewing the sample annotated bibliographies on pages 65, 75, and 158, take a look at the following Web pages:

http://www.writing.utoronto.ca/advice/specific-types-of-writing/annotated-bibliography

http://olinuris.library.cornell.edu/ref/research/skill28.htm

https://owl.english.purdue.edu/owl/resource/614/03

Once you've reviewed the features of annotated bibliographies, try writing a draft of your own.

If possible, ask a classmate, your instructor, or a Writing Center tutor to give you feedback on your draft.

The Steps of a Research Project: Activities from *The Bedford Researcher*

The Bedford Researcher, by Mike Palmquist, includes helpful guides for writing and researching.

Go to **bedfordresearcher.com**, and click on **My Research Project Activities**.

There you will find many downloadable files that will help during the process of planning your English 102 research projects.

We recommend the following, especially:

- Develop and Refine My Research Question
- Conduct a Knowledge Inventory
- Record Searches
- Use Questions to Guide Critical Reading

How to Analyze Primary or Archival Source Materials

If your assignment asks you to find primary or archival materials, use any of the appropriate National Archives worksheets at the links below to analyze the features and to find out more about the particular source material you use.

Each worksheet is available as an interactive .pdf file as well; download the file you want, fill in the blanks, and save and print your completed worksheet.

Written Document

http://www.archives.gov/education/lessons/worksheets/document.html

Photograph

http://www.archives.gov/education/lessons/worksheets/photo.html

Artifact

http://www.archives.gov/education/lessons/worksheets/artifact.html

Cartoon

http://www.archives.gov/education/lessons/worksheets/cartoon.html

Poster

http://www.archives.gov/education/lessons/worksheets/poster.html

Map

http://www.archives.gov/education/lessons/worksheets/map.html

How to Write a Book Review

The most common types of writing about history include essays that draw conclusions based upon your own study of primary and archival sources, and essays that analyze other people's arguments based upon primary sources. The **book review** is a common assignment in history classes, for example, because it requires students to read critically and to think about whether one author's claims or conclusions are warranted and based upon the actual evidence available.

The History Department at Carleton College suggests that you should be sure to analyze how an author draws conclusions from evidence, and they recommend that you answer the following questions:

> How effectively does the author draw claims from the material being presented? Are connections between the claims and evidence made clearly and logically? Here you should definitely use examples to support your evaluation.
>
> What conclusions does the author reach, and how clearly are they stated? Do these conclusions follow from the thesis and aims and from the ways in which they were developed? In other words, how effectively does the book come together?
>
> — "How to Write a Critical Book Review,"
> http://apps.carleton.edu/curricular/history/study/criticalbookreview

The University of Wisconsin–Madison's Writing Center provides several suggestions for how to read and analyze a book that you have been asked to review (see http://writing.wisc.edu/Handbook/CriReadingBook.html). Note especially the following questions:

> What types of evidence or information does the author present to support his or her points? Is this evidence convincing, controversial, factual, one-sided, etc.? (Consider the use of primary historical material, case studies, narratives, recent scientific findings, statistics.)
>
> Where does the author do a good job of conveying factual material as well as personal perspective? Where does the author fail to do so? If solutions to a problem are offered, are they believable, misguided, or promising?
>
> — "Writing the Book Review,"
> http://writing.wisc.edu/Handbook/CriNonfiction_body.html

Visit the above Web pages, and following the suggestions there, write your review.

Once you write a draft of your book review, ask a classmate, your instructor, or a Writing Center tutor to give you feedback.

Obtaining Permission to Conduct Research with People

When you enter a fieldsite and make yourself known, you must follow many courtesies to make yourself and the people you're observing feel comfortable. All places in which you are a participant-observer involve an official process for "negotiating entry." As a beginning researcher, don't enter a site where you feel at risk in the subculture. For the kinds of projects this book suggests, you will not have adequate time to gain entry or insider status in an intimidating group. One of our students, for example, wanted to research a group of campus skinheads. They permitted Jake to hang out on the edges of their subculture, even allowing him to read their "code of honor," which included these statements:

- Be discreet about new recruits; check them out thoroughly.

- For prospects, we must have at least a ninety-day contact period in which we can attest to your character. A probationary period and productivity report will be given.

- Outsiders need no knowledge of what goes on or is said in our meetings.

- No racial exceptions whatsoever! All members must be 100 percent white!

Early on, Jake began to realize that his research position was unworkable, that he was stuck. While the skinheads had let him into their subculture as a potential recruit, he could never fully enter their subculture or worldview. Their code of honor, which excluded minority groups, stood against his personal ethics. In an early portfolio reflection, Jake wrote, "I never hung out with them in public. I never went to an organizational meeting. I realized I was an outsider to this subculture."

Jake's negotiation experience was so dramatic that he was unable to gain full access, and so he was unable to collect the data he wanted. No matter how interested in and enthusiastic we are about a possible fieldsite, we must be conscious of our own comfort levels and even potential dangers in investigating certain groups or places.

Harvey DuMarce, another of our students, experienced difficulty negotiating entry into a fieldsite owing mainly to his own assumption that it would be easy for him

"Obtaining Permission to Conduct Research with People" and "Sample Informed Consent Form" are taken from Bonnie Stone Sunstein and Elizabeth Chiseri-Strater, *FieldWorking: Reading and Writing Research*, Third Edition, pp. 140–143 (Chapter 3, "Reading Self, Reading Cultures: Understanding Texts").

to do so. He is a Native American, a Sioux, who wanted to research a gambling casino on another tribe's reservation. Because of his heritage, he assumed that he would be welcomed. But he wasn't. He had enormous difficulty finding people who were willing to talk to him, and he never really knew whether it was because of his Sioux background or because he was perceived as a student. Eventually, he had a conversation with the woman who ran the gift shop at the casino, and she introduced him to others. As his informant, she helped him gain an insider status in a place where he had assumed he already had it.

Any fieldsite you enter requires that you be conscious of your own personal assumptions and how they reflect your ethics, but you must also be respectful of the people whose lives you are watching. It is common courtesy for researchers to acknowledge time spent with informants with gestures as small as writing thank-you notes or as large as exchanging time (tutoring or babysitting, for example) or obtaining grant-funded stipends to pay them. As you work your way through the process of getting permission or "negotiating entry," be sure to follow these guidelines:

- Explain your project clearly to the people you will study, and obtain the requisite permission from those in charge.

- Let your informants understand what part of the study you'll share with them.

- Think about what you can give back to the fieldsite in exchange for your time there.

Some sites may require official documentation, as in the case of two of our students who collaborated on a study of a day-care center. The center required them to have an interview, submit a proposal describing their project, and sign a document attesting that they had reviewed all of the center's rules and procedures. Entry might be simple, laborious, or even impossible. For this reason, don't wait too long to make yourself visible to the insiders you study. One student we worked with spent over a month in the field observing a Disney store. When she attempted to get official permission to write about this store, however, she was denied entry and could not continue her project.

Once you finalize your site, you might want to check with your instructor to find out your university's policy with respect to research on human subjects. [See UTK policies on classroom research: http://research.utk.edu/forms_docs/human_subjects_classroom.pdf.] For long-term projects, the university's **human subjects review board** usually requires that you file a proposal and submit permission forms from your informants. They are called "**informed consent** forms," and on page 346 we present a sample of one of our own forms as a model. Universities usually have less formal procedures for the kind of short-term fieldwork that you might do for a one-semester course, and often have no requirements for filing permissions. Fieldworkers, no matter what size their projects, are ethically responsible for accurately showing the voices of their informants on the page. We feel strongly that you should receive permission from all the informants whose work you audio or video record as well as from any official person at your fieldsite.

The Ethics of Fieldwork: A Brief History

Whether you're conducting a long-term project with formal permission or a classroom-based study with a short informed consent from each informant, it's important to understand a bit of the history of human subjects' review for research. While institutions' rules differ, the reason for their protective policy never changes, at least for research conducted in the United States. In 1974, the National Research Act established the National Commission for the Protection of Human Subjects of Biomedical and Behavioral Research. Members of the Commission came from diverse disciplines including medicine, law, religion, and bioethics, and their job was to identify the basic ethical principles that should underlie research with human subjects. Prior to this time, there had been far too many cases of research that harmed its subjects. In 1979, five years after their first meeting the Commission published what's commonly called "the Belmont Report," which identifies three basic principles relevant to the ethics of research involving human subjects:

1. **Respect for Persons.** Informants should participate in research studies voluntarily and have enough information to make a decision about their participation. If you expect to interview a nurse, for example, and follow her throughout her clinical day or even meet her at home, you would need to inform her of your plan and see if she is willing and available to give you that much of her time.

2. **Beneficence.** Researchers should protect informants against risk from harm and also from the loss of any substantial benefit that might be gained from research. Let's say, for instance, you're working with a punk rock band that has fallen on hard times. You write an exciting essay about their ups and downs. You sell it to a magazine. In this instance, you are profiting from their story. As an ethical researcher, you should either share the profits or not sell the story.

3. **Justice.** We need to select our informants fairly, without creating undue pressure, especially for people who already experience burdens. In this country, for example, in the 1940s, the Tuskegee syphilis study used disadvantaged, rural

black men to study the untreated course of a disease that is by no means confined to that population.

These three principles from the Belmont Report cover the ethics of research in the United States in all disciplines across research communities. Whether you're working in a lab on stem-cell research, studying the behavior of penguins, working in a soup kitchen, or writing about a punk rock band, the basic ethics are the same—respect for persons, beneficence, and justice.

Sample Informed Consent Form

Mary Smith, Researcher

Dormitory Hall

State University

City, State

Telephone Number/E-mail address

I give my permission to Mary Smith to use my written and spoken words in her research project written for "Composition/English 102" at State University.

I understand that I may read and approve the final draft of the material she uses about me in her project.

Printed Name: _____ Date: _____

Signature: _____

Address: _____

_____

Telephone number/E-mail Address: _____

I prefer to use this pseudonym: _____

Resources for Conducting Interviews, Surveys, and Observations

Use this page from bedfordresearcher.com to locate Web sites that support qualitative research methods, such as interviews, observation, and surveys.

General Resources

Qualitative Research

http://www.uncwil.edu/people/pricej/teaching/methods/interviewing.pdf

Information on types and methods of research is presented in outline form by explaining themes, debates, and uses of qualitative research.

Writing Guides on the Writing Center at CSU

http://writing.colostate.edu/guides

These guides focus on research methods and theories related to empirical research with links to specific information for researchers.

Collecting Data Outside the Library

http://contentselect.pearsoned.com/unit4.html

Pearson Education's ContentSelect gives information on collecting all types of data including interviews, surveys, observations, and experiments.

Conducting Interviews

Northern Illinois University on Conducting Interviews

http://www.engl.niu.edu/wac/interview.html

The University's English Department lists steps involved in planning and conducting interviews for research projects.

Eastern Kentucky University on Conducting Interviews

http://www.president.eku.edu/EqualOp/condinterviews.php

This article details goals, steps, and legal considerations to know when conducting interviews.

General Guidelines for Conducting Interviews

http://www.mapnp.org/library/evaluatn/intrview.htm

This site, written by Carter McNamara, offers information on preparation, type, sample questions, and other resources for conducting interviews.

Peace Corps' Conducting Interviews in the Community

http://www.peacecorps.gov/wws/educators/lessonplans/lesson
.cfm?lpid=207&sid=5

This site offers general interview information along with essential questions
and guides to help students practice interviewing and develop listening skills.

Tips and FAQs for Interviewing

http://www.hr-guide.com/data/G021.htm

This human resources guide offers information about interviewing procedures
with sample questions and links to other resources.

Conducting Observations

**Writing@CSU Guide to Ethnography, Observational Research, and
Narrative Inquiry**

http://writing.colostate.edu/guides/research/observe

Colorado State University's guide discusses types, methods, and commentary
on observational research.

Observation and Inference

http://www.roguecom.com/interview/facts.html

This informational site defines observation and inference along with links to
applications and modules helpful in research procedures.

Designing, Conducting, and Analyzing Surveys

Writing@CSU Guide to Survey Research

http://writing.colostate.edu/guides/research/survey

Colorado State University's Writing Center guide explains survey research and
describes types of surveys and methods for designing, conducting, analyzing,
and reporting survey results.

Creative Research Systems' Survey System

http://www.surveysystem.com/sdesign.htm

Creative Research Systems offers a useful discussion and set of resources for
survey design and analysis. They characterize their site as "an introduction
with many useful do's and don'ts" for researchers.

American Statistical Association's Brochures about Survey Research

http://www.amstat.org/sections/srms/whatsurvey.html

This extensive collection offers clear, helpful brochures on survey research.

How to Create an Interview Protocol

Once you've decided that you'll be conducting an interview for your research project and have designed an interview questionnaire that will answer your research question(s), check to see if your interview protocol is effective by using the outline below, which comes from http://www.stanford.edu/group/ncpi/unspecified/student_assess_toolkit/interviews.html.

An Interview Protocol Checklist

What Should an Interview Protocol Contain?

a. A heading

b. Instructions to the interviewer (opening statements)

c. The key research questions to be asked

d. Probes to follow key questions

e. Transition messages for the interviewer

f. Space for recording the interviewer's comments

g. Space in which the researcher records reflective notes

How to Create Good Interview Questions

Once you've decided that you'll be conducting an interview for your research project, you will need to design an interview questionnaire that will answer your research question(s).

1. The Web site http://ed-web3.educ.msu.edu/digitaladvisor/Research/ interviewing.htm provides helpful, step-by-step information about creating an interview guide (also called a "protocol") and includes specific advice about the types of questions to ask and tips on how to word them.

    Click on "**What Makes a Question Important?**" for an overview. Then, click on "**What Makes a Question Answerable?**" and design your questions following the models given there.

2. Another site, a wiki, also offers some excellent guidelines for creating interview questions. Even though its name, "Idiot's Guide to Qualitative Interviewing," may sound nonacademic, its content is based upon legitimate information.

    Go to the following site: http://kakali.org/qualipedia/index.php?title= IDIOT%E2%80%99S_GUIDE_to_Qualitative_Research_Interviewing#II._ Interviews_.26_Questions

    Click on the "**Grounded Theory Interview Questions**" link to get a downloadable document file that includes sample questions. Adapt several of them for your interview protocol.

Once you've created a draft of your interview questions, ask a classmate, your teacher, or a Writing Center tutor to give you feedback on your questions, and then revise them.

How to Evaluate Interview Questions

On your own or with a classmate, write out answers to the questions below in order to determine whether your interview questionnaire is likely to be successful. The questions, which come from http://www.okstate.edu/ag/agedcm4h/academic/aged5980a/5980/newpage16.htm, should provide you with a sense of how to revise your planned interview.

Evaluation of a Questionnaire or Interview Script

Is the question necessary? How will it be used? What answers will it provide? How will it be tabulated, analyzed, and interpreted?

Are several questions needed instead of one?

Do the respondents have the information or experience necessary to answer the questions?

Is the question clear?

Is the question loaded in one direction? Biased? Emotionally toned?

Will the respondents answer the question honestly?

Will the respondents answer the question?

Is the question misleading because of unstated assumptions?

Is the best type of answer solicited?

Is the wording of the question likely to be objectionable to the respondents?

Is a direct or indirect question best?

If a checklist is used, are the possible answers mutually exclusive, or should they be?

If a checklist is used, are the possible answers "exhaustive"?

Is the answer to a question likely to be influenced by preceding questions?

Are the questions in psychological order?

Is the respondent required to make interpretations of quantities or does the respondent give data which the investigator must interpret?

Revise Your Interview or Survey Questions

Most researchers have to write several drafts of their interview or survey questions before they settle on ones they think will work well to gather people's responses to the subject the researchers are interested in.

After you have drafted your own questions, look at the examples of initial and revised questions on the Purdue OWL's site, http://owl.english.purdue.edu/owl/resource/559/06.

Review your questions to check for the following problems that are common in first drafts of interview and survey questions:

- Are they biased?
- Do they assume what they ask?
- Are they double-barreled?
- Are they confusing or wordy?
- Do they relate to (or note) what you want to learn?

If you find any of the above problems, revise the questions using the models on the Purdue site as a guide.

How to Transcribe an Interview

The Louisiana Voices Folklife in Education project (http://www.louisianavoices.org/unit2/edu_unit2_transcribing_interviewp2.html) offers a step-by-step worksheet for transcribing an interview. Complete the instructions to practice transcribing some of your interview.

Instructions: Select a short portion of [your] tape to transcribe. [. . .] Before starting, write the number on the tape counter at the beginning point. Transcribe until you fill all the lines in the text box. When you have finished [. . .], write the ending number on the tape counter. Here are some points to remember:

1. Write down each word you hear. Stop the tape when needed, [and] rewind occasionally and listen to the same section as you read along, making sure you wrote the words in the correct order. You may need to do this several times. If you can't understand the words, ask another person to listen or simply leave a blank space.

2. Each time a new speaker talks, use their full name and then initials so readers can follow along. Maria Hernandez would be MH, etc.

3. People talk much differently than they write. They begin new sentences without finishing the old one. They may add a lot of extra words (called "crutch words") such as "you know" and "yeah." If you think the words are crutch words and you want to leave these out of your transcript, say so at the beginning. "I removed crutch words and false starts from this transcript." Also say whether you are including all the "uhs" and "ums" and "ahs."

Some hints:

- Sometimes sentences aren't complete. That's okay. Just write what you hear. When a sentence is not complete, put a dash at the end (—).

- To add your own comment or explain something that the interviewee didn't fully say, put brackets [ ] around your words. For example, "I learned how to do it [to crochet] when I was nine years old."

- Don't try to make your transcription sound better by adding your own words or correcting grammar.

- Use standard spelling and don't try to write in dialect or "how it sounds." In other words, write "that" instead of "dat," even if "dat" is what you hear.

- Sometimes it's not easy to hear where one sentence ends and another begins. Just write it the best way you can. The main idea is that the transcript is accurate and comes close to how the speaker really sounds.

- If you can't hear the words, leave a blank and come back to it later or have someone else listen to the tape. If you still can't figure it out, use ellipses . . . three spaced dots . . . to represent something left out.

- If you want to emphasize a word, use italics.

Here's a sample transcript:

1	**Anna Hernandez:** Aunt Maria, I was wondering what kinds of vegetables you
2	use in your chicken soup?
3	**Maria Hernandez:** I like to use celery, parsnips, and carrots mostly, but I
4	always use, see, like these here. I always use carrots. If we have potatoes,
5	of course I put those in. [Tastes the soup].
6	**AH:** How do you cut up the vege . . .
7	**MH:** . . . Carrots — I always put carrots in, you know, in thick slices, but it
8	doesn't much matter how I do the potatoes. No special way, really.

You'll find that transcribing a tape is an art in itself. No two people will transcribe the same tape the same way.

How to Create a Survey

Once you've decided that you'll be conducting a survey for your research project, you have to design an effective survey questionnaire that will answer your research question(s).

The Web site "Social Research Methods/Knowledge Base" includes guidelines for the types of questions to write, the content and wording of the questions, the type of response format to use, and the order of the questions in your survey.

Visit the Web site http://www.socialresearchmethods.net/kb/survey.php and follow the links for:

- Types of surveys
- Types of questions
- Decisions about question content
- Decisions about question wording
- Decisions about response format
- Question placement and sequence

Once you have created a draft of your survey, share it with a classmate, your instructor, or a Writing Center tutor to test it out and revise it.

Create a Visual Presentation of Survey Data

Once you have analyzed your survey data, it's a good idea to try to represent some of the key findings in visual form.

To learn how to create effective visual graphics, check out the tutorial on "Preparing Effective Charts and Graphs" by Roger Munger, accessible at http://bcs.bedfordstmartins.com/techcomm8e/tutorials/chartsgraphs/1a.html.

At the end of the process, create one of the following types of graphics using your survey findings:

1. Pie Chart

2. Gantt Chart

3. 100-Percent Horizontal Bar Graph

4. Vertical Bar Graph

5. Line Graph

How to Analyze Data

The University of Pennsylvania's Anthropology Department offers some good advice on conducting data analysis (http://www.sas.upenn.edu/anthro/anthro/dataanalysis).

According to this advice, researchers should:

- Read through the field notes, notes on interviews, interview transcripts, site documents, or whatever data has been gathered several times. Becoming very familiar with the information at the start helps to proceed.

- Mark the data and take notes on any patterns, connections, similarities, or contrastive points in the data. Does anything stand out as a usual way of doing things at the site? What seems unusual, and why? What becomes clear analytically that was not clear before? [. . .]

- Follow up on what you noticed above by looking for "local categories of meaning" in the data. What terms do the informants have for things? What can you as a researcher identify as themes, even if the informants don't? Remember that the main purpose of ethnography is eliciting "native points of view"; these "local categories" are its components. Try to come up with a list of "local categories" from the data. [. . .]

- Once we have arrived at some conclusions regarding the data gathered, we must consider the question of how to focus on the guiding question which drove the research. Can that question be answered from what we learned? Is another question more appropriate? What other questions has the research provoked? Remembering that the thesis sentence must be an answer to the guiding question, it is important to work back and forth between our emerging conclusions and guiding question to produce a cohesive paper.

When you have completed your collection of interview or survey material, think back to what your initial research question was and start to "code" or analyze your data by following the steps above and those described in Chapter 7, especially the "constant comparison" method.

1. Make a chart of the patterns, similarities, and/or contrastive points you find. (You may need more than one chart.)

2. Come up with a list of "local categories" or themes in your data. If possible, list examples from your data that illustrate those categories or themes.

3. At the end of your process of data analysis, write out a draft of a "thesis sentence" that gives your evidence-based answer to your research question(s).

How to Take Field Notes

Plan where and when you will do your observation, and set aside time to write up your notes afterwards.

As described on the "Qualitative Research Guidelines Project" page of the Robert Wood Johnson Foundation Web site (http://www.qualres.org/HomeFiel-3650.html), "field notes are created by the researcher to remember and record the behaviors, activities, events, and other features of the setting being observed [and] are meant to be read by the researcher to produce meaning and an understanding of the culture, social situation or phenomenon being studied."

The suggestions for taking effective field notes include the following:

- Set aside a specific time to write up notes, preferably immediately after the observation.

- Write down the date, time, place, and details regarding major features of the setting and the people in it.

- Since one cannot always observe everything that is happening, decide in advance what things to look for based upon your research question.

Know specifically the kinds of things you should write down in your notes.

An online textbook for a qualitative research course at Northern Arizona University (http://jan.ucc.nau.edu/~mid/edr725/class/observation/fivedimensions/reading3-2-1.htm) gives suggestions for particular things to observe and record in your field notes:

1. The setting

2. The human, social environment, such as:

   - Characteristics of the subjects (e.g., gender, ethnicity, approximate age grouping, style of dress)

   - Patterns, frequency, direction of interaction and communication

   - Decision-making behaviors

3. Activities and behaviors

4. Informal interactions and unplanned activities

5. The language of program participants

6. Nonverbal communication

7. Documents

8. Observing what does *not* happen and other surprise findings

Finally, write up your notes in an effective and useful way.

For examples of field notes of varying quality, see the examples and comments on field notes offered by Kristen Myers, a sociology professor at Northern Illinois University (http://www.socqrl.niu.edu/myers/field%20notes.htm).

A Template for Writing Up Qualitative Research

A UTK teacher, Ryan Woldruff, created this template for writing up the results of a qualitative research study.

If your instructor allows you to use it (**you must ask!**), follow the format and guidelines for presenting your qualitative information.

Journal of Video Games and Gaming Culture

http://jvggc.inquirypub.com

The Name of Your Study Goes Here: A Qualitative Study

First M. Lastname

Journal of Video Games and Gaming Culture 2010; 1:1

**Journal of Video Games and
Gaming Culture**
Volume 2 Number 1
April 2010 1 - #
© INQUIRY Publications
http://inquirypub.com
hosted at
http://online.sagepub.com

Name of Your Study Goes in This Text Box:

A Qualitative Study

Your M. Lastname

Department of English, University of Tennessee, Knoxville

Write an abstract in this text box. The abstract for your qualitative study should include summary statements about the **purpose** of the study, the **methods (participants, procedures)**, and **findings**.

Here is an **example** from Kutner, Lawrence A., Cheryl K. Olson, Dorothy E. Warner and Sarah M. Hertzog. "Parents' and Sons' Perspectives on Video Game Play: A Qualitative Study." *Journal of Adolescent Research* 23.1 (2008): 76–96. *SAGE*. Web. 12 Feb. 2010.

(**Purpose**) Public policy efforts to restrict children's access to electronic games with violent or sexual content are often predicated on assumptions about parental concerns. (**Methods**) As an initial step in determining whether those assumptions are accurate, the authors conduct focus groups of 21 adolescent boys and 21 of their parents or guardians to explore parents' concerns, compare parents' and children's perceptions, and see whether these are consistent with the focus of proposed legislation and other public policy efforts. (**Findings/Results**) Parents' primary concern is that games not interfere with their children's schoolwork, social skills, and exercise. They worry about exposure to violent content, but definitions of and opinions about what is harmful vary and may not match proposed public policies.

Introduction

Begin your paper by introducing the purpose for your study. What question are you asking? Is your question based on statistics? Observations? Current scholarly debates? Why is your question important? How does your study enter the conversations that are already present in video game literature? Cite other sources in this section to provide foundation for your own work.

Heading II

If you want to use subheadings within your larger sections, italicize them.

Methods

In the second section of your paper, describe the procedures you used to collect data for your project. Did you use a survey? Who, when, and how did you survey? What questions did you ask? Did you observe a setting? Who, what, when, and how did you observe? What questions did you ask after your observation?

You can set this up with subheadings. For example Kutner, Olson, Warner and Hertzong's "Parents' and sons' perspectives on video game play: A qualitative study" use:

Participants

Kutner et al. describe the qualifications for being a participant and how they recruited participants.

Procedures

Kutner et al. discuss the way in which they retrieved information: focus groups with moderators, procedures for discussion, questions that were asked to boys, questions that were asked to parents.

Data Analysis

Data analysis is the process of looking for findings. For example, Kutner et al. state, "After each group, the moderators discussed themes that emerged and noted unanticipated findings. The audio recordings of focus group discussions were fully transcribed. . . . We also created charts of representative participant quotes grouped by theme" (83).

Findings

This section is where you report what you have found as a result of your study. *Refrain from adding personal comments to this section.* Instead, think of it as an index-like entry of what you've found to be important as a result of your study.

For example, from Kutner et al.: "Content analysis of the data revealed four primary areas of parental concern: (a) the balance boys struck between video game play and other activities, (b) the restrictions on video game use imposed by each household, (c) the content of video games, and (d) the influence video games could have on boys" (83,84). Then, Kutner et al, give specific examples/quotations/concerns from the participants.

Discussion

In this section, you analyze your findings. Here, you can present some sort of stance based on the results of your study. Here, you return again to the question that you've introduced at the beginning—based on what you've found, have you gotten any closer to an answer to your question? If so, how so? If not, why not?

Future Work

This last section is where you can state what your findings mean to the future of video game studies. How might future scholars, including yourself, further investigate what you've found to be important in your own study? This section should be 1-2 paragraphs long.

References

If you use references, cite them accordingly here.

Kutner, Lawrence A. , Cheryl K. Olson, Dorothy E. Warner and Sarah M. Hertzog. "Parents' and Sons' Perspectives on Video Game Play: A Qualitative Study." *Journal of Adolescent Research* 23.1 (2008): 76-96. *Sage.* Web. 12 Feb. 2010.

Key Questions for Evaluating Qualitative Research Papers

Before you hand in your qualitative research paper, try to answer the following questions. If you find areas in which you could improve your draft, go ahead and revise one more time before handing it in to your instructor.

Was a qualitative approach appropriate for the study the researcher conducted?

Was the objective of the research to explore, interpret, or obtain a deeper understanding of:

- how people think,

- how people perceive things,

- what people believe, and/or

- how people act?

Does the paper (and especially the introduction) describe an important problem that the paper addresses and state a clearly formulated research question?

One of the first things to look for in any research paper is a statement of why the research was done and what specific question it addressed.

How were the setting and the subjects selected? (Intentionally, with a strong orientation to answering the research question, or randomly?) Is this described in the paper?

Qualitative research studies seek to gain an in-depth understanding of the experience of particular individuals or groups; the researcher should therefore deliberately seek out individuals or groups who fit the bill, rather than selecting interview/survey participants or settings for observation in a random manner.

What methods did the researcher use for collecting data, and are these described in the final paper in enough detail?

- Were the methods used for collecting data a sensible and adequate way of addressing the research question? (Were the interview, survey, and/or observation methods appropriate ways to collect data that would answer the specific research question?)

- Has the reader been given enough information *in the written presentation* about the methods used?

What method(s) did the researcher use to analyze the data, and are those referred to in the paper?

Did the researcher use a systematic way of interpreting the data collected—e.g., constant comparison method, thematic coding, and so forth?

Does the researcher state findings that arose from the interview, survey, and/or observation data?

Does the researcher refer to actual data from interviews, surveys, and/or observations in the written presentation? Are quotes from interviews, charts from survey findings, or quotes from field observations included?

Does the written paper answer the research question? Are the conclusions/answers justified by the actual data collected? (Are the results credible and valid?) (Note: The answer to the research question that the researcher comes to based upon the data is actually stated as the "thesis" in the introduction.)

Generate a List of Alternate Search Terms

Not every source that might be helpful in your research will necessarily use the exact keywords you've used in your research question. To be sure to locate as many useful sources as possible, generate a list of alternative search terms.

As suggested in Chapter 9, you should first identify the keywords in your research question. For each keyword, think of a list of synonyms or related words. For instance, if your research question includes the word "dogs," you might list terms like "canines" and "puppies." (Depending on the focus of your research question, you might also consider "pets," "wolves," "terriers," and so forth.)

Once you've generated a list of alternate search terms, search using these terms connected by the Boolean operator "or." Your search string might look like this:

(dogs OR canines) AND (rabies OR hydrophobia)

Now, try this out on your research question, and make a list of your keywords below. Also make informal notes of what you find when you search using each term.

Browse the Stacks

As noted in Chapter 9, online search engines can be very effective at searching for materials, but many do not allow you to *browse* materials easily. When you have physical, printed texts in front of you, it can be easier to browse and find useful materials that a more focused, online search might not turn up.

Use the a keyword search in the UT Libraries' catalog to locate the titles of two or three books related to your research question; try to find books that are located in different parts of the library (i.e., that have call numbers that are as different as possible from each other). Write down the call numbers for these books, and go to the stacks where they are shelved. Once you're there, spend some time **browsing**— looking at the books that are shelved *near* the books you searched for.

Here are a few questions to consider:

- Can you locate other books near the ones you searched for that seem to be on the same subject?

- How are these books related to the books you searched for?

- Why do you think these books are shelved together? What is their common topic? Try to be as specific as possible.

- How are these books different from the book you searched for? What other perspectives or issues do they deal with?

- In what ways might these books contribute to your research?

- What new questions do these books raise for you in your research?

How to Paraphrase Source Material

One of the reasons you engage in secondary source research is to find out and respond to what others have said about the issue you have chosen to research, so it's natural that as you write you'll want to refer to what other scholars have written. You could quote your sources, of course, but quoting too much takes away from your own writing. Often, it's better to paraphrase from a source that you want to use.

The concept behind paraphrasing is simple: Write down the meaning of a passage from a source in your own words. That phrase, "in your own words," can be tricky, though. It's usually not sufficient simply to replace key words from the original passage with synonyms. For instance, if an original passage read, "The data show that children who experience head trauma are more likely to have undetected complications," and you write, "The data demonstrate that young people who experience head injuries are more likely to have unnoticed complications," that would *not* be an effective paraphrase.

To paraphrase well, you also need to think about the structure of the sentence(s) you want to use. Writers are careful to arrange their ideas in ways that help them achieve their particular purposes in writing, but your reason for writing is likely to be different from that of the source you want to use. Therefore, you'll need to think about how you want to arrange the paraphrased material—that is, what word order and sentence structure you want to use—to best meet your goals in writing.

The following Web sites have good advice for how to paraphrase effectively:

> http://owl.english.purdue.edu/owl/resource/619/01
>
> http://writing.colostate.edu/guides/researchsources/includingsources/paraphrasing/without.cfm
>
> http://library.duke.edu/research/plagiarism/cite/paraphrase.html

Remember, when you paraphrase, you're presenting someone else's ideas in your writing, so it's essential that you identify the source of those ideas. You must cite the source of any material that you've paraphrased, in a parenthetical citation, a footnote, or in your own words, depending on the discipline, genre, and style convention you're following.

How to Integrate Quotations into Your Document

When you want to quote from a source, it's important to do it in a way that helps your reader grasp a point that *you* want to make. There are many ways you can do this, but here is one way that you can use a quotation from a source effectively as evidence in your own writing:

1. Write a topic sentence that states the point you want to make.

2. Write a sentence (or two) that briefly summarizes the source you want to quote from, in a way that shows how the source is related to your topic sentence.

3. Quote the passage you've selected from the source. Be sure to cite the source appropriately.

4. Write a sentence (or two, or more) that explains how the quotation reinforces your topic sentence.

For example, look at the structure of the following paragraph:

Not everyone agrees, however, that these changes have been beneficial. The econo-mist Lori Thompson, for instance, in her book *The Change We Need and the Change We Don't*, argues that the recent alterations to the tax code have hurt the very con-sumers they were meant to help. These policies, she writes, have been "abysmally ineffective" at encouraging economic growth, leaving "the poor and the middle class without any increased confidence in their savings accounts or their political leaders" (211). Thompson's critique suggests that, despite the self-congratulatory rhetoric coming from Washington since the tax changes were introduced, more work needs to be done to ensure a fair and prosperous society.

For more information on integrating quotations into your paragraphs, consult the following Web sites:

http://www.unc.edu/depts/wcweb/handouts/quotations.html

http://www.virtualsalt.com/quotehlp.htm

http://www2.ivcc.edu/rambo/eng1001/quotes.htm

How to Create and Design Effective Posters

As a way of recognizing the excellent research students do in English 102, the First-Year Composition Program, Writing Center, and the UT Libraries sponsor a contest (usually in the Spring) for the best posters that visually communicate English 102 research projects. The prizewinners receive cash awards.

The Four Criteria for the Selection of Prizewinners

1. First Impression

Does the poster stimulate interest and/or discussion?

Is there a memorable and specific "take-home" message?

How specific/adequate is the title?

Is the poster design creative and pleasing?

2. Research Content

Is the research question clearly stated?

Are the results of the research (the "findings") stated and displayed clearly?

Is supporting evidence provided/displayed?

3. Layout and Readability

Can someone read the poster easily from three feet away?

Is it easy for a reader to follow the sequence of information in the poster?

Is the poster too crowded, or is there too much small-print text? (Conversely, is there too much unused space?)

Is font size and style easily readable?

Is the color scheme easy on the eye?

4. Correctness (Note: Posters with *any* errors will *not* be eligible for prizes.)

Are there any grammar, punctuation, spelling, or other sentence-level mistakes?

Is correct parenthetical documentation provided for any outside sources cited?

Is a "Works Cited" page on the back of the poster, also, for any sources cited?

Below are some links about the features of effective posters, how to create them, and some good examples. While the examples refer mostly to displays of scientific research, the guidelines and suggestions should be applicable or adaptable to English 102 research posters.

Creating Effective Poster Presentations (from North Carolina State University)

http://www.ncsu.edu/project/posters/NewSite/index.html

http://www.ncsu.edu/project/posters/examples

Further Resources on Creating a Poster (from Grand Valley State University)

http://www.gvsu.edu/ssd/further-resources-on-creating-a-poster-3.htm

Actual student posters from a previous English 102 Writers' Block Party—See Jenn Fishman's entries on the following Flickr site

http://www.flickr.com/search/?w=all&q=Writers%27+Block&m=text

Supplies

Most students use large foam core posters or heavy-duty paper posters, which are available at the Art & Architecture Building supply store. Alternatively, Jerry's Artarama on Homberg Drive has a great selection of art supplies not too far from campus for those who have access to a car.

For those who wish to use a PowerPoint template to help design the poster, consider using the following free download for 3' x 4' poster: http://www.posterpresentations .com/html/free_poster_templates.html. However, please note that separate, large-format printing is required with this option, so check to see what the cost is at the Copy Center at the University Center or at Kinko's.

D Sample Student Work

✳ Sample Historical Research Paper

The following student paper was written for a 102 course on the topic "Inquiry into Memory and Performance." The instructor, Teresa Hooper, describes the course as follows:

> Whether we like it or not, what we remember — of ourselves, of others, and of past events — is inextricably tied to *how* we remember; what someone recalls in a personal letter to a friend, for instance, will be quite different from the same memory repeated on the witness stand. The genre, the audience, and even our emotional state will drastically change the content of our memories. If this is so, how much can we trust our own memories of the past — or anyone else's, for that matter? And how do we negotiate the limitations of our memories when we live in a society that holds memories in such high regard? This class will explore the complexities of memory and recollection in fields like biology and psychology, in memoirs and comic novels, stage plays, politics, and legal testimony, using both our own memories and those of others for our own investigation.

The assignment for the paper that follows was titled "Inquiry into the Past: Making History from Memories" and asked students to conduct archival research in UT's Special Collections Library. Here is the instructor's assignment:

> **For this assignment, you will use the following resources from Special Collections:**
>
> MS 1334: The Harry Cushing Collection: Folders 1–2
> MS 1161: The John Watkins Papers: Box 1 (letters) and 2 (pictures, personal effects).
>
> Generally, as readers and scholars, we consume our history like we eat fast food: prepackaged, cleaned up, and heavily processed. If you ever wondered what sort of materials historians or ethnographers used in their research and how they use them to reconstruct a piece of history, this paper is your opportunity to try your hand at the real deal. Using the point of view from a long-dead person's letters, you're going to reconstruct a little sliver of Civil War history from the soldiers' and their families' point of view.

The papers you will be working with are collections from two Civil War soldiers who fought in the general Knoxville area — one as an enlisted man, and one as an officer. Both collections contain letters written to various people, and in both, it's *very* surprising how differently the men tell their stories to different people. John Watkins, for example, writes letters home to both his fiancée and her brother. When you read the letters, you would think he was fighting in two different wars.

Note: These are mostly letters that nobody has completed scholarly work on yet. In many cases, you'll be the first person ever to transcribe them. Because nobody has done the dirty work for you, your primary job will be to reconstruct a piece of primary information (a letter) into a readable and usable document for research. What you'll find is that you'll have gaps — ink spots, damage, missing pages, even illegible handwriting — that you won't be able to fix. You will have to decide what is important and what is not, and how to best work around those gaps.

What you will need to do for this assignment:

- Transcribe four single-sided pages of text. (*Note*: See the student's transcription of the letter used for the sample paper on pp. 162–64.)

- Write a historical description of the letter(s), putting it in a historical context using the rest of the collection, historical newspapers available in Special Collections or online, and/or other reference works/databases. Tell your reader (a researcher in Tennessee history) who the people are, what the letter(s) describes, and how the contents of the letter(s) reflect or refer to events happening when they were written. Make a case for one way in which your letter(s) is useful for a researcher — whether he or she is a historian, cultural anthropologist, or literary scholar.

Use a combination of primary and secondary archival information: You can use sources like online archives of old newspapers and magazines, microfilm historical books on the period, and the U.S. official records of the Civil War to help you.

Duncan 1

Beth-Ann Duncan

Teresa Hooper

ENGL 102

14 Mar. 2010

UTK Special Collections, MS 1334:

A Civil War Letter from the Harry Cushing Letters*

The University of Tennessee-Knoxville is the proud holder of a collection
of Civil War letters written by Harry Cushing in the MS Collection 1334. The
letter I transcribed, dated March 30, 1863, is a correspondence from Cushing to
his closest friend, Ned Atwater. The subject matter of the letter is the Battle
of Winchester, which took place near the Shenandoah Valley in the state of
Virginia, and the purpose of the letter is for Cushing to be able to confide in
his friend about the atrocities he'd witnessed upon viewing the aftermath of
the bloody battle. The information gained from this letter would be most helpful to historians interested in the Civil War era, as it gives detailed accounts of
specific areas where the fight was held and descriptions of formations, injuries,
and Cushing's own personal feelings. The letter, which goes into gruesome
detail when describing the battlefield, company units, and wounded men,
is a therapeutic method for Cushing to deal with the horrors of war.

Harry Cushing was a 2nd Lieutenant for the 4th Artillery in the United
States Army. He later rose to the rank of Chief Artillery and was a member of
the William Division, Banks 5th Army Corps (MS 1334). Born in Baltimore,
Maryland on November 8, 1841, he was the fourth son of George and Sarah
Cushing. His eloquent style of writing can be attributed to the fact that he
attended Brown University after his family moved to Providence. Cushing
enlisted in 1861 and was soon promoted to the rank of sergeant and then

The introduction gives contextual information and provides an interpretation of the letter's purpose.

The writer provides good historical information in the second and third paragraphs.

*See the student's transcription of Cushing's letter on pp. 164–64.

second lieutenant. Yet as successful as he was in the war, he chose to end his military career after the war was over in 1865 (Cushing).

The letter I transcribed is addressed to Ned Atwater, on March 30, 1863. The battle being discussed by Cushing is the Battle of Winchester. A part of the Jackson Shenandoah Valley Campaign, the battle took place on May 2, 1862, with the Union troops led by Major Gen. Nathaniel P. Banks, and the Confederate forces by Major Gen. T. J. Jackson. Winchester is said to have been one of the most fought-over locations in the Civil War. It is reported to have shifted between being controlled by the Union and the South over 70 times (*The Battle of Winchester*). The battle was a great success for Major Jackson, as he managed to outflank and overrun the Union troops on Bowers Hill. Many of the Federal troops fled after they realized their error and ran through Winchester and the Potomac River. This was one of the most decisive battles in the Jackson Shenandoah Valley Campaign ("Winchester, First"). It is interesting to learn that Cushing himself never actually fought in the Battle of Winchester. His company was thirty miles away from the scene, but when he arrived the next day, the images of the destruction affected him in such a way that he felt the need to share his knowledge with Atwater.

Cushing starts off his letter to Ned by informing him that he had a present for him. He says, "I write to let you know that I have got you a Secesh musket, one which was picked from a dead rest at the battlefield of Winchester" ("Letter to Ned Atwater"). We can deduce that this rifle was one that belonged to the Confederate Army, as the word "Secesh" was used during the Civil War as a slang term for the Rebel army. "Secesh" was basically a nickname and, at times, was used as an insult for Confederate soldiers (*Urban Dictionary*). He carries on describing the scene that met his eyes as his company found the slaughtered troops of the Battle of Winchester. There are references to damage done by artillery, scattered railings, trampled fences, torn ground, pieces of

> The writer summarizes some of the contents of the letter, quoting actual passages.

> The writer refers to secondary source information to help interpret the letter's context.

Duncan 3

shell casings lying everywhere, splintered fragments of the wooden musket butts, and finally, the gory pile of dead human bodies sprawled out over the terrain. One sentence states, "Their mattered hands clotted with great flocks of gore lawlessly over the dead leaves and their brains ooze out of their mutilated foreheads and mingle with the dust of the earth." It is recorded that a total of 2,419 casualties were reported at the conclusion of the battle. The Union bore the brunt of casualties from the fight, with 2,419 reported dead, compared to the 400 killed from the Confederates ("Winchester, First"). The Union lost six times as many men in that one battle.

In my opinion, the true scope of what Cushing saw can never be expressed on paper. It obviously was a traumatic experience, prompting his letter to Atwater. Another interesting item to ponder is the reason he went into such intricate explanations of the wounded, using flowing language and extensive sentences. Due to the severity of the battle, one can deduce that Cushing was not in the best of spirits. It is hard for anyone to deal with defeat, and during times of war that emotion is amplified. In terms of historical context, Cushing did not emphasize the importance the Battle of Winchester represented to both sides of the army. The people of the Shenandoah Valley were extremely loyal and true not only to Virginia, but The South. It was a fruitful area, largely populated with small farms or towns. A major issue politically was the fact that the region voted 99 percent in favor of secession. And although the area did not boast many slaves due to the low number of plantations, the advantages of agricultural and geographical assets made it a popular item between the two armies in terms of easy access and movement for troops. This is why the inhabitants endured invasions from enemy and friendly troops in search of control of the strategic area (*The Battle of Winchester*). This makes any conflict that occurred in this area important. Cushing, however, had no reference to the great loss endured to the Union that day, merely the significant observations of lives lost.

> The writer refers to secondary source information to help interpret the letter's context.

Duncan 4

In conclusion, I'd like to point out the significance of these letters as a link to the personal experiences felt by the brave men who fought and endured many hardships in order to bring a semblance of freedom and justice to the United States. This letter was a form of release for Harry Cushing. The fact that he had a friend to whom he felt close enough to write of the horrors he'd experienced indicates the great need for soldiers to talk about their experiences. And maybe this paper won't give great in-depth information on the policies of the commanders and their strategies, but it will let anyone who reads it receive insight into the real-life situations of soldiers, Union or Confederate, in the Civil War.

Duncan 5

Works Cited

The Battle of Winchester. We Make History, 2006. Web. 7 Mar. 2010.

Cushing, Harry C. "Letter to Ned Atwater." *Harry C. Cushing Papers: 1861–1865.*
 30 Mar. 1863. MS 1334. Hoskins Special Collections Library, U of Tennessee-
 Knoxville.

"Secesh." *Urban Dictionary.* Urban Dictionary, 2010. Web. 7 Mar. 2010.

"Winchester, First." *CWSAC Battle Summaries.* American Battlefield Protection
 Program, 2010. Web. 7 Mar. 2010.

✳ Sample Historical Research Paper

In her "Inquiry into Romance" section, Dr. Kelly Rivers asks students to conduct archival research to understand the topic from a historical perspective. Her assignment reads:

> Pick an element/issue of romance that you want to know more about; then pick a time period before 1980 (either a specific year or decade). Examine 1–3 primary texts from that era that reflect/illustrate an interpretation/view/perspective of romance. Write a historical analysis that explores the whats, whys, and hows of the text(s) — what clues are there? What do they mean? How are they used? Why are they used? What do we learn about the time period's take on romance?

The following sample paper demonstrates the archival research conducted by Morgan Livingston, who happened to come across some old letters in an antique shop in Tennessee. Her research led her toward a more thorough understanding of the purposes of love letters written during World War II and allowed her to offer close readings of the artifacts themselves.

Livingston 1

Morgan Livingston

Dr. Rivers

English 102

11 Mar. 2011

All My Love Forever, Bill

Although we rarely write them with pen and on paper in the twenty-first century, love letters, historically, have been simple ways for lovers to express their feelings toward each other to create a connection only the two involved can understand. Today, the art of writing love letters seems to have faded with the advent of text messaging and Facebook, but in the past, letters were the only means of communication, especially when it concerned contacting a soldier overseas during war in the early twentieth century. Doris Weatherford's *American Women and World War II* describes how women coped with the absence of their loved ones serving overseas during World War II and how they attempted to run their lives as routinely as possible in disorderly times. To investigate the validity of Weatherford's claims, I examined letters written and exchanged between a World War II couple, Mary Frances Hogan and Lieutenant William C. ("Bill") Brewer. Numerous letters between this couple illustrate how letters allowed couples to develop their relationships despite the distance and strain of war. In these letters, the lovers' repeated desire for normality, their shared interest in religion, and their mutual efforts toward comfort and consolation suggest that expressing their feelings in letters provided stability to their relationship to help it survive the pressures of war and extended separation. An analysis of the letters reveals that writing can help couples endure the emotional strain of war and absence.

One of the ways people maintained a sense of routine in the face of war was by keeping themselves occupied, and in part, they stayed busy so that they did not have time to contemplate how different their lives were from

> The writer lets readers know right away what the focus of the paper is.

> The introduction presents the main "points" the writer will explain in the body of the paper. These points are based upon the writer's analysis of the archival letters.

what they used to be. The demands of war kept the men fighting in Europe or Japan during World War II occupied. For a woman, however, this challenge was more problematic. Before the war, most women stayed at home and worried about domestic affairs, including taking care of their husbands. Like their husbands' and boyfriends' lives, women's lives changed considerably, particularly because they were encouraged to take jobs for the war effort. Weatherford notes that many recommended that women take jobs, of course, and the addition of leisure activities was also crucial to keeping a lonely bride busy while her husband was away (276).

> In this paragraph, the writer provides some context about the times, based upon the material in the external secondary source.

Beyond keeping the wife or girlfriend busy, keeping a routine that simulated life before the war also provided her with subjects about which to write to her soldier overseas. While Mary Frances Hogan does not write about working, she does extensively discuss her daily activities in her letters to Lieutenant Brewer (Figure 1). For instance, she writes about her daily activities (shows, shopping, and playing games with girlfriends) and hobbies that constantly controlled her time. Such details probably allowed Brewer to worry less about the homefront while he was away, because life at home sounded like it was as normal as when he had left it, according to Hogan's letters. This is important for two reasons: it seems Hogan is not only trying to help Brewer feel normal while he is fighting a war, but she is also putting on the appearance of normality for herself by focusing on typical daily activities. In other words, it seems Hogan is trying to convince both Brewer and herself that life has not changed that much. For example, in one letter to Brewer, she bemoans the end of the week and discusses her plans for the next weekend, noting that she plans on going to Asbury Park (Figure 1). She explains that she and a friend hope to get there, but mentions that car troubles might conflict with their plans (Figure 1). The way she talks to Brewer makes it seem like she is continuing an ongoing and ordinary conversation, of which this letter is a smaller piece.

> The writer makes a nice transition from the background context to the letters that are the focus of the paper.

> The writer references and analyzes specific passages from one of the letters.

Livingston 3

Weatherford warns that this focus on an ordinary, even ideal, life back home could have led to less than honest communication between the woman back home and the man overseas. Weatherford suggests that as time passed, men and women might portray themselves and their circumstances unrealistically, hoping to make the civilian life seem more glamorous and desirable (280). Lt. Brewer seems the most at risk for entertaining fantasies about non-war life, particularly when he discusses the future. In one letter written shortly after Christmas, Brewer notes that he wants to come home to the "same Mary Frances I left" (Figure 3). These kind of letters that detail the civilian life as more desirable could prevent the reader from knowing how the other person felt, if he or she were miserable or not. While some might call this practice dishonest, others might argue that this was a way of the writer keeping his/her reader protected and safe from worry. Grasping onto the sense of normalcy allowed soldiers and civilians alike to carry on each day because in "normal" conditions, the war seemed farther away and loved ones grew closer, even if the letters portrayed a happy life that was not actually there.

> The secondary source expert's observation provides a smooth way to transition into mentioning another feature of the letters.

Despite the emphasis on normality, worry constantly paralyzed the thoughts of men and women. Hogan constantly worried about Brewer, but she tried not to think about how he could be a different man when he returned: "I dreamed you were here but wouldn't call me. I certainly hope dreams mean nothing. Darling, it scares me to thing you may have changed--in fact, I just can't think about it" (Figure 2). Lovers struggled to believe in the future of their relationship when forced to deal with vast amounts of distress and anxiety all throughout the war. Brewer refers to Hogan's health in one of the first letters of many: "So you're gaining weight again. Very glad to hear that. Should build up your resistance against colds, etc. Take care of yourself" (Figure 3). Clearly, Brewer worried about Hogan back home just as much as she worried about him. As Weatherford theorized (280), they seemed to grasp

> This paragraph includes effective references to and analysis of actual passages from the letters.

on to the idea that the war would not change either of their personalities, and that they would be reunited with the same lover they knew before the war intervened. Much of a relationship between a soldier and a civilian during wartime was very stressful, with worry becoming very overwhelming. According to Weatherford, this type of relationship was very common between loved ones as they coped with the difficult times.

Another way lovers tried to cope with the strains of war was to discuss their religious beliefs with each other in their letters. Throughout the time they were writing to one another, Hogan and Brewer referred to religion and church on numerous occasions. One point that Brewer emphasizes is the fact that the mass is a widely used tradition in many countries outside North America. For example, on December 27, 1944, he writes, "Religion means so much to one over here. The Latin in the mass is the same and the mass is one of the few things universal in the world today" (Figure 3). He relied on God to carry him through battles, but he also allowed the church to bring him closer to the one he loved. His words reveal how important religion was in retaining a better, stronger relationship at that time, but also how important a common religion was as a sign of the couple's harmony:

> One realizes the material value as well as the aesthetic value of reli-
> gion. [I] still believe that our problems of religious differences can
> be worked out but we must both keep in mind that it'll be a potential
> cause of friction throughout our lives. Your sacrifice will have to be
> much greater than mine. That is the past that worries me most: how
> simple things would be if we both shared the same religious beliefs.
> (Figure 4)

Here, Brewer indicates that a common religious background could be a building block for relationships of the 1940s, because the stress and turmoil of war brought people closer to God and the church. They had to have something to

Livingston 5

rely on, which allowed lovers to have at least one stable thought to grasp onto while they could not be with the ones they loved.

Referring to shared religious beliefs in their letters was only one of the ways in which couples were able to sustain healthy, sane relationships during wartime. Brewer constantly reminds Hogan that he will be home soon and that he will never leave again: "[It] was very difficult to say goodbye but knowing that the next time we see one another there'll be no goodbye, made parting bearable" (Figure 5). The idea that he will return to Hogan helps him fight the war in front of him because he is driven by the power of the idea of love. Hogan also expresses her wishful thinking and hopes in her letters: "All these months I've looked forward only to being with you again--nothing else has mattered" (Figure 2). Without that sense of future connection, long-distance relationships would have struggled to remain intact even more than they already did. The looming idea of married life carried them through those tough, war-stricken years, showing that the idea of love was a major driving force in the 1940s, and the consistent consolation of these ideas of love and well being allowed relationships to remain stable.

These letters serve as a reminder of the importance of communication during stressful times as a way to weather emotional turmoil. A relationship was built upon each letter received by a loved one because any other form of communication was nearly impossible. From Bill Brewer and Mary Frances Hogan's letters, it appears that these were ways to address fear and to provide comfort. Their writing seems to have resulted in creating a stronger, more sustaining relationship. Having something to hold on to, such as past memories, future plans, religious values and sense of ordinary daily routines allowed lovers to remain in stable relationships and kept the idea of normalcy present each day. These letters between Bill Brewer and Mary Frances Hogan provide excellent examples of the importance of writing as a way to survive through wartime and to continue a lasting relationship.

> The transitions from one paragraph to another connect the various points the writer wants to make about the different features and purposes of the letters.

> The conclusion maintains a strong emphasis on the writer's analysis of the letters.

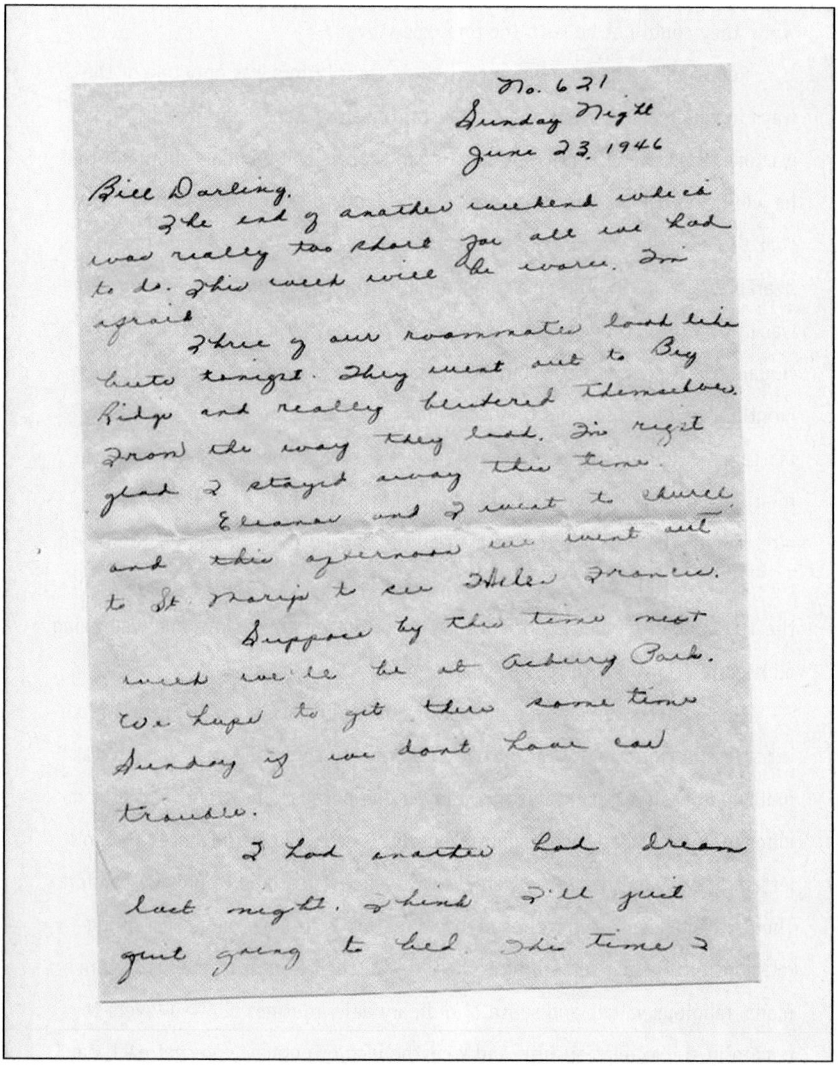

No. 621
Sunday Night
June 23, 1946

Bill Darling,

The end of another weekend which was really too short for all we had to do. This week will be worse I'm afraid.

Three of our roommates look like beets tonight. They went out to Big Ridge and really blistered themselves from the way they look. I'm right glad I stayed away this time.

Eleanor and I went to church and this afternoon we went out to St Mary's to see Helen Francis.

Suppose by this time next week we'll be at Asbury Park. We hope to get there some time Sunday if we dont have car trouble.

I had another bad dream last night. Think I'll just quit going to bed. This time I

Figure 1 Similar to all her letters, Hogan discusses her daily activities and future plans, which cause her to constantly be busy rather than sulking around the house alone.

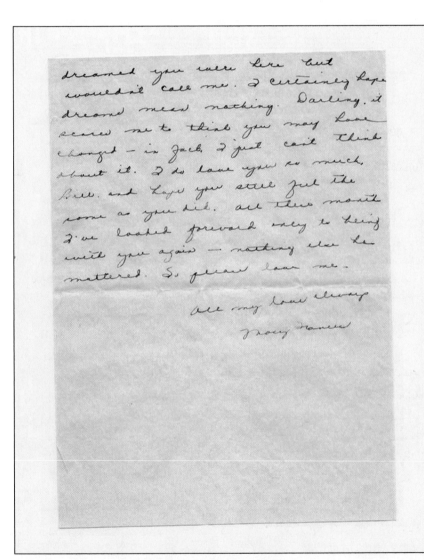

Figure 2 A continuation of the letter from Figure 1, Hogan expresses her distress about Brewer changing into a different person because of the war. She also emphasizes her need to be with him again.

Livingston 8

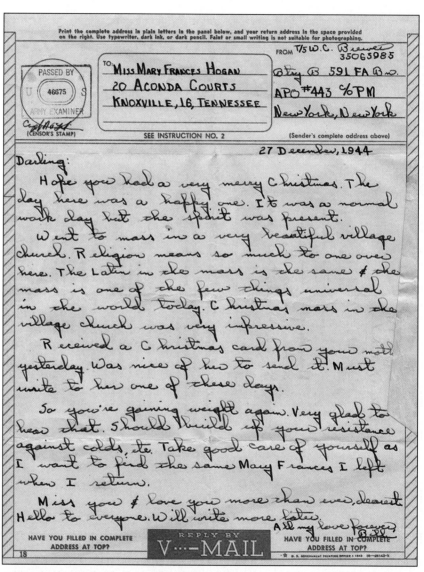

Figure 3 Brewer makes the point of religion being universal and states how important it is to him. He also touches on Hogan's health and wanting to return to the same woman he left.

Livingston 9

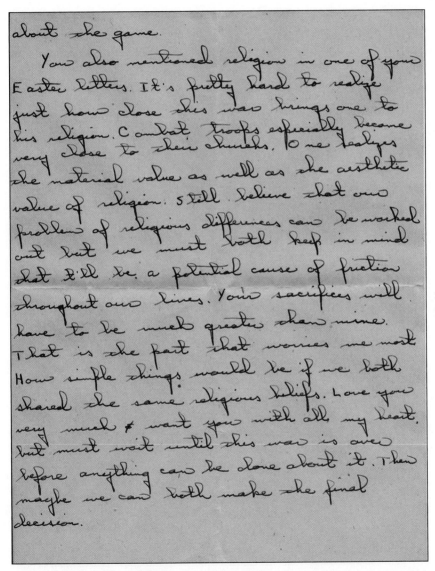

about the game.

You also mentioned religion in one of your Easter letters. It's pretty hard to realize just how close this was brings one to his religion. Combat troops especially became very close to their churches. One realizes the material value as well as the aesthetic value of religion. Still believe that our problem of religious differences can be worked out but we must both keep in mind that it'll be a potential cause of friction throughout our lines. Your sacrifices will have to be much greater than mine. That is the part that worries me most How simple things would be if we both shared the same religious beliefs. Love you very much & want you with all my heart. but must wait until this war is over before anything can be done about it. Then maybe we can both make the final decision.

Figure 4 Brewer accentuates his idea that religion will only make a relationship stronger, which is one aspect that aided in helping him through the war.

Livingston 10

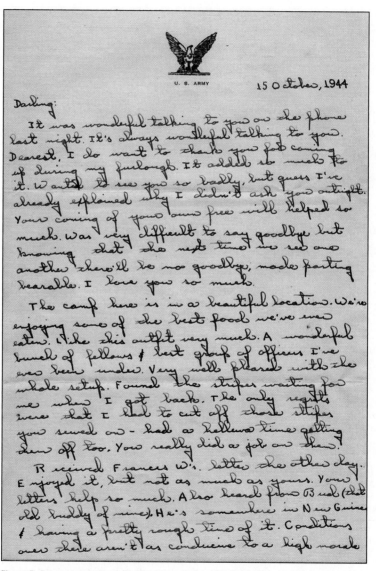

Figure 5 Brewer consoles both Hogan and himself, stating that he knows he will see her again in the near future.

Works Cited

Brewer, William C. "Letter to Mary Frances Hogan." 15 Oct. 1944. MS.

——. 27 Dec. 1944. MS.

——. 15 April 1945. MS.

Hogan, Mary Frances. "Letter to Bill Darling." 23 June 1946. MS.

Weatherford, Doris. *American Women and World War II*. New York: Facts On File,
    Inc., 1990. Print.

Sample Qualitative Research Paper

The following qualitative research paper was written by English 102 student Hannah Esworthy for a section taught by Casie Fedukovich. A shortened version of the assignment, "Unearthing Subcultures," is included below:

> We've been talking in class about the ways cultures differ and how these differences contribute to personal action. The culture in which we live, then, has some power over our actions. Some people choose to embrace fully "mainstream culture," while others choose to buck the system by making themselves a part of a group with differing value systems, modes of dress, languages, rites, rituals, and practices.
>
> For this paper, we're going to step away from "mainstream culture" and look closely at a "subculture" — "a cultural subgroup differentiated by status, ethnic background, residence, religion, or other factors that functionally unify the group and act collectively on each member" (*Dictionary.com*). Using this definition, find a local subculture and conduct *systematic* and *detailed* hands-on research (field observations, interviews, and/or surveys) to discover whether and how this subculture either participates in or rejects American culture. (Subcultures that reject American culture are called "countersubcultures." Think of the "beat" movement of the late 1950s or the "punk" scene in the 1970s.)

The instructor also included some comments about how she might proceed through the assignment:

> I might write about the "gothic" subculture at UT. I would come up with an initial research question and then start my investigations. I could go to a few "goth nights" at a club, interview some people, observe their interactions, and research practices in books and on the Internet. I would read a few "goth" blogs to get a sense of what values the members of this group hold. I would e-mail a few of the blog authors to ask more detailed questions.
>
> After completing the data collection phase, I would print out all of the e-mail correspondence and assemble it with my handwritten or typed interview notes, my "people watching" observations, and other research, and analyze the data using several techniques to see what patterns and themes exist — especially things that would help me develop an answer to my initial research question. Then I would write a draft of the paper and revise it carefully, seeking out help from my classmates, my instructor, and the Writing Center. Before I would hand the paper in, I would gather all of my research data together in a folder with my name on the front. Then, I would turn in that folder along with my paper on the due date!

Now see the paper written by Hannah Esworthy that responds to the "Unearthing Subcultures" assignment. The comments in the margins identify some of the notable features of the paper.

Esworthy 1

Hannah Esworthy

Casie Fedukovich

English 102

26 Sept. 2010

The Subtle Subculture of Vegetarians

A pretty girl in a tight tank top with a preppy purse, a girl with boy-short, dyed hair wearing an "achy breaky heart" T-shirt, a guy with a tiny ponytail and a barrette in his dark hair--on the surface, none of these people appear to have much in common. The unifying force that connects all of these individuals is a similar lifestyle characterized by a diet void of meat. The typical stereotype of a vegetarian is of a fanatical, sign-waving "PETA member" who "bombs fur factories" and eggs fur-sporting celebrities or of a "tree-hugging hippie" who is all about peace and love (Vance). While there may be some vegetarians who meet these criteria, does this image match with the real lives of college-student vegetarians? To discover more about vegetarians, I sent out an online survey through Facebook.com projected towards vegetarians, interviewed both vegetarians and meat-eaters, collected pamphlets, and observed a meeting of the University of Tennessee Vegetarian Student Alliance (VSA). I found that the vegetarian subculture is composed of a truly diverse assortment of people.

Definitions of "Vegetarian"

The basic definition of a vegetarian is one who does not consume meat. It seems straightforward enough, yet there are actually many subcategories and degrees of vegetarianism. A big controversy among vegetarians is whether or not fish is meat. A slight majority of those I asked (14 out of 24) believe that fish is meat and that true vegetarians do not consume fish. They believe this because "to consume a fish you consume its flesh" (Michael) and because "true" vegetarians eat "nothing with a face" (Fleming). According to *The Oxford Dictionary of Food and Nutrition* and *The Oxford Companion to the Body*, those

> This paragraph includes a good presentation of the background information the writer gathered.

> The writer effectively integrates statistics from survey results.

> This is a great example of how to include data from online interviews.

Esworthy 2

who believe that fish are acceptable in a vegetarian diet for whatever reason (10 out of 24) are labeled pescetarians or pescovegetarians. Vegetarians who eat eggs but do not drink milk are called ovo-vegetarians, those who drink milk but do not eat eggs are called lacto-vegetarians, and those who consume both are called lacto-ovo-vegetarians (cited in "Vegetarian"). Oftentimes, these classifications are shortened by omitting the word "vegetarian" and just saying "ovo" or "lacto-ovo" when used in conversation between fellow vegetarians.[1] Another subgroup of vegetarians is vegans, who go to great lengths to avoid all animal products and animal by-products. These include meat, eggs, dairy, leather, honey, silk, wool, and fur. Although there are a significant number of vegans, the majority of the vegetarian population is lacto-ovo-vegetarian.

This paragraph is an excellent example of how to use definitions effectively. It reads like an article one might find in a professional journal!

History of Vegetarianism

Vegetarianism has been around since before recorded history, so no credit can be given for its origin. The earliest records about vegetarianism appear to originate in the eastern religions like Hinduism and Buddhism (although not all Hindus or Buddhists are vegetarian). Even though today only a minority of vegetarians is Buddhist, it is interesting to note that the foundation of their philosophy is to not harm any living thing (Parkinson). While there exist many reasons to follow a meat-free diet, many vegetarians identify with this ethical position, which will be discussed in more detail further on. Until the phrase "vegetarian" was coined in the mid-nineteenth century by the British Vegetarian Society (Bluejay), vegetarians were known as Pythagoreans after Pythagoras, the Greek mathematician (whom many will recognize from the Pythagorean Theorem) (Parkinson). Vegetarianism was not uncommon in Asian countries such as China, but it took until the mid 1800s to really start accumulating support in the western world (Parkinson).

This paragraph gives a good presentation of contextual information relevant to the research problem/question.

This is an interesting fact. It would have helped even more to explain the reason that vegetarians were known as Pythagoreans.

[1]Pseudonyms are used throughout for interview/survey participants.

Esworthy 3

Motivations for Choosing Vegetarianism

The decision to become vegetarian is "highly personal" and multifaceted ("Information Sheet: Going Vegetarian"). There are as many reasons to live a vegetarian lifestyle as there are stars in the night sky. Because of that, the characterization of vegetarians is somewhat nebulous. As a whole, it seems vegetarians tend to be opinionated, especially on issues concerning vegetarianism and including the reasons for being vegetarian. According to a guy at the VSA meeting, "From least offensive to most, the reasons for becoming vegetarian are health, environment, then ethical grounds" (Elliott). Plenty of vegetarians would love to disagree, and many would point out that he left out cultural and societal influences as motives. From what I've gathered in my research, there are four general motives for living a vegetarian lifestyle:

Ethics and Morals: Some vegetarians have moral objections to killing animals for consumption, either because they believe killing animals for human gain is wrong or because they believe the meat industry is inhumane and immoral. When asked how she felt about the current consumer meat industry, Crystal Michael of British Columbia responded, "It's the main reason that I no longer eat any animal flesh--living a life of pain and suffering, just to be killed for the sake of someone's fleeting indulgence . . . it is just pointless." Of the 25 people I surveyed, 21 chose ethics and morals as one of their motives for being vegetarian.

Nutrition: A large percentage of the respondents named nutrition as their primary reason for becoming vegetarian. These people choose to reject meat from their diet (and sometimes fish, eggs, and milk as well, depending on the type of vegetarian) due to the numerous health benefits of reducing fat and cholesterol intake. Of the 25 people I surveyed, 21 identified nutrition as one of their motives for being vegetarian.

> This is good practice: providing the reader with constant reminders of how many of the people surveyed fit into each category.

Environment: A number of vegetarians are concerned about the environmental effects of raising livestock and the use of the world's resources. The mass farming industry is "far too wasteful and unnecessary" (Fitzgereld) and costly in terms of resources--current statistics estimate that "nearly half of the water and 80 percent of the agricultural land in the United States are used to raise animals for food" ("Meat and the Environment"). These vegetarians recognize the risk of feeding the world's resources to livestock while already-rampant starvation is on the rise. Of the 25 people I surveyed, 9 named concern for the environment as one of their motives for being vegetarian.

Upbringing and Religion/Culture: A few vegetarians said they choose their lifestyle based upon their family upbringing, religious beliefs, and/or the demands of their society. Naturally, most vegetarians choose to raise their children as vegetarians, too. "[Meat] wasn't a part of my diet at all when I was very little. It wasn't prohibited exactly, I just didn't know it was an option," says Sarah, who continues to live a vegetarian lifestyle as a 19-year-old college student (Brewer). Of the 25 people I surveyed, 2 chose culture and religion as reasons and 2 were raised as vegetarians.

Vegetarians' Lifestyles

Vegetarians tend to group together. In general they like to associate with each other and form groups including student organizations (the Vegetarian Student Alliance, for example), Facebook groups, regional organizations, online vegetarian dating sites, and other sites designed to connect the vegetarians within a community. Although not a rule by any means, they prefer to date/marry other vegetarians, and in the case of Sarah's parents, her mother wasn't a vegetarian until her husband converted her. Some of these groups aim to share vegetarianism and recruit others to this lifestyle, but just as often their purpose is simply to meet other like-minded people.

Esworthy 5

Beliefs about the Nutritional Value of Vegetarianism

While not cited as the number-one reason for choosing to becoming vegetarian, the belief that a balanced vegetarian diet is healthier than an omnivo-
rous one was shared by 21 of the 24 vegetarians I questioned. "Both can be
healthy," says one of the vegetarians I surveyed, "but I definitely eat more
vegetables and fruits than many of my non-vegetarian friends" (Marks). When I
first started inquiring as to why someone would "go vegetarian," I was naïve
enough to think the single reason was to save animals and to protest a flawed
and cruel system. I had never considered that there might be inherent health
benefits to cutting out such a cholesterol-laden food as meat from one's diet.
A current theory held by many anthropologists is that early humans were not
in fact omnivores, but rather herbivores (Bluejay). Although we have "canine"
teeth like carnivores, we also have molars, which are nonexistent in any other
meat-eaters. Additionally, cardiovascular diseases such as heart attacks and
high-blood pressure are much more prevalent among meat-eaters, suggesting
that our digestive system may not have been designed for meat (Bluejay).
William C. Roberts, M.D., editor of *The American Journal of Cardiology*, asserts,
"When we kill the animals and eat them, they end up killing us because their
flesh, which contains cholesterol and saturated fat, was never intended for
human beings" ("Quotes"). I had never heard of this theory before I started
inquiring about the health benefits of a vegetarian diet, and yet the more I
consider these facts, the more sense it makes. Many vegetarians are extra sen-
sitive about their nutrition and work diligently to eat a balanced diet, often
eating tofu and other soy-based products for protein. "It's so versatile!" says
Crystal Michael, about tofu and soy-based foods. "I had sweet and sour glazed
tofu with fresh mixed veggies on rice for lunch today." Vegetarians are hard to
nail down into neat demographic categories, but from the information I've
gathered, the number of people converting to vegetarianism for health reasons
is on the rise, and for good reason.

> This is a good example of how to include relevant research from a print source.
>
> The writer also demonstrates how to effectively use multiple research methods to answer a research question.

Esworthy 6

Conclusion

The subculture of vegetarians is exceptionally diverse. It is composed of people from every end of the spectrum, from hardcore vegans to casual pescetarians, preppy college girls to graying grandmothers, activists to nutritionists, North Americans to Asians, and beyond. As a vegetarian myself, I thought I already understood this subculture. The more I questioned other vegetarians and probed into its history and stereotypes, the more I realized how mistaken I was. I was astounded at the statistics my surveys came up with; I thought nearly all vegetarians were animal rights activists who wanted to prevent animal suffering, but my research proved otherwise. The only common, definite statement one can make about vegetarians is that they don't eat meat, yet this subculture demonstrates shared ideals, similar lifestyles, and a common origin. Although nobody can be put in a box, measured, and figured out completely, these similarities simply illustrate an array of passionate people whose diet is dictated by their values.

> The conclusion goes beyond a simple rehash of the thesis. It suggests something more: that the writer's findings on the group were not consistent with her initial conception of vegetarians, and that the group cannot easily be quantified. An excellent summation!

Esworthy 7

Works Cited

Bluejay, Michael. "A Short History of Vegetarianism." *Vegetarian Guide*. Michael
 Bluejay, 19 Sept. 2007. Web. 21 Sept. 2010.

Brewer, Sarah. Online interview. 21 Sept. 2010.

Elliott, Daniel. Personal interview. 24 Sept. 2010.

Fitzgereld, Paul. Online interview. 22 Sept. 2010.

Fleming, Chris. Online interview. 21 Sept. 2010.

"Information Sheet: Going Vegetarian." *Vegetarian Society*. Vegetarian Society,
 19 Sept. 2007. Web. 21 Sept. 2010.

Marks, Anna. Online interview. 21 Sept. 2010.

"Meat and the Environment." *GoVeg.com*. PETA, 2010. Web. 20 Sept. 2010.

Michael, Crystal. Online interview. 21 Sept. 2010.

Parkinson, Rhonda. "Vegetarian History in a Nutshell." *About.com: Chinese
 Food*. The New York Times, 2010. Web. 20 Sept. 2010.

"Vegetarian." *Answers.com Reference Answers*. Answers Corporation, 2010.
 Web. 19 Sept. 2010

"Quotes." *Vegetarian Society of East Tennessee*. Vegetarian Society of East
 Tennessee, Aug. 2007. Web. 20 Sept. 2010

Vance, Misty. Personal interview. 18 Sept. 2010.

Sample Student Survey Instrument (Online Survey)

Created by Hannah Esworthy for Her Paper "The Subtle Subculture of Vegetarians"

I'm a college student doing a research paper on vegetarians as a subculture, and I need some first-hand information from fellow vegetarians!

This survey is just intended to collect some general information--your name will not be disclosed in my paper.

To respond, you can copy and paste this into an email, fill it out, and send it to [studentusername]@utk.edu, or you can just paste it into a post and fill it out there.

The structure is in no way meant to be confining, so please feel free to elaborate on any and every question!

What was your main reason for choosing to live a vegetarian/vegan lifestyle?
[ ] ethical/moral grounds
[ ] nutritional benefits
[ ] negative effects on the environment
[ ] cultural/religious beliefs
[ ] other (please specify)

How do you feel about the current consumer meat industry?

Would you consider yourself an animal rights activist?
[ ] yes
[ ] no

Are you a member of PETA?
[ ] yes
[ ] no

In your opinion, is your vegetarian diet healthier than a non-vegetarian diet?

[ ] yes

[ ] no

How often do you eat tofu or other soy-based products?

Are you vegetarian or vegan?

[ ] vegetarian

[ ] vegan

Do you ever eat fish?

[ ] yes

[ ] no

Do you consider pescetarians to be vegetarians?

In your opinion, is sticking to a vegetarian diet difficult for you?

[ ] yes

[ ] no

How many years have you been a vegetarian?

What/who influenced your decision to become a vegetarian?

What kind of reactions do you get from people when you tell them you're a vegetarian?

_____

Thank you so much for taking the time to fill this out! Your input will help me greatly in representing vegetarians and dispelling any misconceptions people have about us.

✱ Sample Qualitative Research Paper

The following student paper was written for English 102, in a section entitled "Inquiry into the History of your Field," taught by Carolyn Wisniewski. The assignment sets up the objectives of the paper as follows:

> This unit of our class is meant to introduce you to different methods of collecting qualitative research, analyzing data, and constructing an effective claim based on data. For this paper, you will formulate a research question that arises from your field of inquiry; you will decide which method of data collection best fits your question — interviews (review pages 184–87 and 197–200), surveys (review pages 188–89 and 202–7), or a combination of both; and you will write a research report from the data you collect.

The instructor outlines the following steps to help students formulate a question and approach to the research project.

Steps:

1. *Research question:* Your research question should be based on a genuine question you have within your selected field or major. Think about what you've read or heard about in your field that seems to be controversial or that you don't know as much about as you wish. Make a list and choose the top one or two that seem most compelling to you. Ask yourself, "How can I add to this body of knowledge?" Your research question should be drawn from the answer to that question.

   Here's a personal example: When I was teaching in my master's program, I noticed a lot of concern about plagiarism from students, faculty, administrators, and the public. I encountered a few cases of plagiarism in my class and was struck by student responses when I spoke to them about their papers. I decided I had a real question here: "What do students think about plagiarism?" To gain a base of knowledge for that question, I read pretty widely. Then, I formulated a survey of fifteen open-ended questions and a eight true/false questions. I decided that I wanted to hear from students at the end of their first year of writing in college and that I wanted as representative a sample as I could get. I then solicited help from my colleagues in distributing a printed survey, from which I received 170 responses. From those responses, I coded my data and formed an analysis, and from that process, I developed my master's thesis.

   Review pages 48–50 and 181–82 as you begin to formulate your research question.

2. *Type of research:* What kind of methodology will best fit your question? In my example, I could have decided to interview students instead of surveying them. While an interview might have yielded more depth, I decided I was more interested in gaining a broad perspective from a larger sample of responses.

3. *Plan for research (timeline):* How long will your research approach take? For instance, setting up, transcribing, and analyzing interviews can be time-consuming, particularly if you need to reschedule interviews. Since you're planning on using people (referred to as "human subjects") in your research, you probably need to obtain some kind of permission and to make sure you are treating your research participants ethically (see "Obtaining Permission to Conduct Research with People" on pages 342–45 in Appendix C), which can be a lengthy process. Take a moment to reflect on the timeline for your research, and retailor your plan if that timeline doesn't line up with the timeline for this paper.

4. *Gathering and analyzing data:* Here's where you'll spend the bulk of your time preparing for this paper. Remember, an analysis is more than just a report. An analysis asks questions of the data, looking for assumptions behind respondents' answers, as well as connections, disparities, and patterns in the data. Think about how the data reveals answers to your overall research questions. As you analyze your data, please revisit pages 188–90 and 209–14.

Following is an example of a qualitative research paper from 102 student Brittany Stanford.

Stanford 1

Brittany Stanford

Carolyn Wisniewski

English 102

22 Mar. 2010

To Read or Not to Read: Examining the Reading Habits

of High School Students

The Adventures of Tom Sawyer, To Kill A Mockingbird, Julius Caesar, The Great Gatsby, Jane Eyre, 1984: These are just a few of the classic pieces of literature that are often included in the curricula of high school English courses. Since most assignments are based on the reading of specific novels, plays, short stories, or poems, it is obvious that reading comprehension is a crucial part of these English classes. With so many outside resources like *CliffsNotes* and *SparkNotes* available through the Internet, however, it is not hard to imagine that some students might ignore their reading assignments and take the easy way out. On the other hand, others may be more responsible and complete what their English teachers expect of them. Although everyone agrees reading is so important, are high school students really doing all that is required? What exactly are the reading habits of high school students, and what effects may those habits have?

Methods

To get a better idea of high schoolers' reading habits, I decided to go straight to the source and conduct my research through a combination of surveys and interviews. Using Facebook, I asked high school students to answer a ten-question survey about how and what they read. I also recruited Thomas Woods,[1] a high school student I know, to distribute physical copies of the survey at Halls High School in Knoxville, Tennessee.

---

[1]Pseudonyms are used for all participants.

> The writer does a good job of moving from the observation of a problem — with many resources, it might be less likely for students to do assigned reading — to a clear research question that can be answered through qualitative research.

> Many students effectively use Facebook to distribute surveys. Talk with your teacher about this option.

Stanford 2

Once I received the completed surveys, I interviewed two students so that I could understand more in-depth the reasoning behind their specific reading habits. I asked two high school students, Kathie Morgan and Karen Skye, a few open-ended questions regarding why they read the way they do, which helped to complete my research.

Results

Thirty high school students completed the reading survey via Facebook. Eight were in 9th grade, two were in 10th, ten were in 11th, and ten were in 12th. The students' GPAs ranged from 2.0 to 4.2. 70% of the students were enrolled in English courses on their grade level and 30% were in courses above their grade level.

When asked how many hours a week the students read for school, nineteen said 0 to 3 hours, five said 4 to 7 hours, five said 8 to 12 hours, and one said 13 to 16 hours. According to their responses, sixteen of the surveyed students have an A in their English course, nine have a B, three have a C, one has a D, and one has an F.

Next, two of the students said they weren't required to read any novels, six were required to read one, four were required to read two, seven were required to read three, five were required to read four, and six were required to read five or more. In response to the question about how many novels they actually read, eleven reported they did not read any, four read one, three read two, four read three, four read four, and five read five or more. For the books read, nine read all that were required without the use of summaries or analyses, nine used summaries and analyses for all that were required, nine used summaries and analyses for some that were required, and three did not read the novels or the summaries. Finally, sixteen of the students said they read for pleasure while fourteen do not. Of the students who do read for pleasure, seven said they spend 0 to 3 hours reading, five spend 4 to 7 hours, three spend 8 to 12 hours, and one spends 13 to 16 hours.

> The variety of research methods the writer uses offers the prospect for both quantitative and qualitative data.

> In this section, the writer presents just the numbers of responses to the survey questions—called the "raw data." If you have more questions and responses, consider using a table or chart to present this kind of information. See page 324 for an example.

Stanford 3

Getting the Grade

The first conclusion or "finding" drawn from the survey is that high school students' poor reading habits do not seem to affect their grades or GPA. While this may not seem to make logical sense, the answers to the survey prove it to be the case. Approximately 80% of the students surveyed have either an A or B in their English course; however, only about half (48%) of the A and B students read all that was required, and about fifteen (60%) spend only 0–3 hours reading for school. This leads to a question: exactly how are these students receiving such good grades? Responses from one of the interviews sheds some light on this. Kathie Morgan, a senior, admitted to only reading two of the four books she was required to read this semester and has a B in the class. When I asked her how she managed this, she replied, "I just do what I need to do to get by. I skim the books, sure, but just to get enough info to get the gist of what's going on. You know, enough to answer the questions on the quizzes." It appears that Kathie is not alone in her approach to reading; it could be this is how other students are passing their classes as well.

*Honor*able Students

The second finding regarding high schoolers' reading habits involves the level of English course in which a student is enrolled. Based on the survey results, students enrolled in classes above grade level, or "Honors" courses, tend to read more of their required readings than students enrolled in classes at grade level. Nine students who completed the survey were in Honors courses. All of them were assigned at least four novels, and all read them. I asked one Honors freshman, Karen Skye, why she chose to read for her English class, and she explained, "I don't know. It's not like I want to read. I mean I really really don't like English, but I have to do it, you know. I guess that's it. I feel like I have to do it, so I do." Karen even told me that she sometimes has her mother read novels to her. Although she is not doing all the reading herself in a con-

> **A good, clear topic sentence helps the reader understand how to make sense of the data from the previous section.**

> **Using a direct quote from an interview can demonstrate something that numbers and percentages cannot.**

> **This detail offers a clear picture of one student's experience.**

Stanford 4

ventional way, she is still using multiple approaches to complete her assignments. It is possible that Karen's responses offer some explanation for why
Honors students tend to have better reading habits than others. The students
in higher-level courses may feel they have a certain standard to live up to and
therefore will do everything they can to succeed.

Everybody Loves *CliffsNotes*

> The writer uses interesting headings throughout the paper.

My research also helped me to find out about the use of online summaries
and analyses. Approximately 60% of the surveyed high school students used
summaries for at least some of their reading requirements--a statistic that is
very revealing. With such outside resources so readily available, many students
simply read the one-page summaries or analyses instead of the entire novels.

> This is good information. It would have been even more helpful to provide responses from interviews to help readers understand more about this practice.

What Would Edward Cullen Read?

Lastly, through my research I found that many high school students do
not read for pleasure either. Fourteen students who took the survey do not consider reading a hobby. Only sixteen (53%) reported that they do read for pleasure, and they tend to read popular young adult fiction like the *Twilight* and
Harry Potter series and various magazines based on individual interests. About
60% of the high school students said they read for pleasure only 0 to 3 hours a
week, so even those who do enjoy reading do not do it that often. Also, the
students who do read for pleasure read more for their classes as well. Could it
be that if more high schoolers began reading for fun, they would not find it as
burdensome to read for class?

Conclusion

The results of my survey and interviews reveal that many high school students tend to ignore reading assignments in their English courses. This conclusion probably does not come as a shock to many people, however, and could be
more representative than the small sample size suggests. When attending high
school, I rarely did my reading assignments and still managed to ace all of my
quizzes and essays. Like many of the students I surveyed, I was able to get by

without having to pick up a book too often. But I now regret the habits I maintained in high school and suspect that current students will one day regret their habits too. These poor habits may carry over to college and therefore cripple a student's learning capabilities. While the short sources many students use may seem like a quick solution to complete last-minute assignments, they do not equip students with all the crucial information found in their required readings. Therefore, however helpful *CliffsNotes* and *SparkNotes* may be, they should not substitute reading all together. So while reading seems insignificant to high school students now, the habits they are forming now may follow them to the end of their academic careers and beyond.

Stanford 6

Works Cited

Morgan, Kathie. Personal interview. 9 Mar. 2010.

Skye, Karen. Personal interview. 14 Mar. 2010.

✱ Sample Student Survey Instrument

Created by Brittany Stanford for Her Paper "To Read or Not to Read: Examining the Reading Habits of High School Students"

> This survey includes a variety of questions. See pages 184–86 and 203–5 for an explanation of types of questions that yield diverse results.

> Answers from multiple-choice questions are easy to code. See pages 189–90 and 209–14 for help with coding data.

> When analyzing responses to surveys, combining some answers — such as those to questions 2 and 3 here — provides a fuller picture than looking at single answers alone.

The following is a series of questions about your reading habits. Please answer each question to the best of your ability. Thank you so much for your participation.

1. What grade are you in currently?
   a. 9th
   b. 10th
   c. 11th
   d. 12th

2. What is your estimated GPA? _____

3. What level English course are you enrolled in this school year?
   a. Below grade level
   b. At grade level
   c. Above grade level (Honors)

4. How many hours a week do you spend reading for school?
   a. 0–3
   b. 4–7
   c. 8–12
   d. 13–16
   e. 17 or more

5. What is your grade in your English course?
   a. A
   b. B
   c. C
   d. D
   e. F

6. How many novels were you required to read in your English course this year?

    a. 0

    b. 1

    c. 2

    d. 3

    e. 4

    f. 5 or more

7. Of those novels, how many did you actually read?

    a. 0

    b. 1

    c. 2

    d. 3

    e. 4

    f. 5 or more

8. If any novels weren't read, did you read summaries or analyses (*CliffsNotes*, *SparkNotes*, etc.)?

    a. No, I read all that was required

    b. Yes, I used summaries for all that was required

    c. Yes, I used summaries for some that was required

    d. No, I didn't read the novels or any summaries

9. Do you do any reading for pleasure (novels, magazines, internet articles, etc.)? If so, please explain exactly what you read.

    _____

    _____

    _____

> A well-placed, open-ended question can produce useful responses, especially if you are not using interviews.

10. How many hours a week do you spend reading for pleasure?

    a. 0–3

    b. 4–7

    c. 8–12

    d. 13–16

    e. Over 17

Sample Secondary Source Research Paper

The following research paper was written by a student in an English 102 section entitled "Inquiry into Your Generation." The instructor, Teresa Saxton, describes the course as follows:

> Today's college students fit into what scholars are starting to term the Millennial Generation. Current discourse about this generation ranges from pessimistic accusations of youthful laziness and beliefs in entitlement to optimistic declarations that the Millennials are hard workers who will "save" America from its current state of decay and revitalize social institutions and moral sensibilities. The goal of this class is to introduce students to these conflicting theories about their generation and to encourage them to understand, analyze, and construct their own definitions of the Millennial Generation. Moreover, this class will offer students a chance to research themselves and their peers, how they interact with the world, and how theirs compares with previous generations. Students will be encouraged to choose a topic of their own interest, incorporate the values of their classmates regarding the topic, trace the trends of the topic during previous generations and their own generation, and finally, offer conjectures about future trends of the topic.

Students in the class wrote secondary source research papers exploring the relationships between Millennials and the following topics: music festivals, video games, Disney marketing, brand names, community service, consumer culture, competition in sports, gambling, hip-hop fashion, Britney Spears/fascination with fame, humor, higher education, drug use, and cell phone use.

Students began their projects by submitting research proposals* that defined their research question about aspects of Millenial life that interested them. They then gathered research sources (which could include surveys and interviews in addition to secondary sources) and presented annotated bibliographies and research papers.

The following is a paper written by James Winston that uses a combination of secondary sources, open-ended surveys, and personal interviews.

*See a sample research proposal on page 68 and a sample annotated bibliography on page 72.

Winston 1

James Winston

Teresa Saxton

English 102

30 Apr. 2010

Millennial Finance: Budgeting Is the New Saving

A trip to the local Wal-Mart on a Saturday serves as a clear indication that Americans do not have the slightest problem spending money. Cart after cart rolls out the door full of groceries, clothing, and consumer electronics, being pushed by individuals scanning their arm's-length receipts. Working at a bank, I see thousands of transactions like these show up everyday on customers' statements. I have seen countless accounts run empty in the days preceding the next payday. It seems that precious few are saving money. According to the Bureau of Economic Analysis, the personal savings rate in America for January 2008 was negative 0.1%. In other words, Americans are spending more money than they earn. As a result, Americans are going into debt and not saving any money. These negative rates have been persistent over the past few years. In 2006, the savings rate was negative 0.6%, the lowest savings rate since the Great Depression (United States). This information is distressing and prompts concern for the nation's youth and young adult population. Having been raised in an environment of excess spending, how do today's young people feel about saving money?

These young people are a part of the Millennial generation. They were born between 1982 and 2001, and their parents are mostly of the storied Boomer generation. Millennials have been raised on technologies like cell phones, computers, and the Internet. With a few clicks of a mouse, they have access to more information than any preceding generation. Considering their access to such vast amounts of information, are Millennials more knowledge-able when it comes to personal finance? Ultimately, inquiry into the Millennial

> The writer identifies the phenomenon/problem he observed about Millenials' lifestyles.

> Secondary source information is offered to verify that others have noted this problem.

> This sentence, along with the last sentence of the previous paragraph, identifies the research questions for the paper.

Winston 2

wallet reveals that despite the importance they place on saving money, Millennials are not doing so because of their misconceptions about saving money.

First, Millennials have access to a good deal of cash, considering their age, and they are using it. According to my survey, 77% of Millennials have about one hundred dollars in spending money per week. This money is left over after bills and other expenses have been paid. 100 dollars a week comes to approximately four hundred dollars in excess cash per month for a single Millennial, who typically lacks a mortgage or children to take care of. With this excess money, nearly 50% of them report eating out two to four times per week. Furthermore, the majority of them go shopping or to the movies once a week, on average. With their access to extra cash, most Millennials are more than willing to spend it on food and entertainment.

However, most of the Millennials who responded to the survey claimed that they were saving money regularly despite their spending habits. Of the survey respondents, 80% indicated that they were saving money on a regular basis. In other words, the great majority of Millennials claim to be saving money while at the same time regularly eating out, shopping, and going to movies. I was confused as to how Millennials could accomplish this. I doubted they would have any left to save after the trips to the mall and McDonald's. I asked Ashleigh Smith, an older Millennial, if she was saving money and if she thought her peers were. Ashleigh, a 25-year-old recent graduate of Carson-Newman College and currently an elementary school teacher, said she is saving money; however, when asked if she thought her Millennial peers were doing so, she too expressed doubt that they were saving money (Smith). With another Millennial besides me feeling doubt, I decided to explore the concept of saving money in an effort to better understand this paradox.

Saving money seems to be a pretty simple concept. It is keeping excess cash in order to have money in the future for emergencies and retirement,

---

Note that the writer conducted a survey and read secondary sources to gather information for the paper.

It would have been more helpful to provide information here regarding the survey — how many were distributed and to whom, how many responded, and so on.

Note that the findings are reported in the context of those who responded to the survey — not in the context of all Millennials.

Winston 3

among other things, as an alternative to spending it all. When posing the question about saving in my survey, I asked each Millennial if he or she was saving money, and what he or she was saving for. The answer choices I gave were quite simple and included items such as retirement, tuition, and a home. I also included a blank for Millennials to insert "other" things that they might be saving for. This "other" became the key to understanding Millennial saving habits.

> This student researcher's survey provided for open-ended responses, which proved helpful in answering the research question.

Apparently, Millennials are saving for other things that would not be considered "true saving." Nicole Grant, a 19-year-old freshman at the University of Tennessee, says it best. She says that she is saving money for her cell phone bill. When asked why saving money is important to her, she answers, "I like to be able to eat and have money for gas." The answers from other Millennials followed this same thinking. Her peers were saving for things like rent, food, gasoline, makeup, and the list goes on. According to Millennials, they are "saving" for imminent expenses that will arise in coming days or weeks, and not for long-term items like retirement or emergencies. Here was the epiphany that I was looking for.

> Here is a good example of how to incorporate quotes from student interviews.

It is important to note that saving money and budgeting for expenses are not the same things. Budgeting is a method of planning one's expenses so bills, food, and other living costs can be met without spending more than one's income. As a part of their budget, some choose to allocate some of their money to savings. To some extent, Millennials are budgeting instead of saving money. In contrast to their parents and other adults who are not saving or budgeting, as judged from negative saving rates, Millennials are budgeting their cash flow for future expenses, but they are not truly setting aside money as savings. Essentially, Millennials have a fundamental misconception about saving money. They believe that because they are not spending it immediately, they are thus "saving" money. Because of this misconception, Millennials will find it nearly impossible to truly save money instead of just budgeting it.

Over the course of many conversations with them, saving money emerged as being very important to Millennials. Even the ones who do not claim to be saving money think it is important. Ginny Watson is a senior at the University of Tennessee at Chattanooga and admits that she is not saving money. Although she is not saving money, she claims that it is important to her, and she intends to start saving in the future. Similarly, Smith adds, "We [Millennials as a whole] know it is important to save, but we just are not doing it." Even though some are not saving money, they still believe that it is important.

Furthermore, the Millennial generation feels the importance of saving money because they think that saving should be a habit that is learned early in life. 30% of those surveyed believe that kids under the age of twelve should be saving money for themselves. Another 60% of Millennials think that saving should begin when they are teenagers between the age of thirteen and eighteen. In other words, 90% of Millennials think that saving should begin before the age of 19. For this group of college students who are not truly saving money, they really do believe that saving should start at a young age. Todd Skelton, a junior at UT Knoxville and a member of the Economics Club, feels strongly about saving while young and even in college. He says, "Saving now sets one up well so that he or she could function in the 'real world.'" Skelton feels that saving is so important that individuals should start early and continue through college and beyond.

Also, Millennials recognize the importance of saving for retirement. Several Millennials who said they were saving commented that they were saving for retirement. Some are concerned about the future of retirement programs such as Social Security and believe that they will need to save their own money for retirement. Smith commented that in her opinion Social Security may not be around for young people when it becomes their time to retire. Skelton is worried not only for the future of Social Security but about its current inad-

Winston 5

equacies as well. He said, "I am worried about retirement because so many seniors are struggling to live on Social Security now because they do not have other savings to support it." The emphasis placed by these Millennials on saving for retirement shows that they clearly understand the importance of saving money.

Despite their misconception about saving money and in light of the importance they put on saving money, the Millennial generation should be able to save. Many Millennials are in college, and they do not have lots of extra money. College is very expensive; tuition increases frequently and all too often requires loans to pay for it. According to Millennial Watson, the cost of college is keeping her from saving. Because of tuition, books, and other costs, she claims that she does not have enough left over to save any money. She adds, "I do not have a job or a steady income that would allow me to do so."

Even though Williams is short on money, young cash-strapped Millennials should be able to save money. Michelle Miller-Adams writes in her 2002 book, *Owning Up: Poverty, Assets, and the American Dream*, about a study of poor Americans' ability to save. Her study revealed that even those living on limited incomes could save money. Her study essentially argued that a lack of money does not mean that one is unable to save. Of those participating in the study, 88% were considered low income. The participants, through support of local businesses and organizations, were given an account in which to save money to buy a home, pay for education, or save for retirement. In addition, these individuals were offered classes and training in financial literacy. Miller-Adams concluded that these poor individuals would save if encouraged to do so and were given access to places to save money (Miller-Adams 152). For poor college students at the University of Tennessee, there are many financial institutions on the nearby Cumberland Avenue or in the downtown area. Ultimately, Millennials are financially able to save money, but they do not understand how.

Winston 6

Millennials are not saving money due to their misunderstandings, which are the result of a lack of education. Fiscal responsibility is simply not being taught in schools or at home. Millennial Ashleigh Smith agrees that no one has taught Millennials how to save: "Kids only have the example that has been set by their parents to follow." Through mortgages, credit cards, and other loans, parents become overextended financially. The Cuellar family of Elk River, Minnesota, a town approximately 30 miles north of Minneapolis, is a current example. According to an article in the *Elk River Star News*, the family took on an excess of debt in the form of a mortgage. Now faced with foreclosure on their home, the children are suffering. This improper borrowing has forced the kids to deal with changing schools, making new friends, and the financial problems of their parents that constantly surround them (Cook). Although basic financial lessons about saving money and proper borrowing should be taught by parents, schools need to step in because some parents are not doing their part. Skelton feels that "a class in high school would go a long way in teaching youth about saving, spending, and borrowing properly" since some parents are only setting a bad example for kids. Keen Babbage, the author of *Extreme Economics: The Need for Personal Finance in the School Curriculum*, explains exactly what the title of the book suggests, stressing the importance of teaching personal finance to students at all levels of schooling. Babbage explains that while "teenagers have not caused the current financial crisis, they will inherit this difficulty" (viii). Also, Skelton and the Economics Club organized a financial literacy fair to teach fellow UT students about fiscal responsibility. He thought that college students especially are lacking basic financial skills. It is no wonder that they have such a misunderstanding, because no one is regularly and systematically teaching Millennials about saving money.

Furthermore, government spending is fueling Millennial misconceptions about saving money. The U.S. government does not operate on a balanced budget, and, as a result, the United States is trillions of dollars in debt. Congressman John J. Duncan, Jr., representative for the second congressional district of Tennessee, which includes Knoxville, writes about his frustration in his February 2008 newsletter. In reference to both personal and governmental budgeting, he comments that "we need to get our fiscal house in order" (Duncan 1). Essentially, representatives who operate government, like Congressman Duncan, are citizens. They run the government, and if America's "leaders" cannot balance the budget, why would an individual be expected to behave otherwise? In the same way, if individuals cannot handle their own money, why would these individuals who run the government be expected to balance the budget? It is a circle of futility. The fact of the matter is, it is hard to point a finger at a single cause, because fiscal responsibility at both the personal and governmental level is lacking. This is a terrible example that has been set for young Millennials.

After years of observing poor budgeting and saving techniques, Millennials are adopting these bad habits. Millennial Skelton acknowledged this problem and noted that "there is this idea that if the government can do it, so can individuals." In other words, if the government can spend billions of dollars, I can spend a hundred dollars on shoes and not feel bad about it. However, Skelton continued, "There has to be a balance. A person and the government can only be in so much debt before they get into trouble." In the end, government spending is not necessarily driving personal spending, but both are negatively influencing the Millennial generation. Since no one is teaching proper saving habits to Millennials, they are only learning from bad examples. It is painfully apparent why they do not understand saving money.

Fortunately, there is still hope for the future because Millennials are so young. The youngest ones are still in grammar school, and Millennial notions on saving money can still change. Obviously, one has to have money in order to be able to save any. As such, as Millennials get older and obtain jobs, their ability, but not necessarily their aptitude, to save money will increase. Also, more people are starting to push for financial education to be included in school curriculums. Some high schools already offer optional financial planning courses. In response to this push, the Tennessee State Board of Education will require high school students to complete a personal finance class in order to graduate (Tennessee 2). In addition, organizations like Skelton's Economics Club are getting increasingly involved in teaching personal finance skills to students on a less formal basis. If the Millennial generation is to avoid the fiscal irresponsibility that has plagued their parents, they will need all of this education to reverse the tide of negative savings rates.

Winston 9

Works Cited

Babbage, Keen. *Extreme Economics: The Need for Personal Finance in the School Curriculum*. Lanham, MD: Rowman & Littlefield Education, 2007. Print.

Cook, Elizabeth. "Residents, Pets Need New Homes." *Star News*. EMC Publishers, 8 Apr. 2008. Web. 28 Apr. 2008.

Duncan, Jr., John J. "Legislative Update." *Congressman Duncan's Washington Report*. Feb. 2008. Web. 1 Apr. 2010

Grant, Nicole. Personal interview. 4 Apr. 2010.

Miller-Adams, Michelle. *Owning Up: Poverty, Assets, and the American Dream*. Washington, D.C.: Brookings Institution Press, 2002. Print.

Skelton, Todd. Personal interview. 5 Apr. 2010.

Smith, Ashleigh. Personal interview. 1 Apr. 2010.

Tennessee State Board of Education. *High School Transition Policy, Rule*. 25 Jan. 2008. Web. 15 Apr. 2008

United States. Dept. of Commerce. Bureau of Economic Analysis. *Personal Income and Outlays*. 28 Mar. 2008. Web. 29 Mar. 2008.

Watson, Ginny. Personal interview. 1 Apr. 2010.

Sample Student Survey Instrument

Created by James Winston for His Paper "Millennial Finance: Budgeting Is the New Saving"

Survey Results (**Bold** represents number of respondents out of 103 total surveyed)

Gender: M **45**   F **58**   Age: _____

1. After bills and other expenses, how much money do you have per week to use for eating out, clothes, entertainment, etc?
   a. Less than $50   **33**
   b. Between $51 and $100   **46**
   c. Between $101 and $150   **10**
   d. More than $150   **13**

2. Where do you get the majority of this money?
   Parents **37**   Job **46**   Credit cards/loans **5**
   Other (please specify) **15** _____

3. On average, how many times a week do you do the following?

	0–1	2–4	5+
Eat out	**40**	**52**	**11**
Go to the movies	**98**	**5**	**0**
Go shopping	**85**	**18**	**0**

4. Do you have credit cards?   Yes **57**   No **46**
   If yes, who pays for them?   Myself **29**   Parents **28**

5. When should people start saving money for themselves?

   Child (0–12) **33**   Teenager (13–18) **66**   Young Adult (18–24) **4**

   Adult (25–50) **0**   Senior (50+) **0**

6. Currently, are you saving any money on a regular basis?   Yes **82**   No **21**

   If yes, what are you saving for?

   Home **3**   Car **9**   Tuition **12**   Retirement **8**

   Other (please specify) **50** (**Responses:** gas, cell phone, makeup, rent, etc.)

   If no, why not?   Don't have enough to save **13**   Don't want to save **4**

   Don't need to save **4**   Other (specify) **72** _____

Sample Secondary Source Research Paper

Instructor Ryan Woldruff asks his students to contribute to an ongoing scholarly conversation regarding video games and gaming culture for his section on "Inquiry into Gaming":

> If you enjoyed Game Analysis, consider expanding your earlier response into a longer inquiry. If you enjoyed Game History, consider looking there for larger topics. If you enjoyed the Game Design Challenge, what might you research concerning game design that would provide a fruitful inquiry?
>
> **Like all of your writing, your secondary source research paper should include:**
>
> - A strong argumentative/analytical thesis (a little description/summation is fine, but the majority of your paper should include *your* analysis and argument).
>
> - A thorough investigation of secondary source material that demonstrates your ability to find, read, evaluate, and use relevant sources.
>
> - A fully developed introduction, body, and conclusion with a logical, planned arrangement, an attention to overall coherence, paragraph unity, sentence clarity, and transitions.
>
> - A context in which to ground the significance of your argument as well as a balanced integration of various perspectives and voices into your own argument.
>
> - A tone that seems appropriate for the assignment—in this case, more "academic."

His students must include at least five secondary sources that are either books or scholarly articles.

The following paper, written by 102 student Christopher Sharpe, offers an example of a research paper that makes an argument based upon secondary sources.

Sharpe 1

Christopher Sharpe

Ryan Woldruff

English 102

20 Apr. 2010

Game World Immersion: Steadily Improving

Perhaps the greatest challenge in designing a video game is how to translate a concept or environment from the designer's mind into an image on a television or computer screen--and, even more challenging, to create games that are more realistic, both visually and theoretically, to better encourage gamers' immersion in the game world. Matt Barton, a professor of English, whose 2008 article "How's the Weather: Simulating Weather in Virtual Environments" appeared in the *Game Studies Journal,* believes immersion is both graphical and aural:

> Immersing players in believable, coherent virtual worlds--complete with
> their own physics and ecology--has remained an elusive, yet lucrative,
> goal for the game industry. Game makers often privilege their games' inno-
> vations towards cinematic realism over all other factors. . . . Modern video-
> games . . . make the realism of their three-dimensional virtual worlds a key
> selling point. These worlds are represented both graphically and aurally
> in multiple dimensions, and players must navigate them in a manner
> designed to simulate real-life. (Barton)

Similarly, in his book *An Introduction to Game Studies,* Franz Mäyrä says video games captivate us by their variety of sensory, imaginative, and challenge-based immersions (108). Sensory immersion, according to Mäyrä, is achieved through "the powerful overall quality of the interactive moving images and sounds," and he describes imaginative immersion as gameplay that allows the player to become "emotionally as well as intellectually absorbed in the game world" (108). There are some very effective ways in which game designers lead players to become more immersed in virtual game worlds. However, while

This paragraph identifies the subject and introduces some of the scholarly conversation taking place about it.

Sharpe 2

it's clear that video game designers want to immerse players into a game's world to ensure consumers will enjoy the game experience and are making "progress" towards that end, fully realizing that goal seems, still, to be somewhat elusive.

> The thesis presents the writer's analysis regarding how successful game designers have been in achieving "immersion."

One way in which designers create an immersive game world is by creating games with physics that mirror life on Earth. In her article "Video Game Space and the Player," game designer Laurie Taylor mentions that players interpret what happens during gameplay as "procedural outcomes of geometrically articulated orders derived from using program code and the physics of game engines" (Taylor). If the physics or images produced by the video game are in any way unrealistic--when the game's intention is realism--the player will recognize this flaw. One of the earliest games in the first-person shooter genre (or FPS) was *Marine Doom*, which put the player in the role of a soldier who had to fend off enemies and could interact with soldiers from the player's platoon. However, the game was produced before realistic graphics and complicated physics algorithms were a standard part of video games, so the game world did not attain the desired sensory immersion for the game's intended audience (Taylor).

> The writer provides direct quotes from relevant secondary sources.

Manhunt 2, for the Nintendo Wii, is a good example of a game that takes advantage of the technological advancements made in video game design. While like many games its content and the virtual actions in it may be disturbing to some, its technical skill in achieving the immersive experience is worth noting. *Manhunt 2* forces the player to "act out" (with the Wiimote) repeated acts of slaughter towards non-player characters (NPC's) by gruesome means. For example, the player must more "actively" engage in parts of the act of killing, rather than just pressing a button. The game's astonishingly personal connection of life-like physical activity and images seen on the screen produces an emotional effect not felt in many video games. Scholar Mark Sample notes that players typically come away from playing *Manhunt 2* repulsed at their own

Sharpe 3

actions (Sample), an effect that comes from combining visual images that allow the player to comprehend what is happening on-screen with very powerful imaginative immersion that makes the player feel the acts they are engaged in.

> The writer emphasizes his overall thesis at the end of this paragraph.

Weather is another factor video game designers have begun paying more attention to in order to better immerse players, even if this approach has not yet been very successful. Barton states, "Unfortunately, the game industry's achievements in spatial realism has been consistent only in its lack of consistency; we now have the ability to render individual blades of grass blowing in the wind, but a realistic mud puddle still seems years away" (Barton). While games have much room for improvement in achieving realism with weather, many games have already incorporated certain weather elements as vital parts, primarily in the form of sensory immersions. Andrew Hutchison mentions that the first game in the adventure series *Myst*, released in 1993, had bodies of water that never even so much as moved, but *realMyst*, released in 2000, featured moving water that even foamed as it came closer to shore (Hutchison).

> The writer uses a transition sentence that, again, keeps the focus on the overall argument of the paper, and he carefully chooses key words and phrases such as "immerse" and "not yet . . . successful."

Developers use weather scenes as a way to achieve imaginative immersion. Barton recalls that the game *A Change in the Weather* actually uses weather to affect the plot, which changes the player's decisions (Barton). Other more recent games, such as *Call of Duty 4: Modern Warfare*, feature inclement weather to make difficult levels seem even more severe. In the opening level, players must drop onto a cargo ship in the middle of the ocean during a large thunderstorm, which makes the environment very dramatic and stirs up a feeling of anxiety in the player. The player knows something is about to happen but does not know when or where this is going to occur.

> The writer includes good details that serve as examples for the reader.

Sports games, famous for attempting to mirror every tangible aspect of realism, have jumped on the bandwagon of improving variety in weather conditions. EA Sports' football franchises, *NCAA Football* and *Madden NFL*, have part-

Sharpe 4

nered with the Weather Channel to provide up-to-the-minute, real-time weather conditions for games if the player has an Internet connection. Portrayals of changes in weather also affect the strategy behind many players' decisions. If the player chooses to play a football game in rainy or snowy conditions, wide receivers will have a more difficult time catching passes; if players choose to have winds of up to 20 mph at their stadium, they will have to account for this fact when lining up a field goal ("EA and the Weather Channel"). The same concept is applied to the *Tiger Woods PGA Tour* series: heavy wind will affect where the ball travels once hit into the air. These features allow for some interesting immersive possibilities during gameplay and offer new and often less easily controllable elements for players who master the game under ideal weather conditions.

One way in which game designers have achieved strong imaginative immersion and improved the overall gaming experience is by the use of gigantic game worlds, better known as "sandboxes." Games like the *Grand Theft Auto* (or *GTA*) series, or even the *Spider-Man* series, allow the player total freedom in movement and only restrict players once they advance too far into a body of water. If a player so chooses, he or she could spend an infinite amount of time just roaming around the game world, doing nothing aside from wandering and interacting occasionally with NPC's. The *GTA* series has gained most of its popularity and critical acclaim because of this feature, drawing praise from players and reviewers alike (Miller). One reviewer included this feature as a strong selling point for *GTA IV*: "From the tiniest of details to the broadest touches, there is a vibrancy and almost tangible reality to the play area that takes the breath away. For the first twenty minutes of play all I found myself doing was wondering the streets gawping like a tourist" (Jones). As for the *Spider-Man* series, GameSpot game reviewer Jeff Gertsmann says that while there is not much to do while roaming around New York City in *Spider-Man 2*, the combination of excellent physical mechanics when Spider-Man swings from building to building

Again, the writer provides details — in this case more than just one example — to better develop his point.

The last sentence of this paragraph is an effective paraphrase of a secondary source.

Sharpe 5

and the freedom to stray wherever the player wishes is enough to keep people playing the game for hours (Gertsmann).

While current video games offer consumers a more immersive experience than ever before, they still have much room for improvement. Once again, Barton provides an insightful analysis of challenges that current games face:

> When game developers, theorists, and critics discuss what features are most important when creating a realistic virtual world, they tend to focus on aesthetics and kinetics, or, in simpler terms, graphics and animation. Some aspects of "reality," such as lighting effects and shadows, draw more attention than other, less dramatic, natural phenomena. The end result is that even the most realistic games offer a hodgepodge of realistic and very unrealistic effects. (Barton)

Similarly, Sample argues that some gameplay elements, while feeling realistic, are not entirely accurate portrayals of real-life choices and situations. Although the visual aspects of certain games are quite realistic and offer good sensory immersion, Sample argues that players will have a hard time immersing themselves imaginatively in a game that does not consider the consequences of such actions.

Fortunately, video game designers realize their games do not always connect with consumers in the ways they intended, and they gather information about gamers' experiences in an effort to improve the games. In an interview with lecturer and game designer Celia Pearce, Maxis co-founder and designer of *SimCity* Will Wright explained how Maxis consults customer feedback when designing updates of games. The *SimCity* series of games has been retooled several times over the last twenty years since the original release, and many of the changes have come about as a result of suggestions sent in by people who bought the game. Wright said that Maxis even created a website for people who play *The Sims* to upload their families and show them to other people who play the game, but he said the company also uses the website

> Even when the writer includes a longer quote, the source material never outweighs the writer's own analysis and argument.

to determine information about the families these people are designing in the games. Wright also said they included a discussion forum for consumers to use and talk about their game experience and interact, but the game designers also use the forum to view any complaints or suggestions consumers may have (Pearce). By gathering this kind of information, game designers seek to better immerse their audience and create a more enjoyable and realistic game experience.

Designers must take into account exactly who they are designing their games for, and this typically determines what they will emphasize or ignore in the game world. The most effective games tend to be those that attempt to immerse the player through multiple combinations of sensory and imaginative features, as seen with the *Manhunt* example, although it is possible to intrigue the player with only one kind of immersion in mind. Barton mentioned that *Microsoft Flight Simulator* has only one goal in mind and that is to recreate the experience of flying a plane for those who do not have the means or skills necessary to actually fly a plane. As a result, Barton argues, this game has some of the most realistic weather simulation technology ever invented, allows players to download up-to-the-minute weather updates (like the EA Sports games), and even differentiates between three different kinds of clouds. Players can fly through these clouds like an actual airplane would, and the clouds even feature shading and will merge into other clouds nearby (Barton). By enhancing the visual and simulated motion experience to the limits of modern technology, Microsoft effectively created a game that immersed its target audience and brought players as close to piloting a plane as possible without leaving their homes.

Game designers have a plethora of options when deciding how to immerse their audience in the game world. Whether they choose to have stunning graphics, intellectually stimulating puzzles, or even just gruesome realism within the game, designers want players to feel totally involved in the game-play and to keep buying the games the designers produce. With the technological advancements in video games over the last twenty-five years, designers need only have a strong idea of what emotion they want to convey in their games in order to effectively immerse players. No doubt they will continue to work on achieving even greater feelings of immersion in years to come.

Works Cited

Barton, Matt. "How's the Weather: Simulating Weather in Virtual Environments." *Game Studies* 8.1 (2008): n. pag. Web. 12 Apr. 2009.

"EA and the Weather Channel Interactive Present Real-Time Weather in NCAA Football 2008." *Electronic Arts*. Electronic Arts, 2009. Web. 16 Apr. 2009.

Gerstman, Jeff. Rev. of *Spider-Man 2*. *GameSpot*. CBS Interactive, 2009. Web. 13 Apr. 2009.

Hutchison, Andrew. "Making the Water Move: Techno-Historic Limits in the Game Aesthetics of *Myst* and *Doom*." *Game Studies* 8.1 (2008): n. pag. Web. 12 Apr. 2009.

Jones, Owen. Rev. of *Grand Theft Auto IV*. *Sffworld.com*. Sffworld, 2009. Web. 16 Apr. 2009.

Mäyrä, Franz. *An Introduction to Game Studies: Games in Culture*. Los Angeles: Sage Publications, 2008. Print.

Miller, Kiri. "The Accidental Carjack: Ethnography, Gameworld Tourism, and Grand Theft Auto." *Game Studies* 8.2 (2008): n. pag. Web. 11 Apr. 2009.

Pearce, Celia. "Sims, BattleBots, Cellular Automata God, and *Go*: A Conversation with Will Wright." *Game Studies* 2.1 (2002): n. pag. Web. 11 Apr. 2009.

Sample, Mark L. "Virtual Torture: Videogames and the War on Terror." *Game Studies* 8.2 (2008): n. pag. Web. 11 Apr. 2009.

Taylor, Laurie. "When Seams Fall Apart: Video Game Space and the Player." *Game Studies* 3.2 (2003): n. pag. Web. 16 Apr. 2009.

Acknowledgments